Also by Variorum:

CHRISTOPHER WALTER
Art and Ritual of the Byzantine Church

In the Collected Studies Series:

CYRIL MANGO
Studies on Constantinople

CYRIL MANGO
Byzantium and Its Image

ANTHONY CUTLER
Imagery and Ideology in Byzantine Art

JULIAN GARDNER
Patrons, Painters and Saints in Medieval Italian Painting

ALEXANDER KAZHDAN
Authors and Texts in Byzantium

ROBIN CORMACK
The Byzantine Eye: Studies in Art and Patronage

CLIVE FOSS
History and Archaeology of Byzantine Asia Minor

JOSEPH GUTMANN
Sacred Images: Studies in Jewish Art from Antiquity to the Middle Ages

MACHIEL KIEL
Studies on the Ottoman Architecture of the Balkans

NICOLAS OIKONOMIDES
Byzantium from the Ninth Century to the Fourth Crusade

ANGELIKI E. LAIOU
Gender, Society and Economic Life in Byzantium

PAUL MAGDALINO
Tradition and Transformation in Medieval Byzantium

ROBERT S. LOPEZ
Byzantium and the World Around It

ROBERT BROWNING
History, Language and Literacy in the Byzantine World

Prayer and Power
in Byzantine and Papal Imagery

Dr Christopher Walter

Christopher Walter

———

Prayer and Power
in Byzantine and Papal Imagery

———

VARIORUM

Published by VARIORUM
        Ashgate Publishing Limited
        Gower House, Croft Road,
        Aldershot, Hampshire GU11 3HR
        Great Britain

        Ashgate Publishing Company
        Old Post Road,
        Brookfield, Vermont 05036
        USA

ISBN 0-86078-363-4

British Library Cataloguing in Publication Data

        Walter, Christopher
        Prayer and Power in Byzantine and Papal Imagery.
        — (Variorum Collected Studies Series; CS 396)
        I. Title II. Series
        949.5

Printed by   Galliard (Printers) Ltd
               Great Yarmouth, Norfolk
               Great Britain

COLLECTED STUDIES SERIES CS396

CONTENTS

This volume contains xii + 307 pages

PREFACE

In 1977, Variorum paid me the compliment of publishing my *Studies in Byzantine Iconography* in their Collected Studies series. This volume has long been out of print. The articles collected here cover a longer period, from 1970 to 1990. They are not presented chronologically but in relation to the research projects which were the occasion of writing them. Although there is inevitably some overlap, they can be divided roughly into three groups.

The first three articles are excursuses connected with my book *Art and Ritual of the Byzantine Church* (Variorum 1982). This study received a warm welcome in Eastern Europe. It has been republished in a Polish translation, and I am told that a translation into another Slav language circulates as a *samizdat*! Reactions in the West were more reticent. For example Thomas Mathews reviewed it very unfavourably in *The Art Bulletin* (March 1984).

The first article on 'Expressionism and Hellenism' develops a theme which could be mentioned only briefly in the book: that traditional methods used in the study of art history – assuming the validity of a stylistic continuum as well as the transcendental value of Hellenism – distort our appreciation of Byzantine art. Development can be traced more plausibly in terms of the function of the artefacts and the message which they were destined to communicate.

In the second article I was concerned with the function of portraits of local bishops. In spite of the frequent disputes over authority in the Early Church, pictures were not used at first to propagate local claims to autonomy. Local bishops were represented in sanctuaries rather than in cathedrals. The situation changed in the ninth century. There is a striking difference between pope Leo III's presentation of the Petrine claim to universal jurisdiction in the *triclinia* which he built at St John Lateran and the implicit notion of collegiality in the echelon of bishops in St Sophia, Constantinople. In later Byzantine tradition, the claims of local bishops were promulgated by integrating their portraits into programmes in which the established Fathers of the Church already had a place. In passing, I should mention that Robert Markus pointed out to me in a private letter that I was wrong to claim St Vitalis as a local martyr of Ravenna. It must be said that his early history is somewhat confused (G. Lucchesi, 'Vitale, Valeria ed Ursicino', *Bibliotheca sanctorum* 12, 1229–1231).

Biographical scenes of Dionysius the Areopagite, the subject of the third article, were somehow omitted from *Art and Ritual of the Byzantine Church*. I attempt here to explain the enigmatic miniature of Dionysius observing the Crucifixion in the Chludov Psalter, to identify from their portrait types the bishops reputed to have been present with Dionysius at the demise of the Virgin Mary, and to trace the passage of the *kephalophoros* saint from West to East. The prodigy of Dionysius walking two *millia*, carrying his severed head, originated in the West but was first represented in Byzantine art. *Céphalophorie* would receive quite different connotations in East and West, a subject which I am investigating further.

The next five articles form part of series of studies of imperial or official iconography which I have never attempted to put together to form a book. Some such articles were republished in my earlier volume of collected studies (see the list in a note at the beginning of article VI of this volume). Since the appearance of article IV in 1978, a number of pictures of coronation have been published in more detail: Milutin and Simonida themselves at Gračanica by B. Todić, *Gračanica slikarstvo* (Belgrade no date); the despot Stefan at Ljubostinja, S. Djurić, *Ljubostinja* (Belgrade 1985), and the frontispiece to the Barberini Psalter (see below). To these should be added the recently discovered fresco of Stefan Dušan at Pološka, Macedonia, C. Grozdanov & D. Ćornakov, 'Istorijski portreti u Pološkom', *Zograf* 14 (1981), 60–67; 15 (1984), 85–93.

In connection with the articles on the iconography of marriage, Gary Vikan's more far-reaching studies of objects connected with marriage should be mentioned: 'Art, Medicine and Magic in Early Byzantium', *Dumbarton Oaks Papers* 38 (1984), 65–86; 'Art and Marriage in Early Byzantium', *Ibidem* 44 (1990), 145–163.

My study of papal political imagery (VIIa,b) was undertaken on the suggestion of the late André Grabar. Recently Vojislav Djurić has republished, with Pavle Ivić and Sima Ćirković, the Esphigmenou charter of the Despot Djuradj, *Esfigmena pobelja despota Djurdja* (Belgrade 1989). I have also fulfilled a promise to consider in more detail the lost picture of the coronation of Lotharius III at St John Lateran in a paper given at the symposium, Byzantium and Its Neighbours from the Mid-9th till the 12th Centuries, held at Bechyně, Czechoslovakia, in September 1990 (printing).

Other recent studies of this subject are an article by Ingo Herklotz, 'Die Beratungsräume Calixtus' II. im Lateranpalast und ihre Fresken, Kunst und Propaganda am Ende des Investiturstreits', *Zeitschriftd für Kunstgeschichte* 52 (1989, p. 145–214, and a book by Mary Stroll, *Symbols as Power. The Papacy following the Investiture Contest* (Leiden 1991).

The remaining articles are connected, directly or indirectly, with the preparation of an edition of the Barberini Psalter, the last of the great Byzantine marginal psalters to have remained unpublished. The project upon which I began work in 1983 was finally brought to fruition, with the help of P. Canart and J. Anderson, in 1989, *The Barberini Psalter, Codex vaticanus barberinianus graecus 372* (Belser Verlag Zürich). Articles IX, X and XI are primarily concerned with Christological and hagiographical themes in the marginal psalters. In attempting to identify their literary counterparts, I had inevitably to consider the question of development. This development is fairly clear for the Christological themes, whose literary counterparts range from the New Testament through the Patristic commentators up to eighth-century writers. However I also detected changes in the conception of the Psalter, notably that from being regarded primarily as a compendium of prophecies it was considered in the eleventh century rather as the just man's book of prayer.

I also succumbed to the temptation – despite Anthony Cutler's warning in a memorable phrase that, in so doing, I would be "attempting to resolve insoluble questions with unverifiable answers" – of speculating about lost models. I was already toying with the hypothesis that the ninth-century marginal psalters derive from an eighth-century model executed in Palestine, when F. Boespflug invited me to contribute a paper to a volume commemorating the twelfth centenary of the second council of Nicaea (article VIII). I argue here that there is little evidence for the second council of Nicaea exercising a direct impact on image-making at the time – and probably none on the ninth-century marginal psalters. I also availed myself of the opportunity of updating what I had written earlier on the iconography of councils: *Iconographie des conciles dans la tradition byzantine* (Paris 1970) and 'Konzilien', *Reallexikon zur byzantinischen Kunst* (Stuttgart 1990 but actually written in 1978). A further article on post-Byzantine icons of councils is due to appear in the *Deltion tis christianikis archaiologikis etaireias*, volume 16.

Finally article XII, written at the request of V. Vavřínek, attempts to make some sense of Ode illustration which is, with rare exceptions, at once so heterogeneous and so banal. The general rule was to choose either an author portrait or an iconographical theme deeply rooted in Early Christian art. Some of the more intriguing miniatures, concerned with the prophet Habakkuk, are treated in my article 'The Iconography of the Prophet Habakkuk', *Revue des études byzantines* 47 (1989), 251–260. Since a number of the Odes are attributed to prophets, John Lowden's *The Illuminated Prophet Books* (Pennsylvania State University 1988) is relevant to the subject, notably for what he has to say about Ulpius the Roman, Habakkuk and Isaiah.

I should like to finish this preface with some remarks about approach and methodology. Scholars began to study Byzantine art scientifically in the nineteenth century. To my mind the soundest approach was that of the Russians. It has been recently contrasted lucidly by J.-M. Spieser with Western approaches in a paper entitled 'Hellénisme et connaissance de l'art byzantin au XIXᵉ siècle', ʽΕΛΛΗΝΙΣΜΟΣ. *Quelques jalons pour une histoire de l'identité grecque*, edited S. Said (Strasbourg 1989), p. 337–362. I quote from his article a passage which he himself quotes (p. 360) from a translation from the Russian which was published in the *Revue archéologique* in 1850:

> Dans l'iconographie byzantine, l'art ne sert pas de but, mais de moyen; il est soumis à la vérité et à la tradition, de même que l'idée artistique est soumise à l'idée religieuse . . . Si les images saintes, quant à leur valeur esthétique, ne correspondent pas toujours aux règles de l'art, c'est que leur but unique est de rendre fidèlement l'idée religieuse . . .

This approach, shared by later Russian scholars such as D.V. Ainalov and rendered familiar in the West by A. Grabar, has not always been understood by those art historians who accept the transcendental value of Hellenism. Spieser quotes another nineteenth-century scholar, L. Vitet, to the effect that "des notions de rythme, de mesure, d'équilibre, d'intelligente imitation, qui sont l'essence même de l'art grec" were maintained in the Athonite monasteries "comme (dans) une autre arche de Noé" (p. 353). However, even in our time, some art historians are satisfied with an approach which looks on Byzantine art as a subspecies of that of the Renaissance.

Others, who have escaped from the ivory tower but who are not particularly sympathetic towards the Russian approach, seek inspiration in sociology, a procedure which offers interesting insights but which runs the risk of ceasing to be art history at all.

There are no doubt connections between approaches and methodology in the study of Byzantine art. However it is not my intention to explore them here, only to note that Byzantine art historians often show remarkable versatility in their search for methodologies. I suspect that they are motivated, at least in part, by the disproportion between the relatively small quantity of artefacts which have survived and the vast number which are lost for ever. In consequence they are haunted – not to say obsessed – by the following dilemma: to attempt to reconstruct what is lost and so risk producing unverifiable answers to insoluble questions or to ignore entirely what is lost and so risk falsifying their presentation of what does still exist.

The elaboration of methodologies is based on analogy. There is nothing spectacular about this, for the same procedure is used in theology, philosophy, physics and, no doubt, other sciences. However it is necessary to be circumspect and to recognize that, at a certain point, all analogies break down.

One methodology which has proved fruitful is to apply to the transmission of subjects in manuscript illumination the principles of textual criticism. Some years ago, I attempted a critique of this method, 'Liturgy and the Illustration of Gregory of Nazianus's Homilies', *Revue des études byzantines* 29 (1971), pp. 183–212 (reprinted in *Studies in Byzantine Iconography*). The analogy broke down, I argued, because, unlike texts, series of miniatures are rarely, if ever, transmitted *en bloc* from a primordial archetype. Furthermore the use of this method may lead to greater importance being given to what no longer exists – if it ever did – than to those manuscripts which do exist and are available to us.

It has been hinted to me that, in my articles on the marginal psalters (IX, X, XI), I have come back on my earlier position by paying too much attention to lost models. I have, in fact, postulated two lost models, one an eighth-century marginal psalter illuminated in Palestine and the other an eleventh-century marginal psalter which would have been available in the monastery of Saint John Studius for the illuminators of the London and the Barberini Psalters.

The two cases are rather different, even if my motivation in postulating the two models is the same: to explain how the miniature cycles developed in the extant illuminated psalters.

The three surviving ninth-century psalters are related but not interdependent. It is obviously most implausible to treat them as autochthonous productions of their century for several strata can be discerned in the choice of their miniature subjects. One of these is the subjacent Iconophile theology which has its counterpart in the writings of eighth-century Palestinians. Other earlier strata correspond to Psalm interpretation by earlier writers. Consequently, by analogy with developments in Psalm commentary, a hypothesis of development in the illustrative programme may be formulated. This would have occurred by accretion, as in the Psalm commentaries. I do not postulate a pre-Iconoclast archetype. On the other hand I would suggest that in the late eighth century, the illustrative programme was recast, in order to give it an explicitly Iconophile slant. This marginal psalter would have been the model for the three extant ninth-century psalters.

As for the lost eleventh-century illuminated psalter which I postulate – and not I alone – everything depends on the dating of the Barberini Psalter. Most of those who have studied it have placed it later than the London Psalter. Nothing certain can be deduced from the portraits in the frontispiece. Consequently the psalter's miniatures have to be dated by their style. J. Anderson sets out the arguments lucidly in our joint edition of the Psalter (see above). If his arguments in favour of a late eleventh-century date are probative, then a lost psalter, painted before the London Psalter, has to be postulated, in order to explain the relationship between the ninth- and the eleventh-century illuminated psalters. If it could be proved that the Barberini Psalter was painted earlier than the London Psalter, then, of course, the whole situation would change: the model would disappear and be replaced by the Barberini Psalter! In practice the psalter which I describe in article XI *is* the Barberini Psalter, for it would in any case have been a faithful copy of the lost model.

It remains to thank Variorum for accepting this volume in their series of Collected Studies, and more particularly John Smedley for the diligent work that he has put into its production.

CHRISTOPHER WALTER

Athens
Ascension Day, 1992

PUBLISHER'S NOTE

The articles in this volume, as in all others in the Collected Studies Series, have not been given a new, continuous pagination. In order to avoid confusion, and to facilitate their use where these same studies have been referred to elsewhere, the original pagination has been maintained wherever possible.

Each article has been given a Roman number in order of appearance, as listed in the Contents. This number is repeated on each page and quoted in the index entries.

I

EXPRESSIONISM AND HELLENISM

A Note on Stylistic Tendencies in Byzantine Figurative Art from *Spätantike* to the Macedonian " Renaissance "

The specific qualities of Byzantine art are described by scholars in widely differing, even contradictory, terms. For some it is 'the last of the great hieratic arts of Antiquity', in which 'the immobility is more apparent than changes and developments'[1]. It is restrained by an 'ever-present law', which 'forbids rhetoric and lends to the artistic language the stately grandeur of a liturgy'[2]. For others, its 'lifegiving activating force is its Greek heritage'[3]. Although it deviates from the ideals of classical art, it forever returns to them, such that it is possible to 'speak of a perpetual renaissance or of perennial Hellenism'[4]. Some of those who are impressed by the stately grandeur of Byzantine art maintain that it belongs to the aesthetic category of the sublime, inspiring awe and wonder[5]. Most of those who stress the importance of its Greek heritage

---

1. June & D. WINFIELD, *Proportion and Structure of the Human Figure in Byzantine Wall-Painting and Mosaic*, Oxford 1982, p. 1.

2. O. M. DALTON, *Byzantine Art and Archaeology*, London 1911, p. 33-35.

3. O. DEMUS, *Byzantine Art and the West*, London 1970, p. 7-9.

4. *Ibid.*, p. 3 ; E. KITZINGER, The Hellenistic Heritage in Byzantine Art, *DOP* 17, 1963, p. 95-115 ; IDEM, The Hellenistic Heritage in Byzantine Art Reconsidered, *XVI. Internationaler Byzantinistenkongress, Akten* I/2 (= *JÖB* 31/2, 1981), p. 657-675. In his earlier article, Kitzinger is more *nuancé* : Byzantium's own aesthetic ideal was polarized by two powerful magnets, the medieval and the essentially classical (p 115).

5. P. A. MICHELIS, *Αἰσθητικὴ Θεώρηση τῆς Βυζαντινῆς τέχνης*, second edition, Athens 1974.

maintain, at least implicitly, that when it remains faithful to classical ideals, it belongs to the category of the beautiful, inspiring delight. Advocates of these two contrasted approaches may exemplify their appreciation from the same monument. Thus Michelis, for whom all Byzantine art was sublime, chose the Pantocrator at Daphni to typify this aesthetic category[6], while, for Demus, the Christ of the Transfiguration in the same church is particularly redolent of Hellenism[7].

These differing approaches continue to inform art historians in their interpretation of their subject, as may be seen in two recently published studies reviewed in these pages. Maguire, far from supposing that Byzantine artists eschewed rhetoric, maintains that they were consciously or unconsciously influenced by it, assimilating its techniques from the literary texts, composed according to its rules, which were the iconographical source of their compositions[8]. He attributes particular importance to ecphrasis, which 'can truly be described as a hidden long-lasting spring of Hellenism in Byzantine art'[9]. Winfield, on the other hand, bases his study of human proportion on the 'immobility' and 'ever-present law', which are for him characteristic of Byzantine art[10].

Such differing assessments are obviously, to some extent, tributary of the aesthetic taste and sensibility of those who make them. However, the discipline of art history is necessarily based upon aesthetic principles, which serve, often, as criteria in deciding what works are worthy of serious study. It is not so long since Byzantine art was considered by some to be barbarous or decadent[11]. While recognition that much Byzantine art may be considered to belong to an 'alternative convention' has helped to promote its study, it seems more fashionable to-day to concentrate rather on the survival and renewal of its Hellenic qualities. The former view may claim some support in literary texts which describe the φρικτὸς experienced by the beholder of some works of art: the Last Judgment and scenes of martyrdom[12]. However the vast majority of Byzantine descriptions of works of art insist on their conformity to the classical canon: imitation

---

6. P. A. MICHELIS, *Esthétique de l'art byzantin*, Paris 1959, p. 11.

7. DEMUS, *op. cit.* (note 3), p. 7-9 ; see also KITZINGER, *art. cit.* (note 4), p. 661.

8. H. MAGUIRE, *Art and Eloquence in Byzantium*, Princeton 1981 ; see below, p. 344.

9. *Ibid.*, p. 52.

10. WINFIELD, *op. cit.* (note 1) ; see below, p. 350.

11. MICHELIS, *op. cit.* (note 5), p. 19.

12. DOROTHÉE DE GAZA, *Vie de Dosithée*, edited L. RÉGNAULT & J. DE PRÉVILLE (Sources chrétiennes 92), Paris 1963, p. 126, ἐκπληττόμενος (amazed, astonished) by a picture of hell ; Wanda WOLSKA-CONUS, Un programme iconographique du patriarche Tarasios ?, *REB* 38, 1980, p. 247-254, for a plethora of emotions experienced in beholding pictures of martyrdom (which may be summed up as compunction) ; THEOPHANES CONTINUATUS IV, 15, Bonn, p. 164 (= C. MANGO, *The Art of the Byzantine Empire 312-1453*, Englewood Cliffs, N.J., 1972, p. 190-191), φόβος, ἔκπληξις (fear, amazement) inspired by a picture of the Last Judgment. In passing it should be noted that the modern use of the term sublime derives from eighteenth-century interpretations of the treatise

of nature, liveliness, beauty[13]. Yet it may be objected that these descriptions are conventional literary exercises, couched in language destined to conceal rather than manifest the writer's sentiments.

The present article is inspired by the conviction that neither way of describing the specific qualities of Byzantine art is satisfactory. A serious obstacle to a proper appreciation of them has always been the practice of applying to Byzantine art notions and conceptions taken from the study of art of other periods. Thus the notion of an 'alternative convention' is taken from the study of art produced at a time of rupture with the classical canon: *Spätantike*, Mannerism, Baroque or even latter-day Expressionism[14]. Indeed, some art historians consider Byzantine art in the period before Iconoclasm to be a continuation of *Spätantike*[15]. On the other hand, those who are sensitive to the Hellenic qualities of Byzantine art concentrate upon periods where classical revival is more evident, notably upon the ninth and tenth centuries. If this period is conceived as a renaissance, then it is difficult to avoid interpreting its art in terms which have proved fruitful in studying the art of the Italian Renaissance.

In the course of this article, an attempt will be made to re-assess the debt of early Byzantine art to *Spätantike*, followed by a re-examination of the specific qualities of the classical revival after the Triumph of Orthodoxy. However, since its primary aim is to provide a critique of the conceptual framework and theoretical approaches currently used in Byzantine art history, it is necessary to begin by making some observations about the language and methodology associated with them. In the conclusion, another version will be proposed of the specific qualities of Byzantine art. It needs, of course, to be controlled and verified, with particular reference to the art produced from the eleventh century onwards. This control and verification lie outside the scope of the present article.

1. CONCEPTUAL FRAMEWORK AND THEORETICAL APPROACH

The following observations are concerned with *figurative* works of art. Such works are ambivalent. Since they have a subject, they are significant. The Dormition is readily distinguishable from the Rescue of Andromeda, although

---

attributed to Longinus, G. FAGGIN, Sublime, *Enciclopedia filosofica* IV, 1031-1034. With the possible exception of ἔκπληξις, see below p. 287, note 113, it is unlikely that these words, any more than φρικτός or ὕψος, were used by the Byzantines in an aesthetic sense.

13. MANGO, *op. cit.* (note 12), XIV-XV.

14. R. BIANCHI BANDINELLI, Espressionismo, *Enciclopedia dell'arte antica* III, 460-461. The term is a neologism used by a group of late nineteenth-century German artists to characterize their rupture with conventional academic art.

15. R. BIANCHI BANDINELLI, Spaetantike, *ibid.* VII, 428.

sometimes a title may be necessary to confirm an identification. Figurative works of art also re-create the physical world, and it is this aspect which has generally interested art historians. It is also the aspect which tends to dominate in works produced according to the classical canon. Re-creation of the physical world in a work of art has two aspects. Firstly, there is the aspect of scientific exploration of physical space, which has no necessary connection with artistic production: optics, the analysis of light and colour, anatomy. Secondly, there is the aspect of technical exploration, which *is* specific to artistic production: perspective, composition, the plastic rendering of the human figure. Sometimes these two kinds of exploration are undertaken concurrently, such that the scientific influences the technical. For example, investigation of optics and anatomy in the Quattrocento and the Cinquecento influenced the technical development of linear and tonal perspective as well as of plastic rendering of the human body. At other times, technical exploration is undertaken independently of scientific exploration. Such art tends to be 'academic'. Its practitioners may continue to observe the physical world, or they may concentrate on imitating renderings of it in works produced by their predecessors. Either way they are resistant to developments in technique deriving from advances in scientific exploration. For example, Impressionist works exploiting new analyses of light and colour were rejected by nineteenth-century academic artists.

The various technical means used by artists to re-create the physical world — light, colours, perspective, plasticity, composition — predominate in descriptions of their individual *style*. Art historians who study figurative works as re-creations of the physical world focus upon the concept of style. They may consider style to be *autonomous*, such that the history of art may be plotted in terms of influences, developments and reactions. This approach is fruitful in periods when artists were directly interested in scientific or technical exploration. However, it encounters difficulties when artistic production consists mainly in copying or adapting existing works.

The vast majority of figurative works of art, even of those produced in periods when the classical canon prevailed, were not intended primarily to be re-creations of the physical world but to be significant. In many such works — most obviously representations on coins or medals — re-creation of the physical world is reduced to the minimum necessary to make them significative. Such works tend — or tended — to be excluded from the repertory of the art historian, because they do not enter into the category of the 'fine arts'. When art history became a serious discipline, the repertory of the fine arts was somewhat restricted, for Winckelmann's view was still dominant that the art of fifth- and fourth-century Greece was the paragon of absolute beauty, and that all subsequent art was decadent[16]. The repertory has been widened, not only by art historians

16. R. BIANCHI BANDINELLI, La crisi artistica della fine del mondo antico, *Archeologia e cultura*, Milan/Naples 1961, p. 189.

who were tolerant of alternative conventions but also by those who have been influenced by subversive forces operating outside the strict discipline of art history: Marxists, focussing attention on the social and economic factors which determine art production; Freudians, disciples of de Saussure and ultimately semiologists focussing attention on significance. Nevertheless, in spite of the amount of studies devoted to iconography, it seems that in the field of Byzantine art history the focal point is still style. The traditional conceptual framework and theoretical approach are maintained.

Style, of course, may itself be significant. Works respecting the classical canon may presuppose a Humanist ideology, according to which man is at the centre of the universe and potentially capable of mastering it. However, its significative value may become formal when artists challenge the classical canon. This point will require further development when the debt of early Byzantine art to *Spätantike* is discussed. Provisorily it may be illustrated by reference to Mannerist and Baroque art. Its creators used the results of scientific exploration undertaken during the Renaissance, but technically they exploited them in order to signify the existence of a non-spatial mode of being. They abandoned the harmony and proportion of perfectly formed self-sufficient human beings in favour of others, strained and contorted, striving towards this non-spatial existence. They moved the vanishing point outside the perspectives of man's physical surroundings, so that, for example, in Pozzi's ceiling in the church of Sant'Ignazio, Rome, an illusion is created of the building being open to the heavens above.

These brief observations may be helpful in the discussion which is to follow. If art history is to be focussed upon the concept of style, it is necessary to ask, nevertheless, how its constituent elements were assembled. Did the artist use the results of scientific as well as technical exploration of space? Did he look at nature or work from models? Was style for him formally significative? What balance did he attempt to strike in his work between a re-creation of physical space and the transmission of a message?

2. THE ART OF *Spätantike* AND OF THE EARLY BYZANTINE PERIOD

In the third century, there was a stylistic upheaval, particularly in Roman art. The classical canon disintegrated and there emerged radically conceptual forms, either abstracted from the canon or imposed on it[17]. Artists ceased to be interested in reproducing athletes with perfectly proportioned figures[18]. They no longer set their figures in a harmoniously structured space, nor were their figures set in relation to each other with proper respect for perspective. The pioneers of art history were inclined to interpret these departures from the

17. E. KITZINGER, *Byzantine Art in the Making*, London 1977, p. 7-21.
18. BIANCHI BANDINELLI, *art. cit.* (note 16), p. 204.

classical canon in terms of decadence: third-century artists lacked the competence and their patrons lacked the taste of their predecessors. However, a different interpretation was proposed in the early years of this century, notably by Riegl[19], who introduced the concept of *Spätantike*, and by Rodenwaldt, who introduced that of Expressionism[20]. They argued that these departures, far from being symptomatic of incompetence, were motivated by and corresponded to changes in contemporary taste. Subsequent scholars, notably Bianchi Bandinelli, in whose studies of art history the subversive influence of Marxism is particularly evident, liberated themselves entirely from the aesthetic *aprioris* of Winckelmann's disciples. They have vastly enlarged the repertory of Roman art, and from these previously unconsidered works they have been able to show that the antecedents of the art of *Spätantike* are to be sought in works destined for more modest patrons during the centuries when commissions for imperial or aristocratic patrons were executed in accordance with the classical canon.

The stylistic developments in the art of *Spätantike* may be described in terms of technical exploration. Narrative works, such as the reliefs on the columns of Marcus Aurelius and of Trajan, called for different techniques from those used in a free-standing composition. Once a work of art is being used to 'tell a story', lucidity in the narrative becomes more important than the re-creation of the physical world. Consequently the chief person in a scene may be made to stand out by representing him as larger than the other figures, so violating the laws of perspective. Since the face is the most expressive part of the human figure, it may be executed in detail, while the body is rendered without particular attention to its plasticity. This lack of consideration in the art of *Spätantike* for perspective and anatomy has been described as a passage from the plastic to the pictorial[21]. Notably, bas-relief, instead of being associated with sculpture in the round, is now assimilated rather to painting, such that contrasts of light and shade replace the natural contours suggested by moulding. The contrast between a plastic and a pictorial rendering of the same subject may be exemplified by two representations of a lionhunt. In one, on a sarcophagus in the Palazzo Giustiniani, the lion's mane has been rendered plastically by moulding. In the other, on a sarcophagus in the Catacombs of Saint Sebastian, the lion's mane has been rendered by drilling, so as to give a pictorial illusion of light and shade[22].

This abandonment of the classical canon has been explained as symptomatic of the intellectual climate of *Spätantike*[23]. Confidence had been lost in the

19. R. BIANCHI BANDINELLI, Riegl, *Enciclopedia dell'arte antica* VI, 683-686.

20. V. HAUSMANN, Rodenwaldt, *ibid.*, 740-742 ; G. RODENWALDT, The Transition to Late Classical Art, *Cambridge Ancient History* XII, edited S. A. COOK, Cambridge 1939, p. 544-570.

21. BIANCHI BANDINELLI, *art. cit.* (note 16), p. 190.

22. *Ibid.*, plate 22 a, b.

23. *Ibid.*, p. 198.

power of the human reason to create the conditions of a perfect life in the context of the physical world.   From the third century, it has been noted, both religious practice and philosophical teaching are marked by a common tendency to mysticism.   The human mind may attain 'reality', but this reality lies outside the physical world observable by the senses.   What is given in sensation — and, *a fortiori*, artistic representations of it — have no autonomous existence.   They serve only as an intermediary, a vehicle for ideas.   It is by means of ideas that the human spirit enters into contact with eternal Being and essential Truth.

The possible influence of the most eminent third-century exponent of such notions, not only upon contemporary artistic production but also on early Byzantine and Medieval art, has frequently been examined[24].   Plotinus (205-270) certainly reflected profoundly both on the nature of art and on the concomitant conditions, intellectual and social, of its production.   Given the influential position held by Plotinus at the court of Gallienus, it seems reasonable to take note of the ways in which his ideas may have been reflected in the artistic production of the third century.   However, before pronouncing on his influence upon early Byzantine or Medieval art, it is necessary to establish how this influence would have been transmitted.

The observations which Plotinus makes about art, except as a means of contact with eternal Being, are not presented systematically.   They are rather *obiter dicta*, which can easily be over-interpreted.   His basic anthropology is pessimistic: man diminishes; his body weakens; he will not escape the consequences of disease[25].   Man's fulfilment consists in liberating himself from the prison of his body by entering into contact with eternal Being, the universal soul[26].   One means of establishing this contact, wellknown to the oldtime sages, was to make statues of the gods, because the representation, in the form of an image, of something undergoes the influence of its prototype, whose appearance may be grasped in the image as in a mirror[27].   Such a process implies that the artist himself has contemplated eternal Being, that he has entered into the rhythm of eternal life, ascending towards pure vision and descending to give it sensible expression[28].   Thus the artist acts as mediator between the sensible and the

24. *Ibid.*, p. 204 ; S. Ferri, Plotino e l'arte del III secolo, *La critica d'arte* 1, 1936, p. 166-171 ; Idem, Plotino, *Enciclopedia dell'arte antica* VI, 250-252 ; M. Cagiano de Azevedo, Il colore nella Antichità, *Aevum* 28, 1954, p. 160-161 ; A. Grabar, Plotin et les origines de l'esthétique médiévale, *L'art de la fin de l'Antiquité et du Moyen Age* I, Paris 1968, p. 15-29.

25. G. Figgin, Plotino, *Enciclopedia filosofica* III, 1458-1459; F. Bourbon di Petrella, *Il problema dell'arte e della bellezza in Plotino*, Florence 1956 ; *Enneads* I iv 14, *Plotini opera*, edited P. Henry & H.-R. Schwyzer, Paris/Brussels 1951-1959 (cited hereinafter Henry/Schwyzer), I, p. 95-96.

26. Figgin, *art. cit.* (note 25), 1455.

27. *Enneads* IV iii 11, Henry/Schwyzer II, p. 28-29.

28. Figgin, *art. cit.* (note 25), 1458.

intelligible. The image which he makes is not a personal creation, the product of his imagination; rather it is an objective revelation, incapsulating his intuition of eternal Being. His production ($\pi o \acute{\iota} \eta \sigma \iota \varsigma$) is contemplation ($\theta \varepsilon \omega \rho \acute{\iota} \alpha$)[29]. In modern terms, it may not distort the thought of Plotinus too gravely to suggest that for him the value of a work of art consists in its capacity to signify; it enables the observor to possess the object signified (eternal Being), and to identify himself with it. In this context one might adduce his fascination for Egyptian hieroglyphs, each one of which was a 'science'[30].

Such notions are far removed from Plato's theory of art as imitation ($\mu \acute{\iota} \mu \eta \sigma \iota \varsigma$) of nature[31]. They also limit strictly the autonomy of the artist, who is not required to be original, since his function is purely instrumental. Yet Plotinus was not indifferent to sensible appearances, although he described them from the point of view of someone who considered the material to be an obstacle to the attainment of the intelligible. Thus for Plotinus profundity is an aspect of the material and consequently obscure[32]. The intellect is directed rather towards colour and light, a notion which may be reflected in the contemporary passage from a 'plastic' to a 'pictorial' style in bas-relief[33]. Sensible impressions occur at the place where the object is situated: the closer the eye to the object, the more exactly the eye grasps it[34].

This notion may be compared with the common practice in third-century art of grouping figures in the foreground in the same plane. It may also be compared with the less common practice known by art historians, but not by Plotinus, as presenting a scene in inverse perspective[35]. When the more important figures, although larger in size, are not represented in the foreground, it is as if the artist had envisaged the scene from the point of view of these persons. The rest of the scene, smaller in scale but placed in the foreground, is in false perspective for the beholder. In consequence he cannot maintain a distance between himself and the scene. In order to grasp it correctly, he has to identify himself with the more important persons, who, for the artist, are the real beholders.

In sum, Plotinus spoke of art in terms which are opposed to the principles of the classical canon. He situated 'reality' outside the physical world; he regarded a work of art as a means of attaining this non-physical reality; his exploration of the sensible world is in terms of light and colour rather than of depth, painterly rather than plastic. However, these notions, even if they derive

29. *Ibid.*, 1459.

30. *Enneads* V viii 6, HENRY/SCHWYZER II, p. 390.

31. L. STEFANINI, *Il problema estetico in Platone*, Turin 1926 ; P.M. SCHUHL, *Platon et l'art de son temps*, Paris 1933.

32. *Enneads* II iv 5, HENRY/SCHWYZER I, p. 186-188.

33. BIANCHI BANDINELLI, *art. cit.* (note 16), p. 190 ; CAGIANO DE AZEVEDO, *art. cit.* (note 24), p. 160-161.

34. *Enneads* II viii 1, HENRY/SCHWYZER I, p. 220-222.

35. GRABAR, *art. cit.* (note 24).

from his search for non-physical 'reality', do not constitute a structured whole, such that if one is rejected the others fall with it. Art may be considered as primarily significative (the production of hieroglyphs), without necessarily being exploited as a means of attaining non-physical 'reality'. It is also possible to produce a significative work of art independently of Plotinian notions of sense perception as well as of the technical means proper to the third century. These considerations must be borne in mind when attempting to assess the influence of Plotinus on early — and *a fortiori* later — Byzantine art. The following paragraphs offer only the *status quaestionis* of a problem which merits full investigation in all its complexity.

If Plotinus exercised an influence on Byzantine art, it could have been directly by his writings or indirectly by the intermediary of third-century works of art. So far as direct influence is concerned, there are, of course, no surviving manuscripts of the *Enneads* earlier than the twelfth century[36]. There is no evidence of copies having been made during the period of the first Byzantine humanism, although Photius refers twice to Plotinus in his *Bibliotheca*, coupling his name with that of Origen as disciples of Ammianus[37]. On the other hand a number of fourth- and fifth-century Church Fathers, as well as philosophers, copied extracts from his teaching. Further extracts are preserved in the tenth-century compilation known as the *Souda* and again in the writings of Nicephoras Gregoras (*ca* 1295-1359/60)[38]. Other Church Fathers, notably Gregory of Nyssa and Dionysius the Areopagite, betray a familiarity with the *Enneads*, extending to quotation, although they do not actually mention his name[39].

The interest of the Fathers was above all in Plotinian epistemology. His terms could be used in order to explain how man, by contemplation, may attain the Godhead[40]. However, whereas Plotinus considered that man was ultimately absorbed into eternal Being, Gregory of Nyssa insisted upon a necessary and radical separation between man and God. An exegesis of the term 'image' was necessary in order to explain both the relationship of the Son to the Father, and the way in which the pure in heart 'see' God, reflected in the soul as in an untarnished mirror[41]. For this exegesis Plotinus was a more reliable master

---

36. P. HENRY, *Les manuscrits des Ennéades*, second edition, Brussels 1948.

37. PHOTIUS, *Bibliotheca*, PG 103, 705 ; 104, 77 ; P. LEMERLE, *Le premier humanisme byzantin*, Paris 1971, makes no reference to manuscripts of the Enneads being copied during the period treated in his study.

38. P. HENRY, *Les états du texte de Plotin*, Brussels 1937 ; for the *Souda*, see LEMERLE, *op. cit.* (note 37), p. 297-299.

39. J. DANIÉLOU, *Platonisme et théologie mystique*, Paris 1944, p. 211-217 ; R. ROQUES, *L'univers dionysien*, Paris 1954, *passim*.

40. DANIÉLOU, *op. cit.* (note 39), p. 212-213.

41. *Ibid.*, p. 215-216 ; see also J. KIRCHMEYER, Grecque (Eglise), *Dictionnaire de spiritualité* VI, 812-822, with ample bibliography but no reference to the influence of Plotinus.

than Plato, for whom the notion of image, as that of mimesis, had pejorative connotations, the representation, as the imitation, being an inferior, adulterated or deceptive version of the original.

However, the Cappadocian Fathers did not exploit their exegesis of the term image when describing works of art. The good work of art, *pace* Plato, was an exact mimesis of nature, although, by this very fact, it could be a more effective means of telling a story or conveying a message than language itself. In other words, it may well be that the writings of Plotinus continued to exercice an influence on art production, but above all, because he considered art to be a means of communication. When the qualities of the work of art were assessed, the Greek Fathers remained faithful to the criteria of the classical ecphrasis, particularly to that of exact imitation of nature[42].

Patristic exegesis of the notion of image was later exploited by the Iconophiles to explain how Christ was present in his image on an icon. However, again, their preoccupation was epistemological and not aesthetic. Although the contrary is often maintained, it does not seem that the Iconophiles were at all concerned to assess the quality of specific icons or representations of Christ[43]. Fidelity to the prototype imposed constraints and probably favoured the practice of copying, but it was not a criterion of aesthetic quality. This separation between the epistemological and the qualitative assessment of figurative art may be exemplified by Photius's ecphrasis of the image of the Virgin in Saint Sophia: 'Sight... having somehow... touched and encompassed the object..., sends the essence of the thing seen to the mind'. Yet the picture itself is a 'lifelike imitation... You might think (the Virgin) not incapable of speaking'[44].

There is no doubt that Plotinian influence could have been mediated by third-century works of art, which served as models for early Byzantine artists. Stylistic resemblance can be detected in works like reliefs conceived pictorially rather than plastically with the figures all in one plane, in statues whose faces are executed in great detail while the body has been executed summarily, and in scenes presented in inverse perspective. However, such resemblance by no means extends to all the artistic production of the early Byzantine period. Stylistically speaking early Byzantine art, far from being uniform, is remarkably eclectic.

---

42. MANGO, *op. cit.* (note 12), p. 34, 36-37.

43. For the exploitation by the Iconophiles of Patristic exegesis of the notion of image, see C. VON SCHOENBORN, *L'icône du Christ. Fondements théologiques élaborés entre le Ier et le IIe concile de Nicée (325-787)*, second edition, Fribourg 1976. For the development of an aesthetic from exegesis of the notion of image, see L. OUSPENSKY, *Essai sur la théologie de l'icône dans l'Eglise orthodoxe*, Paris 1960 ; P. EVDOKIMOV, *L'art de l'icône. Théologie de la beauté*, Paris 1970. See also the pertinent remarks by Suzy DUFRENNE, *L'icône dans la pensée et la piété orthodoxe d'après le témoignage du monde byzantin*, in *Aspects de l'orthodoxie*, edited M. SIMON, Paris 1981, p. 31-41.

44. PHOTIUS, *Homily XVII 2, 5*, MANGO, *op. cit.* (note 12), p. 187, 190.

Artists copied models which respect the classical canon as readily as ones which flout it. This eclecticism requires some explanation.

Further, with the advent of Constantine, a radical change took place in the social climate of the Roman Empire. Men no longer despaired at the possibility of finding their fulfilment in their terrestrial life. On the contrary, it seemed that, with the official recognition of the Christian Church, an ordered, stable society could be restored. Since Christians were no longer a persecuted sect, they no longer felt obliged to focus the message of their art on the theme of the afterlife[45]. Celestial life was, indeed, a continuing and dominant theme of Christian art, but it was not contrasted with terrestrial existence as an opposition between the intelligible and the sensible. Early Byzantine art stresses the analogies between celestial and terrestrial life rather than the differences. The mediating theme was that, thanks to Constantine, the reign of Christ had been established on earth. Further, to represent Christ in heaven, Christian artists adapted models which to contemporaries would have vividly recalled the fact that they lived in the terrestrial, physical world, pictures taken from imperial imagery, proclaiming the reality of imperial power[46].

Probably few art historians to-day would maintain that there is any correlation between the stylistic upheaval of *Spätantike* and the artistic patronage of the Christian Church[47]. On the other hand official recognition by Constantine of the Christian Church, since the emperor was the principal patron of the arts, must have progressively encouraged an enormous increase of artistic production, consisting of works intended to be a vehicle of religious and political propaganda[48]. In such works significance was more important than the re-creation of the physical world. Already in the third century Christians, like other sects, were using figurative art as a means of propagating their doctrines. Some such works are assimilable to hieroglyphs. For example, in the catacombs of Priscilla, the dove with an olive branch from Noah's ark is juxtaposed, as a sign of liberation, to the Three Youths in the fiery furnace. Although such composite 'messages' are exceptional, the practice persisted. In the Rossano Gospels, in illustration to the parable of the Wise and Foolish Virgins, four rivers, the sign of Paradise, are represented inside the bridegroom's dwelling[49].

If a case is to be made for the influence of Plotinus on early Byzantine art, the most convincing argument would be that he formulated most clearly the notion

---

45. Ch. WALTER, *Art and Ritual of the Byzantine Church*, London 1982, p. 2-4.
46. A. GRABAR, *L'empereur dans l'art byzantin*, Paris 1936, p. 196-243.
47. See above, note 17.
48. R. KRAUTHEIMER, The Constantinian Basilica, *DOP* 21, 1967, p. 115-140.
49. Ch. WALTER, Liturgy and the Illustration of Gregory of Nazianzen's Homilies, *Studies in Byzantine Iconography*, London 1977, p. 193-195. This point is developed with regard to narrative and interpretative pictures in my paper delivered at the IVe Symposium International sur l'Art Géorgien, Tbilissi 1983, *Le culte, les légendes et l'iconographie de saint Georges* (printing).

that the essential value of a work of art is its capacity to signify. On the other hand the systematic use of art for propaganda purposes would seem to be a Constantinian innovation, bringing about a rupture between the art of *Spätantike* and that of the early Byzantine period. Henceforward, throughout the Byzantine period, the figurative arts would be 'conceptualist', giving primacy to significance. Early Christian artists did not invent new signs to propagate their doctrines. They borrowed and adapted them from existing works. It is likely that a model for every theme of early Byzantine iconography may be identified in pre-Christian works[50]. This helps to explain why early Byzantine art is eclectic. Artists consulted the repertory of available models as a lexicon rather than as a pattern book. However, in transposing the 'sign', they also copied its style.

This explanation does not, of course, purport to be complete. Individual taste may well have sometimes determined the choice of a model. Moreover, it is evident that a choice of style could be in itself significant, as, for example, in the case of the late fourth-century neo-pagan ivories[51]. However, it would be difficult in the early Byzantine period to relate stylistic trends to the results of scientific or technical exploration. The artist's function had been established as that of a copyist or adaptor, whose field of vision was virtually limited to such works of art as might prove to be useful models. Whether the model or the resulting work was classical or expressionist in style probably mattered less to contemporaries than to modern art historians. Our aesthetic sensibility is offended by the violent contrast of style between the second- and fourth-century reliefs on the Arch of Constantine[52]. If the fourth-century beholder was primarily concerned to read the message of the reliefs, he may have barely noticed the difference.

3. THE MACEDONIAN 'RENAISSANCE'

There is a consensus among art historians that there was a revival of Byzantine art after the Triumph of Orthodoxy. However, there is not a consensus as to how this revival should be defined and described. For example, Loumyer wrote of a Second Golden Age, beginning in the reign of Basil I (867-886) and lasting for three centuries[53]. Frolow wrote of a renaissance beginning at the end of

---

50. A. GRABAR, *Christian Iconography. A Study of Its Origins*, London 1969.

51. Ch. WALTER, Marriage Crowns in Byzantine Iconography, *Zograf* 10, 1979, p. 84-85 ; KITZINGER, *op. cit.* (note 47), p. 34-38.

52. KITZINGER, *ibid.*, p. 7. It may be observed that in modern advertising, in many respects the heir of conceptualist traditions in art, juxtapositions of this kind frequently occur without apparently offending the potential client.

53. G. LOUMYER, *Les traditions techniques de la peinture médiévale*, Brussels/Paris 1920, p. 59.

the ninth century, continuing to the end of the eleventh century and extending into the more troubled epoch of the Comneni; it was remarkable for the quality and quantity of the works of art produced[54]. Generally art historians attribute a shorter duration to this renaissance. Weitzmann, for example, dates its beginning to the late ninth or tenth century but does not allow it to continue into the eleventh century[55].

So far as the quantity of artistic production is concerned, it seems that there was a large increase in the ninth century, motivated in part at least by the need to restore damage and destruction during the period of Iconoclasm, followed by a recession in the tenth century and a new increase of production in the eleventh. However, those who attribute a shorter duration to this renaissance connect it with the style of the works produced. From the late ninth to the end of the tenth century there was a marked preference for a style which resembles that of works produced in Antiquity in accordance with the classical canon, implying an intensified study of the classical repertory of forms.

In this sense, the word is also applied to the art of other periods. Scholars have discerned a Gallienic Renaissance in the third century[56]. Another short renaissance, associated with the production of neo-pagan ivories and the patronage of the court of Theodosius I (379-395), occurred in the late fourth century[57]. Yet another occurred in the reign of Justinian II (685-695; 705-711)[58]. A further 'Late Byzantine Renaissance' took place under the Palaeologan dynasty[59]. Probably this list is not exhaustive.

The hazards of using the term renaissance, introduced into art history to denote the fifteenth-century cultural renewal in the West, in other contexts but with the same connotations, are now generally recognized. Many scholars now place the word renaissance between inverted commas, to signify that it must be interpreted with circumspection. Mango has even proposed that a term used by Panofsky for Western art history should also be used by Byzantinists: other classical revivals should be distinguished from the fifteenth-century Western

54. A. FROLOW, La renaissance de l'art byzantin au 9ᵉ siècle et son origine, *Corsi di cultura sull'arte ravennate e bizantina* 9, 1962, p. 269.

55. K. WEITZMANN, The Classical in Byzantine Art as a Mode of Individual Expression, *Studies in Classical and Byzantine Manuscript Illumination*, Chicago/London 1971, p. 151-175 ; The Character and Intellectual Origins of Byzantine Art, *ibid.*, p. 176-223 ; The Classical Mode in the Period of the Macedonian Emperors : Continuity or Revival ?, *The Classical Heritage in Byzantine and Near Eastern Art*, London 1981.

56. BIANCHI BANDINELLI, *art. cit.* (note 16), p. 200.

57. See above, note 51.

58. D. WRIGHT, The Classical Revival in Art at the Court of Justinian II, *Résumés der Kurzbeiträge, XVI. Internationaler Byzantinistenkongress*, Vienna 1981, 10.1 : 'A truly Justinianic Renaissance'.

59. For some references : *Art et société sous les Paléologues*, Venice 1971 ; KITZINGER, *art. cit.* (note 4), p. 669-672.

278

Rinascimento dell' Antichità by the use of the term renascence[60]. His example has not been generally followed, perhaps because the danger still remains of attributing some of the connotations of the word renaissance to the word renascence. The following connotations need particularly to be scrutinized: a renaissance (or renascence) is inspired by a direct study of the art of Antiquity; a renaissance is a period of progress and creativity; a renaissance is a heyday in the history of art.

Art historians do not have a monopoly of the term renaissance. Historians of Byzantine literature also use it, notably to designate the Humanist revival in letters in the ninth and tenth centuries[61]. Fortunately, this revival has been studied in depth. In spite of Lemerle's modest disclaimers, it is unlikely that the conclusions to his 'notes et remarques' on this Humanist revival will need to be modified substantially[62]. It is useful to recapitulate his conclusions briefly, for, although there are analogies between the literary and the artistic classical revival in the ninth and tenth centuries, there are also points of difference. Lemerle notes that, in the period preceding the ninth century, there was, if not a rupture, at least a suspension of study of classical letters[63]. From the fifth or sixth century to the ninth, very few Greek manuscripts were copied and possibly no literary texts[64]. Public instruction ceased to exist in Constantinople[65]. Leo the Mathematician, the first authentic 'homme de la Renaissance', had to seek out a teacher on the isle of Andros and to continue his instruction alone by reading such ancient texts as he could find[66]. The decisive date in the re-establishment of public teaching was his appointment by Bardas shortly after 855 as director of the school founded in the Magnaura palace[67]. Photius was the real founder of Byzantine classicism, which was not genuinely Hellenic, since Photius frequented mainly Greek writers of the Christian era[68]. He was more interested in classical rhetoric than in the sciences. His successors did not modify greatly his approach. Lemerle suggests that one consequence of the condamnation of Iconoclasm was the suppression of an 'esprit scientifique' and of any 'originalité créatrice'. No progress was made in the different branches

60. C. MANGO, Antique Statuary and the Byzantine Beholder, *DOP* 17, 1963, p. 53-75 ; E. PANOFSKY, *Renaissance and Renascences in Western Art*, second edition, Uppsala 1965.

61. For the most recent *status quaestionis*, see *Byzantium and the Classical Tradition*, edited Margaret MULLET & R. SCOTT, Birmingham 1981.

62. LEMERLE, *op. cit.* (note 37), p. 301-307.

63. *Ibid.*, p. 303.

64. *Ibid.*, p. 8.

65. *Ibid.*, p. 303.

66. *Ibid.*, p. 148-176.

67. *Ibid.*, p. 303.

68. *Ibid.*, p. 304.

of knowledge, nor in the *humaniores litterae*[69]. The encyclopedic movement of the tenth century completed the dossier of relevant classical texts[70]. Interest in them was motivated by a spirit of conservation rather than creative development. They were points of reference, to be commented and controlled by reference to Christian dogma.

Several differences between this 'first Byzantine humanism' and that of the Western Renaissance are immediately evident. Western humanism was genuinely anthropocentric, inspired by a renewed confidence in man's ability to explore and master his environment, and accompanied by a critical attitude to the theocentric culture of the Middle Ages. Scholars exploited Antique culture selectively, in order to develop lines of research which existed independently of it. The style of their literary composition was intimately connected with their research. By contrast, Byzantine humanism during the Madeconian 'Renaissance' in no way challenged the prevailing theocentric culture. On the contrary its adepts sought rather to conserve and reinforce the corpus of dogmatic certainties which were the fruit of the decisions of the seven oecumenical councils. They were not interested in exploring and mastering their environment. There was no intimate connection between their theological lucubrations and their assiduous practice of rhetoric. Moreover their frequentation of classical texts which could serve as models for their own literary composition may often be more correctly designated as mimesis rather than as rhetoric[71]. This distinction between rhetoric and mimesis is no doubt important in the study of the Byzantine attitude to its Hellenic literary heritage. It is capital in the study of its attitude to its Hellenic artistic heritage. If the aspect of Hellenic culture which was particularly valued during the Macedonian 'Renaissance' may be generically designated as style, it is necessary to use the term with considerable circumspection.

The ensuing paragraphs are intended only to raise a number of issues relevant to the study of style during the Macedonian 'Renaissance'. Some questions cannot yet be definitively answered, because the source material has yet to be published; others, probably, can never be definitively answered, because the source material either does not or never did exist. Nevertheless, these questions should be asked. The points at issue are: conditions of artistic production; scientific and technical exploration; the status of the artist and his capacity for individual expression.

Artistic production during the Western Renaissance is sufficiently well documented for it to be possible to reconstruct its organisation independently of the

69. *Ibid.*, p. 302, 305. This arrest of speculative thinking extended to theology, notably as to the possibility of establishing an analogy between the Eucharistic species and a figurative representation as 'icons' of Christ, WALTER, *op. cit.* (note 45), p. 186-189.

70. LEMERLE, *ibid.*, p. 304-305.

71. H. HUNGER, On the Imitation ΜΙΜΗΣΙΣ of Antiquity in Byzantine Literature, *DOP* 23-24, 1969-1970, p. 17-38. He recalls that Greek Antiquity and the Byzantine Middle Ages cared very little for « original genius ».

internal evidence provided by the paintings themselves. Schools, workshops, individual artists may be identified, making possible the reconstitution of objective structures, which may serve as a basis for the study of stylistic relationships: influences, original developments and so on. Such documentation is virtually non-existent for the Macedonian 'Renaissance'. The art historian may be tempted to assume that the structures of art production in Constantinople were similar to those in the West. If, however, he is prudent, he will exploit the model cautiously. For example, the wellknown accounts by Theophanes Continuatus and Liutprand of Cremona of the artistic patronage of Constantine VII (913-959) make no reference to manuscript illumination[72]. Yet it is largely on the evidence of miniature painting that the notion of a Macedonian 'Renaissance' is based. It is hardly likely that Constantine VII did not maintain a permanent scriptorium under his patronage. However, even for the eleventh and twelfth centuries, from which a far greater number of illuminated manuscripts have survived, scholars are now less willing to suppose that the miniatures were executed in a workshop attached to the scriptorium[73]. Even when illuminated manuscripts may be grouped together by reason of stylistic resemblances, the inference that they were produced in the same workshop is not certain. With regard to the Palaeologan group of illuminated manuscripts which are associated with Theodora Raoulaina, the scholars who have studied them so assiduously have not been able to relate them either to an earlier or to a later group, although their dependence on tenth-century models can be demonstrated[74]. Other art historians, emulating their assiduity, will no doubt establish similar groups for the tenth century. Yet it may still remain impossible to establish that workshops for manuscript illumination formed part of the structure of Constantinopolitan art production during the Macedonian 'Renaissance'. It may prove difficult to refute the hypothesis that artists were assembled to execute specific commissions, and that such production was contingent and occasional.

The point was made earlier that, during the Western Renaissance, stylistic development was closely related to scientific and technical exploration. The first Byzantine humanists, however, studied rhetoric in abstraction from the sciences. What can we know about the way in which their contemporaries conceived the technical problems of art production? The term *prospettiva* is an invention of the Florentine Quattrocento, used to distinguish the rules for representing recession in a picture from the laws governing recession in optics[75].

72. THEOPHANES CONTINUATUS VI, 18-28, Bonn, p. 449-452 ; MANGO, *op. cit.* (note 12), p. 207-210.

73. Suzy DUFRENNE, Problèmes des ateliers de miniaturistes byzantins, *XVI. Internationaler Byzantinistenkongress, Akten* I/2 (= *JÖB* 31/2, 1981), p. 445-470.

74. Such is the conclusion of H. BUCHTHAL & H. BELTING, *Patronage in Thirteenth Century Constantinople*, Washington 1978, for the group of Palaeologan manuscripts analysed in this study.

75. D. GIOSEPPI, Perspective, *Encyclopedia of World Art* XI, 184.

If, therefore, it is an anachronism to use the term perspective when describing Byzantine painting, nevertheless there can be no doubt that Byzantine artists, like their Antique predecessors, were versant with perspective *avant la lettre*. Moreover treatises concerning arithmetic, geometry and astronomy were copied in the ninth and tenth centuries. Arethas had a manuscript of Euclid copied, *Bodleian d'Orvill.* 301, which was finished in 888[76]. School manuals which treat these subjects are unfortunately for the most part unpublished[77]. However, the use made by Byzantine artists of the Macedonian 'Renaissance', both to set their compositions in perspective and to compensate, in monumental painting, for distortion due to the angle of vision of the beholder, has to be established on internal evidence. Some scholars have attempted to reconstruct the lines of recession in Byzantine paintings but so far on too limited a scale[78]. In general, classicizing works, particularly miniatures, of this period are not composed with a single vanishing point. They are constructed piecemeal from details taken from models, whose perspective is retained but not unified in the new composition. This is particularly evident in portraits of Evangelists set against a classical architecturescape[79]. The effects of recession are derivative and not the result of deliberate technical exploration on the part of the artist.

The plastic rendering of the human figure in Western Renaissance art derived in part from the study of anatomy and in part from the imitation and adaptation of classical statuary. The extent to which anatomy was studied during the Macedonian 'Renaissance' requires investigation[80]. For practical purposes, Byzantine artists needed some working rules for representing the human figure[81]. The unique surviving text, the treatise composed by Ulpius the Roman in the

76. LEMERLE, *op. cit.* (note 37), p. 170-171, 224-225. G. MATHEW, *Byzantine Aesthetics*, London 1963, p. 23-27, discusses the use of mathematics by Byzantine artists, and maintains that Euclid's *Optics* was available to them, thanks to Pappus Alexandrinus (*fl.* late third century). Pappus commented the *Optics* in Συναγωγαί VI, but this treatise does not figure in the *Bibliotheca* of Photius, nor is it mentioned by Lemerle as having been copied by the first Byzantine Humanists. MATHEW, *ibid.*, p. 31, writes : 'If a Byzantine artist is primarily concerned with height and width, it is because his primary task to provide surface decoration'. Would this explanation extend to miniature painting ?

77. LEMERLE, *op. cit.* (note 37), p. 133.

78. E. PANOFSKY, Die Perspektive als symbolische Form, *Vorträge der Bibliothek Warburg*, 1921-1925 ; MICHELIS, *op. cit.* (note 5), p. 174-195.

79. For example, the portraits in the Gospel Book *Athos Stavronikita* 43, illustrated by WEITZMANN, Character and Intellectual Origins, *art. cit.* (note 55), figs. 180, 203.

80. LEMERLE, *op. cit.* (note 37), gives no reference to copies of classical treatises on anatomy.

81. E. PANOFSKY, The History of the Theory of Human Proportions as a Reflection of the History of Styles, *Meaning in the Visual Arts*, New York 1955, p. 55-107 ; WINFIELD, *op. cit.* (note 1), who suggests that nose-length provided the basic unit for human proportion in Byzantine art.

ninth or tenth century, is unfortunately laconic[82]. His directions for rendering most figures is limited to the observation that they were tall, of middle stature or short. Exceptionally, he gives precise measurements for Adam, 'the first man created by God', which, if they could be convincingly interpreted, might provide information as to the ideal proportions of the human figure during the Macedonian 'Renaissance'.

To supplement this meagre information on Byzantine notions of human proportion, scholars have sometimes worked on the assumption that the treatises of Denys of Fourna and Manuel Panselinus incorporate traditions dating back to the Byzantine epoch[83]. However, the remarks of Denys of Fourna on human proportions are difficult to interpret. Hetherington has suggested that they were originally formulated by 'piecemeal observation of existing painted figures rather than on a mathematical basis'[84]. If so, it seems that, in this respect at least, he was indeed following an ancient tradition. Again the hypothesis remains open that the plasticity of the human figure in Macedonian 'Renaissance' painting is derivative. Moreover, it does not derive from the abundant examples of classical statuary available in tenth-century Constantinople. As Mango has shown, the Byzantine attitude to these statues was ambivalent[85]. Yet in no case did they stimulate the same interest as classical literature. Nor did artists resort to them as models, even when their composition required the presence of a classical statue[86]. The plastic human figures of Macedonian painting derive from earlier copies in manuscript illumination or the minor arts.

82. M. CHATZIDAKIS, 'Εκ τῶν 'Ελπίου τοῦ 'Ρωμαίου, *Studies in Byzantine Art and Archaeology*, London 1972, p. 409 ; MANGO, *op. cit.* (note 12), p. 214-215 ; WALTER, *op. cit.* (note 45), p. 106-107.

83. The confidence placed by art historians in the *Hermeneia* is surprising. E. BERGER, *Beiträge zur Entwicklungsgeschichte der Maltechnik* III, Munich 1897, p. 65-92, attributes the text of Panselinus, 'Ερμηνεία τῆς ζωγραφικῆς τέχνης, edited A. PAPADOPOULOS-KERAMEUS, Saint Petersburg 1909, p. 237-253, following M. DIDRON, *Manuel de l'iconographie chrétienne*, Paris 1845, p. 7, to the twelfth century. LOUMYER, *op. cit.* (note 53), p. 59, recognizes that there are additions to the 'fond médiéval' ; he maintains that they can be easily separated but he does not explain how. PANOFSKY, *art. cit.* (note 78), also considers that the *Hermeneia* embodies authentic Medieval traditions. However, the *Hermeneia* is poor evidence for Byzantine Medieval practice so long as no critical edition is available. Meanwhile, the annotations of P. HETHERINGTON, *The Painter's Manual of Dionysius of Fourna*, London 1974, are shrewd and penetrating. For Manuel Panselinus there is now a considerable bibliography : HETHERINGTON, *op. cit.*, p. 91 ; M. RESTLE, Athos, *Reallexikon zur byzantinischen Kunst* I, 411-412. See especially A. XYNGOPOULOS, *Thessalonique et la peinture macédonienne*, Athens 1955 ; IDEM, *Manuel Panselinos*, Athens 1956. There is no reference to Panselinus in the sources earlier than 1744, when the tradition is first attested that he was the artist from Thessaloniki who painted frescoes in the Protaton, Karyes.

84. HETHERINGTON, *op. cit.* (note 83), p. 95.

85. MANGO, *art. cit.* (note 60).

86. *Ibid.*, p. 73-75.

During the Western Renaissance, the social status of artists steadily improved. An activity which had been artisanal became the occupation of men of wide culture with distinctive personalities, on a par with men of letters. It seems that over the centuries a similar improvement occurred in the social status of Byzantine artists. Whereas an imperial decree, issued in 337, ranked artists with stone-masons and blacksmiths[87], the *œuvre* of the twelfth-century Eulalius inspired epigrams and learned puns[88]. Yet references to painters by their names are infrequent in the literary sources, particularly before the twelfth century. If Lazarus the icon-painter is remembered, it is less because his painting was of outstanding quality than because he refused to be suborned by the Iconoclasts[89].

However, the personality of one artist of the Macedonian 'Renaissance' can be tentatively reconstructed. In the *Life* of Athanasius the Athonite, it is told how a certain Pantoleon was commissioned to copy an icon[90]. One of the illuminators of the *Menologium of Basil II* is also called Pantoleon[91]. An idiosyncracy has been detected in his miniatures. He had a *penchant* for introducing classical statues (idols) into his miniatures quite gratuitously. Yet he did not copy them from extant classical statues but rather from representations of them, whether in other miniatures or in the minor arts[92]. It cannot be proved that the name Pantoleon refers to the same artist. Yet it is significant that in each case the artist was commissioned to copy another work rather than to produce an original one, and that in the latter case he was free to follow in a limited degree the dictates of his personal taste.

Nevertheless, in contrast to the Western Renaissance and contemporary humanist letters, ninth- and tenth century artistic production remained artisanal. Works were produced, in which mosaic tesserae were set or colours layered with consummate skill. Yet the more plausible hypothesis is that the subjects as well as the stylistic models were chosen by patrons rather than the artists themselves. It is unlikely that the way in which models were transmitted can ever be exactly established. The rare surviving *bozze* are palimpsests, which were readily expendable[93]. However, comparisons with earlier works suggest that, in monumental painting however the model was transmitted, artists turned to early Byzantine art rather than directly to whatever remained of Antique

87. *Cod. Theod.* XIII iv 2, MANGO, *op. cit.* (note 12), p. 15.

88. *Ibid.*, p. 229-232.

89. THEOPHANES CONTINUATUS, Bonn, p. 102-103 (= MANGO, *ibid.*, p. 159) ; Ch. WALTER, Saints of Second Iconoclasm in the Madrid Scylitzes, *REB* 39, 1981, p. 310-311.

90. MANGO, *ibid.*, p. 213·214.

91. I. ŠEVČENKO, The Illuminators of the Menologium of Basil II, *DOP* 16, 1962, p. 243-276 ; IDEM, On Pantoleon the Painter, *JÖB* 21, 1972, p. 241-249.

92. MANGO, *art. cit.* (note 60), p. 73-74.

93. H. BUCHTHAL, The '*Musterbuch*' of Wolfenbüttel and Its Position in the Art of the 13th Century, Vienna 1979. In the Kekelidze Institute of Manuscripts, Tbilissi, there are three large folios with uncial script, which have served as palimpsests for sketches of an angel and two saints.

monumental painting and mosaic[94]. Here again the preference of Photius for literature of the Christian era should be recalled[95].

In answer to one of the questions which were raised, it may, then, be said that the artists of the Macedonian 'Renaissance' did not, unlike those of the Western Renaissance, study directly the art of Antiquity. To another of the questions raised, whether this was a period of progress and creativity, it is more difficult to give a straight answer, because the criteria used for the Western Renaissance hardly apply. In Western art stylistic development can be measured in terms of scientific and technical exploration, but, since, apparently, there was no such exploration during the Macedonian 'Renaissance', strictly speaking there was no development, any more than in the preceding centuries. Art historians register and designate changes in style; they even plot them out, but the pattern which emerges is often abstruse and convoluted: 'spirals and not regular spirals at that'[96]. These changes reflect usually fashion in the choice of models. In their exploitation the artist, lacking the culture of his literary contemporaries, practised 'mimesis' rather than 'rhetoric'. Yet although it is authorized by no literary text, it is certainly useful to explore the analogies between literary and artistic composition[97]. An artist could exercise a measure of independence in embellishing his composition, rather than leave it in the rudimentary state of those widely scattered works painted in what is called, unjustifiably it would seem, the 'monastic' style[98]. He might even resort to antithesis. Rarely indeed, during the Macedonian 'Renaissance' does the embellishment of his composition reveal direct familiarity with literary use of rhetoric. Whatever may be the case during the 'Late Palaeologan Renaissance', during the ninth and tenth centuries inspiration hardly gushed from this 'hidden spring of Hellenism'[99]. In sum, progress and creativity are not useful concepts for describing the fashions of ninth- and tenth-century Byzantine art.

4. Conclusion

The principal aim of this article has been to describe and explain the difficulties which arise when an attempt is made to present a coherent interpretation of

94. The dependence of ninth-century art on surviving works from the sixth and seventh centuries rather than from Antiquity is argued by R. CORMACK, Painting after Iconoclasm, Iconoclasm, edited A. BRYER & Judith HERRIN, Birmingham 1977, p. 147-163 ; see also KITZINGER, art. cit. (note 4), p. 661-663.

95. LEMERLE, op. cit. (note 37), p. 304.

96. DEMUS, op. cit. (note 3), p. 3.

97. KITZINGER, art. cit. (note 4), p. 674, with references, advocates the use of the term rhetoric, understood analogically, in describing original stylistic elements in Byzantine works of art.

98. C. MANGO, Lo stile cosidetto 'monastico' della pittura bizantina, *Habitat Strutture Territorio*, Galatina 1978, p. 45-63.

99. MAGUIRE, op. cit. (note 8), p. 52.

Byzantine figurative art up to the 11th century in terms of style as this word is normally understood in art history. For the early period, the principal reason for the extreme diversity of style is probably to be sought in the dominant motivation for art production: the need to create a coherent system of signs in order to communicate the 'messages' of Christianity. This system was built up from the iconography of earlier figurative art. The style of the works from which this iconography was borrowed was of secondary consideration; the artist's function, which did not change in succeeding centuries, was primarily that of a copyist or adaptor.

Focus on the 'message' of figurative works of art is undoubtedly in large part responsible for what one might call the introverted character of Byzantine art[100]. It is almost entirely divorced from the world of nature. If artists looked beyond existing works for inspiration, it was usually to another form of communication: ritual and ceremony[101]. Consequently, in order to seek an explanation of the style of a work of art, it is necessary first to identify the model and account for its choice; after this, there may be still the possibility of demonstrating on occasions that the artist elaborated his own 'personal' rhetoric[102].

These observations may also apply to the art of the Macedonian 'Renaissance'. However, during this period, new factors come into play, which are possibly more easier to identify in the contemporary revival of interest in classical literature: an arrest of speculative enquiry; the establishment of a corpus of authoritative texts; the assiduous study of rhetoric. These factors have their correlatives in artistic production: conservative iconographical programmes; a preference, at least at first, for models taken from the centuries immediately preceding Iconoclasm; a continuous preference, in spite of variations in fashion, for a 'Hellenic' style recalling works executed in conformity with the classical canon.

However, this 'Hellenic' style was abandoned, almost abruptly, in the eleventh century. There was a return to a style recalling rather models which flout the classical canon; one might call it 'expressionist'. This change of style coincides with a widening of the iconographical repertory, in which the innovations may

100. Compare Lemerle's expression, *op. cit.* (note 37), p. 306 : 'connaissance du dedans'. He continues : 'Elle s'est... enfermée dans le monde sans communication, dans le cercle clos du discours théologique'.

101. O. TREITINGER, *Die oströmische Kaiser- und Reichsidee*, second edition, Darmstadt 1956. Performance of ceremony, in order to maintain an eschatological mode of existence, no doubt reinforced the boundaries of the 'cercle clos' (see preceding note). However ceremony, particularly ecclesiastical ceremony, was developed and modified. I have argued that liturgical development was one of the contributing causes of iconographical renewal in the eleventh century, WALTER, *op. cit.* (note 45), p. 189-192. This renewal was accompanied by a raising of the embargo on speculation about the Eucharist, see above, note 69. Consequently it is not quite exact to write of a 'discours théologique inlassablement, indéfiniment répétitif', LEMERLE, *op. cit.* (note 37), p. 306.

102. K. WEITZMANN, *Illustrations in Roll and Codex*, second printing, Princeton 1970, p. 205.

in large part be traced back to ecclesiastical and, in some cases, imperial ritual and ceremony. This coincidence of a return in the eleventh century to an 'expressionist' style and an iconographical renewal was the starting point of the present enquiry[103]. Once again, it marks a difference between the specificity of Byzantine art and that of the Western Renaissance, when iconographical renewal coincided with a return to the classical canon.

In an art which is primarily conceptualist, it is not surprising that the stimulus to creative renewal should derive from the need to construct new 'messages'. Moreover a coherent interpretation of development in Byzantine art in terms of iconographical programmes presents far fewer difficulties than an interpretation of development in terms of style. For this reason, it may be correct to describe style in Byzantine art as epiphenomenal.

At this point, an answer may be attempted to a question which had been left in suspense: was the Macedonian 'Renaissance' a heyday in the history of Byzantine art? For those who concentrate their attention on the survival of Hellenism, the answer is clear. The Macedonian 'Renaissance' was a 'peak', while the eleventh century was a 'valley', a 'period of estrangement from the classical tradition'[104]. Yet such a proposition is reversible. In terms of iconographical development, the eleventh century was a 'peak' and the Macedonian 'Renaissance' a 'valley'.

Even if Byzantine art was introverted and its style epiphenomenal to its iconographical content, it may still be possible to establish and explain the relationship in different periods between content and style. In the early Byzantine period, in spite of its stylistic eclecticism, which has been explained in terms of the relative indifference of artists to the style of their models, provided that they could be adapted to the communication of the Christian message, the late fourth-century 'renaissance' stands out as a period when the choice of style was ideologically motivated. In different contexts a classical style could 'communicate', because it was associated with nostalgia for a past epoch[105]. Ninth-century copying of the style of monuments surviving from the pre-Iconoclast period was also ideologically motivated. However, it is possible that in the later decades of the Macedonian 'Renaissance' the relative stability of iconographical programmes encouraged artists to exercise a limited measure of initiative in adapting their Hellenic models. On the other hand, when eleventh-century artists were required to construct new 'messages', they were too preoccupied by the need to select or improvise appropriate signs to give much

103. WALTER, op. cit. (note 45), p. 5-6 ; IDEM, Résumés der Kurzbeiträge, XVI. Internationaler Byzantinistenkongress, Vienna 1981, 10.1 ; IDEM, Style an Epiphenomenon of Ideological Development in Byzantine Art, ibid., Akten II/5 (= JÖB 32/5, 1982), p. 3-6. See also my review of KITZINGER, op. cit. (note 17), REB 37, 1979, p. 291-293.

104. KITZINGER, art. cit. (note 4), p. 660-661.

105. See above, note 51.

attention to producing an illusion of physical reality. Thus it may be argued that in the history of Byzantine art what is determinant is the need to communicate. On the other hand it cannot be argued that iconographical renewal was invariably associated with an expressionist style. To plot the history of stylistic development in terms of perpetual expressionism does not make better sense than to plot it in terms of perpetual Hellenism.

Associated with the expressionist style of the eleventh century is an increase of versatility in decorative motifs particularly in manuscript illustration. This tendency is even more marked in the twelfth century. It is necessary only to cite the Homilies of Gregory of Nazianzus, *Sinaï*. 339, and the manuscripts associated with it[106]. The miniatures are virtually swamped by the richly decorated borders surrounding them. This may serve as a reminder that a proper appreciation of style in Byzantine figurative art cannot be dissociated from a consideration of its setting. An ecphrasis of a church usually describes the figurative paintings summarily: their subject and their lifelikeness[107]. There may also be some observations on their function, which was, from Nilus of Sinaï[108] to Symeon of Thessaloniki[109], invariably to communicate: to instruct the illiterate and to impress all who beheld them[110]. However, when the writer describes the setting, he has difficulty in restraining his admiration and raptures. The point hardly requires to be laboured. Byzantine taste found its delight in gleam and glitter: shining marble, dazzling gold tesserae, silk and pearls[111]. The luxurious surviving monuments, from the churches of Justinian to the Kariye Cami, confirm that this is not mere verbiage. In church decoration at least what counted was the overall effect. The writer of the *Life* of Basil I was struck time after time by the 'beauties' of the New Church[112]. When he moved on to the Kainourgion he succumbed to another emotion, stupor or amazement (ἔκπληξις)[113]. Or did he? Perhaps for the Byzantine beholder the sublime and the beautiful were not mutually exclusive[114].

106. J. C. ANDERSON, The Illustration of Cod. Sinaï. Gr. 339, *The Art Bulletin* 61, 1979, p. 167-185.

107. MANGO, *op. cit.* (note 12), p. 60-72, 80-91, 107-108, 184-190, 192-205, etc.

108. *PG* 79, 577-580 (= MANGO, *ibid.*, p. 32-33).

109. *Dialogus contra haereses*, 23, *PG* 155, 112 (= MANGO, *ibid.*, p. 253) : '(Icons) instruct us pictorially by means of colour and other materials'.

110. WOLSKA-CONUS, *art. cit.* (note 12), p. 248 : 'l'image qui serait mise sous les yeux de tous comme un livre'.

111. MANGO, *op. cit.* (note 12), p. 3.

112. *Vita Basilii*, 83-85, THEOPHANES CONTINUATUS V, Bonn, p. 325-327 (= MANGO, *ibid.*, p. 194-195).

113. *Vita Basilii*, 89, *ibid.*, p. 332, line 5 (= MANGO, *ibid.*, p. 197).

114. FAGGIN, *art. cit.* (note 12), 1032. In the Περὶ ὕψους, 'il concetto di sublime non sembra implicare nessuna distinzione di valore fra κάλλος e ὕψος'.

PORTRAITS OF LOCAL BISHOPS:
A NOTE ON THEIR SIGNIFICANCE

Early Christian and Byzantine art was, for the most part, inspired by the needs of religious cult. This could be the cult of the triumphant Christ, of the saints or of the dead. No attempt was made to devise in the early centuries a sign language which could set forth in pictorial form the rights and status of the universal or local Church. This is surprizing considering the frequency and acerbity of disputes whether about doctrine or about jurisdiction. So far as Christendom had its 'official imagery' in these early centuries, it was that of the *oikoumene*, in which the principal rôle in the divine providential plan was attributed to the emperor.[1]

Nevertheless circumstances did arise in which a local Church chose to call attention to its special claims. Whether such claims were limited to prestige or extended to jurisdiction over other episcopal sees, they had to be expressed within the limits of available imagery, that of Christian cult or of the imperial court. An appreciation of these special uses of imagery is best focussed upon the representation of local bishops, the more so that their portraits have been assiduously studied in recent years.[2] The present article does not present any new material. It is intended rather to be interpretative. After a consideration of pictures from the early centuries, which are found in shrines when they proclaim the status of the local Church, it passes to changes in the 9th century, when new iconographical themes are found in cathedrals. Since these themes were concerned with the universal status of the Church, it now became necessary to devise new ways of expressing local claims in imagery.

The most usual way in Early Christian art of introducing a local bishop into an iconographical programme was to represent him as a donor. Examples of such pictures have survived at Rome, Poreč and Ravenna.[3] In this last centre may be cited, besides the surviving portrait of bishop Ecclesius (522—

---

[1] Ch. Walter, *Art and Ritual of the Byzantine Church* (London, 1982), 179 ff.

[2] Svetlana Tomeković, 'Les évêques locaux dans la composition absidale des saints officiant', *Byzantinisch-Neugriechische Jahrbücher* 23 (1981), 65—88.

[3] Walter, *Art and Ritual*, 179—180; W. Oakeshott, *The Mosaics of Rome* (London, 1967), *passim*; Jovanka Maksimović,'Ikonografija i program mozaika u Poreču', *ZRVI* 8₂ (1964), 247—262; F. W. Deichmann, *Ravenna Hauptstadt des spätantiken Abendlandes* (Wiesbaden, 1969—1974), *passim*.

—532) in San Vitale, a lost portrait of him presenting the church in Saint Mary Major, and of Maximian (546—556) in Saint Stephen.[4] In other cases the bishop's munificence was commemorated by a simple portrait: John Angeloptes (477—494) in the cathedral Ursiana and in Saint Agatha;[5] Peter II (494—519) in the archiepiscopal chapel;[6] Agnellus (557—570) in Sant' Apollinare Nuovo.[7] Sometimes, it seems, the commemorative portrait was put up by the bishop's successor. In one case, that of the 'Domus quae vocatur Tricoli', the bishop who terminated the work had portraits set up of five earlier bishops who had contributed to it.[8]

Some scholars have attempted to read into such series of portraits an affirmation of the apostolicity of the see and hence of its privileged status. This hypothesis is implausible. Such series witness only to a well-established cult of the local bishops. An analogy is supplied by the effigies made when the remains of dead bishops were deposed in the Stephania in Naples.[9] Similarly effigies of past popes were executed in Rome in the restored tomb of pope Cornelius and in the church of Saint Chrysogonus.[10]

Rather than to his successors, it was to the founder-bishop or protector himself that the status and claims of a local Church were related. This practice may well have been widespread. It is known that both Epiphanius and Spyridon were represented in their respective shrines in Cyprus, and that Cyprus claimed to be an autocephalous Church.[11] However no connection can be established between the descriptions of these lost pictures and the local Church's claims. The case is otherwise for three Western sees: Milan, Ravenna and Rome.

From the 5th century Saint Ambrose was regarded as the protector of the see of Milan. It is therefore not surprizing that in the chapel of Saint Victor at his shrine, he is represented between the martyrs Nabor and Felix.[12] Another bishop, Maternus (*ca.* 316—*ca.* 328), figures between the martyrs Gervase and Proteus. It was during the episcopate of Maternus that Milan, as an imperial residence and administrative centre, became the capital of the diocese of Italia Annonaria.[13] The bishop acquired jurisdiction over

---

[4] Deichmann, *op. cit.*, I, 234—248; II ii, 343; II ii, 372—374.

[5] *Ibid.*, II i, 9—11; II ii, 292—294.

[6] *Ibid.*, II i, 198.

[7] *Ibid.*, II i, 127.

[8] *Ibid.*, II i, 197—198: Aurelianus (519—521); Ecclesius (522/3—532/3); Ursicinus (534/5—536/7); Victor (536/7—544/5); Maximian (546—556). These are Deichmann's dates. The latest list is that of G. Orioli, 'I vescovi di Ravenna. Note di cronologia e di storia', Bollettino della Badia Greca di Grottaferrata 32 (1978), 45—75, but this may not be definitive. See Ch. Walter, 'Was Ravenna an Imperial or a Papal Fief? The Evidence of the Mosaics', *Bulletin de l'Association Internationale pour l'Etude de la Mosaïque Antique* 8 (1980), 93 note 2.

[9] John the Deacon, *Chronicon episcoporum sanctae neapolitanae ecclesiae*, *Rerum italicarum scriptores*, ed. L. A. Muratori (Milan, 1725), II ii, 315.

[10] G. Ladner, *I ritratti dei papi nell'antichità e nel medioevo* I (Vatican, 1941), 38—59; Walter, *Art and Ritual* (note I), 168—169.

[11] Nancy Patterson-Ševčenko, *The Life of Saint Nicholas in Byzantine Art* (Bari, printing); Tomeković, 'Evêques locaux' (note 2), 84; P. Van Den Ven, *La légende de saint Spyridon, évêque de Trimithonte* (Louvain, 1953), 88—91.

[12] Marguerite Van Berchem & E. Clouzot, *Mosaïques chrétiennes du 4e au 10e siècle* (Geneva, 1924), 111—112, figs. 125—126.

[13] F. Dvorník, *The Idea of Apostolicity in Byzantium and the Legend of the Apostle Andrew* (Cambridge, Massachusetts, 1958), 24—25.

ecclesiastical dioceses which had previously been subject to Rome. The new status of the Church of Milan was confirmed by the emperor Constantine in 323. It was therefore appropriate that the bishop then reigning should be represented along with the more renowned Ambrose.

Yet more significant is the lost programme of the central apse of Saint Ambrose.[14] According to 17th-century engravings, there were originally two scenes in the conch associating the cult of Ambrose with that of Martin of Tours.[15] Below the two scenes was a series of pictures of enthroned bishops representing the sees which fell under the jurisdiction of Milan. One of the sees represented was that of Genoa which later became independent. However, unfortunately the separation cannot be used to establish a *terminus ante quem* for the execution of the mosaics. The Italian scholar F. Reggiori was able to examine the remaining mosaics minutely during their restoration after damage incurred in the Second World War. He proposed a 9th-century date with 11th-century restorations, although he did not preclude the possibility that some fragments had been transposed from the apse of the earlier basilica to the present one.[16] The lost series of portraits of suffragan bishops, possibly copying an earlier one, would have been more appropriate to our minds, as A. Grabar remarked, in the decorative programme of a cathedral rather than of a shrine.[17] Nevertheless, as the next examples show, pictures setting forth the claims of a local Church were regularly placed in a shrine.

A consciousness of its local status seems to have developed only slowly in the Church of Ravenna. Its bishops did not seek to become independent of Roman jurisdiction. In fact Ravenna was cited by pope Gelasius in his letter to the bishops of Dardania (495) as one of the cities whose priests did not usurp, on its becoming an imperial residence, anything besides the honours received in ancient times.[18] Although Peter Chrysologus (432——450) has been likened to Ambrose of Milan, there is no evidence that he was particularly venerated.[19] Apparently he discovered the founder-bishop's tomb at Classe and initiated his cult.[20] Yet the portrait of Peter Chrysologus does not figure among the bishops of Ravenna in the later mosaic in Sant' Apollinare in Classe.[21]

In fact it was at about the time that pope Gelasius was congratulating the clergy of Ravenna on the modesty of their ambitions that local tradition began to acquire more importance. The cult of the Ravenna martyrs Vitalis and Ursicinus began at the end of the 5th century.[22] During the episcopate

[14] P. Toesca, *Pittura e miniatura nella Lombardia* (Milan, 1912), 128—129; new edition (Turin, 1966), 68—71, figs. 91—93.

[15] G. P. Puricelli, *Sancti Satyri Confessoris et Sanctorum Ambrosii et Marcellinae fratris Tumulus...* (Milan, 1664); engraving reproduced, *ZRVI* 8₂ (1964), after 168.

[16] F. Reggiori, 'Il mosaico della grande abside di Sant' Ambrogio alla luce di recentissime osservazioni', *Studi in onore di A. Calderini e R. Paribeni*, III (Milan, 1956), 815——817.

[17] A. Grabar, 'Deux témoignages archéologiques sur l'autocéphalie d'une Eglise: Prespa et Ochrid', *ZRVI* 8₂ (1964), 166.

[18] PL 59, 71—72; Dvorník, *Idea of Apostolicity* (note 13), 112.

[19] Eva Teà, 'I committenti d'arte a Ravenna nel V e VI secolo', *Studi Calderini* (note 16), 747.

[20] Deichmann, *Ravenna Hauptstadt* (note 3), I, 21.

[21] *Ibid.*

[22] *Ibid.*, I, 25.

of Ursicinus (533—536) the construction began of a shrine for Apollinarius.[23] After the conquest of Ravenna by Belisarius in 540, the cult of saints popular in Constantinople was introduced, notably of John the Baptist, Stephen and Euphemia.[24] Nevertheless the two churches whose programmes are ecclesiologically significant were dedicated to local saints: Vitalis and Apollinarius.

A comparison might be attempted between the lost church of Saint John the Evangelist, commissioned by the empress Galla Placidia, and that of San Vitale. In the former, the patron saint was represented receiving a book from Christ, a variant of the *Traditio legis*.[25] Below were portraits of members of the imperial family, presumably as donors, while a votive picture of Peter Chrysologus recalled his vision of an angel. In San Vitale, the programme is built up around the central theme of offering.[26] Typological scenes of the Eucharist, taken from the Old Testament, provide the link between Justinian and Theodora presenting their gifts, accompanied by bishop Maximian, and the celestial scene above. Here the local bishop, Ecclesius, presents the church to Christ, who himself crowns the local martyr Vitalis. The theme of offering thus provides the imagery with which to present the integration of the local Church both into the celestial Church through the mediation of Ecclesius and Vitalis and into the *oikoumene* through the mediation of Maximian. This well-structured programme contrasts with the piecemeal disposition of subjects in Galla Placidia's church.

If the programme of San Vitale proclaims the integration of the local Church of Ravenna into the *oikoumene* after Justinian's reconquest, that of Sant' Apollinare in Classe suggests that the local Church nevertheless maintained a certain independence. If so, it was probably due to Maximian (546—556), who consecrated the church in 549.[27] The importance of having a shrine of the founder-bishop was evident. The choice of the four local bishops who also figure in the apse must be significant. Severus (*fl.* 342) was the first 'historical' bishop of Ravenna, whose name figures among those present at the council of Sardica;[28] Ursus (399—426) moved the episcopal see from Classe to Ravenna;[29] Ecclesius (521/2—532/4) initiated the cult of the local martyr Vitalis;[30] Ursicinus (533—536) began the construction of the church.[31] If Peter Chrysologus was not included, it may be because he failed to manifest a spirit of independence.

Yet this programme does no more than reflect the prestige of the local Church. Maximian had received the pallium on his consecration by pope

---

[23] *Ibid.*, I, 21.
[24] *Ibid.*, I, 25.
[25] *Ibid.*, II i, 110, 120—121.
[26] Walter, *Art and Ritual* (note 1), 179—181.
[27] Deichmann, *Ravenna Hauptstadt* (note 3), I, 21.
[28] H. L. Gonin, *Excerpta Agnelliana, The Ravennate* Liber Pontificalis *as a Source for the History of Art* (Utrecht, 1933), 40.
[29] Deichmann, *Ravenna Hauptstadt* (note 3), II ii, 262.
[30] *Ibid.*, I, 25.
[31] *Ibid.*, I, 25. It is noteworthy that no bishop of Ravenna who was venerated as a saint (for example Probus, Eleucadius and Calogerus) figures in the church apart from the founder.

Vigilius in 546.[32] He was later to receive from Justinian the title of arch-bishop, such that Ravenna passed 'from anomalous not quite metropolitan to anomalous super-metropolitan status.[33]' The title is first recorded in a papyrus of 553, but in the consecration inscription Maximian is called *beatissimus*, an adjective normally applied only to patriarchs, archbishops and metropolitans.[34] Maximian was in Constantinople in 548, the previous year, the most likely date for the conferment of the title.[35] Although the title was not recognized nor used in correspondence with the bishops of Ravenna by Rome, nevertheless Pelagius I (556—561) called Ravenna an 'apostolic' see.[36] Yet this, again, would seem to be an honorific title, admitting by implication that Apollinarius had genuinely been a Syrian disciple of Saint Peter who consecrated him first bishop of Ravenna.[37] It is, indeed, unlikely that either the emperor Justinian or pope Vigilius would have favoured any claim at that time for Ravenna to be freed from Roman jurisdiction. Its bishops were their instruments in their common policy of fighting schism in the dioceses of Milan and Aquileia.[38]

Over a century later a mosaic was added to the shrine of Sant' Apollinare in Classe, which clearly records the see of Ravenna's claim to a privileged status, even if the precise nature of the privilege is not specified.[39] Relations between Rome and Ravenna had become strained in the time of pope Gregory I. Two bishops appointed by him to Ravenna, John and Marinianus, Roman by origin and the pope's own protégés, continued to use the title of archbishop and wore the pallium abusively.[40] However, rupture only occurred in 666, when Reparatus sought and received the privilege of autocephaly from Constans II for bishop Maurus (648—671).[41] Maurus was buried in Sant'Apollinare in Classe, where his epitaph, due to his successor Reparatus (671—677), recorded that *Maurus archiepiscopus... liberavit ecclesiam suam de iugo Romanorum servitutis.*[42]

Obviously the mosaic gains in interest if it does indeed record the conferment of autocephaly, such that the imperial figures would be Constans II, Constantine IV, Heraclius and Tiberius, while the bishop in the background, extending his arms in a gesture of protection, would be Apollinarius

---

[32] R. A. Markus, 'Carthage — Prima Justiniana — Ravenna: an Aspect of Justinian's Kirchenpolitik', *Byzantion* 49 (1979), 294.

[33] *Ibid.*, 293.

[34] *Ibid.*, 298.

[35] *Ibid.*, 298.

[36] R. A. Markus, 'Ravenna and Rome 554—604', *Byzantion* 51 (1981), 567.

[37] The earliest documentary evidence for the existence of Apollinarius seems to date from the 5th century, G. Lucchesi, 'Apollinare', *Bibliotheca sanctorum* 2, 239—246. This was probably known to and developed by Agnellus in the 9th century, PL 106, 475——477; Gonin, *Excerpta Agnelliana* (note 28), 59. Agnellus also maintained that, up till the 5th century, bishops of Ravenna had been Syrian in origin.

[38] Markus, 'Carthage — Prima Justiniana — Ravenna' (note 32), 298.

[39] Deichmann, *Ravenna Hauptstadt* (note 3), II ii, 273—279, argues the case closely in favour of the mosaic commemorating the conferment of autocephaly in 666.

[40] Markus, 'Ravenna and Rome' (note 36), 575—578. Just as Maximian, a native of Istria and a protégé of Justinian, these two bishops acquired a sense of local patriotism.

[41] F. Dölger, *Regesten der Kaiserurkunden des oströmischen Reiches*, I (Munich/ /Berlin, 1924), no. 232. The 'scandal' of autocephaly ended in the pontificate of Leo II (682—683), when the newly elected bishop of Ravenna went to Rome to be consecrated, *Le Liber pontificalis*, I (2nd edition, Paris, 1955), 360.

[42] Deichmann, *Ravenna Hauptstadt* (note 3), II ii, 278.

himself. This interpretation has, however, been disputed.[43] Less open to dispute is the view that the mosaic of Old Testament sacrifices was added at the same time as that commemorating the conferment of a privilege.[44] The model was most likely to have been the lower part of the programme of San Vitale. Thus the privilege mosaic is associated with another whose theme is oblation, ineptly in Sant' Apollinare in Classe, for Apollinarius himself is not represented as a donor nor as the recipient of a martyr's crown but as a 'visionary', contemplating Christ and associated with the Transfiguration.

The third example of imagery being related to the founder-bishop in order to set forth the claims and status of a local Church is provided by the lost programmes of the Roman shrines of Saint Peter and Saint Paul.[45] In both the original basilicas dedicated to these saints, there was a series of clipeate portraits of popes. However, whereas other series of local bishops' portraits were not complete, those in Rome go back to the origins of the see. The model for such series was provided by antique series of clipeate portraits set up in a temple.[46] Pliny the Elder describes the series of his ancestors' portraits set up by Appius Claudius in the temple of Bellona.[47] Some idea of their presentation may be formed from the picture of the Basilica Emiliana on coins.[48] The distribution of shields along the architrave above the column was the same as that of the clipeate portraits of popes in the basilicas of Saint Peter and Saint Paul. Thus preceding popes were presented as ancestors, stretching back in an unbroken line to Saint Peter, founder of the see.

Once initiated, the practice continued of adding successive clipeate portraits of popes to those of their predecessors. The question arises when the practice began. Wilpert attributed it to pope Liberius, no doubt because the 'Liberian catalogue', dated 354, is one of the earliest lists to place Saint Peter at the head of the bishops of Rome.[49] However, Ladner rather favoured Leo I (440—461).[50] Not only did the original series of portraits on the south wall of Saint Paul outside the Walls end with Leo I, but also there are references to work undertaken by him in the two basilicas in the *Liber pontificalis*.[51] The ecclesiological climate of Leo I's pontificate seems parti-

[43] See especially S. Mazzarino, 'Da Lollianus ed Arbetio al mosaico storico di S. Apollinare in Classe', *Rivista di studi bizantini e neoellenici* 2—3 (1965—1966), 111—114.

[44] Deichmann, *loc. cit.*, 273.

[45] Ladner, *Ritratti* (note 10), 38ff., 52ff. L. De Bruyne, *L'antica serie di ritratti papali della Basilica di S. Paolo fuori le Mura* (Rome, 1934). For the series at Saint Peter, see the facsimile edition of Giacomo Grimaldi's sketchbook, *Descrizione della basilica antica di S. Pietro in Vaticano, codice barberini latino 2733*, ed. R. Niggl (Vatican 1972), especially figs. 51, 52, 57, 58. Tomeković, 'Evêques locaux' (note 2), refers to a gallery of portraits of popes at San Crisogono, 67 note 2. But this is an exaggeration. See M. Mesnard, *La basilique de Saint-Chrysogone à Rome* (Vatican, 1935) 110.

[46] Ladner, *loc. cit.* (note 45).

[47] Pliny, *Histoire naturelle*, translated M. E. Littré, II (Paris, 1883), 463—464.

[48] G. Fuchs, 'Zur Baugeschichte de Basilica Aemilia in republikanischer Zeit', *Mitteilungen des Deutschen Archäologischen Institut, römische Abteilung* 63 (1956), 19—20, pl. 8.

[49] Dvorník, *Idea of Apostolicity* (note 13), 42; J. Wilpert, *Die römischen Mosaiken und Malereien* (Freiburg im Breisgau, 1917), III, 560 ff.

[50] Ladner, *Ritratti* (note 10), 54—55.

[51] *Liber pontificalis* (note 39), I, 239, 240.

cularly suited to the decoration of these basilicas with pictures setting forth the claim of Rome to be *the* apostolic see. At the council of Chalcedon, with its 28th canon, the rivalry between Constantinople and Rome was expressed in the two opposing theories of the way in which the prestige of a local Church was determined. Constantinople based its claims on the fact that it was the imperial capital and the New Rome. Old Rome, in the person of Leo I, for the first time invoked the Petrine claims to justify its superiority as a see to Constantinople.[52]

The evidence, sparse though it is, favours the view that the pretensions of a local Church were, when expressed in imagery, directly attached in the early Christian period to the cult of the founder-bishop or protector of the see. There may have been a break with this tradition in the 9th century, both in the West and in the East. Pope Leo III (795—816) marked his rupture with the Byzantine imperial court and his quest for a new relationship with Charlemagne and his successors by building two *triclinia* at Saint John Lateran.[53] Both were decorated with mosaics. In one there were scenes of the apostles preaching to the Gentiles. In the other, known in part from later copies, there was an apse scene of the Mission of the Apostles, while, to one side on the triumphal arch, Saint Peter was represented investing Charlemagne with the vexillum and Leo III with the pallium.[54] What should be particularly noted is that Saint Peter himself is also wearing the pallium. Thus Leo III is confirmed as the successor of Saint Peter, while Charlemagne receives the office of protector of 'the Universal Church, particularly the Roman Church.'[55] Essentially the imagery is traditional. What is new is that it has been transferred from a shrine to a seat of government, that is to say to the papal palace and cathedral. The decoration of these two *triclinia* was the starting point for a whole series of Roman programmes, in which the central theme is no longer the cult of Saint Peter but rather the authority of the current occupant of the see of Rome.[56]

The echelon of bishops in Saint Sophia, Constantinople, dates from later in the 9th century, probably from the years after the earthquake of

---

[52] Dvorník, *op. cit.*, 98.

[53] Ch. Walter, 'Papal Political Imagery in the Medieval Lateran Palace', *Cahiers archéologiques* 20 (1970), 157—160, 170—176.

[54] *Ibid.*, 158, fig. 1. No certainty is possible as to the subject of mosaic on the other side of the triumphal arch, although Grimaldi reported a tradition that it had been Saint Paul. This is plausible, the more so that in the nearby church of San Clemente, consecrated in 1128, when, presumably, the *triclinium* mosaic was still extant, Saint Peter and Paul figure to either side of the triumphal arch, G. Matthiae, *Mosaici medioevali delle chiese di Roma* (Rome, 1967), I, 279—304, II, pl. 228. The authenticity of the drawing upon which the later restoration was based, was already doubted by contemporaries, E. Müntz, 'Notes sur les mosaïques chrétiennes de l'Italie, 8, Le triclinium du Latran et Léon III', *Revue archéologique* (1884), 9—12. H. Belting makes no reference to this article, nor to mine, in his paper, 'I mosaici dell'aula leonina come testimonianza della prima „renovatio" nell'arte medioevale di Roma', *Roma e l'Età Carolingia* (Rome, 1976), 169—182. Moreover he accepts apparently without question the authenticity of the later restoration.

[55] G. B. Ladner, 'Aspects of Medieval Thought on Church and State', *Review of Politics* 9 (1947), 406.

[56] Walter, 'Papal Political Imagery' (note 53), continued in *Cahiers archéologiques* 21 (1971), 109—136. It may be noted that a series of portraits of popes was later represented in Saint John Lateran under pope Nicolas III (1277—1280), Ladner, *Ritratti* (note 10), 57. Meanwhile a series of portraits of bishops of Ravenna had been represented in the Cathedral Ursiana, dated 1112, Deichmann, *Ravenna Hauptstadt* (note 3) II i, 9.

14

869.[57] Without being the formal answer of the Constantinopolitan Church to the Roman claim to primacy as expressed in Leo III's mosaics, it nevertheless well exemplifies the very different way in which Eastern ecclesiology was developing. Whereas the programme of Leo III's mosaics gives universal force to the claims of a local Church, the programme in Saint Sophia gives universal force to the claims of the whole communion of bishops. In the *triclinium* the pope alone figures as the successor to Saint Peter. In Saint Sophia, the whole college of bishops figures as succeeding to the college of apostles.

The constitution of an echelon of bishops can be traced in the preceding dialectics in the form of imagery.[58] It was, it seems, during the reign of Justinian (527—565) that the practice began of displaying publicly pictures of orthodox bishops and destroying pictures of those who were considered to be heterodox. The latest testimony to this practice dates from the reign of Theodosius III (715—717), who replaced a picture at the Milion of the third council of Constantinople destroyed by Philippicus (711—713).[59] The absence of further testimonies may suggest that, with the Triumph of Orthodoxy, a synthesis had been achieved. The echelon of saintly bishops began to figure regularly in Eastern church decorative programmes below the angels, prophets and apostles. It may be suggested tentatively that, although this practice became general, it was likely to have been originally conceived for the decoration of cathedrals.

Once the echelon of saintly bishops had become a regular theme of Byzantine apse decoration, new ways had to be invented of setting forth the status and claims of a local Church. The most common practice was to introduce saintly bishops who received a local cult among those who were universally venerated in the Byzantine Church.[60] Usually they were ancient

---

[57] C. Mango & E. J. W. Hawkins, 'The Mosaics of Saint Sophia at Istanbul. The Church Fathers in the North Tympanum', *Dumbarton Oaks Papers* 28 (1972), 1—41. Ch. Delvoye, 'La signification des mosaïques posticonoclastes de Sainte-Sophie de Constantinople', *Problèmes d'histoire du christianisme* 9 (1980), *Hommages à Jean Hadot*, 45—55 (presented briefly at the Byzantine Congress in Vienna, 1981) gives a further explanation of the reasons for choosing individual bishops, but has little new to add with regard to the over-riding criteria.

[58] Walter, *Art and Ritual* (note 1), 169—170, where all the literary references known to me are given. The reference in the *Parastaseis* to the Arians destroying images of Metrophanes, Alexander and Paul in the Forum of Constantinople, together with an icon of the Virgin and Child, dates from after 741, and is probably anachronistic, C. Mango, *The Art of the Byzantine Empire, 312—1452* (Englewood Cliffs, N. J., 1972), 16.

[59] Ch. Walter, *L'iconographie des conciles dans la tradition byzantine* (Paris, 1970), 20—21. R. Cormack has suggested that there may, in fact, have heen inscriptions at the Milion, like those in the church of the Nativity, Bethlehem, rather than pictures, 'The Arts during the Age of Iconoclasm', *Iconoclasm*, edited A. Bryer & Judith Herrin (Birmingham, 1977), 42. Further evidence of the 'dialectical' use of imagery may be available at Faras, Nubia, where the local Church was Monophysite until *ca.* 1000. Bishop John then introduced the Melkite rite. In their portraits, bishops Cyrus (866—902) and Peter (973——999) are wearing the *šamla*. Marian (1005—1037) is represented without the *šamla*. See T. Golgowski, 'Z problematyki ikonografii biskupów Pachoras', *Rocznik Muzeum Narodowego w Warszawie* 11 (1967), 175—191; K. Michałowski, 'Open problems of Nubian Art and Culture in the Light of the Discoveries at Faras', *Kunst und Geschichte Nubiens in christlicher Zeit*, edited E. Dinkler (Recklinghausen, 1970), 14.

[60] Tomeković, 'Evêques locaux', (note 2), 73—88.

bishops, although occasionally more recent local bishops were chosen.[61] The general sense of the inclusion of local saintly bishops among the others must be that the local Church was in communion with the other orthodox Churches.

The most original adaptation of the echelon of bishops to the situation of a local Church was that of the church of Saint Sophia, Ohrid.[62] Here, as Grabar justly remarked, the choice and number of bishops represented was inspired not by the claims of Ohrid to autocephaly as Prima Justiniana but by its recent reintegration into the Constantinopolitan sphere of influence.[63] In this respect its situation resembled that of Ravenna in the 6th century. However, whereas the Church was conceived in Justinian's time as the *oikoumene*, in which the emperor had a leading rôle, in the 11th century its structure was entirely clerical. In Saint Sophia, Ohrid, the principal bishops represented are John Chrysostom as exemplar of wisdom and Basil of Caesarea as author of the principal Constantinopolitan liturgy.[64] Unlike other echelons of saintly bishops in apse programmes, that in Saint Sophia, Ohrid, is not inspired uniquely by their cult. An explicitly ecclesiological significance may be attributed to their choice and disposition. The patriarchates of the Pentarchy are all represented, with pride of place given to the saintly bishops of Constantinople.[65] Two local bishops, Cyril the Philosopher and Clement of Ohrid, are relegated to an unimportant place on the

[61] Desanka Milošević, 'Ikonografija svetoga Save u srednjem veku', *Sava Nemanjić — Sveti Sava, istorija i predanje*, edited V. Đurić (Belgrade, 1979), 279—315. There have so far been published only two examples of recently dead Greek bishops figuring among those who officiate at the altar. One, Michael Choniates, in Saint Peter, Kalivia-Kouvara, has long been known, Nafsika Coumbaraki-Pansélinou, *Saint Pierre de Kalivia-Kouvara et la chapelle de la Vierge de Mérenta* (Thessaloniki, 1976), 67—70, pls. 11—12. The other, of John Kaloktenes of Thebes (12th century) in the crypt of Saint Nicolas, Kambia (Boeotia), was published recently by Maria Panagiotide, Οἱ τοιχογραφίες τῆς κρυπτῆς τοῦ ἁγίου Νικολάου στὰ Κάμπια τῆς Βοιωτίας, *Actes du 15e congrès international d'études byzantines, Athènes 1976*, II, *Art et Archéologie*, Communications (Athens, 1981), 601, 614, fig. 5. John Kaloktenes of Thebes figures frequently in the correspondence of the patriarchs of Constantinople. He was also considered to be a saint by so elevated a personality as Gregory Palamas, *Regestes des actes du patriarcat de Constantinople*, Index *sub nomine*. For Slav bishops recently dead, see below note 67.

[62] V. Đurić, *Vizantijske freske u Jugoslaviji* (Belgrade, 1974), 9—10, with earlier bibliography, especially S. Radojčić, 'Prilozi za istoriju najstarijeg ohridskog slikarstva', *ZRVI* 8₂ (1964), 355—381; Ann Wharton Epstein, 'The Political Content of the Paintings of Saint Sophia at Ohrid', *Jahrbuch der österreichischen Byzantinistik* 29 (1980), 315—329; Walter, *Art and Ritual* (note 1), 175—176, 193—198.

[63] Grabar, 'Deux témoignages' (note 17), 166—168. Ann Epstein, *art. cit.* (note 62), develops Grabar's thesis, but carries it too far. Strictly the pictures have no 'political' content, for their themes are entirely religious, although no doubt Leo's appointment to Ohrid was intended to facilitate the political reintegration of the city into the Byzantine Empire. Epstein fails to notice the local bishops (see note 67 below). Her interpretation of the Christ child as a deacon in the apse, as well as of the Communion of the Apostles, is open to doubt. Finally the scene on the north wall of the sanctuary next to that of Basil celebrating the liturgy can now only be understood as John Chrysostom receiving the gift of wisdom, C. Grozdanov, 'Slika javljanja premudrosti sv. Jovanu Zlatoustom u sv. Sofiji Ohridskoj', *ZRVI* 19 (1980), 147—155.

[64] Walter, *Art and Ritual* (note 1), 193—196.

[65] Radojčić, 'Prilozi' (note 62), 365—369.

south wall of the diaconicon.[66] Thus the latent autocephaly of Ohrid was strictly contained!

A new situation arose in the late Byzantine epoch, for which no exact analogy exists in Eastern Christendom in the pre-Iconoclast period, when a claim to autocephaly was associated with national autonomy. So far as the national Church was concerned, such a claim did not imply the rupture of ecclesiastical communion with Constantinople. On the contrary, local saintly bishops — Cyril the Philosopher, Clement of Ohrid, Sava I and Arsenije of Serbia — were represented concelebrating with the saintly bishops of the Constantinopolitan Church.[67] Thus the theme of apse programmes remained the cult of the communion of orthodox bishops.

When an explicitly ecclesiological notion concerning the status of a national Church had to be expressed in pictorial form, this was done in the narthex or at least not in the apse. A local bishop might be represented wearing the *sakkos*, a vestment originally reserved to patriarchs of Constantinople but later extended to major archbishops.[68] Nicolas Cabasilas of Ohrid was represented in the church of Saint Clement wearing the *sakkos* in 1295. Sava I, founder of the Serbian autocephalous Church, was represented wearing the *sakkos* in the Bogorodica Ljeviška, Prizren (1308/9).[69] Other vestments could also serve as a sign of the prestige of a local bishop. Thus, in the church of the Dormition, Volotovo (ca. 1380), Moses and Alexius of Novgorod were represented wearing a phelonion decorated with crosses, although the patriarch Philotheus of Constantinople had expressly forbidden Alexius to wear this vestment.[70]

Another way of expressing the claims of the local Church was to represent a series of bishops in the narthex. For the late Byzantine period, all the surviving examples are in Serbian churches.[71] The absence of analogies elsewhere makes it difficult to determine the exact significance in every case. The earliest series of portraits of Serbian archbishops was executed in the South Chapel of the shrine of Symeon Nemanja at Studenica (1233——1235).[72] The anachronism of placing it in a shrine may be explained by the exceptional veneration offered by the Serbian nation to the Nemanjić dynasty.

[66] *Ibid.*, 368; C. Grozdanov, 'Pojava i prodor portreta Klimenta Ohridskog u srednjovekovnoj umetnosti', *Zbornik za likovne umetnosti* 3 (1967), 53—55.

[67] Mirjana Ćorović-Ljubinković, 'Odraz kulta Ćirila i Metodija u balkanskoj srednjevekovnoj umetnosti', *Simpozium 1100-godišnina od smrtta na Kiril Solunski* I (Skopje, 1970); 123—130; Milošević, 'Ikonografija sv. Save' (note 61), 290, 299—300; Walter, *Art and Ceremonial* (note 1), 107—108, 223—224. One of the officiating bishops in the apse of Sopoćani is generally identified by Serbian scholars as Sava II (1263—1271). They date the decoration of the church to his lifetime, Đurić, *Vizantijske freske* (note 62), 196 note 41. However, the argument is tenuous, for no other example is known of a living bishop being represented among those who officiate in the apse.

[68] Walter, *Art and Ritual*, (note 1), 16—19.

[69] C. Grozdanov, 'Prilozi poznavanju srednjevekovne umetnosti Ohrida', *Zbornik za likovne umetnosti* 2 (1966); 199—207; Draga Panić & Gordana Babić, *Bogorodica Ljeviška* (Belgrade, 1975), 129, pl. 4.

[70] V. Lazarev, *Old Russian Murals and Mosaics* (London, 1966), 165—166, figs. 140—142; *Regestes* (note 61) nos. 2364, 2583; Walter, *Art and Ceremony* (note 1), 14—15.

[71] Gordana Babić, 'Nizovi portreta srpskih episkopa, arhiepiskopa i patrijaraha u zidnom slikarstvu (13—16 v.)', *Sava Nemanjić* (note 61), 319—340.

[72] *Ibid.*, 320—321.

The series of portraits of Serbian archbishops in the cathedral churches of Arilje (1296) and Prizren (1307—1313) affirm that the local Church is in communion with the other Serbian eparchies.[73] When a series of local bishops figured there as well, as at Arilje and Prizren, then the independent traditions of the local eparchy were affirmed along with its juridical subordination to the Serbian major archbishops.

In conclusion it may be suggested that the use of imagery to affirm the status and claims of a local Church was always the exception rather than the rule. In the earlier period these claims were invariably related to the cult of the saintly patron or patrons of the local see and the pictures expressing these claims were placed in their shrine. Evidence is available from the 9th century of divergences in the use of imagery in the East and West to set forth the rôle of the Church in the divine providential plan. In the Constantinopolitan sphere of influence, emphasis was placed upon the communion of all orthodox bishops, whereas in Rome it was placed on the privileged status of the local 'apostolic' see. In Byzantine iconography, the cult of the whole communion of orthodox bishops becomes the central theme of apse decoration. When a local Church gave a special interpretation to this universal theme, it did so in order to emphasize the fact that it was in communion with other orthodox bishops. Pictures expressing the juridical status of the local Church were placed elsewhere than in the apse of the church, normally in the narthex. Thus the distinction regularly made in ecclesiastical matters between the orthodoxy and communion of local Churches on the one hand and their respective canonical status on the other was also made in the decoration of churches, both in the choice of iconographical themes and in their emplacement.

---

[73] *Ibid.*, 335—340.

III

THREE NOTES ON THE ICONOGRAPHY
OF DIONYSIUS THE AREOPAGITE

Among the hagiographical traditions of the Byzantine Church that which concerns Dionysius the Areopagite is not the least complex[1]. The beginnings are, indeed, modest. Dionysius is mentioned once in the Acts of the Apostles 17,34, as a follower of Saint Paul. Eusebius recorded a tradition that, according to Dionysius of Corinth (fl. 171), he was appointed the first bishop of Athens[2]. This was also noted in the Apostolic Constitutions[3]. However the situation changed when the *Corpus dionysiacum* appeared some time before 533[4]. Some of these works, notably the *De divinis nominibus* and the Letter to Polycarp, contain biographical details which were developed in two later texts, doubly spurious, the Letter to Apollophanes and the Autobiography. From John of Scythopolis's *scholion* to a passage in the *De divinis nominibus* the tradition spread that Dionysius had been present at the Dormition of the Virgin. Finally, when Dionysius had been identified with the founder bishop of Paris and the *Post beatam* translated into Greek, information became available about his Western apostolate and his martyrdom.

---

1. There is no full study of the hagiographical tradition of Dionysius in the East. Both the late R. Loenertz and P. Canart intended to undertake such a study but were regrettably obliged to set it aside. Some texts — possibly important — remain unpublished : *BHG* 555c, d, e, m, 556b, 557. Only those which are published are exploited here. From the plethora of general studies of (Pseudo-) Dionysius the Areopagite may be cited : M. DE GANDILLAC, *Œuvres complètes du Pseudo-Denys l'Aréopagite*, Paris 1943, Introduction, p. 7-60; Denys l'Aréopagite (Le Pseudo-), *Dictionnaire de spiritualité* 3, 244-430, especially A. RAYEZ, Utilisation du Pseudo-Denys en Orient, 286-318 ; G. O'DALY, Dionysius Areopagita, *Theologische Realenzyklopädie* 8, 772-780.

2. EUSÈBE DE CÉSARÉE, *Histoire ecclésiastique*, IV, xxiii, edited G. BARDY, Paris 1952, p. 203 = *PG* 20, 385 (*Clavis* 3495).

3. *Constitutiones apostolicae*, 7, 46 : *PG* 1, 1053 (*Clavis* 1730).

4. DE GANDILLAC, *op. cit.* (note 1), p. 14.

Although Dionysius the Areopagite never rivalled the Three Hierarchs in the esteem of the Byzantine Church and although he was less appreciated as a theologian in the East than in the West, nevertheless he had a certain standing. He was introduced into the Byzantine calendar of feasts about 800[5]. He figures among the bishops named in the Letter to the Three Patriarchs[6], as well as in Ode 9 for the Saturday τῆς Τυρινῆς in the *Triodion* along with his teacher Hierotheus[7]. In the Letter attributed to Photius addressed to the Armenian catholicos Zacharias he is also counted among the Greek bishops who evangelized the world[8]. Ulpius the Roman provided a description of his features which also appears in the *Synaxaria* and the *Menaia*[9]. Later he merited the distinction of a Metaphrastic Life and quotation by Euthymius Zigabenus in his *Panoplia dogmatica*[10].

In consequence representations of him in Byzantine art are fairly frequent. He appeared in the echelon of bishops in Saint Sophia, in illuminated manuscripts of the October volume of Metaphrastic Lives, in the Lectionary Vatican *graec.* 1156, f. 255[v], in Menologia, wall-calendars and in two manuscripts of Zigabenus's *Panoplia*. However I have only recorded one example of him among the officiating bishops in apse programmes[11]. Most of these pictures are conventional portraits or scenes of decapitation. Yet three iconographical themes, derived from the apocryphal texts about his life, depart from the ordinary. These are his vision at Heliopolis, his presence at the Dormition of the Virgin and the prodigy which occurred at his death when he picked up his head and carried it two *millia*. It is with these themes that the following notes are concerned.

1. THE VISION AT HELIOPOLIS

The Chludov Psalter contains three miniatures of the Crucifixion : f. 45[v], f. 67 and f. 72[v][12]. The first of the these miniatures differs from

5. V. GRUMEL, Autour de la question pseudo-dionysienne, *REB* 13, 1955, p. 48.

6. L. DUCHESNE, L'iconographie byzantine dans un document grec du 9e siècle, *Roma e Oriente* 5, 1912-1913, p. 354.

7. *Triodion*, Rome 1879, p. 96.

8. Ch. WALTER, *Art and Ritual of the Byzantine Church*, London 1982, p. 173.

9. See below, note 68.

10. *PG* 130, 19-1362.

11. At Staro Nagoričino, Gordana BABIĆ and Ch. WALTER, The Inscriptions upon Liturgical Rolls in Byzantine Apse Decoration, *REB* 34, 1976, p. 275; R. HAMANN-MAC LEAN and H. HALLENSLEBEN, *Die Monumentalmalerei in Serbien und Makedonien*, Giessen 1963, fig. 280.

12. Marfa ŠČEPKINA, *Miniatjuri Hludovskoj Psaltyri...*, Moscow 1977, at folio number.

the other two in several respects (figure 1). Only in this one is Christ flanked by two other crucified figures, one to the right with his head hanging down and the other to the left looking up at Christ. The latter figure must be the Good Thief. It therefore follows that the artist sought his inspiration for this miniature in Saint Luke's Gospel 23,33 ..., for only Luke recounts the incident of the Good Thief.

Only in this miniature is the scene of the Crucifixion augmented by two other groups of figures. To the right, beside the centurion, is a group of figures, two of whom are represented wearing the *loros*. Yet further to the right is another group composed of three figures. Two, engaged in conversation, are bearded and of mature age; one holds three *codices* in his left hand. Behind them, partly concealed by the figure to the right, is a youth who looks towards the Crucifixion, his right hand extended in that direction. In the margin beside this group is a legend : ΕΛΛΗΝΕΣ ΗΓΟΥΝ ΔΙΟΝΥΣΙΟΣ[13].

No other marginal Psalter is illustrated with the full scene, although the Crucifixion is represented beside the same Psalm in the Barberini and Hamilton Psalters[14]. Nor has the full scene survived elsewhere in Byzantine art. It is a *hapax* and, as such, not susceptible of an absolutely certain interpretation. Tikkanen and Kondakov both drew attention to it, but Malickij was the first to read the name of Dionysius and to refer the miniature to his vision at Heliopolis[15]. However, he wrongly connected it with Psalm 45,4 : « The mountains have been troubled by this might. » In fact there is an indicative sign beside verse 7 : « The nations were troubled ; the kingdoms tottered. He uttered his voice ; the earth shook. »

The earliest account of the vision at Heliopolis is to be found in Dionysius's Letter to Polycarp[16]. According to this he witnessed an eclipse of the sun which could not be explained as a natural phenomenon. Later, on meeting Saint Paul in Athens, Dionysius discovered that the eclipse had occurred exactly at the time of Christ's death, corresponding to the account in Saint Luke's Gospel 23,44-45 : there was darkness from the sixth hour (midday) for three

13. Ἕλληνες ἤγουν Διονύσιος. Neither Tikkanen nor Malickij nor even Ščepkina (although it is clearly legible in her illustration of the miniature) transcribed this legend correctly.

14. J. ANDERSON, P. CANART and Ch. WALTER, *The Barberini Psalter*, Stuttgart 1989, at f. 79ᵛ ; Ch. WALTER, Christological Themes in the Byzantine Marginal Psalters, *REB* 44, 1986, p. 275 ; Suzy DUFRENNE, *Tables synoptiques des 15 psautiers médiévaux*, Paris 1978, at Psalm 45.

15. J. J. TIKKANEN, *Die Psalterillustration im Mittelalter*, Helsingfors 1895-1900, reprinted, Soest 1975, p. 58 ; N. MALICKIJ, Remarques sur la date des mosaïques de l'église des Saint-Apôtres à Constantinople, décrites par Mésarites, *Byz.* 3, 1926, p. 145-146.

16. *PG* 3, 1077-1084 (*Clavis* 6610).

hours, the sun having disappeared. The passage in the Letter to Polycarp was commented in a *scholion* by John of Scythopolis[17] and developed later in the Letter to Apollophanes[18].

The connection between the Psalm verse, the miniature and Dionysius's vision is so far somewhat tenuous, being limited to the fact that the texts refer to the account of the phenomenon in Luke's Gospel and that the miniature derives from Luke's account of the Crucifixion. In the Psalm verse there is no reference to an eclipse. The connection becomes considerably stronger if another text attributed to Dionysius is taken into consideration, the account of the vision in the Autobiography. This work, which has not survived in Greek, is nevertheless known in Coptic, Syriac, Armenian, Arabic and Georgian[19]. Kugener published two recensions of the Syrian text, one of which is in a manuscript dated 804[20]. According to this, Dionysius, in spite of his youth, was sent from Athens to judge a priest at Heliopolis in Syria. While everyone was assembled in the theatre, there was a great earthquake, the sun was obscured and there was darkness from the sixth to the ninth hour[21].

"I saw", Dionysius added, "with the eye of the spirit, Christ hanging from the cross in the land of Judaea. I learnt that he was the god who had become incarnate"[22].

Dionysius returned to Athens. Fourteen years later, when Saint Paul visited the city, he heard the account of Christ's death, of the eclipse, the earthquake and the God who died in the flesh[23].

The author of the Autobiography has evidently borrowed from the more developed accounts in Saint Matthew's and Saint Mark's Gospels of the phenomena which occurred at the time of Christ's death. Now it is clear that the connection between the miniature, the Autobigraphy and the Psalm verse is the earthquake : "The earth shook." Moreover it can be established that a Greek version of the

17. *PG* 4, 536-541 (*Clavis* 6852, 7708).

18. *PG* 3, 1119-1122; cf. *PL* 106, 33-34 (*Clavis* 6630); P. CANART, En marge de la question aréopagitique : La lettre XI de Denys à Apollophane, *Byz*, 41, 1971, p. 18-27.

19. P. PEETERS, La vision de Denys l'Aréopagite à Héliopolis, *An. Boll.* 29, 1910, p. 302-322; IDEM, La version géorgienne de l'autobiographie de Denys l'Aréopagite, *ibidem* 31, 1912, p. 5-10; IDEM, La version ibéro-arménienne de l'autobiographie de Denys l'Aréopagite, *ibidem* 39, 1921, p. 277-313.

20. M. A. KUGENER, Une autobiographie syriaque de Denys l'Aréopagite, *Oriens christianus* 7, 1907, p. 292-348 (*Clavis* 6633). The two recensions are contained in London British Library Additional 12151 ('A', dated 804), and 14645 ('B', dated 936).

21. *Ibidem*, recension 'A', § 8, p. 303.

22. *Ibidem*, § 10, p. 307.

23. *Ibidem*, § 12-13, p. 309-311.

Pl. I

III

Figure 1. — Vision of Dionysius, Chludov Psalter, f. 45ᵛ.

Figure 2. — Dormition, Hypapante, Meteora.

Autobiography existed as early as the first decades of the ninth century, for Michael the Syncellus used it in his panegyric on Dionysius. Before quoting lengthily from the Letter to Polycarp, he summarizes the account of the phenomena in the Autobiography, giving only one phrase *verbatim* : Ὁ ἄγνωστος, ἔφη, σαρκὶ πάσχει Θεός, δι' ὃν τὸ πᾶν ἐζόφωταί τε καὶ σεσάλευται (The unknown God suffers in the flesh, on account of which the universe is deprived of light and shaken)[24].

This phrase, while corresponding to the Syriac, seems closest to the Coptic, which Peeters rendered thus : *Omnis istae terrae motus et astrorum perturbatio quae acciderunt propter Deum qui crucifixus est*[25]. Grabar remarked on its relevance to the Iconophile cause[26]. If Michael the Syncellus composed the panegyric between 821 and 833, then we have a *terminus ante quem* for the composition of the Greek version of the Autobiography[27].

To return to the miniature, it may now be possible to elucidate other problems that it poses. The group in the centre no doubt represents the troubled nations and tottering kingdoms, but who are the figures to the right? The legend beside them can only be translated : "(The) Greeks, that is to say Dionysius." The words may be part of a phrase of which the rest is obliterated. Nevertheless they affirm that one of the figures is Dionysius. Which one? Now in the account of the vision in the Autobiography only one person actually sees Christ hanging on the cross, Dionysius himself. Equally only one figure is actually looking towards and pointing at the scene of the Crucifixion, the young man standing behind the two others. It is affirmed in the Autobiography that Dionysius was young when he visited Heliopolis. There are consequently reasons for arguing that the young man is, in fact, Dionysius.

Who, then, are the other two? In the Autobiography, the elucidation of the phenomena which occurred fourteen years earlier is placed more or less in parallel to the actual account of them. It may be that the parallel is taken up in the miniature. In other words, Dionysius may be represented *twice*. The figure wearing a mantle and holding three scrolls, who partly obscures the youthful figure, would be the mature Dionysius. He would be explaining to a Greek, no doubt Apollophanes, the cause of his conversion[28].

---

24. *PG* 4, 625-628 (*BHG* 556).

25. PEETERS, *art. cit.*, 1910 (note 19), p. 304.

26. A. GRABAR, *L'iconoclasme byzantin*, Paris 1957, p. 230.

27. R. LOENERTZ, Le panégyrique de S. Denis l'Aréopagite par S. Michel le Syncelle, *An. Boll.* 68, 1950, p. 97.

28. Cf. the account in the *Souda* (*BHG* 558), *Suidae Lexikon*, edited Ada ADLER, II, Leipzig 1931, p. 106-109 = *PG* 4, 608-612.

Since the miniature is a *hapax*, this explanation remains conjectural, but at least it takes into account all the elements of its perplexing iconography.

2. The Presence of Dionysius at the Dormition of the Virgin

Although good studies of the iconography of the Dormition exist, they do not enter exhaustively into all its complexities[29]. The subject, for which the earliest surviving examples date from the tenth century, did not remain stable. New elements were successively introduced until, in the Palaeologan period, a whole cycle was developed, beginning with the annunciation to the Virgin of her imminent demise and ending with her corporal *metastasis* from earth to heaven. Artists, therefore, or their patrons, regularly had recourse to the rich apocryphal literature about the Dormition, borrowing from it new iconographical details.

The earliest dated example of the Dormition in which bishops figure is that in the church of Saint Sophia, Ohrid (1037-1056)[30]. Subsequently — and possibly earlier[31] — they are represented, either mourning or participating in the funeral rites. There may be four, three or two bishops; rarely there is only one[32]. It is well known that their presence was also inspired by the literary sources. Globally they can be identified as Dionysius the Areopagite and Hierotheus of Athens, James Adelphotheos of Jerusalem and Timothy of Ephesus. However, when it comes to identifying the individual bishops, art historians are hesitant or speculative.

Here are some examples, taken more or less at random, of identifications proposed. At Asinou (1105/6) there are two bishops, one with dark hair and a short rounded beard, the other with white hair and a longer pointed beard. Cormack suggested that "perhaps the older figure with a white beard is Saint James and the other Dionysius". On the other hand for the Dormition at Lagoudera (1192), where there are three bishops all represented with the same

29. Ludmila WRATISLAW-MITROVIĆ and N. OKUNEV, La Dormition de la Sainte Vierge dans la peinture médiévale orthodoxe, *Byzantinoslavica* 3, 1931, p. 134-174; Karoline KREIDLE-PAPADOPOULOS, Koimesis, *Lexikon zur byzantinischen Kunst* 4, 136-182.

30. V. DJURIĆ, *Vizantijske freske u Jugoslaviji*, Belgrade 1974, p. 9-11, 197 note 3.

31. The Phocas Lectionary, with a miniature of the Dormition, is usually dated around 1000. See below note 79.

32. V. N. LAZAREV, *Istorija vizantijskoj živopisi*, Moscow 1986, fig. 519, a 14th-century icon at Saint Catherine's Mount Sinaï.

features, white hair and a medium pointed beard, Cormack refrained from an identification[33]. For the Dormition at Kurbinovo (1191), where there are two bishops, one with grey hair and a shortish beard and the other with dark hair and a rounded beard, Hadermann-Misguich wrote that "ces prélats... dont Denys l'Aréopagite... Jacques, premier évêque de Jérusalem, ainsi qu'éventuellement Hiérothée et Timothée[34]". For the Dormition in the King's church at Studenica (1314), where one bishop has a long, forked grey beard and the other shaggy hair and a beard, Babić proposed Dionysius and James Adelphotheos[35].

For the Dormition in the Kariye Cami (1315-1320/1), two different interpretations may be noted. Del Medico proposed for the two bishops to the left, one of whom is bald with a long pointed beard and the other of whom has full grey hair and a beard, Dionysius and Hierotheus respectively, while for the bishop to the right, with a short dark beard and hair, he proposed Timothy[36]. Underwood, however, with the proviso that bishops in Dormition scenes cannot be firmly identified because they vary from picture to picture, suggested that the bishop holding a book was James Adelphotheos while one of the others was probably meant to be Dionysius[37].

These examples illustrate well Underwood's point that there is not absolute consistency in the portrait types of bishops in Dormition scenes any more than there is consistency in the number represented. This may be because artists were sometimes ignorant of or indifferent to the identity of the bishops. Another reason might be that there was a variety of iconographical traditions. Nevertheless it seems that, if all the literary and iconographical evidence is taken into consideration, artists can be shown to have been in many cases both conversant with the legends of the Dormition and exact in their representation of the bishops concerned. A survey of the material will entail a revision of the identifications proposed for some of pictures which have just been cited.

The presence of bishops at the Dormition is attested in two apocryphal traditions which develop parallel and then converge. Legends about the Dormition first appear in the fifth and sixth centuries[38]. A liturgical feast of the Dormition became widespread in

33. R. CORMACK, *Writing in Gold*, London 1985, p. 174, fig. 62-64.

34. Lydie HADERMANN-MISGUICH, *Kurbinovo*, Brussels 1975, p. 184.

35. Gordana BABIĆ, *Kraljeva crkva u Studenici*, Belgrade 1987, p. 166.

36. H. E. DEL MEDICO, La mosaïque de la κοίμησις à Kahrie Djami, *Byz.* 7, 1932, p. 128-129.

37. P. A. UNDERWOOD, *The Karije Djami*, New York 1966, p. 15 (date), n° 185, p. 166-167, fig. 320-327.

38. M. JUGIE, *La mort et l'assomption de la Sainte Vierge*, Vatican 1944, p. 103-171.

the early decades of the seventh century, inviting the composition of homilies for the occasion[39]. However the early texts make no allusion to the presence of bishops. The only reason for supposing at this stage that any bishop was present would be the attribution of one apocryphal account to James, bishop of Jerusalem[40]. Moreover many of the subsequent homilies also omit any reference to bishops. They are mentioned neither by John of Thessaloniki (fl.. 610-649)[41], nor by Modestus of Jerusalem (died 634)[42], nor by Germanus of Constantinople (died 733)[43], nor by John Damascene (died 749)[44].

Among the treatises which make up the *Corpus dionysiacum* is the *De divinis nominibus*, addressed to the priest Timothy, which recounts how Dionysius, Hierotheus and James Adelphotheus met with others to contemplate «the body origin of life and residence of the divinity"[45]. As is well known, John of Scythopolis, commenting this passage in the sixth century, suggested that "perhaps" it referred to the body of the Virgin and that the occasion of the meeting was her Dormition[46].

It is at this point that the two traditions first converge. That an eyewitness account of the Dormition existed was of moment to hagiographers. For Andrew of Crete (died 740) "perhaps" became certitude. In his homily on the Dormition he cited the passage from the *De divinis nominibus* with the names of the three episcopal witnesses, adding Timothy to their number[47]. The same passage was used in the *Historia euthymiaca*, according to which "there were present with the apostles the holy apostle Timothy, first bishop of Ephesus, and Dionysius the Areopagite[48]". Hierotheus and James

---

39. *Ibidem*, p. 175-194.

40. *Ibidem*, p. 121-122.

41. *Clavis* 7924, *BHG* 1144. I wrote erroneously, *op. cit.* (note 8), p. 141 note 138, that John of Thessaloniki mentioned the presence of bishops.

42. *Clavis* 7876, *BHG* 1085.

43. *Clavis* 8010-8012, *BHG* 1119, 1135, 1155.

44. *Clavis* 8061-8063, *BHG* 1114, 1126n, 1089.

45. *PG* 3, 681 (*Clavis* 6602).

46. *PG* 4, 236 (*Clavis* 6852, 7708). Jugie, *op. cit.* (note 38), p. 99-101, was quite certain that the passage does *not* refer to the Dormition!

47. *PG* 97, 1061-1068 (*Clavis* 8181, *BHG* 1122).

48. This text is most easily accessible in editions of John Damascene's homily, S. Jean Damascène, *Homélies sur la Nativité et la Dormition*, edited P. Voulet, Paris 1961, p. 168-175 = PG 96, 748-752. However, it exists independently in *Sinaït.* 491, f. 246ᵛ-251 (8th-9th century); A. Wenger, *L'assomption de la T. S. Vierge dans la tradition byzantine du vɪᵉ au xᵉ siècle*, Paris 1955, p. 136-139. E. Honigmann, Juvenal of Jerusalem, *DOP* 5 1950, p. 270, dated it between 518 and 980. A probable *terminus post quem* would be John of Scythopolis's *scholion* (fl. 536-550), and the *terminus ante quem* the homilies of Cosmas Vestitor who knew the text (first half of the 9th century) : Wenger, *op, cit.*, p. 137.

Adelphotheos are also mentioned, but their episcopal status is not stressed. The *Historia euthymiaca* had the good fortune to be interpolated into John Damascene's homily in the second half of the ninth century; otherwise it might have been ignored[49]. As it was, the whole text is likely to have been one of the principal sources for the iconography of the Dormition.

Another text which may have been influential was the discourse of John the Geometer (died after 989)[50]. Accepting the authenticity of the passage in the *De divinis nominibus*, as an account of the Dormition, he made full use of his imagination in developing it. He attributed considerable importance to the ceremonial aspect, stressing the rôle of the "hierarch" Hierotheus, but also referring to Dionysius, James Adelphotheos and Timothy. Symeon the Metaphrast also mentions all these names, although he calls only Timothy a bishop[51]. In the Synaxary of Constantinople, Dionysius, Hierotheus and Timothy are explicitly mentioned at the date of the feast of the Dormition, while in the Menaia at the same date only James Adelphotheos is mentioned[52]. Later Nicephorus Callistus Xanthopoulos (ca 1256-ca 1335) mentions the presence of Dionysius, Hierotheus and Timothy, adding that James Adelphotheos was also there[53].

In the parallel tradition for the Life of Dionysius himself, Michael Syncellus wrote in his panegyric that Dionysius was present at the Dormition with James Adelphotheos[54]. Symeon the Metaphrast mentions his presence too but names no other bishops[55]. The *Souda* makes no allusion to his presence at the Dormition[56], nor does the Synaxary of Constantinople at the date of his feast (October 3rd)[57]. However in the *Menaia* for the same date the presence of Dionysius, Hierotheus and Timothy is mentioned in a *theotokion*[58].

Curiously, although the presence of Hierotheus at the Dormition is noted in the Menologium of Basil II and the Synaxary of Constantinople at the date of his commemoration (October 4th)[59], no hagiogra-

49. JUGIE, *op. cit.* (note 38), p. 160-162, demonstrated that the passage is an interpolation.

50. WENGER, *op. cit.* (note 48), p. 185-205, 371-373 (*BHG* 1102g). See also V. LAURENT, Jean le Géomètre, *Catholicisme* 6, 604-606.

51. Reading for August 15th : *PG* 115, 547-550 (*BHG* 1047).

52. *Syn. CP*, 893; *Menaia* 6, Rome 1901, p. 410.

53. *PG* 145, 812.

54. *PG* 4, 653-655.

55. Reading for October 3rd : *PG* 4, 593.

56. See above, note 28.

57. *Syn. CP*, 101-102.

58. *Menaia* 1, Rome 1888, p. 329; compare *PG* 4, 584.

59. *PG* 117, 89 (*BHG* 751); *Syn. CP*, 103. See also V. GRUMEL, Hiérothée, *Catholicisme* 5, 728.

pher, not even Nicodemus Hagioreitus, thought of mentioning the presence of Timothy and James Adelphotheos in notices concerning their respective Lives[60].

With such diversity in the texts, it is not surprizing that there should be diversity in the iconography. Nevertheless some generalisations can be made. When only two bishops are represented, they are likely to be Dionysius and Timothy or Dionysius and James Adelphotheos. When three are represented, they are likely to be Dionysius, Hierotheus and Timothy[61].

We may now consider the evidence provided by the tradition of portrait types outside pictures of the Dormition. Hierotheus is represented in the Menologium of Basil II, p. 88, with white hair and a medium pointed beard[62]. There is little attempt at individualisation. James Adelphotheos is represented in the same manuscript, p. 131, with grey hair and a beard which is slightly shaggy[63]. This portrait is similar to the one in Vatican *graec.* 1679, f. 248^v, and to the one at Hosios Loukas[64]. His portraits at Nereditsy and in the Baltimore *Praxapostolos*, W. 533, f. 89, while similar, are more individualized, for he now has a slight curl in the middle of his forehead (figure 5)[65]. Timothy in the Menologium of Basil II, p. 341, and in the similar miniature in the Baltimore Menologium, W. 521, f. 203, has dark short hair and a dark rounded beard[66]. He is

60. So far as I have been able to control them : Timothy *BHG* 1848, 1848b, 1848n ; James Adelphotheos *BHG* 765, 766m.

61. Dionysius of Phourna gives these three bishops as figuring in representations of the Dormition : Ἑρμηνεία τῆς ζωγραφικῆς τέχνης, edited A. Papadopoulos-Kerameus, Saint Petersburg 1909, p. 144.

62. *Il Menologio di Basilio II*, edited C. Stornajolo and P. Franchi de' Cavalieri, Vatican/Milan 1907, p. 88, also reproduced in illustration to J.-M. Sauget, Geroteo, *Bibliotheca sanctorum* 6, 275-276. Hierotheus's features are similar in the Oxford Menologium, Bodleian *gr. th. f.* 1, f. 12 (1322-1340) : I. Hutter, *Corpus der byzantinischen Miniaturen-handschriften*, I, *Oxford Bodleian Library* 2, Stuttgart 1978, fig. 19. For other representations of Hierotheus, not easily exploitable, see P. Mijović, *Menolog*, Belgrade 1973, *sub nomine*. For Dionysius of Phourna, *ed. cit.* (note 61), p. 155, Hierotheus is to be represented as an old man with a long beard.

63. *Ed. cit.* (note 62).

64. Vatican *graec.* 1679 : Ch. Walter, The Triumph of Saint Peter in the Church of Saint Clement at Ohrid and the Iconography of the Triumph of the Martyrs, *Zograf* 5, 1975, p. 31. Hosios Loukas : P. Lazaridès, *Le monastère de Hosios Loukas*, Athens 1987, fig. 22. For Dionysius of Phourna, *ed. cit.* (note 61), p. 154, James is to be represented as an old man with curly hair and a long beard.

65. Nereditsy : V. N. Lazarev, *Old Russian Murals and Mosaics from the XI to the XVI Century*, London 1966, p. 117, fig. 94. Baltimore W. 533 : Sirarpie Der Nersessian, The Praxapostolos of the Walters Art Gallery, *Gatherings in Honor of Dorothy E. Miner*, edited Ursula Mc Cracken, Baltimore 1974, p. 43, fig. 1.

66. Vatican *graec.* 1613 : *ed. cit.* (note 62), p. 341. Baltimore W. 521 : Walter, *op. cit.* (note 8), fig. 43 (with incorrect legend).

Pl. III

Figure 4. — Timothy, Dormition (detail), Omorphi Ekklesia, Athens.

Figure 3. — Timothy and Paul, Baltimore Praxapostolos, f. 239.

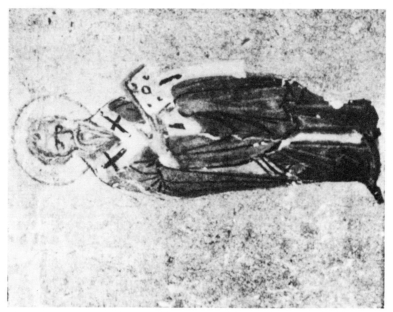

Figure 6. — Dionysius and Catula, calendar-icon (detail), Saint Catherine's, Mount Sinai.

Figure 5. — James Adelphotheos, Baltimore Praxapostolos, f. 89.

represented four times in the Baltimore *Praxapostolos* with similar features (figure 3)[67]. Of these three bishops he has the most distinctive portrait type.

For Dionysius there is a detailed description in the text of Ulpius the Roman : white complexion, sallow skin, somewhat flat-nosed, puckered eyebrows, hollow eyes,(an air of) continual concentration, big ears, long grey hair, a fairly long beard of sparse growth[68]. The same text occurs in the Synaxary of Constantinople and in the *Menaia*[69]. However, in spite of its accessibility, artists do not seem to have referred to it often. There is no resemblance, for example, between this description and any of the figures in the Chludov Psalter miniature, f. 45[v] (figure 1); Salzenberg's drawing of the lost mosaic in Saint Sophia, Constantinople, is perhaps too academic to be reliable[70]; in the Menologium of Basil II, p. 82, Dionysius has grey hair and a short beard (figure 7)[71]. Later pictures, with one exception, are also disconcertingly different from Ulpius's description, as that in Moscow GIM *graec.* 175, f. 28, where he a dark beard and hair, or in the Vienna Metaphrast, *hist. graec.* 6, f. 3, where he has a longish dark beard and copious hair[72]. The exception is his portrait among the doctors of the Church in the frontispiece to the Panoply of Zigabenus, Vatican *graec.* 666, f. 1[v][73]. One could well suppose that in this case the artist was familiar with Ulpius.

Of these bishops, the one who is most easily recognized is Timothy with his dark hair and short beard. It is consequently necessary to revise the identifications proposed by Cormack for the bishops at Asinou and by Hadermann-Misguich for those at Kurbinovo. In both

67. DER NERSESSIAN, *art, cit.* (note 65), f. 239, 255[v], 262[v], 287, fig. 8, 9, 10, 11. For Dionysius of Phourna, *ed. cit.* (note 61), p. 364, Timothy is to be represented as a young man with a flattened beard.

68. M. CHATZIDAKIS, Ἐκ τῶν Ἐλπίου τοῦ Ρωμάιου, *EEBS* 14, 1938, p. 412, reprinted *Studies in Byzantine Art and Archaeology*, Variorum London 1972; C. MANGO, *The Art of the Byzantine Empire, 312-1452*, Englewood Cliffs 1972, p. 148.

69. *Syn. CP*, 102. Delehaye had already noted the similarity with Ulpius, *ibidem*, lxvi. CHATZIDAKIS, *art. cit.* (note 68), p. 402-403, considered that Ulpius's text was earlier. The problem still remains where he found it if he did not compose it himself. See also *Menaia, PG* 4, 587.

70. C. MANGO, *Materials for the Study of the Mosaics of St. Sophia at Istanbul*, Washington 1962, p. 49-51, figure 57-59.

71. *Ed. cit.* (note 62), p. 82. For Dionysius of Phourna, Dionysius was to be represented as an old man with curly hair, and a shaggy forked beard, *ed. cit.* (note 61), p. 154.

72. P. BUBERL and H. GERSTINGER, *Die illuminierten Handschriften und Inkunabeln der Nationalbibliothek in Wien*, IV, Leipzig 1930, p. 38-43, fig. 13-15.

73. WALTER, *op. cit.* (note 8), p. 40, fig. 11 ; I. SPATHARAKIS, *The Portrait in Byzantine Illuminated Manuscripts*, Leiden 1976, p. 122-129, fig. 78, 83 (with the copy in *Mosqu. graec.* 387, f. 5[v]).

these pictures Timothy is represented. Moreover this identification is confirmed by the evidence of the painting in the Omorphi Ekklisia at Athens (second half of thirteenth century). Here Timothy's portrait, with the dark hair and beard, is accompanied by a legend specifying his name (figure 4)[74]. Other examples of the Dormition with two bishops, one of whom has Timothy's features, are those in the Martorana, Palermo (1146-1151)[75], at Saint Nicolas *tou Kasnitzi*, Kastoria (1164-1191)[76], in the church of the Virgin, Studenica (1208/9)[77], in the Hypapante, Meteora (1366/7) (figure 2)[78], and in the Phocas Lectionary, f. 134[v], in the skevophylakion of the Great Lavra[79].

There is no consistency in the way that the second bishop, who must be Dionysius, was represented in these pictures. This was to be expected since, outside Dormition scenes, no clear tradition had been established for this portrait type. Nevertheless it should be noted that the second bishop in the miniature of the Skevophylakion Lectionary closely resembles the Dionysius in Vatican *graec.* 666, f. 1[v] , which corresponds to Ulpius's description of him. Furthermore the second bishop at Kurbinovo and in Saint Nicolas *tou Kasnitzi* is represented as being bald. This portrait type recurs at Staro Nagoričino (1316/8)[80], Lesnovo (before 1349)[81], at Markov manastir (1376-1381)[82] and at Saint Athanasius *tou Mouzaki*, Kastoria (1384/5)[83]. It is therefore

74. Agapi Vasilaki-Karakatsani, Οι τοιχογραφίες της Όμορφης Εκκλησίας στην Αθήνα, Athens 1971, p. 51, fig. 36, 37. Legends accompanying the bishops in pictures of the Dormition are rare. G. de Jerphanion read the names of Dionysius and Timothy on the fresco at Saint Basil, Cemil, *Les églises rupestres de Cappadoce*, II, Paris 1936, p. 124-125, but unfortunately he did not reproduce it.

75. O. Demus, *The Mosaics of Norman Sicily*, London 1949, p. 82, fig. 56; Lazarev, *op. cit.* (note 32), fig. 379.

76. S. Pelekanides and M. Chatzidakis, *Kastoria*, Athens 1985, p. 63, fig. 16.

77. Djurić, *op. cit.* (note 30), p. 31-33. Restored 1568, Gordana Babić, O kompoziciji Uspenja Bogorodičinog u Studenici, *Starinar*, n. s., 13-14, 1965, p. 261-265.

78. G. Subotić, Počeci monaškog života i crkva manastira Sretenja u Meteorima, *Zbornik za likovne umetnosti* 2, 1966, p. 143-176.

79. K. Weitzmann, Das Evangeliar im Skevophylakion zu Lavra, *Seminarium Kondakovium* 8, 1936, p. 83-93, plate III 1, reprinted *Byzantine Liturgical Psalters and Gospels*, Variorum London 1980; *The Treasures of Mount Athos*, III, edited S. Pelekanides, etc., Athens 1979, fig. 8.

80. Hamann-Mac Lean, *op. cit.* (note 11), fig. 285. The same portrait type is used for Dionysius in the wall-calendar, Mijović *op. cit.* (note 62), fig. 28, but not for him as an officiating bishop (see above, note 11)!

81. Djurić, *op. cit.* (note 30), p. 64.

82. *Ibidem*, p. 38.

83. Pelekanides and Chatzidakis, *op. cit*, (note 76), p. 115, fig. 9.

likely that this bald-headed portrait type was developed for Dionysius, although it is not clear why[84].

A certain number of representations of the Dormition exist with two bishops, neither of whom are of the portrait type of Timothy. At Daphni[85] and in the Dionysiou Lectionary, f. 163[v 86], the two bishops are not individualized. Both have conventional white hair and beards. Not only do they resemble each other but also the portraiture in the two pictures is extremely close. At Saint Nicolas, Prilep (1298), both bishops have letters inscribed on their haloes[87]. One has the letters ΔΙ, so that he must be Dionysius. The other has the letters ΔΑ (an error for IA ?). This latter bishop has a slight curl in the middle of his forehead, which recalls the portraits of James Adelphotheos in the Baltimore *Praxapostolos* and at Nereditsy (figure 5). We can therefore be fairly sure of his identity. The same portrait type recurs in two other churches in which the Dormition is represented with only two bishops, at Lesnovo and at Pološko (after 1350)[88]. It recurs again in representations of the Dormition with more than two bishops, at Saint Clement (Peribleptos), Ohrid (1294/5)[89], at Saint Nikita, Čučer (before 1316)[90], and at Saint Nicolas, Psača (after 1354)[91].

In view of these considerations, the names proposed by Babić for the two bishops in the Dormition in the King's church at Studenica can be confirmed. The bald-headed bishop would be Dionysius. The other is certainly not Timothy. On the other hand, while his features are less individualized than in the examples mentioned above, they are close enough to the portrait type of James Adelphotheos. For the bishops in the Kariye Cami mosaic, del Medico's identifications are to be preferred to those of Underwood. The bishop to the right certainly has the features attributed to Timothy, while, when three bishops are represented, the other two are likely, according to the texts, to be Dionysius and Hierotheos.

---

84. Dionysius is also represented as bald in his martyrdom scene in the Oxford Menologium, f. 11[v], HUTTER, *op. cit.* (note 62), fig. 18.

85. P. LAZARIDÈS, *Le monastère de Daphni*, Athens 1987, fig. 15.

86. *Treasures*, I, Athens 1973 (cf. note 79), fig. 272; Ch. Walter, The Date and Content of the Dionysiou Lectionary, Δελτίον της χριστιανικής αρχαιολογικής εταιρείας 4 13, 1985-1986, p. 186 (dating the Lectionary around 1100).

87. DJURIĆ, *op. cit.* (note 30), p. 19.

88. Gordana BABIĆ, Quelques observations sur le cycle des grandes fêtes de l'église de Pološko (Macédoine), *CA* 27, 1978, p. 175-176, fig. 8, 9. With the discovery and publication of the donor portraits, these frescoes can now be dated between 1343 and 1345 : C. GROZDANOV and D. ĆORNAKOV, Istorijski portreti u Pološkom (I), *Zograf* 14, 1983, p. 60-67.

89. DJURIĆ, *op. cit.* (note 30), p. 17-19, plate XV.

90. HAMANN-MAC LEAN, *op. cit.* (note 11), fig. 232.

91. V. PETKOVIĆ, *La peinture serbe du Moyen Age*, II, Belgrade 1934, fig. CLXIX.

268

There are, nevertheless, limits to the possibility of identifying the bishops. It has already been noted that there was no attempt by the artist concerned to individualize the bishops at Daphni or in the Dionysiou Lectionary. At Saint Sophia, Ohrid, the three bishops have similar features[92]. At Sopoćani (ca 1265), their features differ but only slightly ; there is no clear correspondence with the established portrait types[93]. Further, although the presence of Hierotheus may sometimes be inferred, no individualized portrait type seems to have been developed for him. Cormack was therefore right not to suggest names for the bishops at Lagoudera.

To conclude, it may be affirmed, in spite of these reservations, that artists were often concerned to portray the bishops present at the Dormition according to their portrait type. For Hierotheus they could do no more than delineate an elderly man with white hair and beard. For James Adelphotheos a clearer portrait type existed, with shaggy hair and beard and a curl in the centre of his forehead. Timothy of Ephesus was evidently considered to be younger, with dark hair and short beard. Finally there seems to have developed a consensus that Dionysius, in spite of the fact that a detailed description of his features existed in the literary sources, should be represented as bald.

These criteria may be extended to the less usual cases, where four bishops are represented as present at the Dormition. For example, on a Crusader icon at Saint Catherine's, Mount Sinaï, all the bishops can be identified, while in the painting of the Dormition in Saint Nicolas Orphanos, the features of Dionysius and Timothy are clearly delineated, although the other two bishops, James Adelphotheos and Hierotheos, are too similar for it to be possible to distinguish them[94].

3. SAINT DIONYSIUS 'KEPHALOPHOROS'

In Byzantine art the death of Dionysius the Areopagite was sometimes represented as a banal scene of decapitation. This is the case, for example, in Vatican graec. 1679, f. 25^v[1], the Oxford Menologium, Bodleian gr. th. f. 1, f. 11^v[2], and in the wall-calendars at

92. HAMANN-MAC LEAN, op. cit. (note 11), fig. 26.

93. DJURIĆ, op. cit. (note 30), p. 39-41, plate XXVIII.

94. Crusader icon : K. WEITZMANN, The Icon, London 1978, p. 118, plate 40. Saint Nicolas Orphanos : Anna TSITOURIDOU, Ο ζωγραφικός διάκοσμος του αγίου Νικολάου Ορφανού στη Θεσσαλονίκη, Thessaloniki 1986, p. 105, fig. 30.

1. WALTER, art. cit. (note 64), p. 30.

2. See above, note 62.

Pl. V

Figure 7. — Martyrdom of Dionysius, Menologium of Basil II, p. 82.

Figure 8. — Dionysius, Moscow Metaphrast, f. 28.

Figure 9. — Denys of Paris (detail), Musée du Louvre.

Cozia and Peć[3]. However there are at least four examples of the martyr holding his severed head in his hands : Vatican *graec.* 1613, p. 82[4], Moscow GIM *graec.* 175, f. 28[5], a calendar icon at Saint Catherine's monastery, Mount Sinaï[6], and the wall-calendar at Dečani[7] (figures 7, 8, 6). These pictures, each of which has its individual characteristics, will be discussed in due course. Before doing so, it is useful to consider briefly what was written about 'kephalophoroi' saints in general and Dionysius in particular in the literary sources both Western and Eastern.

There is no doubt that the legend of Dionysius walking for two *millia* holding his severed head in his hands is of Western origin. It reached Byzantium after Denys the founder bishop of Paris had been identified with Dionysius the Areopagite by means of the Greek translation of the Latin Life *Post beatam*, the first in which the prodigy was recounted[8]. In the earlier Latin Life, the *Gloriosae*, it is told that Denys, with his companions the priest Rusticus and the deacon Eleutherius, was sent by pope Clement to France[9]. After their martyrdom a pagan matron buried their bodies in a field. Later a mausoleum was built for them and finally a shrine. It seems that the *Gloriosae* dates from about 475 when the first shrine in honour of Saint Denys was built.

The *Post beatam* modifies the story by identifying Denys with Dionysius of Athens. Dionysius, already a bishop consecrated by Saint Paul, went to Rome and thence to Paris where he was martyred along with his two companions. Denys/Dionysius then walked two *millia* carrying his head in his hands. Later the same pagan matron, now called Catula, recovered their bodies and buried them. She was converted by the intercession of the martyrs to Christianity.

The *Corpus dionysiacum*, with its attribution to Dionysius the Areopagite, had reached France as early as 758-763. Another copy was brought to Paris from Constantinople by ambassadors of Michael II in 827. However the *Post beatam* does not exploit any of the biographical material available in the *Corpus dionysiacum*. It is

---

3. MIJOVIĆ, *op. cit.* (note 62), p. 350, 363.

4. See above, note 71.

5. V. D. LIKHACHOVA, *Byzantine Miniature*, Moscow 1977, p. 16.

6. G. and Maria SOTIRIOU, Icônes du Mont Sinaï, Athens 1958, p. 121-123, fig. 38 ; K. WEITZMANN, *Ikone*, Belgrade 1983, p. 17, 50.

7. Vl. PETKOVIĆ, *Dečani*, II, Belgrade 1941, p. 9, fig. CVIII ; MIJOVIĆ, *op. cit.* (note 62), p. 317, 320.

8. *Acta sanctorum octobris* IV, Brussels 1780, 792-794 (*BHL* 2178) ; *PG* 4, 669-684 (*BHG* 554).

9. *PL* 88, 577-583 (*BHL* 2171) ; R. J. LOENERTZ, La légende parisienne de S. Denys l'Aréopagite, sa genèse et son premier témoin, *An. Boll.* 69, 1951, p. 217-237.

therefore not certain that its author was aware of its existence and of its attribution to Dionysius the Areopagite. Further, his introduction of the *céphalophorie* is quite gratuitous[10].

The prodigy was not first recounted of Denys/Dionysius. The earliest recorded example is that of the child martyr Saint Just of Auxerre, whose Passion is attested as early as the seventh century[11]. In this Passion the reason for the prodigy is evident : Saint Just tells his family where he is to be buried and what is to be done with his head. The same motivation for introducing the prodigy is clear in the hundred or so Lives of Western 'kephalophoroi' saints, who indicate the shrine where their relics are to be venerated[12]. However Denys/Dionysius was buried at Saint Denis, six *millia* from Paris, whereas he only walked for two *millia* carrying his head !

That the Greek translation of the *Post beatam* (Μετὰ τὴν μακαρίαν) existed before 833 is evident, because it was used discreetly by Michael the Syncellus[13]. He accepted the story that Dionysius went to Paris where he was martyred, but does not recount the prodigy of the *céphalophorie*, nor does he mention Catula. He also drew largely on the biographical material available in the *Corpus dionysiacum* and, as we have seen, the Autobiography. The *Souda* is yet more discret. It does not refer to Dionysius's journey to Paris, nor to the circumstances of his death, although it cites Michael the Syncellus[14].

In the brief notice in the Menologium of Basil II, the *Post beatam* is exploited but considerably modified[15]. No reference is made to the journey to Paris ; Dionysius's two disciples are mentioned but not named. The martyrdom takes place in Athens, and here — it seems to be the first time — a new detail is introduced : Dionysius, having

---

10. H. MORETUS-PLANTIN, Les Passions de saint Denys, *Mélanges offerts au R. P. Ferdinand Cavallera*, Toulouse 1948, p. 215-230, dated the *Post beatum* to 757 (p. 228). LOENERTZ, *art. cit.* (note 9), mainly on the grounds that Toulouse is mentioned as being in Aquitaine, only true after 817, refused the earlier dating. Neither scholar discusses the fact that Dionysius and his companions are said to chant the Creed with the *Filioque, Acta sanctorum, vol. cit.* (note 8), 793. This anachronism would surely not have been perpetrated before the synod of Frankfurt, 794 ! The *Filioque* was, of course, omitted in the Greek translation, *PG* 4, 680.

11. M. COENS, Aux origines de la céphalophorie. Un fragment retrouvé d'une ancienne Passion de S. Just, martyr de Beauvais, *An Boll.* 74, 1956, p. 86-114 ; IDEM, Nouvelles recherches sur un thème hagiographique : la céphalophorie, *Recueil d'études bollandiennes (Subsidia hagiographica* n° 37), Brussels 1969, p. 9-31 (*BHL* 4590).

12. P. SAINTYVES, Les saints céphalophores, *Revue de l'histoire des religions* 99, 1929, p. 158-231 ; H. MORETUS-PLANTIN, *Les Passions de saint Lucien et leurs dérivés céphalophoriques*, Namur 1953.

13. See above, note 27.

14. *Ed. cit.* (note 28), p. 108.

15. *PG* 117, 84-85.

carried his head two *millia*, presents it to a Christian woman. His two disciples are beheaded after him. It seems that the author was puzzled by the gratuitous nature of the *céphalophorie* in the *Post beatam*. He therefore gives it a purpose, which becomes more explicit in later accounts.

Thus in the notice in the Constantinopolitan Synaxary, in which Rufinus and Eleutherius are mentioned by name but without being attributed a clerical status, Dionysius gives his head to the woman, named Catula in the text, as a sacred treasure (τὸν ἱερὸν θησαυρόν)[16]. In the Metaphrastic Life, the *Post beatam* is exploited far more abundantly. Rusticus is called a priest and Eleutherius a deacon. The martyrdom takes place explicitly in Paris. Dionysius again gives his head to a woman, whom, it is explained, was Catula, the person responsible for the burial of the martyrs. Moreover the language used about Dionysius's severed head is more hyperbolic : a prize..., a trophy ..., a treasure ... (βραβεῖον ..., τρόπαιον ..., θησαυρόν ...)[17]. Nicodemus Hagioreitos seems to have followed the Metaphrastic Life closely. He refers to the most sweet miracle and the treasure (θαῦμα γλυκύτατον, ὡς ἕνα θησαυρόν)[18].

The Western motivation for introducing the prodigy of *céphalophorie* into the Life of a saint being unknown in the East, Byzantine hagiographers adapted the prodigy as recounted in the *Post beatam* in order to assimilate it to their own tradition, according to which the head was the most prized relic of a decapitated martyr. A clear witness to this tradition is provided by Saint John Chrysostom in his Homily in honour of Saints Juventinus and Maximinus, who were beheaded under Julian the Apostate. He wrote that the severed head of a martyr was more terrifying to the devil than when it was able to speak. He adduced the case of the head of Saint John the Baptist, which was more awe-inspiring when placed on a dish than when he was alive. He compared soldiers showing their wounds received in battle to the emperor with martyrs holding their severed head in their hands and presenting it to Christ[19]. Among the severed heads prized as relics, that of Saint John the Baptist was obviously pre-eminent[20].

16. *Syn CP*, 101-102.

17. *PG* 4, 605.

18. Nicodemus Hagioreitos, Συναξαριστής, I, Athens 1868, p. 96.

19. *PG* 50, 575-576 (*Clavis* 4349, *BHG* 974). H. Delehaye, *Cinq leçons sur la méthode hagiographique*, Brussels 1934, p. 135-138, rejected peremptorily — but no doubt rightly — the hypothesis that this text of Chrysostom's was at the origin of Western *céphalophorie*. However, subsequent research necessitates the revision of several of his statements.

20. Ch. Walter, *The Invention of John the Baptist's Head in the Wall-calendar at Gračanica. Its place in Byzantine Iconographical Tradition*, *Zbornik za likovne umetnosti* 16, 1980, p. 71-83 ; M. Chatzidakis, *Une icône avec les trois inventions de la tête du Prodrome à Lavra*, *CA* 36, 1988, p. 85-97.

However, the example of Saint Auxentius should also be adduced. Great was the grief when his severed head was found to be missing, until it was discovered in a tree, to which it had been carried by a bird[21].

It was therefore the severed head as a trophy which was the focal point of Byzantine interest in Dionysius's *céphalophorie*. The rôle of Catula was to take charge of the precious relic, and this is what she does in three of the pictures of Saint Dionysius 'kephalophoros'.

The earliest of these is in the Menologium of Basil II, p. 82. Dionysius's two companions have already been beheaded — or so it seems, although, according to the text, Dionysius was beheaded first (figure 7). They wear simple tunics, but then the text does not say that they were respectively a priest and a deacon. On the other hand, although Dionysius is said explicitly to have been consecrated bishop of Athens, he is not represented wearing episcopal costume. The excutioner, having severed Dionysius's head, is replacing his sword in its sheath. Dionysius, leaning forward, holds his head in his covered hands; blood falls from it to the ground. To the right stands the Christian woman, one hand covered, waiting to receive the head.

The scene on the calendar icon at Saint Catherine's, Mount Sinaï, which Soterios dated to the second half of the eleventh century, is more simple (figure 6). The executioner and the companions are missing. Dionysius, wearing episcopal dress, holds his severed head in his hands. Catula, facing him, extends her uncovered hands to receive it. At Dečani (1346/7) Dionysius's companions are also omitted. The excutioner stands in the background to the left, his unsheathed sword still raised. In the foreground to the right, Dionysius, episcopally dressed, is slightly inclined. Catula, facing him, has taken his head in her hands.

The scene in the Moscow Metaphrast, f. 28, differs from the others (figure 8). Moreover it has little relation to the text. Catula is omitted. Dionysius is represented frontally in episcopal costume holding his severed head in his hands. Haloed, as in the previous examples, the head has more the aspect of a trophy, resembling that of Saint John the Baptist in later pictures of him represented 'kephalophoros'. Blood gushes from Dionysius's neck. To the left stands the excutioner who is replacing his sword in its sheath. To the right stand two figures, haloed and episcopally dressed. The one nearer to Dionysius extends his right hand towards him. Their presence is curious. If they are Rusticus and Eleutherius, the artist has perpetrated an anomaly in representing them as bishops. Moreover it does not seem that they

---

21. *PG* 116, 488-489 (*BHG* 646); WALTER, *art. cit.* (note 20), p. 76.

Figure 11. — Deacon 'kephalophoros', Platanistasa.

Figure 10. — Heads of Oreb and Zeb, Vatopedi 602, f. 421ᵛ.

Figure 12. — Saint Paul 'kephalophoros', Krina.

too are to undergo martyrdom, since the executioner is sheathing his sword[22].

Although the legend of the *céphalophorie* came from the West, there can be no doubt that the iconography, at least for the three first examples, was an Eastern invention, because in Western tradition Catula does not receive Dionysius's head. The frontal portrait of Dionysius in the Moscow Metaphrast is closer to Western examples, like the fifteenth-century picture in the Louvre, in which Denys of Paris, also represented frontally with blood gushing from his neck, accompanies Charlemagne (figures 8, 9)[23]. However the Moscow Metaphrast is an eleventh-century manuscript and consequently earlier than any known Western picture of a 'kephalophoros' saint.

Thus the *céphalophorie* of a martyr, in the literal or historical sense, is restricted in Byzantine tradition, unlike that of the West, to Dionysius. It does not seem that Byzantine martyrs were in the habit of displacing themselves after their death. There is, perhaps, a near equivalent in the description of a picture in the Life of the patriarch Tarasius by Ignatius the deacon. According to this text, the martyr was represented, his severed head reunited to this body, walking on the sea as if it was land. I was unable to establish to which martyr Ignatius was referring[24]. The severed head could, of course, be represented as a trophy in quite another context, when it was the head of an enemy. For example in the thirteenth-century Octateuch, Vatopedi 602, f. 421^v, and the twelfth-century Vatican *graec.* 746, f. 480^v, two soldiers present the heads of Zeb and Oreb to Gedeon (figure 10). The illustration corresponds literally to the text, Judges 7,24-25[25].

On the other hand from the thirteenth century onwards there exists a number of examples of *céphalophorie* in the figurative or symbolic sense. In the pictures in question the saints all differ from Dionysius in that they have *two* heads, one placed on their shoulders and the other, held as a trophy, in their hand. In these cases the severed head

---

22. For Dionysius of Phourna, the martyrdom of Dionysius was to be represented with him as an old man holding his head in his hands, *ed. cit.* (note 61), p. 194. In the wall-calendar at Markov manastir, there are, at the date of Dionysius's feast, two busts, one of a man and the other of a woman. Mijović, *op. cit.* (note 62), p. 346, suggested that the woman was Damaris, whom he calls Dionysius's wife (!). It seems more likely that she is Catula.

23. A. W. Ritter, Dionysius (Denis) von Paris, *Lexikon der christlichen Ikonographie* 5, 61-67 ; G. Kaster, Kephalophoren Heilige, *ibidem* 6, 307-308.

24. Wanda Wolska-Conus and Ch. Walter, Un programme iconographique du patriarche Tarasios ?, *REB* 38, 1980, p. 249-250, 255.

25. J. Lowden, The Production of the Vatopedi Octateuch, *DOP* 36, 1982, p. 124-125, fig. 25, 26.

274

is to be interpreted as an attribute of martyrdom. There is no question of the saint having displaced himself, carrying his severed head.

Possibly the earliest of these pictures is that of Saint Paul in the church at Krina, Chios, dated between 1197 and 1296 (figure 12)[26]. In the old metropolis at Veroia, six bishops are represented 'kephalophoroi'[27]. Saint John the Baptist appears for the first time as 'kephalophoros' at Arilje (1296)[28]. Other examples exist in four-teenth-century wall-painting, while post-Byzantine icons of him 'kephalophoros' are common. In the church at Platanistasa, Cyprus (1494?), an anonymous deacon holds his severed head in a veil (figure 11)[29]. Finally I have noted seventeen examples of Saint George 'kephalophoros' in post-Byzantine art[30].

To conclude, although the legend of Dionysius's *céphalophorie* was Western in origin, it received a new interpretation in Byzantine tradition. The head was considered to be a trophy, and, in the case of a martyr, as a prized relic. However, Dionysius was the only martyr, whose *céphalophorie* was understood literally. For all the others represented in Byzantine art the sense was symbolic.

26. Unpublished. Information communicated by Ch. Pennas.

27. Unpublished. Information communicated by I. Ath. Papangelos, 11th ephoria for Byzantine antiquities, Veroia.

28. Ch. Walter, Saint John the Baptist 'Kephalophoros', a New Iconographical theme of the Palaeologan Period, Ἔνατο συμπόσιο Βυζαντινῆς καὶ Μεταβυζαντινῆς ἀρχαιολογίας καὶ τέχνης, Athens 1989, p. 85-86.

29. A. and Judith Stylianou, *The Painted Churches of Cyprus*, London 1985, p. 186 (date), 217.

30. Ch. Walter, Saint George 'Kephalophoros', *Mélanges Manolis Chatzidakis* (printing).

Credit lines : figure 1, Photothèque Gabriel Millet, Paris ; figure 2, Gojko Subotić ; figure 3, 5, Der Nersessian, *art. cit.* (note 65) ; figure 4, Vasilaki-Karakatsani, *op. cit.* (note-74) ; figure 6, Weitzmann, *op. cit.* (note 100) ; figure 7, Biblioteca apostolica vaticana : figure 8, Likhachova, *op. cit.* (note 99) ; figure 9, Giraudon, Paris ; figure 10, Lowden, *art. cit.* (note 25) ; figure 11, A. Stylianou ; figure 12, Ch. Pennas.

THE ICONOGRAPHICAL SOURCES FOR THE CORONATION OF MILUTIN AND SIMONIDA AT GRAČANICA

Among the schools of art which developed within the sphere of Byzantine influence during the Middle Ages, that of Serbia is particularly important. Thanks to the dynamism of the Ne-manjić dynasty, numerous churches were built or restored. In many of them the donors were represented. I am particularly concerned here with the portraits of Milutin and Simonida in the church of Gračanica[1]. They are represented together in the central archway between the narthex and the nave. Milutin wears a *sakkos* with the *loros*, or *diadema* as it was called in the XIVth century; on his head he has a *stemma* with lappets and in his hands he holds a model of the church[2]. Simonida wears a mantle over her tunic; her *tympanion*, wider at the top than at the base, is decorated with the triangular *pinnae*, which figure on the headdress of an empress as early as the VIth century[3]. It is to be noted, however, that the *thorakion* has disappeared[4].

Each portrait is accompanied by an inscription[5]:

Milutin

Left	Right
стєфанк оүро	самодоⷬжцк
ш хоү воү вѣ	вⷭѣхк срькⷭс
рьнк матию	кихк землⷭ
божию кⷬалк	и поморьскихк
	и хтиторк

Simonida

Left	Right
симони	дьши цⷬіа
да кⷬа	андроника
лица и па	палеѡлоⷢа
леологина	

---

[1] S. Radojčić, *Portreti srpskih vladara u srednjem veku*, Skoplje 1934, p. 44—45, pl. XIX no 17; P. Mijović, *O hronologiji gračaničkih fresaka*, in Starine Kosova i Metohije 4—5, 1971, p. 179 and 191, pl. 6.

[2] J. Ebersolt, *Les arts somptuaires de Byzance*, Paris 1923, p. 120—129; Pseudo—Kodinos, *Traité des offices*, ed. J. Verpeaux, Paris 1966, passim, especially p. 252—273; Gordana Babić, *L'icono-graphie constantinopolitaine de l'Acathiste de la Vierge à Cozia*, in Zbornik radova, 14—15, 1973, p. 185,

[3] Ebersolt, *op. cit.* (note 2), p. 126—128; J. Deér, *Die heilige Krone Ungarns*, Vienna 1966, p. 55. pl. XXXII—XXXV.

[4] G. de Jerphanion, *Le „thorakion", caractéristique iconographique du XIe siècle*, in La voix des monuments (nouvelle série), Rome/Paris 1938, p. 263—278.

184

Milutin's epigraph, which differs slightly from the one accompanying his portrait at Studenica, nevertheless closely resembles those in use at that time at Constantinople[6]. For example, in the profession of faith made by the emperor, according to Pseudo-Codinus, on the occasion of his coronation, the following formula was used: ὁ [δεῖνα] ἐν Χριστῷ τῷ Θεῷ πιστὸς βασιλεὺς καὶ αὐτοκράτωρ Ῥωμαίων[7].

This is how I translate the two inscriptions at Gračanica:

Stefan Uroš (Milutin), faithful to Christ, by divine grace sole despot (autocrator)[8] of all the Serbs by land (Raška) and by sea (Zeta) and founder.

FIG. 1.
CORONATION OF MILUTIN
AND SIMONIDA,
GRAČANICA
(AFTER DJ. BOŠKOVIĆ)

[5] I give the transcription of S. Radojčić, *op. cit.* (note 1), p. 44. He observes that in 1934 the inscription was well preserved (dobro očuvan). Since then it has deteriorated and some letters are no longer visible. The transcription due to Lj. Stojanović, *Stari srpski zapisi i natpisi,* III, Belgrade 1905, p. 77, n⁰ 5091, differs somewhat for Milutin. The inscription for Simonida, clearer than that for Milutin even to-day (Stojanović p. 78, n⁰ 5095), presents no problem to the reader.

[6] Stojanović, *op. cit.* (note 5), III, p. 86, n⁰ 5093; Radojčić, *op. cit.* (note 1), p. 36.

[7] Pseudo—Kodinos, *op. cit.* (note 2), p. 252, lines 19—21.

[8] G. Ostrogorsky, *Avtokrator i samodržac,* in Glas srpske kraljevske akademije, 164, 1935, p. 95—187, reprinted in *Vizantija i Sloveni,* Belgrade s. d., p. 281—364.

Simonida Palaeologa, queen, daughter of Andronicus Palaeologus.

In the centre of the arch, above the heads of the two Serbian sovereigns, Jesus Christ is represented in a mandorla. He extends both hands, his fingers bent in the gesture of benediction, towards Milutin and Simonida. Outside the mandorla, each side of Christ, is an angel holding a crown; they are descending towards Milutin and Simonida. In each case the crown is identical with that which the sovereign already wears. It is evident that the crowns are being presented by Christ to the Serbian sovereigns. What is the significance of this scene?

In an article published before the war, Dr Bošković linked these portraits to the Last Judgment scene, represented in the narthex: „Il est évident que les couronnes portées par les anges ne sont pas des couronnes royales, mais bien les 'couronnes de vie'."[9] With regard to a somewhat similar scene in the *Theodore Psalter* (*Londin. Addit.* 19352, f. 21), in which an angel places a second crown upon the head of Hezekiah, I proposed independently an interpretation along the same lines: „What meaning are we to give to this second crown? I suspect that the explanation is to be sought in the Antique distinction between the crown as attribute of victory and the diadem as attribute of authority."[10] (Plate 10a)

Dr Mijović has also published an interpretation of the portraits of Milutin and Simonida[11]. He notes the originality of the Last Judgment scene in the narthex. Its central theme is Christ Light of the World. The ray of light issuing from the Hand of God, in which are the souls of the just, extends as far as the portrait of Milutin. Dr Mijović deduces that Milutin does not figure here as awaiting judgment, but rather that he considers himself to have been redeemed from the moment that he opted for Christ.

There are, in fact, in Serbia a number of portaits of sovereigns receiving a crown from Christ, sometimes by the intermediary of an angel. (Plate 17). The Bulgarian Tsar John Alexander is represented in the same fashion. (Plate 16 a, b). The introduction of this theme into the official iconography of the Serbian and Bulgarian rulers was probably due to the initiative of Milutin. However, as I have noted, the theme already existed in Byzantine art. In interpreting Milutin's portrait at Gračanica, it is necessary to take these other examples of official portraiture into account. In this paper I propose, first of all, to discuss two basic themes: the distinction between the crown and the diadem in Byzantine iconography and the rôle of angels in coronation scenes. After that I shall present a short dossier of dedicatory portraits in which angels crown. Finally I shall reconsider the portraits of Milutin and Simonida in the context of XIVth-century portraits of the same genre.

I. CROWNS AND DIADEMS IN BYZANTINE ICONOGRAPHY

It is not possible here to do more than enumerate briefly the problems involved in attempting to distinguish in iconography between a crown and a diadem.

The first problem is one of language. Whereas in Antique usage it seems clear what was the difference between the στέφανος and the διάδημα, this is not the case for Byzantine usage.

[9] Đ. Bošković, *Deux „couronnes de vie" à Gračanica.* in Annales de l'Institut Kondakov, 11, 1939, p, 63—64.

[10] Review of Sirarpie Der Nersessian's edition of this *Psalter* (see below note 55), in Revue des études byzantines, 30, 1972 p. 369—370.

[11] P. Mijović, *Carska ikonografija u srpskoj srednjovekovnoj umetnosti,* in Starinar XVIII, 1967, p. 104—107.

186

The next problem is one of material form. Crowns and diadems no doubt differed in their basic aspect but also had, within each genre, numerous variants. Further, in Byzantine tradition not only does the form of the diadem change but also different kinds of ceremonial headdress existed, corresponding to different ranks[12].

In Antique usage the crown was a circlet made of leaves or flowers, natural or copied in precious metal[13]. Such a crown figured in marriage and funerary rites; it was given as a prize at contests, whether artistic or sportive. In Roman triumphal ceremonial, a crown was held over the head of a *triumphatus*, or presented to the emperor who would then wear it on ceremonial occasions. Apart from the marriage crown, whose significance at the beginning was probably festal, all these crowns were presented as the reward of victory.

By contrast in Antiquity the diadem was a band bedecked normally with pearls; it could be ornamented with lappets and a large jewel in front[14]. It was the sign of royalty *par excellence*, and, as such, notoriously abhorred by the Romans. The distinction between the crown and the diadem is quite clear on Roman coins (Plate 1 a, b). During the first centuries Roman emperors are represented wearing a crown; it was only when they began to imitate Oriental potentates, that they had themselves represented wearing a diadem.

In Antique, as in Early Christian iconography, the distinction is normally clear, from the form and the context, between a diadem and a crown. For example, on the Boscoreale cup in the Louvre, the attendant standing behind Tiberius in the quadriga is placing a crown on his head[15] (Plate 2). On the Barberini ivory, also in the Louvre, the emperor is wearing a diadem, while the angel of victory offers him a crown[16]. Similarly in the Adventus scene on the plate from Kersch now in the Hermitage, the emperor wears a diadem, while the angel of victory preceding him carries a crown[17] (Plate 3). The diadem, in both these examples, is the sign of his imperial status, while the crown is the reward of success in battle.

In an apotheosis scene, such as that represented upon a cameo in the Cabinet des médailles of the Paris Bibliothèque nationale, Germanicus, like Ganymede, is carried aloft by an eagle; he holds a *lituus* and a *cornucopia*[18] (Plate 4 a). The angel flying towards him carries a crown,

[12] E. Amann, in *Le Protoévangile de Jacques le Mineur er ses remaniements latins*, Paris 1910, p. 186, defines the *diadem* thus: un bandeau plus ou moins orné, servant à retenir les cheveux, qui, fixé au bas de la tiare perse, devient un ornement royal. It was taken over by Alexander from the Great Kings as a sign of his sovereignty over Asia, cf. H.—W. Ritter, *Diadem und Königscherrschaft*, Munich/Berlin 1965, especially p. 125—127. For the *modiolus*, cf. P. Charanis, *The Imperial Crown Modiolus and its Constitutional Significance*, in Byzantion 12, 1937, p. 189—195; *The Crown Modiolus Once More*, ibid., 13, 1938, p. 377—383. The word στέμμα originally denoted a garland made of wool, but from the IXth century at least (for example in the *Book of Ceremonies* of Constantine Porphyrogenitus) it denotes the imperial diadem. Pseudo—Codinus observes that by his time the word διάδημα was used rather for the imperial girdle or λῶρος, *op. cit.* (note 2), p. 199. For different views on the meaning of στέφανος in Byzantine usage, see Verpeaux's important note, *op. cit.* (note 2), p. 199. For the translation of these words into Slavonic,

cf. Gordana Babić, *L'iconographie constantinopolitaine de l'Acathiste de la Vierge à Cozia (Valachie)*, in Zbornik radova, 14—15 1973, p. 185.

[13] *Dictionnaire des antiquités grecques et romaines*, I 2, Paris 1887, ed. C. Daremberg and E. Saglio, 1520—1537 (Corona) and 1080—1086 (Certamina). for a recent *status quaestionis*, cf. R. Turcan, *Les guirlandes dans l'Antiquité classique*, in Jahrbuch für Antike und Christentum, 14, 1971, p. 92——139.

[14] Ibid. II 1, 119—121 (Diadema).

[15] Inez Scott Ryberg, *Rites of the State Religion in Roman Art*, Rome 1955, p. 141—142, pl. L fig. 77a.

[16] D. Talbot Rice, *Art byzantin*, Paris/Brussels 1959, n° 19.

[17] Alisa Bank, *Vizantiiskoe iskusstvo*, Leningrad/Moscow 1969, n° 1, p. 277.

[18] E. Babelon, *Guide illustré au Cabinet des Médailles et Antiques de la Bibliothèque Nationale*, Paris 1900, p. 116.

(A) CROWN

(B) DIADEM

PLATE 1: ROMAN COINS

(C) CROWN AND DIADEM COMBINED

IV

PLATE 3: KERSCH PLATE, HERMITAGE, LENINGRAD.

PLATE 2: BOSCOREALE CUP, LOUVRE, PARIS.

PLATE 4 (A): CAMEO, CABINET DES MÉDAILLES, PARIS.

PLATE 4 (B): MINIATURE, RABBULA GOSPELS, LAURENZIANA, FLORENCE.

PLATE 5: MOSAIC, NORTH APSE, BASILICA EUPHRASIANA, POREC.

PLATE 6 (A): BASE OF COLUMN OF THEODOSIUS I,
HIPPODROME, CONSTANTINOPLE.

PLATE 6 (B): MOSAIC, APSE, SAN VITALE, RAVENNA.

which must signify the reward of eternal life. It is with a similar triumphal significance that two angels hold out (Plate 4 b) crowns towards Christ in the Ascension scene of the *Rabbula Gospels*[19].

Another type of scene in which the crown of victory commonly occurs is that in which the theme of triumph in the Hippodrome is represented. The victor may be represented actually being crowned, by another personage on the diptych of Areobindus at Besançon[20], or by a winged victory on the Porphyrius bases in Istanbul[21]. As is wellknown, the Early Christians compared the perseverance of the Christian with that of the athlete, with this difference that the Christian received an imperishable crown, a crown of glory or a crown of life[22]. This metaphor has its equivalent in iconography, for example at Poreč, where Christ holds a crown over the heads of two martyrs[23] (Plate 5).

The most striking adaptation of Hippodrome iconography to Christians ends is probably that at San Vitale in Ravenna[24]. (Plate 6b). Here the crown, which is heavily bejewelled and therefore at one remove from the crown which figures in Hippodrome scenes, is extended by Christ, seated in majesty, towards the martyr Vitalis. One easily recognizes the prototype in the scene of the emperor Theodosius standing in the *kathisma* with a crown in his hand to be presented to the victor, which figures upon the base of his column in Istanbul[25] (Plate 6a). John Chrysostom, so prolific in his use of imperial and sporting analogies, explains in one of his homilies that, just as athletes are not crowned in the stadium but „above" (presumably in the imperial *kathisma*), so Christians struggle here below, but receive their reward „above" (in heaven)[26].

Thus far the distinction between the crown and the diadem is easy enough to make and to explain, the more so that the rite of investiture with a diadem, represented in Iranian art, does not, apparently, exist in Hellenistic art[27]. Confusion begins with the introduction of new themes into imperial iconography by Constantine. For example Constantine is represented on coins wearing a headdress which combines the leaves of a crown with the bejewelled band of a diadem (Plate I c). Although his successors were to abandon this in favour of a headdress which is clearly a diadem, it seems that, from the time of Constantine, the emperor's majesty ($\beta\alpha\sigma\iota\lambda\varepsilon\iota\alpha$) and his triumph are jointly symbolized by his headdress. Another Constantinian innovation in this kind of iconography, is that of the Hand of God emerging from a mandorla, and extending a crown towards the personage represented below (Plate 7a). Thus on a medal now in

[19] C. Cecchelli, *The Rabbula Gospels*, Olten/Lausanne 1959, f. 13ᵛ, p. 71—72.

[20] R. Delbrueck, *Die Consulardiptychen und verwandte Denkmäler*, Berlin/Leipzig 1929, p. 72; Tafeln, V pl. 10. This detail only occurs in the Besançon version of the diptych of Areobindus.

[21] A. Cameron, *Porphyrius the Charioteer*, Oxford 1973, p. 43—44, fig. 8. This book is a mine of useful information upon the ceremonial and imagery of the Hippodrome.

[22] *Dictionnaire de la Bible*, II, Paris 1899, 1083——1087 (Couronne); I *Corinthians* 9, 25; I *Peter* 5, 4; *Apocalypse* 2, 10, etc...

[23] Marguerite Van Berchem and E. Clouzot, *Mosaiques chrétiennes*, Geneva 1924, p. 181—182.

[24] Christa Ihm, *Die Programme der christlichen Apsismalerei vom vierten Jahrhundert bis zur Mitte des achten Jahrhunderts*, Wiesbaden 1960, p. 163——165.

[25] G. Bruns, *Der Obelisk und seine Basis auf Hippodrom zu Konstantinopel*, Istanbul 1935; Cameron, *op. cit.* (note 21), fig. 19.

[26] John Chrysostom, *In epistola ad Philippenses commentarius*, PG 62, 272; cf. P. Van der Aalst, *Christus Basileus bij Johannes Chrysostomus*, Nijmegen/Utrecht 1966, p. 1—30.

[27] Investiture scenes, dating back to the IIIrd century A. D., have survived at Naqsh-i Rustan, the religious and funerary centre of the Achemenids and the Sassanids. The iconographical formula remains constant: the god puts a diadem into the hands of the king. Cf. R. Ghirshman, *Parthes et Sassanides*, Paris 1962, p. 10, 119, 133, etc... Ghirshman comments (p. 133): une vision artistique traduit sur la pierre la titulature du prince, qui se dit dieu et d'essence divine. (I thank Mme Nicole Thierry for drawing my attention to these scenes.).

Vienna Constantine stands between two of his sons; one is crowned by an angel of victory, the other, probably, by a personification[28]. Thus far no innovation is introduced. However the hand with a crown above Constantine himself implies that he is directly crowned by God. The title Θεοστεφής was later to be applied regularly to emperors, although the first literary witness to it is, apparently, in Sophronius of Jerusalem's *Life* of Saints Cyr and John. The text is relevant to the present enquiry. According to Sophronius, the monk Senuphius gave Theodosius II his baculus and maphorion; Theodosius is qualified here as Θεοστεφής. He wore the maphorion in battle and thereafter preferred it to any other διάδημα[29].

The Hand of God holding a crown over the head of Christ appears on the lid of the *Capsella africana*, conserved in the Museo sacro of the Vatican[30] (Plate 7 b). Christ, like a victorious charioteer, holds one crown in his hand, while from above another hand extends a crown towards him. André Grabar aptly quotes, with respect to this scene, the African doctor Cyprian: *Dominus... ipse in certamine nostri et coronat et coronatur*[31]. However, the sense may not be that Christ is going to present the crown which he holds in his hand; we may have here two successive scenes: God presenting the crown and Christ holding it. Be this as it may, there is no question here of a diadem, any more than in the texts, of which one attributed to George of Pisidia dating from the first half of the VIIth century seems to be the earliest[32], in which a martyr is qualified also as Θεοστεφής.

One consequence of the conversion of Constantine was that the Hellenistic and Roman concepts of βασιλεία were further enriched by Jewish notions of Messianic kingship[33]. The ceremony of imposing a diadem on the emperor's head, if first attested in a military context, early became an ecclesiastical one[34]. In the coronation ritual published by Goar, the patriarch recites a prayer paraphrasing *Psalm* 20 (21), of which verse 3 is ἔθηκας ἐπὶ τὴν κεφαλὴν αὐτοῦ στέφανον ἐκ λίθου τιμίου[35]. This is, no doubt, another sign that the symbolism of the crown and the diadem are now united in the imperial headdress, which receives the name of στέμμα[36]. The verb στεφανόω is used for the imposition both of a crown and of a diadem[37]. George Cedrenus,

[28] Maria R. Alföldi, *Die constantinische Goldprägung*, Mainz 1963, p. 168 n° 148 and pl. XV fig. 214. Cf. the medal now in the Hermitage, A.Grabar, *Un médaillon en or provenant de Mersine en Cilicie*, in L'art de la fin de l'Antiquité et du Moyen Age, Paris 1968, I, p. 200—211 and III, pl. 24. The Hand of God seems to be a theme of Jewish origin; cf. A. Grabar, *Christian Iconography, a Study of its Origins*, London 1969, p. 40.

[29] *Life of Cyr and* John, para. 14, PG 87³, 3686——3688 (earlier than 638). Cf. the inscription concerning the donation of a saltpan by Justinian II to the sanctuary of Saint Demetrius at Thessalonika: δεσπότου Φλαυίου Ἰουστινιανοῦ τοῦ θεοστεφοῦς, A. Vasiliev, *An Edict of the Emperor Justinian*, September 688, in Speculum, 18, 1943, p. 5, and S. G. Mercati, *Sull'uso di* θεόστεπτος, in Collectanea byzantina, II, Bari 1970, p. 370——371.

[30] H. Buschhausen, *Die spätrömischen Metallscrinia und frühchristlichen Reliquiare*, Vienna 1971, p. 242—243, pl. 49; A. Grabar, *Martyrium*, II, Paris 1946, p. 56—57, gives the correct explanation of the iconography of this reliquary. Buschhausen did not recognize Christ and, apparently, did not know Grabar's study.

[31] Cyprian, Letter X, para. 4, *Opera omnia* (C.S.E. L., III ii), Vienna 1871, p. 494, lines 11—12.

[32] *Contra Severum*, line 553, PG 92, 1664.

[33] F. Dvornik, *Early Christian and Byzantine Political Philosophy*, I, Washington 1966, p. 278—402.

[34] It seems that Julian's military „coronation" is the first of which a written account exists; cf. O. Treitinger, *Die oströmische Kaiser- und Reichsidee*, Darmstadt 1956², p. 7, and that the patriarch intervened for the first time at the coronation of Leo I in 457; cf. W. Ensslin, *Zur Frage der ersten Kaiserkrönung durch den Patriarchen und zur Bedeutung dieses Artes im Wahlzeremoniell*, in Byzantinische Zeitschrift, 42, 1942, p. 370.

[35] J. Goar, *Rituale Graecorum*, Paris 1647, p. 925.

[36] See note 12.

[37] The examples cited by Ducange, *Glossarium*, 1445, and by G. W. H. Lampe, *A Patristic Greek Lexicon*, Oxford 1961, 1258, are concerned with crowns (in the Antique sense), but it is evident from the epigraphs accompanying miniatures that the word was also used for the imposition of a diadem.

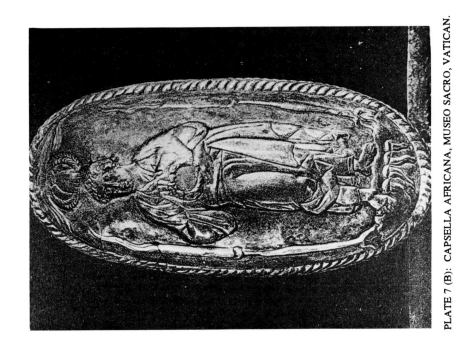

PLATE 7 (B): CAPSELLA AFRICANA, MUSEO SACRO, VATICAN.

PLATE 7 (A): MEDALLION, KUNSTHISTORISCHES MUSEUM,
VIENNA.

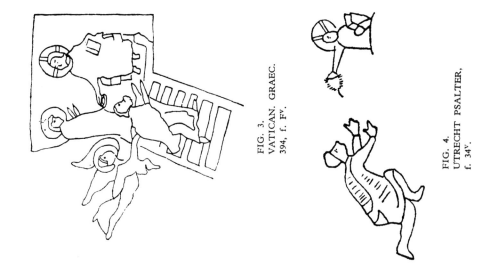

FIG. 3.
VATICAN. GRAEC.
394, f. FV.

FIG. 4.
UTRECHT PSALTER,
f. 34v.

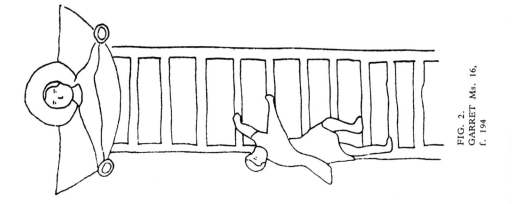

FIG. 2.
GARRET Ms. 16,
f. 194

indeed, distinguishes clearly between the marriage crown and the imperial diadem[38]. For the coronation of an emperor, Pseudo—Codinus uses the word στεφηφορία[39].

Before returning to the specific problems of iconography, one final source of possible confusion must be mentioned: the difficulty in establishing precisely the significance of the Byzantine rite of coronation[40]. Although the ceremony became increasingly important, particularly in the period of the Paleologi, it was „doubled" by others: raising on a shield, acclamation and proclamation[41]. These other rites marked an accession to power. Unless he was a usurper, an emperor was not normally crowned at the beginning of his reign but during that of his predecessor. A parallel may perhaps be drawn with the consecration and investiture of patriarchs. Coronation, conferred the grace of the state of βασιλεία, a capacity to reign; the authority to reign was conferred by the other ceremonies. As the patriarch's prayer in the rite of coronation makes clear, these graces of state included the divine favour: long life (immortality), glory, majesty, honour and help against enemies[42].

These divine favours were not, however, reserved to the state of βασιλεία. In fact it is important to call attention to a group of pictures illustrating *The Heavenly Ladder* of John Climacus in which crowns are awarded for perseverance in the practice of the virtues[43]. Christ, in fact, is represented at the top of the heavenly ladder, conferring crowns upon the monks approaching the last rung. In Hippodrome iconography, the crown is normally held downwards vertically; in scenes where a co-emperor is crowned, the diadem is held horizontally, ready to be imposed on the head. It is interesting to note that both variants occur in Climacus manuscripts: In *Garrett* MS 16, f. 194 (Princeton University Library), dated 1081, for example, Christ holds the crowns vertically, while in *Sinaït*. 423, f. 10ᵛ, dated to the XIIth century, he holds the crowns horizontally, as again in the XIVth-century frontispiece added to *Vatican. graec.* 394, f. Fᵛ[44].

The explanation of this apparently indifferent use of crowns and diadems may be that crowns of the Antique form conferred as prizes in the Hippodrome were no longer in use by the XIth century. However another explanation may be that, whereas in one case the artist had the New Testament uses of Hippodrome imagery in mind, in the other it was perhaps rather *Wisdom 5*, 15—16.

The just live for ever... Royal splendour shall be theirs, and a fair diadem from the Lord himself.

In sum the distinction between the royal diadem and the crown of victory, which is clear in Antiquity, subsequently becomes blurred. Byzantine artists and writers, particularly when

---

[38] *Chronicle*, II, Bonn 1839, p. 315 line 22—24: ἅμα δὲ τῷ νυμφικῷ στεφάνῳ καὶ τὸ τῆς βασιλείας διάδημα αὐτῇ ἐπετίθετο.

[39] *Op. cit.* (note 2), p. 252. On the other hand the word στεφάνωμα is used for the marriage of an autocrator. Aikaterini Christophilopoulou, Περὶ τὸ πρόβλημα τῆς ἀναδείξεως τοῦ βυζαντινοῦ αὐτοκράτορος, in Ἐπιστημονικὴ ἐπετηρὶς τῆς φιλοσοφικῆς σχολῆς τοῦ Πανεπιστημίου Ἀθηνῶν, 13, 1962—1963, p. 395.

[40] For the most recent *status quaestionis*, cf. A. Failler, *La déposition du patriarche Calliste Iᵉʳ (1353)*, in Revue des études byzantines, 31, 1973, p. 146——156.

[41] Ibid., p. 149—152.

[42] Goar, *op. cit.* (note 35), p. 925.

[43] J. R. Martin, *The Illustration of the Heavenly Ladder of John Climacus*, Princeton 1954, p. 16—17. The heavenly crown as a reward for perseverance on earth was a commonplace of Byzantine spirituality. Cf. P. Gautier, *Les lettres de Grégoire, higoumène d'Oxia*, in Revue des études byzantines, 31, 1973, p. 212—214. Writing to Alexius Comnenus, a cousin of the emperor Manuel I, Gregory consoles him on the death of his wife by saying that the sufferings which she bore on earth have merited for her innumerable crowns in heaven.

[44] Martin, *op. cit.* (note 43), p. 175—177 and fig 66; p. 190 and fig. 23; p. 177—181 and fig. 67

they are concerned with the symbolism of crowns and diadems, are not consistent. Consequently the exact significance of a crown or diadem in a particular case can only be determined by a study of the genre of picture, the context and the accompanying inscriptions.

II. THE ROLE OF ANGELS IN CORONATION SCENES

In matters of coronation, English is not less ambiguous than Greek. Henceforward I use the word 'coronation' indifferently for the imposition of a crown or a diadem. It is evident that the presence of angels in coronation scenes derives from their rôle in Antique triumphal imagery. To the examples already noted, we may add the cuirass of a IInd century imperial statue found at Stobi, upon which are represented two angels placing a crown on the emperor's head[45].

The most obvious Christian adaptations of this kind of scene occur in the iconography of the martyrs. According to the *Passion* of Saint Demetrius, in its IXth century version, the saint killed a scorpion with the sign of the cross. The angel of the Lord then came and placed a crown upon the saint's head, saying to him: Peace be with you, athlete of Christ[46]. No earlier version of this scene for Saint Demetrius occurs than the XIVth-century frescoes of the saint's Life in the Metropolis, dedicated to him, at Mistra[47]. However, the theme recurs fairly often in late Byzantine art. We may cite the ikon attributed to the XVth century in the monastery of the Transfiguration at the Meteora[48], and the painting over the West door of the monastery of Marko at Sušica, in which Demetrius, seated on horseback, is being crowned and invested with armour (Plate 8) Earlier than these is the ikon of the warrior saint Procopius in the monastery of Saint Catherine, Sinaî, attributed, by the Sotiriou to the XIIIth century[49] (Plate 9) The crown, whether or not imposed by an angel, becomes a regular attribute of warrior saints in late Byzantine iconography, perhaps reflecting the theme of Tertullian's treatise *De corona militari*, which praises those Christian warriors who preferred martyrdom to the igonominy of wearing a military crown fraught with pagan associations[50].

In a manuscript of the Heavenly Ladder, *Sinaït*. 418, there are three miniatures, in which angels impose a crown[51]. The miniature on f. 164 portrays two angels crowning a poor man, for, according to the text illustrated, the monk who is poor is lord of the world[52]. In this case the crown must have the sense of an imperial diadem. On f. 170 the monk who prays instead of sleeping is crowned by an angel[53]. Here the crown is evidently the reward of perseverance. Finally on f. 279 an angel crowns the monk who practises the virtue of charity. This virtue entitles the poor man to sit with the princes of the angels. Only in the last case does the text contain an explicit reference to angels[54]. It seems, then, that their presence is to be derived from their rôle of servants of the Lord; there is no direct association with Antique angels of victory.

[45] *L'art en Yougoslavie de la préhistoire à nos jours*, catalogue of exhibition, Paris 1971, n° 92.

[46] *Passio altera*, para. 6, PG 116, 1177.

[47] G. Millet, *Monuments byzantins de Mistra*, Paris 1910, pl. 68, 3; Suzy Dufrenne, *Les programmes iconographiques des églises byzantines de Mistra*, Paris 1970, p. 7—8; cf. my article, Saint Demetrius: *The Myroblytos of Thessalonika*, in Eastern Churches Review, 5, 1973, p. 169—170.

[48] *L'art byzantin*, catalogue of exhibition, Athens 1964, n° 240.

[49] G. and Maria Sotiriou, *Icônes du Mont Sinaï* I, Athens 1958, p. 171—173; II, pl. 188.

[50] *Tertulliana opera*, II, *Opera montanistica*, ed. E. Kroymann, Tournai 1954, p. 1039—1065; *De corona*, ed. M. J. Fontaine, Paris 1966; J. Bayet, *En relisant la De corona*, in Rivista dell' archeologia cristiana, 43, 1967, p. 21—32.

[51] Martin, *op. cit.* (note 43), fig. 198, 200, 214.

[52] *Scala paradisi*, 17, PG 88, 928.

[53] Ibid., 19, PG 88, 937.

[54] Ibid., 29, PG 88, 1152.

PLATE 8: FRESCO, MONASTERY OF MARKO, SUSICA.

PLATE 9: ICON, MONASTERY OF SAINT CATHERINE,
MOUNT SINAÏ.

IV

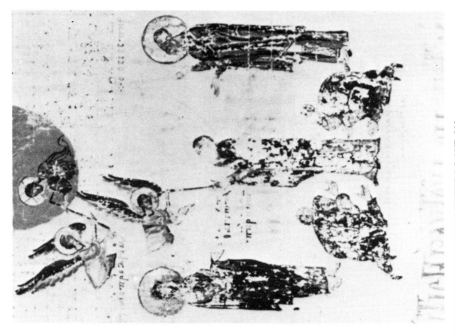

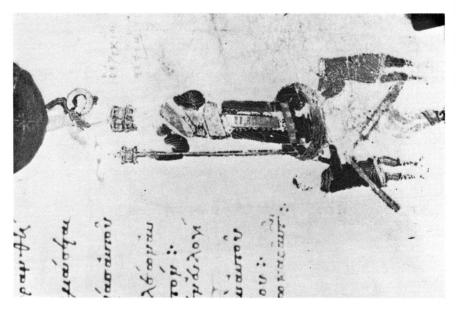

PLATES 10 (A & B): MINIATURES, THEODORE PSALTER, BRITISH MUSEUM, LONDON.

Finally there is the miniature of Hezekiah in the *Theodore Psalter*, to which I alluded at the beginning of this paper (*Londin. Addit.* 19352, f. 21)[55]. (Plate 10 a) The text illustrated is, it will be recalled, *Psalm* 20 (21), v. 4: Thou set a crown of fine gold upon his head. In the *Chludov Psalter* (*Mosquen. addit. graec.* 129, f. 18ᵛ), Hezekiah, dressed in imperial robes, is raised on a shield; the inscription merely says: 'Εζεχίας ὁ βασιλ(εύ)ς. The *Barberini Psalter* (*Vatican. barb. graec.* 372, f. 30ᵛ) adds to the *Chludov* miniature a standard held by Hezekiah in his right hand, an angel descending from a mandorla to place a *single* crown on his head and a more detailed inscription: ὁ 'Εζεχίας στεφόμενος[56]. Another variant occurs in the *Bristol Psalter* (*Londin. Addit.* 40731, f. 33), in which David (not Hezekiah), raised on a shield, is crowned by a personification called Βασιλεία[57]. The miniature in the *Theodore Psalter* only differs from that in the *Barberini Psalter* in that the angel imposes a second crown.

The artist responsible for illustrating the *Chludov Psalter* was, then, content to illustrate this Psalm with the standard picture used to mark the beginning of a reign in Old Testament history. The *Bristol Psalter* makes it clear that the state of βασιλεία is being conferred by placing a crown on David's head. This must also be the sense of the miniature in the *Barberini Psalter*, with the difference that βασιλεία comes from God by the intermediary of his angel. Can the hypothesis still be maintained that the second crown in the *Theodore Psalter* modifies the sense of the miniature?

In the *Utrecht Psalter*, f. 34ᵛ, illustrating *Psalm* 60 (61) v. 7: *Dies super dies regis adicies, annos eius usque in diem generationis*, the king, wearing a diadem, stretches his arms towards Christ in the gesture of prayer[58]. Christ extends towards him a crown with fillets of the Antique kind. In this case, the crown, distinguished from the diadem, no doubt symbolises God's favour, while the diadem symbolises the kingly state. However, in the *Theodore Psalter*, given the fact that the two crowns are identical, and given the preceding illustrations of this Psalm, it seems impossible to maintain the interpretation that I had proposed before. It seems more plausible, to my mind, to interpret the miniature as representing two successive scenes: the angel descending with a crown, and the king wearing the crown. Both crowns here have the connotations of a diadem.

Probably the scene of coronation by an angel has been transposed from another miniature portraying a Byzantine emperor. Indeed, there is a legend, which Constantine Porphyrogenitus recounts in the *De administrando imperio*, that the first imperial diadem was sent by an angel to the first Constantine: These robes of state and the diadems... were not fashioned by men..., but when God made emperor that famous Constantine the Great, he sent him these robes by the hand of his angel, and the diadems...[59].

[55] Sirarpie Der Nersessian, *Illustrations des psautiers, grecs du Moyen Age*, II, Londres, Add. 19.352, Paris 1970, p. 22, 78—79. It is not certain that this Psalm evokes the occasion when the crown of Milcom, king of Rabba, was placed upon David's head (II *Samuel* 12, 30—31).

[56] Ch. Walter, Raising on a shield in Byzantine iconography, *Revue des études byzantines*, 33, 1975, p. 149—150 and plates 4—5.

[57] Suzy Dufrenne, *L'illustration des psautiers grecs du Moyen Age*, I, Paris 1966, p. 55—56, pl. 49; Eadem, Le Psautier de Bristol et les autres psautiers byzantins, in Cahiers archéologiques, 14, 1964, p. 174, fig. 28.

[58] E. T. De Wald, *Illustrations of the Utrecht Psalter*, Princeton 1932, p. 28. (I thank Mlle Suzy Dufrenne for this, and other references; also for having allowed me to present the subject of this paper in her seminar at the Ecole pratique des hautes études on May 18th, 1974).

[59] Constantine Porphyrogenitus, *De administrando imperio*, ed. Gy. Moravcsik and tr. R. Jenkins, Budapest 1949; p. 66—67; ibid., *Commentary*, ed. R. Jenkins, London 1962, p. 64—65. Cf. Michael Psellus: ὁ δὲ ... βασιλεύς, ᾧ τὸ στέφος οὐκ ἐξ ἀνθρώπων οὐδὲ δι'ἀνθρώπων ἀλλ'ἄνωθεν ἐνήρμοσται προσφυῶς ... , *Letter* 207, in Μιχαὴλ Ψελλοῦ ἱστορικοὶ λόγοι ἐπιστολαὶ καὶ ἄλλα ἀνέκδοτα, ed. C. N. Sathas, Μεσαιωνικὴ βιβλιοθήκη V, Venice/ Paris, 1876, p. 508—509.

Our next task must, then, be to examine a number of Byzantine miniatures, in which Christ is represented presenting a crown to an emperor by the intermediary of an angel.

III. CORONATION BY ANGELS IN BYZANTINE DEDICATORY PICTURES

The four miniatures which I propose to analyse in this section are all extremely wellknown[60]. However in each case previous publication has left something to be desired. For this reason I give a full description of each miniature and transcribe the epigraphs.

1. Homilies of Gregory of Nazianzen, Paris. graec. 510, f. C^v, Basil I.

The miniature, executed between 880 and 883, portrays Basil I between the archangel Gabriel, called ἀρχιστράτηγος, placing a diadem on his head, while the prophet Elias presents him with a standard[61]. The miniature is, unfortunately, badly damaged, for which reason I add a drawing

FIG. 5.
PARIS. GRAEC. 510. f. C^v.

---

[60] A. Grabar, *L'empereur dans l'art byzantin*, Strasbourg 1936 (reprinted photographically, London 1971, with an updated bibliography, p. i—ν), p. 112—122. Related to the pictures discussed here are those where Christ himself crowns, or blesses or extends his protection to the royal personages represented, as well as those where the Virgin or a saint replaces Christ. For additional comparative material, cf. S. Lambros, Λεύκωμα βυζαντινῶν αὐτοκρατόρων, Athens 1930; H. Belting, *Das illuminierte Buch in der spätbyzantinischen Gesellschaft*, Heidelberg 1970; J. Barker, *Manuel II Palaeologus*, Rutgers University (New Jersey) 1969, and the contributions of H. Belting, *Die Auftraggeber der spätbyzantinischen Bildhandschrift*, and Tanja Velmans, *Le portrait dans l'art des Paléologues*, in Art et société à Byzance sous les Paléologues, Venice 1971. I thank Father Joseph Munitiz for valuable remarks concerning the literary genre of the verses which accompany the miniatures.

[61] H. Omont, *Fac-similés des miniatures des plus*

anciens manuscrits grecs de la Bibliothèque Nationale, 1902 and 1929, p. 13, pl. XIX; Sirarpie Der Nersessian, *The Illustration of the Homilies of Saint Gregory of Nazianzus, Paris, graecus 510*, in Dumbarton Oaks Papers, 16 1962, p. 198; G. Moravcsik, *Sagen und Legenden über Kaiser Basileios*, in Dumbarton Oaks Papers, 15 1961, p. 104 and fig. 11. Moravcsik does not, to my mind, increase our understanding of this picture by relating it to the ceremonial coronation of Basil. Basil was, in fact, crowned twice, once as the adopted son of Michael III and once as co-emperor (Cedrenus, *op. cit* note 38), p. 181, 200; cf. Aikaterini Christophilo-. poulou, Ἐκλογή, ἀναγόρευσις καὶ στέψις τοῦ βυζαντινοῦ αὐτοκράτορος, Athens 1956, p. 90—92). On the occasion of his proclamation there was no further coronation ceremony; it would have been superfluous. The coronation represented here is, therefore, purely symbolical; it sets forth the source of Basil's authority without explicit reference to the historical coronation(s).

PLATE 11 (A): MINIATURE, PSALTER OF BASIL II, MARCIANA, VENICE.

† τὸ θαῦμα καινὸν ὧδε τῶν ὁρωμένων·
χριστὸς προτείνει δεξιᾷ ζωηφόρῳ
ἐξ οὐρανοῦ τὸ στέμμα σύμβολον κράτους,
πιστῷ κραταιῷ δεσπότῃ βασιλείῳ·
κάτωθεν οἱ πρῶτοι τῶν ἀσωμάτων·
ὁ μὲν λαβὼν ἤνεγκε καὶ χαίρων στέφει·
ὁ δὲ προσάπτων τῷ κράτει καὶ τὰς νίκας·
ῥομφαίαν· ὅπλον ἐκφοβοῦν ἐναντίους,
φέρων δίδωσι χειρὶ τῇ τοῦ δεσπότου·
οἱ μάρτυρες δὲ συμμαχοῦσιν ὡς φίλῳ,
ῥιπτοῦντες ἐχθροὺς τοὺς ποσὶ προκειμένους·

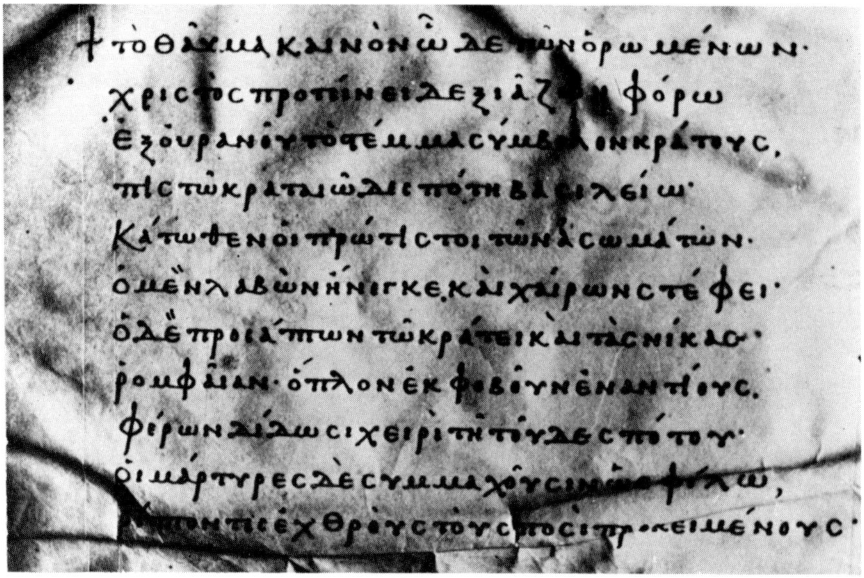

PLATE 11 (B): DEDICATORY POEM, PSALTER OF BASIL II, MARCIANA, VENICE.

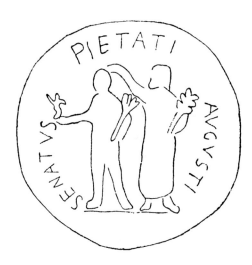

FIG. 6.
AE OF SERVIUS
SULPICIUS GALBA.

of the essential part. (figure 5) Of the quatrain in dodecasyllables, the line running across the top of the miniature is hardly decipherable. The other three lines run thus:

ὁ Γαβριὴλ δὲ τὴν χαρὰν προμηνύων
Βασίλειε στέφει σε κόσμου προστάτην.
νίκην κατ'ἐχθρῶν Ἡλίας ὑπογράφει

(Gabriel, announcing joy, crowns you, Basil, ruler of the world; Elias underwrites victory over enemies.).

The two themes of *Psalm* 20 recur: βασιλεία and victory over enemies. However, it is the standard which is regarded particularly as an emblem of success in battle, while the imposition of a crown is the central theme. This would have been more evident still had the miniature on f. B^v not been suppressed. Traces of a sketch are just visible under the substituted miniature: Gabriel and Elias jointly crown Basil.

The formula for the coronation of Basil is that which was used in Antique art when the crown was imposed by a personification. An example may be seen on an AE of Servius Sulpicius Galba, dated 68/69 A. D., on which the emperor is crowned by a personification of the Senate[62].

It does not seem to have been used in Byzantine iconography earlier than this miniature. From the Xth century, however, it figures on Byzantine coins[63], and is used also, for example, on Leo VI's sceptre[64]. It only recurs in dedicatory pictures when Christ crowns directly.

2. Psalter, Venice Marc. graec. 17, f. III, Basil II.

In this miniature, executed about 1019, Basil II is portrayed in armour standing upon a *scabellum*[65]. (Plate 11 a) In the foreground a number of personages are making a *proskynesis*. To left and right are busts of warrior saints: George, Procopius, Demetrius, Mercurius and the two Theodores. Above Basil's head, in a half circle, is a bust of Christ, who holds out a crown horizontally, not vertically as does the hand of Gold. Two angels figure in this scene; one places a crown on Basil's head, while the other presents him with a lance. Like the warrior saints they are named: Michael (left) and Gabriel (right). Basil himself is called: Βασίλειος ἐν Χριστῷ πιστός βασιλεὺς Ῥωμαίων ὁ νέος (Basil II, faithful in Christ, emperor of the Romans).

Before discussing the significance of this scene, it would be well to examine the eleven-line poem in dodecasyllables on the page facing the miniature: (Plate 11 b)

τὸ θαῦμα καινὸν ὧδε τῶν ὁρωμένων.
Χριστὸς προτείνει δεξιᾷ ζωηφόρῳ

[62] R. Brilliant, *Gesture and Rank in Roman Art*, New Haven (Connecticut) 1963, p. 87, 90, 201.

[63] The first representation of a coronation on a Byzantine coin seems to be due to Alexander (912——913), who is crowned by his patron saint (W. Wroth, *Catalogue of the Imperial Byzantine Coins in the British Museum*, II, London 1908, p. 450, pl. LII 1). John Tzimisces (969—976) is crowned by the Virgin; in one variant the Hand of God is also portrayed (Ibid., p. 474, pl. LIV 10—12). From the time of Alexius I Comnenus the coronation

motif recurs frequently; cf. M. F. Hendy, *Coinage and Money in the Byzantine Empire, 1081—1261*, Washington 1961, *passim*.

[64] Talbot Rice, *op. cit.* (note 16), n⁰ 96.

[65] Reproduction in colour, Talbot Rice, *op. cit.* (note 16), pl. XI; cf. p. 306; Sirarpie Der Nersessian, *Remarks on the Date of the Menologium and the Psalter written for Basil II*, in Byzantion, 15, 1940——1941, p. 115; V. Lazarev, *Storia della pittura bizantina* Turin, 1967, p. 141, 174 note 57, pl. 128—130.

194

ἐξ οὐρανοῦ τὸ στέμμα σύμβολον κράτους
πιστῷ κραταιῷ δεσπότῃ βασιλείῳ.
κάτωθεν οἱ πρώτιστοι τῶν ἀσωμάτων.
ὁ μὲν λαβὼν ἤνεγκε καὶ χαίρων στέφει,
ὁ δὲ προσάπτων τῷ κράτει καὶ τὰς νίκας
ῥομφαῖαν, ὅπλον ἐκφοβοῦν ἐναντίους,
φέρων δίδωσι χειρὶ τῇ τοῦ δεσπότου
οἱ μάρτυρες δὲ συμμαχοῦσιν ὡς φίλῳ
ῥίπτοντες ἐχθροὺς τοὺς ποσὶ προκειμένους.

(What new wonder is to be seen here!/ Christ extends in his lifebearing hand / from heaven
the crown, symbol of power, / to the despot Basil, faithful and mighty./ Below (are) the princes
of the angels./ One (angel), having taken (the crown), has carried (it) and joyfully crowns./
The other (angel), linking to power victories as well,/ (the) lance, weapon which terrifies adversaries,/ having carried (it), he gives (it) into the ruler's hand./ The martyrs fight with him as
with a friend,/ throwing down enemies prostrate at his feet.)[66].

This text, which, from the style of the script, is certainly contemporary with the miniature,
removes a certain number of ambiguities in the iconography. The prostrate figures are said
explicitly to be enemies. A similar formula is used for representing conquered enemies in the
Theodore Psalter[67]. In this case it is a reasonable deduction to suppose that they are Bulgars[68].
The two crowns are not different; in fact two successive actions are represented: Christ extends
the crown, and the angel, having taken it, places it on Basil's head. Moreover the crown is
said explicitly to be a symbol of power (κράτος); the adjectival form of the word (κραταιός)
being repeated in the poem to qualify Basil. However, as in the previous miniature, success
in battle is joined to power; this success is symbolized by a lance, not by a crown of victory.

Were there any doubt as to the significance of the two crowns in this scene, one could dispel
it by adducing the miniature in the Theodore Psalter (*Londin. Addit.* 19352, f. 192), in which
the set-out of the scene is virtually the same[69]. (Plate 10) The only difference is that here

[66] Transcribed from the photograph belonging to
the Institut des textes, Paris, kindly put at my
disposition by Father Joseph Paramelle. This epi-
gram was previously published by J. Morelli,
Bibliotheca manuscripta graeca et latina, Bassani
1802, p. 34—35 (information kindly supplied by
Monsieur J. N. Olivier of the Institut des textes),
and by I. Ševčenko *(The illuminators of the Menologium of Basil II*, Dumbarton Oaks Papers, 16,
1962, p. 272 note 92). It should be compared with
the poem (n⁰ 81), in *Marc. graec.* 524, f. 36, concerning a lost portrait of Manuel I Comnenus,
published by Sp. P. Lampros, 'Ο Μαρκιανὸς κῶδιξ
524, in 'Νέος 'Ελληνομνήμων, 8, 1911, p. 43—44
The poem is attributed to Andronicus Kamatirus
(fl. 1150; cf. *Lettres et discours de Georges et Dèmè-
trios Tornikès*, ed. J. Darrouzès, Paris 1970, p. 43
—49), and perhaps describes a pictore over the
entrance to Manuel Comnenus's new palace (cf.
R. Janin, *Constantinople byzantine*, Paris 1964, p.
126—128), which was decorated with pictures representing Manuel Comnenus's wars. See also below, note 94.

[67] Der Nersessian, *op. cit.* (note 55), p. 22 and
fig. 32. For the place of this miniature in prosky-
nesis/scabellum iconography, cf. my article, *Papal
political imagery in the Medieval Lateran Palace*,
in Cahiers archéologiques, 21, 1971, p. 109—115.
For its association with warrior saints, cf. my
art. cit. (note 47), p. 175.

[68] The deduction is reasonable, because Basil II's
principal victories were over the Bulgars, earning
him the dubious title of Bulgaroctonos. It is, however,
to be noted that J. Ivanov, in his article, *Le costume
des anciens Bulgars*, in L'art byzantin chez les
Slaves, Paris 1930, p. 324—333, adduces no con-
clusive proof from an examination of their dress
that the prostrate personages are Bulgars.

[69] Der Nersessian, *op. cit.* (note 55), p. 59, 71—72
and fig. 301. Cf. the similar scene serving as frontispiece to the Liturgical Roll n⁰ 1, in the Library of
the Leningrad Academy of Sciences (formerly at
the Russian Institute in Constantinople). The two
miniatures are reproduced by Suzy Dufrenne,
Deux chefs d'oeuvre de la miniature du XIe siècle, in
Cahiers archéologiques, 17, 1976, p. 189, fig. 16, 17.

all ambiguity has been eliminated, for the angel actually receives the higoumene's staff from Christ, before presenting it to the higoumene.

3. John Chrysostom's Commentary on Saint Matthew, Sinaït. 364 (373), f. 3,
Constantine IX Monomachus, Zoë and Theodora.

Constantine IX married Zoë in 1042[70]; consequently this miniature must date from about the middle of the century[71] (Plate 12) Facing it (f. 2ᵛ), is another miniature, in which Matthew presents his Gospel to John Chrysostom[72].

The emperor is not dressed in armour, as was Basil in the preceding miniature, but in *sakkos*, *loros* and *stemma*. The two sisters wear the *thorakion* and the *tympanion* (woman's crown), ornamented with *pinnae*. The three portraits are accompanied by inscriptions (from left to right): Ζωὴ εὐσεβχστάτη αὐγούστ(α) ἡ φορφυρογέννητ(η). Κωνσταντ(ίνος) ἐν Χ(ριστ)ῷ τῷ θ(ε)ῷ πιστὸς βχσιλε(ὺς) αὐτοκράτ(ωρ) Ῥωμαίων ὁ μονομάχος. Θεοδώρα αὐγούστα ἡ πορφυρογέννητ(η). (Zoë, most revered Augusta, born in the purple. Constantine, in Christ God faithful Basileus, autocrator of the Romans, Monomachus. Theodora Augusta, born in the purple.).

Above the imperial personages, Christ is seated upon a rainbow in a mandorla. From his hands and feet, rays of light descend towards the heads of the figures below. A crown is suspended above the head of Constantine, while, to left and right, is an angel holding a crown and bâton.

Around the border of the minature, runs a quatrain in dodecasyllables:

ὡς τῆς τριάδος σῶτερ εἷς παντοκράτωρ
σκέποις κράτιστον δεσπότην μονομάχον
ὁ μαιμόνων ζεῦγος τὲ φορφύρας κλάδ(ον)
τῶν γῆς ἀνάκτων τὴν φαιηνὴν τριά(δα)

(As one of the Trinity, Saviour Pantocrator,/ may you protect the mightiest despot Monomachus,/ the pair of sisters and offspring of the purple,/ the shining trinity of the rulers of the earth.).

In spite of a certain similarity with the preceding miniature, there are differences of detail, which, to my mind, modify considerably its significance. In the first place, there are no military allusions. The central theme is government. Secondly, an analogy is established between the Trinity in heaven, represented by the all-powerful Saviour, and the Trinity on earth, among whom figures the mightiest despot Monomachus. The use of the analogy between the terrestrial and the celestial Trinity is, in fact, relatively common in the Byzantine imperial tradition[73].

---

[70] G. Ostrogorsky, *History of the Byzantine State*, Oxford 1968, p. 326.

[71] V. Benešević, *Catalogus codicum manuscriptorum graecorum qui in monasterio Sanctae Catherinae in monte Sina asservantur*, I, Saint Petersburg 1911, p. 205—206; Idem, *Monumenta sinaïtica archaeologica et palaeographica*, I, Leningrad 1925, pl. 30; K. Weitzmann, *Illustrated Manuscripts at St. Catherine's Monastery on Mount Sinaï*, Collegeville 1973, p. 16, pl. XIII.

[72] Benešević, *op. cit.* (note 71), pl. 29; Weitzmann, *op. cit.* (note 71), pl. XII.

[73] This subject merits a monograph. When Heraclius and Tiberius were to be associated with Constantine IV as co-emperors, the citizens of Nicomedia acclaimed them: εἰς τριάδα πιστεύομεν. Τοὺς τρεῖς στέψωμεν, Theophanes, *Chronographia*, ed. De Boor, Leipzig 1883, p. 352 lines 14—16; Zonaras, ed. Bonn, III, 1897, p. 222 lines 12—15. Cf. Treitinger, *op. cit.* (note 34), p. 37—39. For the representation of three angels above the author portrait of John Cantacuzenus, *Paris. graec. 1242*, *f. 123ᵛ*, cf. Belting, *op. cit.* (note 60), p. 86—88, fig. 51.

Secondly, the apocalyptic presentation of Christ, linked to the rays of light and the stars, which may just be seen in the trajectory of the light rays, introduces a theme to be more fully developed, as Dr Mijović noted, in the narthex of Gračanica. Again the analogy between Christ Light of the World and the emperor is relatively common in the Byzantine imperial tradition[74].

Finally, the three crowns suspended above the imperial personages, while resembling each other, do not resemble those which they are actually wearing. In fact they recall rather the votive crown of Leo VI in the Treasury of Saint Mark's at Venice[75]. (Plate 13) Another kind of crown was known in Byzantine tradition. Although there was, as we have seen, no question of offering an imperial diadem to barbaric rulers, others, who were admitted into the Byzantine family, might be presented with a crown[76]. Unfortunately one cannot be sure as to its exact form. However we do know that Constantine Monomachus, who is represented in this miniature, sent such a crown to Andrew I, king of Hungary[77]. I suggest, therefore, that the crowns represented here are to be explained in terms of a third analogy: Constantine Monomachus, the mightiest despot, considered his relationship to other rulers on earth, such as the king of Hungary, to be analogous to the relationship between Christ, Pantocrator, and himself.

4. Psalter, Vatican. barb. graec. 372, f. 1, Alexius I Comnenus, Irene and John (?).

The two emperors, dressed in *sakkos* and *loros*, hold standard in the right hand and stand on a *scabellum*. (Plate 15) The empress, also standing on a *scabellum*, wears the *thorakion*. In a half mandorla, Christ is enthroned. In his left hand he holds, as usual, a book, while in his right hand he holds a crown of the same rounded style as that which is worn by the emeperor in the preceding miniatures, except for the lappets and the cross in pearls surmounting it.

Below are three angels. Each one places a crown on the head of one of the imperial personages. The empress has the normal *tympanion*. However the two emperors wear a crown with a globe of a kind which hitherto we have not met; it is quite different from that which Christ is holding in his hand.

Around the miniature runs a quatrain in dodecasyllables:

οὓς ἡ τριφεγγὴς ἔνθεος μοναρχία
πολλοῖς φυλάξει καὶ γαληνίοις χρόνοις
εἰρηνικῇ τὲ καὶ σοφῇ καταστάσει
διεξάγειν τὰ σκῆπτρα τῆς εξουσίας

(... whom (may) the triply brilliant divine monarchy / protect during long and serene times / in a peaceful and wise state / to wield the sceptres of authority.).

The preceding folio is now lost. De Wald has suggested that the verses, which begin abruptly on this folio with a relative pronoun, in fact continue from the preceding page[78]. It would have

---

[74] This subject also merits a monograph. Cf. my article, *Two Notes on the Deësis*, in Revue des études byzantines, 26, 1968, p. 332.

[75] A. Grabar, *Opere bizantine*, in Il Tesoro e il Museo di San Marco, Florence 1971, n° 92, p. 81, pl. LXXII—LXXV; Deér, *op. cit.* (note 3), pl. XXI fig. 46.

[76] Tretinger, *op. cit.* (note 34), p. 202—204; Deér, *op. cit.* (note 3), p. 139—149; G. Ostrogorsky, *Die byzantinische Staatenhierarchie*, in Zur byzantinischen Geschichte, Darmstadt 1973, p. 119—141.

[77] Grabar, *op. cit.* (note 60), p. 7 note 3 (additional bibliography in edition of 1971, p. iv).

[78] E. De Wald, *The Comnenian Portraits in the Barberini Psalter*, in Hesperia, 13, 1944, p. 80.

PLATE 12: MINIATURE, JOHN CHRYSOSTOM'S COMMENTARY ON MATTHEW,
MONASTERY OF SAINT CATHERINE, MOUNT SINAÏ.

PLATE 13: CROWN, TREASURY, SAN MARCO, VENICE.

PLATE 14: MINIATURE, BARBERINI PSALTER, VATICAN.

been on the missing folio that the names of the personages represented would have been inscribed. However this may be, the identification, made independently by De Wald and de Jerphanion, with Alexius I Comnenus, Irene and their son John, is now generally accepted. The date 1092, when John was crowned, may be advanced[79]. De Wald has also suggested that the book which John holds in his hand is, in fact, this Psalter, illuminated for the occasion.

By analogy with the miniature of the coronation of Hezekiah on f. 30^v mentioned above, the coronation may be interpreted as conferment of the state of βασιλεία. The Trinity analogy is introduced but not in so developed a form as in the previous miniature. There remain, then, only the contrasting style of crowns and the gesture of the angel above the head of Alexius Comnenus to be explained.

The contrasting style of the crowns may be summarily despatched as a „non-lieu". In a lecture delivered at the Conférence Gabriel Millet (Paris) on January 11th 1975, John Spatharakis called attention to the fact that the crowns had been repainted. In February 1975 I was able to examine myself the manuscript in Rome. The crown of the empress has not been repainted since the angel's hand is clearly visible. On the other hand, the angel's hand has been painted over in the case of the two emperors. Originally, therefore, the two emperors were represented wearing crowns of the same type as that which Christ holds in his hand. Consequently, the crowns offer no argument in favour of an association of the miniature with the reign of Alexius Comnenus, when the globe was introduced[80]. All that we can infer is that the repainting of the miniature cannot be earlier than the reign of Alexius Comnenus.

The gesture of the angel, whose left hand is extended towards Christ, while the right hand places the crown on the head of Alexius, resembles that of the Virgin in certain versions of the Deësis[81]. In her rôle of Advocate, the Virgin extends one hand towards the person whose petition she is to present and the other towards Christ who is to receive it. If we interpret the angel's gesture in this miniature in the same way, then Alexius, who is, in fact, ruling emperor is being particularly commended to Christ.

*

The analysis of these miniatures and the confrontation of their iconography with the accompanying texts permit us to draw certain conclusions. Firstly, the imposition of a crown or diadem has as its primary sense the conferment of power or authority. This comes from Christ by the intermediary of an angel. The notion of victory or triumph, which is primary in Roman and Hellenistic coronation scenes, as in other genres of Christian scenes, notably the triumph of the martyr and perseverance in the practice of virtue, is secondary in these imperial portraits. When it is explicitly present, as in the portraits of the two Basils, a military investiture accom-

---

[79] De Jerphanion, art. cit. (note 4), p. 270—271. Sirarpie Der Nersessian, op. cit. (note 55), p. 63 and V. Lazarev, op. cit. (note 65), p. 249 note 28, accept this identification. De Wald, art. cit. (note 78), p. 80, draws attention to the use in the verses of expressions characteristic of the acclamations made on the occasion of a coronation; cf. Constantine Porphyrogenitus, Book of Ceremonies, chapters 38 and 39, I, ed. Bonn 1829, p. 192 line 14; p. 195 lines 14—15; p. 196 lines 3—4. Cf. also P. Maas, Metrische Akklamationen der Byzantiner, in Byzantinische Zeitschrift, 21, 1912, p. 28—51. It is to be noted that, in the acclamations, the symbol of government is the sceptre, not the crown (e.g. Maas, p. 39 para. 5).

[80] Anna Comnena, Alexiad, III iv. 1, ed. B. Leib, Paris 1937, p. 113—114; cf. Deér, op. cit. (note 3), p. 69; R. Guilland, Recherches sur les institutions byzantines, II, Berlin/Amsterdam 1967, p. 1—2.

[81] Cf. the gesture of the Virgin on an ikon in the collection of the Hellenic Institute at Venice, nº 8 (218) and the votive mosaic of George of Antioch in the Martorana at Palermo, illustrated in my art. cit. (note 74), p. 316, 320 and fig. 6, 7.

panies the imposition of the crown. On the other hand further developments of the notion of authority are possible. By reason of the special links between the emperor and the members of the Trinity, authority may be accompanied by divine illumination. Further the relationship between the emperor and other princes may provide an analogy for his relationship with Christ.

IV. CORONATION BY ANGELS IN SLAV DEDICATORY PICTURES.

It is possible now, I think, to give a clear and certain interpretation of the picture of the coronation of Milutin and Simonida at Gračanica. My suggestion that the double coronation as an iconographical theme is derived from the distinction between the crown and the diadem in Antiquity cannot be rigorously maintained. Nor, it seems, can the distinction made by Dr Bošković between the diadem and the crown of life. The primary sense, in all these official portraits, is that imperial authority is derived from Christ; where the two crowns are identical, two successive stages are represented in the conferment of the crown by Christ.

It seems that Milutin was the first Serbian ruler to make use of this iconographical theme — and this right at the end of his reign. One may ask why he should have adopted it at this time. Earlier Serbian rulers were represented more modestly in the churches which they built. They were aware that their status was inferior to that of the Byzantine emperor. Stefan Prvovenčani was, indeed, proud of his subordinate title of sebastocrator[82]. However since his time the Nemanjić family had risen in the world.

In his earlier foundations Milutin is also represented with a relative modesty. At Arilje, where he figures with Dragutin, the two Nemanjić princes, in imperial dress, are blessed by Christ (1293—1295)[83]. At this time Milutin had been already master of Byzantine territory in the Skoplje region for more than a decade[84]. After 1299 his social status was further enhanced by his marriage with Andronicus II's daughter Simonida[85]. Not only did this marriage mark the beginning of an intensive influence of Byzantine culture on the Serbs, but it also raised Milutin socially far above the general run of Serbian nobles. Although, apparently, he did not himself adopt the title of Tsar, the time was not far off when Stefan Dušan would do so[86]. Meanwhile the iconography of the portrait at Gračanica suggests that Milutin was already attributing himself the same kind of relationship with Christ as that of the Byzantine emperors. He is receiving what is virtually the $\beta\alpha\sigma\iota\lambda\epsilon\acute{\iota}\alpha$ from Christ as they did.

If Milutin was the first Serbian prince to lay claim to so exalted a status, he had been preceded in Sicily by William II. There are two dedicatory mosaics in the cathedral of Monreale; both date from between 1180 and 1194[87]. In one king William II presents the church to the Virgin. In the other Christ is enthroned, holding a book inscribed with the following words: *Ego sum lux mundi; qui sequitur me*, taken from *John* 8, 12. Christ, in fact, crowns the king himself, but two angels descend with a sceptre and an orb (Plate 15). The picture, if closer to Western tradition than those in Serbia, nevertheless depends from Byzantine models. A century before Milutin, a Sicilian king was laying claim to derive his authority directly from Christ.

[82] Ostrogorsky, *art. cit.* (note 76), p. 125.

[83] Radojčić, *op. cit.* (note 1), p. 55—56, pl. XVII 25.

[84] Ostrogorsky, *op. cit.* (note 70), p. 464.

[85] Ibid., p. 489—490.

[86] In the Gospel of Hilandar (1346) Stojanović, *op. cit.* (note 5), I, Belgrade 1902, p. 35, nᵒ 89;

in an inscription at Dečani, ibid., III, Belgrade 1905, p. 79, nᵒ 5110; on the Nemanjić genealogilac tree at Dečani, (about 1350), Radojčić, *op. cit.* (note 1), p. 58, pl. XVI 24.

[87] O. Demus, *The Mosaics of Norman Sicily*, London 1949, p. 118, p. 163 note 314, pl. 7a; Lazarev *op. cit.* (note 65), p. 239.

PLATE 15: MOSAIC, CATHEDRAL, MONREALE.

IV

PLATE 16 (A & B): MINIATURES, CHRONICLE OF MANASSES, VATICAN.

PLATE 17: DESPOT STEFAN, FRESCO, LJUBOSTINJA.

PLATE 18: NEMANJIC FAMILY TREE, FRESCO, GRACANICA.

John Alexander II (1331—1371) was to do the same. In two miniatures of the Chronicle of Manasses (*Vatican. slav.* 2, f. 1ᵛ and f. 91ᵛ), illuminated at Tirnovo between 1344 and 1345, the Bulgarian ruler is represented being crowned by an angel[88]. In the first (f. 1ᵛ), Christ is called Tsar of Tsars and eternal Tsar, while John Alexander is called faithful to Christ God, Tsar and autocrator of all the Bulgars and Greeks (Plate 16). The text upon Christ's roll is from *John* 8, 12: I am the Light of the world. Further the angel holds a circlet over John's head, while John wears a diadem with a globe[89]. I. Dujčev proposes as a model for the illuminations of this manuscript a Byzantine original probably from the time of Manuel I Comnenus (1143 —1180)[90]. If the frontispiece was changed only by the substitution of John Alexander's portrait for that of Manuel I, then there is good reason to interpret the iconography in the same way as that of the Sinaï and Barberini frontispieces: Christ illuminated the ruler and, by the intermediary of his angel, presents him with a crown of the kind offered to subordinate rulers, a sign that his authority derives from Christ.

In the second miniature (f. 91ᵛ), which illustrates a panegyric on John Alexander, substituted for that on Manuel I in the Byzantine original, the angel presents the Bulgarian Tsar with a crown identical to that which he is already wearing[91] (Plate 16). Beside him stands king David with an unrolled scroll upon which is inscribed the following phrase: г҃и сил҄ож твоеѫ (Oh Lord in thy might...). It is the beginning of *Psalm* 20 (21), that which is illustrated by a coronation in the *Bristol*, *Theodore* and *Barberini Psalters*, and which is paraphrased in the prayer recited by the patriarch in the rite of coronation. There is no doubt that we have here two successive stages of the same scene: the angel brings the crown and Tsar John Alexander wears the crown. This miniature, therefore, is to be interpreted in the same way as the portraits of Milutin and Simonida at Gračanica.

To return now to Serbia, we may note that Milutin's innovation was copied by his successors. Stefan Dušan with his wife Jelena are portrayed at Lesnovo sometime after 1346 being offered crowns by Christ[92]. In the following century, towards 1405, the despot Stefan was represented being crowned by two angels[93] (Plate 17). They place a crown upon his head, while one of the angels also presents him with a sword. At that time, when the Turks were advancing ineluctably across the Balkans, the Serbian despot needed the qualities of a warrior as well as those of a ruler.

The portraits of Milutin can be treated as belonging to a series. They can be inserted chronologically into the line of coronation pictures which stretches back to Antiquity and contiunes after their time. This, however, is not the only way of treating them. They should also be considered in the context of the rich iconographical vocabulary created during Milutin's reign[94].

[88] B. D. Filow, *Les miniatures de la Chronique de Manassès*, Sofia 1927, p. 10—15; I. Dujčev, *Miniature Manasijevog letopisa*, Sofia/Belgrade 1965, p. 23—24; Belting, *op. cit.* (note 60), p. 7 note 19, p. 21—22.

[89] Filow, *op. cit.* (note 88), p. 29—30, pl. 1; Dujčev, *op. cit.* (note 88), n⁰ 1.

[90] I. Dujčev, *Le miniature bulgare medioevali*, in Corsi di cultura sull'arte ravennate e bizantina, 15, 1968, p. 124—125.

[91] Filow, *op. cit.* (note 88), p. 51—52; Dujčev, *op. cit.* (note 88), n⁰ 33. The text of both panegyrics is given by Filow, ibid., p. 10, notes 6 and 7. Cf. also the portrait of John Alexander in the narthex of the funerary chapel at Bačkovo, in which he

is crowned by angels and protected by the Virgin and Child (after 1344 when John Alexander conquered the region of Plovdiv). A. Grabar, *La peinture religieuse en Bulgarie*, Paris 1928, p. 282—283; A. Vasiliev, *Bačkovskata kostnica*, Sofia 1965, fig. 41.

[92] Radojčić, *op. cit.* (note 1), p. 55—56, pl. XVII 25.

[93] Ibid., p. 66—68, pl. XXIII 33.

[94] V. Đurić, *Tri događaja u srpskoj državi XIV veka i njihov odjek u slikarstvu*, in Zbornik za likovne umetnosti, 4, 1968, especially p. 68—76, Kralj Milutin „izbi Turki", in which he develops the military aspects of Milutin's official imagery, interpreting the picture of Milutin and Saint George at Staro Nagoričino as a military investiture, analogous to that of Manuel Commenus by Sain

The theme of coronation, itself so full of overtones, entered well into a repertory of official imagery, the theme of which was the divinisation of the Nemanjić family. Dr S. Ćurčić has shown how, in Milutin's church at Studenica, the ancestors of Christ, Saints Joachim and Anna, are placed parallel to members of the Nemanjić family[95]. The adaptation of the Tree of Jesse to the genealogy of the Nemanjić family was also, it seems, an innovation due to Milutin. Represented in the narthex of Gračanica, it has at the summit Milutin, in imperial costume, to whom angels are proferring a crown and a *loros*[96]. (Plate 19) To link the theme of coronation to that of Christ Light of the World presented no difficulty; indeed, as we have seen, the Byzantine imperial family had already done so. To his claim to have received the βασιλεία Milutin could well add that of immortality. Indeed *Psalm* 20 (21), to which we have already so frequently alluded, continues: He asked of thee life, and thou didst give it to him, length of days for ever and ever.*

Theodore Tyron now lost (see above, note 66). Idem, *L'art des paléologues et l'état serbe*, in Art et société, *op. cit.* (note 60), p. 177—191.

[95] S. Ćurčić, *The Nemanjić Family Tree in the Light of the Ancestral Cult in the Church of Joachim and Anna at Studenica*, in Zbornik radova, 14—15 1973, p. 191—195.

[96] Radojčić, *op. cit.* (note 1), p. 42—43, pl. X 15.

* *Note (1978)*. The text of this article has not been altered since 1975. Although they do not, in my opinion, necessitate any important modification of what I have written here, it seems worth while listing here the four folloving studies which have subsequently come to my notice:

I. Spatharakis, *The Portraits and the Date of the Codex Par. gr. 510*, Cahiers archéologiques 23, 1874, p. 97—105.

Idem, *The Portrait in Byzantine Illuminated Manuscripts*, Leiden 1976.

Ioli Kalavrezou-Maxeiner, *The Portraits of Basil I in Paris. gr. 510*, Jahrbuch der österreichischen Byzantinistik 27, 1978, p. 19—24.

A. Cutler, *The Psalter of Basil II*, Arte Veneta 30, 1976, p. 9—19; 31, 1977, p. 9—15.

I add a complement concerning the marriage connotations of the coronation of Milutin and Simonida in the forthcoming number of *Zograf* dedicated to the memory of the later professor Svetozar Radojčić.

V

THE DEXTRARUM JUNCTIO OF LEPCIS MAGNA
IN RELATIONSHIP TO THE ICONOGRAPHY OF MARRIAGE

In the course of his academic career, Monsieur Jean Lassus has worked in many countries on several continents. In the present article we shall not be following him on all his travels, nor, however, shall we be remaining the whole time on the continent of Africa. The monument with which we are here particularly concerned, the Triumphal Arch at Lepcis Magna, constructed and decorated in the first decade of the third century, was probably decorated by sculptors from the East and certainly reflects, in its iconographical programme, Roman political and religious notions. We too, in consequence, shall be obliged to turn our attention both to Constantinople and to Rome.

The excavation of the site of Lepcis Magna between 1923 and 1942 has proved to be one of the most rewarding archaeological enterprises of this century [1]. It seems that the triumphal arch commemorates the visit of Severus to the city where he had been born of a wealthy provincial family about 146 A.D. The most recent dating of the arch is that of V.M. Strocka, who proposes the years 206-209 [2]. We are particularly concerned here with the relief on the South-West side (fig. 1). In this relief Septimius Severus and Caracalla hold each other's right hand. Julia Domna and Geta also figure in the scene, together with a number of personages, real and mythological. It is not our intention here to enter into the detail of the composition, in which, as is generally the case in Roman official art, ceremonial, realism and the

---

* Coins to which reference is made in this article are cited almost exclusively from *The Coins of the Roman Empire in the British Museum,* edited by R.A.G. Carson and H. Mattingly, volumes I-VI, London, 1923-1962. The citation is made thus : *British Museum,* number of volume, number of plate, number of coin. The article by KANTOROWICZ (E.H.), *On the Golden Marriage Belt and the Marriage Rings of the Dumbarton Oaks Collection,* Dumbarton Oaks Papers, t. 14, 1960, p. 1-16, is cited thus : KANTOROWICZ, *Marriage Belts.* I take the opportunity of expressing my gratitude to Madame Cécile Morrisson, Mademoiselle Claude Brenot and Mr R.A.G. Carson for their help with the coins.

[1] BARTOCCINI (R.), *L'Arco quadrifronte dei Severi a Lepcis (Leptis Magna).* Africa italiana, t. 4, 1931, p. 32-152, especially p. 116-129 ; WARD-PERKINS (J.B.), *Severan Art and Architecture at Lepcis Magna.* The journal of Roman Studies, t. 38, 1948, p. 59-80, especially p. 72-80 ; ID., *The Art of the Severan Age in the Light of Tripolitanian Discoveries.* Proceedings of the British Academy, t. 37, 1951, p. 269-304 ; TOYNBEE (Jocelyn M.C.), *Picture-Language in Roman Art and Coinage.* Essays in Roman Coinage Presented to Harold Mattingly, edited by R.A.G. Carson and C.H.V. Sutherland, Oxford 1956, p. 205-226, especially p. 207-209.

[2] STROCKA (V.M.), *Beobachtungen an den Attikareliefs des severischen Quadrifons von Lepcis Magna.* Antiquités africaines, t. 6, 1972, p. 147-172, especially, p. 157-160.

Fig. 1. — Lepcis Magna, Relief, South-West attic of the Arch of Severus.

supernatural are combined. We intend rather to concentrate upon the central gesture of Severus and Caracalla, the socalled *Dextrarum junctio*. Its particular interest is due to the fact that it seems to be the unique surviving example of this gesture represented on an imperial Roman monument.

Hitherto the *Dextrarum junctio* has been studied almost uniquely in the context of the iconography of marriage. The pioneer study of August Rossbach, published over a century ago, is still valuable [1]. However, it has been superseded by the excellent article due to Louis Reekmans, which includes a virtually exhaustive repertory of this theme in marriage scenes [2]. He traces the theme from the fourth century B.C., when it seems to have first appeared in Etruscan funerary art, through the period of the Roman Republic and Empire, noting the adaptations introduced when the theme is introduced into Christian art. However he is manifestly unconcerned by the known examples of the *Dextrarum junctio*, which have no relationship to marriage [3].

---

[1] ROSSBACH (A.), *Römische Hochzeits- und Ehedenkmäler*. Leipzig, 1871

[2] REEKMANS (L.), *La « dextrarum junctio » dans l'iconographie romaine et paléochrétienne*. Bulletin de l'Institut historique belge de Rome, t. 31, 1958, p. 23-95.

[3] Thus, in his article *Dextrarum junctio* in *Enciclopedia dell'arte antica*, t. 3, Rome 1960, col. 82, Reekmans defines this subject as « La rappresentazione dei due coniugi nell'atto di stringere la mano destra ».

It may well be that the first examples of the *Dextrarum junctio* occur in marriage scenes. However, if the evidence of coinage may be adduced, it could be argued that, in Roman art at least, the *Dextrarum junctio* was originally exploited mainly in a military context [1]. It seems to have been first represented in periods of civil war, with the desire to propagate the notion that military unity was a condition of civil peace. In its earliest form, dating back to Augustus (B.C. 8), the *Dextrarum junctio* is represented as a pair of clasped hands, holding, the caduceus [2] (fig. 2). An example of 68 A.D. has the legend : PAX ET LIBERTAS [3]. The replacement of clasped hands by two standing soldiers making this gesture and holding legionary eagles seems to date from the reign of Vespasian, (69-70 A.D.), when the picture is accompanied by the legend : CONSENSUS EXER-CITUS [4]. The way was now open for extending the theme to propagate the notion of agreement between members of the imperial family or rival emperors. Thus Titus and Domitian are represented together joining right hands in the presence of a figure who may be Pietas or Concordia on a coin of 80-81 A.D., with the legend : PIETAS AUGUST(ORUM) [5]. Later (after 161 A.D.), Marcus Aurelius and Verus are represented together in the same way with the legend : CONCORDIA AUGUSTOR(UM) [6]. These examples may be multiplied. For example, from the

FIG. 2. — Clasped hands and caduceus, coin of Antonius Pius (Cabinet des médailles, Paris).

period of the construction of the Arch of Lepcis Magna, we have coins on which Caracalla and Geta are represented joining their right hands, with the legend : CONCORDIA AUGUSTORUM or FELICITAS SAECULI [7]. However, before the middle of the third century, the theme of standing figures joining right hands disappears, apparently, from coinage, while, around 238 A.D., a pair of clasped hands is re-introduced, with an legend such as CONCORDIA or FIDES MUTUA or PIETAS MUTUA AUG(USTORUM) [8]. Only one later example seems to have survived, dating from 321-324, in which Crispus and Constantine II join hands, with Fausta as Concordia [9].

Meanwhile, for the period of the reign of Commodus, there had been a transitory but luxuriant exploitation of the *Dextrarum junctio*. It merits our attention. From about 186 A.D. Commodus is represented in military dress with four soldiers in front of him ; the two in the centre join their right hands

[1] KÖTTING (B.), *Dextrarum junctio, Reallexikon für Antike und Christentum*, t. 3, Stuttgart, 1957, col. 881-886. ROSSBACH, *op. cit.*, p. 21 wrote of « die schöne Münze aus der Zeit Alexanders des Grossen .. ». However, I have found no example with a *dextrarum junctio*.

[2] *British Museum* I, pl. 20, 2, n° 204.

[3] *British Museum* I, pl. 50, 15, n° 27 ; compare IV, pl. 3, 2, n° 85 (Antoninus Pius, 139 A.D.).

[4] *British Museum* II, pl. 14, 11-13, n° 414-416.

[5] *British Museum* II, pl. 49, 2, n° 177.

[6] *British Museum* IV, pl. 53, 15, n° 9.

[7] *British Museum* V, pl. 34, 19, n° 312.

[8] *British Museum* VI, pl. 47, n° 67-74. For the theme of Pietas see the article of CHRISTOL (M.), *La Pietas de Constance Chlore : l'empereur et les provinciaux à la fin du III*ᵉ *siècle*. Bulletin de la Société française de Numismatique, t. 10, 1975, p. 858.

[9] KANTOROWICZ, *Marriage Belts*, p. 7, note 31, fig. 20.

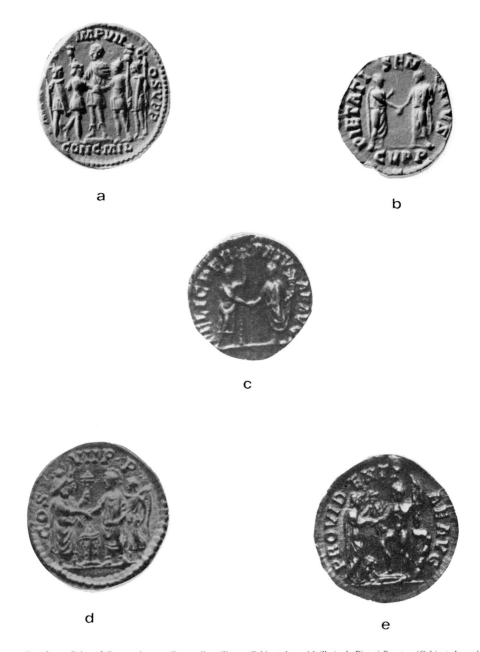

a

b

c

d

e

FIG. 3. — Coins of Commodus : *a*, Concordia militum (Cabinet des médailles) ; *b*, Pietati Senatus (Cabinet des médailles) ; *c*, Commodus and Felicity (British Museum. London) ; *d*, Commodus and Serapis (British Museum) ; *e*, Commodus as Hercules and Africa (British Museum).

(fig. 3, a). The legend reads: CONC(ORDIA) MIL(ITUM) [1]. Another example shows Commodus dressed in a toga joining hands with a personification of the Senate, the legend: PIETATI SENATUS [2] (fig. 3, b). Yet another shows him holding a cornucopia and joinging right hands with a personification of Felicity, the legend: FELIC(ITAS) PERPETUAE AUG(USTORUM) [3] (fig. 3, c). In a different register, Commodus is represented joining hands with Serapis, accompanied by Isis, over a lighted altar, while Victory crowns him [4] (fig. 3, d). Similarly, he is represented, dressed as Hercules, joining right hands with a personification of Africa, the legend: PROVIDENTIAE AUG(USTORUM) [5] (fig. 3, e).

These examples from the reign of Commodus are important partly because the range of meaning of the *Dextrarum junctio* seems to have been extended, but also because the connotations have become richer. We are confronted with developed scenes such as we find on the arch at Lepcis Magna. A legend is not necessarily a direct « translation » of the iconographical type which it accompanies, but it is certainly related to it. It may either render more explicit or implement the picture's meaning. Thus the words *consensus, concordia, mutua* would seem to render more explicit the sense of the joined hands : that two separate entities are united. Other words, such as *pietas, felicitas, fides,* suggest the conditions or consequences of this union of two separate entities. Commodus, however, on his coins seems to go beyond the evident notion that unity in the army or between rulers is a necessary condition of peace and prosperity. He is identifying himself with Felicitas and Pietas, and proclaiming the union in his person of Egypt and Africa with Rome.

We must see if the intentions of Severus at Lepcis Magna were as magnificent. First, however, it would be well to recall that, from the reign of Antoninus Pius, coins are minted on which the *Dextrarum junctio* commemorates an imperial marriage: Antoninus and Faustina in 141 (fig. 4), Marcus Aurelius and Faustina II after 145, Caracalla and Plautilla after 201 [6]. In the last case we find as legends : CONCORDIAE AETERNAE, CONCORDIA FELIX, PROPAGO IMPERI. Thus the marriage coins enter into the same range of meaning. Moreover they appear just at the period when it became part of the Roman marriage ceremony to offer sacrifice before the statues of the emperor and empress, *ob insignem eorum concordiam* [7]. Concord is thus celebrated as a virtue of both public and private life.

FIG. 4. — Antoninus and Faustina, coin of Antoninus Pius (Cabinet des médailles).

Programmes decorating private — notably funeral — monuments could include elements taken from the imagery of imperial cult [8]. Thus a group of sarcophagi, on which the marriage *dextrarum junctio* is associated with sacrifice, enters into the category of monuments where Concord is celebrated at once

[1] *British Museum* IV, pl. 96, 2, n° 197.

[2] *British Museum* IV, pl. 96, 17, n° 237.

[3] *British Museum* IV, pl. 99, 17, n° 337.

[4] *British Museum* IV, pl. 99, 15, n° 335.

[5] *British Museum* IV, pl. 100, 7, n° 355.

[6] *British Museum* IV, pl. 7, 13, n° 298 ; IV, pl. 43, 4, n° 1787 ; V, pl. 33, 16, n° 271.

[7] REEKMANS, *art. cit.,* p. 35.

[8] SCOTT RYBERG (Inez), *Rites of the State Religion in Roman Art,* American Academy in Rome, Memoirs 22, Rome 1955, p. 163-167.

FIG. 5. — Annona sarcophagus, Museo dei Termi, Rome (detail).

as a private and a public virtue (fig. 5). However, as Reekmans has shown, the *dextrarum junctio* was easily integrated into other funeral programmes, both pagan and Christian, which are not imperial in origin. These private monuments do not provide examples of the *dextrarum junctio* except as the marriage *Iugum* [1]. Consequently we have to have recourse to imperial monuments in order to determine the generic sense of this theme.

The starting-point for determining this generic meaning should be, I suggest, the culminating scene of the four great friezes which once decorated the attic of the Arch of Lepcis Magna. Although we cannot argue, in the absence of surviving examples, that the *dextrarum junctio* figures regularly on imperial monuments, the widespread use of the theme on coins confirms its place in the imperial iconographical repertory. The four reliefs show, first, the state entry of Septimius, Caracalla and Geta into Lepcis ; then the triumphal cortege of Caracalla and his mother ; there follows a sacrifice, and, finally, the *dextrarum junctio*. Dr Jocelyn Toynbee writes of « specific ceremonies enacted at Lepcis on the occasion of the imperial family's visit » [2]. This must not, of course, be taken too literally, the more so that she notes, a few lines later, that « supernatural beings... participated fully in the action ».

Would it be excessively sceptical to ask whether a ceremonial performance of the *dextrarum junctio* did take place at all on such occasions ? Did Septimius Severus, ceremonially, present Caracalla to the citizens of Lepcis Magna as co-Augustus and publicly join hands with him ? We may be certain that Septimius did not present Caracalla to the Tychai of the cities of Lepcis, Sabratha and Oea, as he is represented doing on another relief of the arch ! [3] Moreover it seems unlikely that all the representations of the *dextrarum junctio* on coins recall an actual historical ceremony. When Commodus joins hands with a personification, we may be sure that the historical elements have been subordinated to the symbolical. When Caracalla joins hands with Geta, we must reserve judgment on the question whether a historical event has indeed been represented. However, if the *dextrarum junctio* is used symbolically as well as historically, then, clearly, the idea which this gesture conveys is more important than its historical enactment. The Arch therefore stood in Lepcis Magna, not just to commemorate the brief visit of a former citizen who had risen to become emperor, but to put on record permanently the notion that joint rule is not divided rule : Septimius Severus and Caracalla constitute one single entity.

If we have spent some time considering whether the *dextrarum junctio* at Lepcis Magna represents a real ceremony, it is because the same question must be put with regard to representations of marriage

---

[1] KROLL (W.), *Iuga, Paulys Realencyclopädie der classischen Altertumswissenschaft*, t. IX b, col. 2506 : Iuga, Beiname der Iuno. Sie heisst so wohl von der *dextrarum iunctio*. Compare *Ibidem*, t. X a, col. 1117-1118, Iuno, paragraph 7.

[2] TOYNBEE, *art. cit.* (note 1, p. 271), p. 207.

[3] *Ibid.*, p. 208.

by the same iconographical theme. At first sight this question seems easy to answer. The rite of *dextrarum junctio* exists to this day in the Christian marriage ceremony ; it is an expression of mutual consent and of reciprocal fidelity. It would be pleasant to read back this meaning into the surviving early Christian representations of the *dextrarum junctio*. However, there are two difficulties. Firstly, in the Western Christian tradition, there stands in the way another rite, whereby the father or *mundualdus* made over the *puella* to her future spouse. In the 12th-century *Pontifical* of Lyre, this *traditio puellae* is represented by the gesture of her future spouse taking her by the right hand [1]. R. Metz sees in this rite a Germanic use, which fell into desuetude, or rather changed its meaning, when children were no longer obliged to accept the marriage arranged for them by their father or guardian.

However, this explanation gives rise to a second difficulty. Where did the Germanic liturgists find this rite of the *dextrarum junctio* ? Metz supposes that they rediscovered it in ancient Roman usage. Consequently for Metz the *dextrarum junctio* symbolizes the act whereby the Roman father or guardian handed over to her husband the girl promised to him at their betrothal : « ce rite serait à l'origine de l'expression *convenire in manum*. » [2] Unfortunately iconographical and epigraphical evidence hardly favours such an explanation. As we have seen, the significance which it attributes to the *dextrarum junctio* is wider and more fundamental. We are left with two other possible explanations : either Germanic liturgists rediscovered the *dextrarum junctio*, possibly from funeral monuments, but misunderstood it, or they gave the rite a different meaning in their own marriage ceremonial from that which it had in Roman liturgical tradition.

This consideration of Western tradition does not give us an answer to the question whether the *dextrarum junctio* actually formed a part of the Roman pre-Christian marriage ceremony. Possibly Byzantine evidence is more helpful. We have a description by Theophylact Simoncatta, written in the early 7th century, of the marriage of the emperor Maurice (583-602) [3]. The patriarch of Constantinople presided. After imploring the divine blessing, he took the hands of the imperial couple and joined them ; then he pronounced the nuptial blessing and imposed nuptial crowns on their heads. Eight centuries later, in his mystagogical commentary of the marriage liturgy, Symeon of Thessalonika explains that the priest unites the right hands of the couple, in order to signify that they are united in Christ and that they become one entity in him [4]. The meaning which Symeon attributes to the *dextrarum junctio* in the Byzantine marriage ceremony is, then, close to that which we are attributing to this theme at Lepcis Magna.

Nevertheless, we are inclined to follow Reekmans, who himself follows Rossbach, and to see in the *dextrarum junctio* in Roman art, whether pagan or Christian, a symbolical act rather than a representation of a specific rite of the marriage ceremony [5]. The introduction of the *dextrarum junctio* into the marriage ceremony would be due to Christian initiative probably not earlier than the fifth century and certainly not later than the sixth. Of course it is not possible to prove this conclusively ; however some arguments can be advanced, whose value the reader must judge for himself.

The last Roman marriage issue with a *dextrarum junctio* was for Severus Alexander and Orbiana in 225, with the legend : CONCORDIA AUGUSTORUM [6]. Over two hundred years later there were three marriage issures with the *dextrarum junctio* in fairly rapid succession : for Eudoxia and Valentinian

---

[1] Metz (R.), *La consécration des vierges dans l'Eglise romaine*. Paris, 1954, Appendice 1, Le rituel du mariage, origine et évolution historique, p. 363-410, especially p. 387 : tunc detur femina a patre vel amicis suis, quam vir recipiat in fide Dei... et per manum dextram teneant (*sic*) eam (*Pontifical* of Lyre).

[2] *Ibid.*, p. 377.

[3] Theophylact Simocattas, *Historiae*, I 10, edited by C. De Boor, Leipzig 1887, p. 57 line 13 = Bonn, p. 51 line 14 ; Anné (L.), *Les rites des fiançailles et la donation pour cause de mariage sous le bas-empire*. Louvain, 1941, p. 157.

[4] Symeon of Thessalonika. *De honesto et legitimo conjugio*. Migne, PG 155, 509.

[5] Rossbach, *op. cit.* (note 1, p. 272), p. 9-11 ; Reekmans, *art. cit.* (note 2, p. 272), col. 82.

[6] *British Museum* VI, pl. 10, n⁰ˢ 299-301.

FIG. 6. — Eudoxia and Valentinian III, coin of Theodosius II (British Museum).

III in 437 (fig. 6), with Theodosius II as Pronubus, for Marcian and Pulcheria in 451 and for Anastasius I and Ariadne in 491 ; in the latter two cases Christ appears as Pronubus [1]. Round about the same time Santa Maria Maggiore was built and decorated with mosaics. The artists, although Christian, unselfconsciously adapted pagan models in a way which, a century earlier, would hardly have been possible [2]. Thus they use the *dextrarum junctio* for the marriage of Jacob with Rachel and of Moses with Sephora [3]. What genre of Antique monument would have given the artist his model ? Obviously he could have adapted a coin or a sarcophagus. However these marriage scenes definitely have the air of a court ceremony. Although the scale is much smaller, the Marriage of Moses and Sephora recalls the two mosaics in San Vitale of the Offering respectively of Justinian and of Theodora. Sephora stands to the left of the scene, imperially dressed and accompanied by her ladies-in-waiting, while Moses stands to the right, accompanied by his *garçons d'honneur*. A figure much larger in scale (Sephora's father ?) stands behind the couple who join hands. On the one hand it seems that the artist was familiar with contemporary court marriage ceremonial, as represented, for example, on the coin commemorating the marriage of Eudoxia and Valentinian III ; on the other hand he is more likely to have known also a representation of a similar ceremony in imperial Roman art.

I do not, of course, suggest that he knew the reliefs of the Arch of Lepcis Magna, but rather related monuments which no longer exist. We can, indeed, demonstrate a similarity between the triumphal art of the Later Roman Empire and the decoration of the triumphal arch of Santa Maria Maggiore (fig. 7). There is the same fusion — or confusion — of personages of different orders of being [4]. In the scene of the Presentation, the two groups of personages converge in the same way as those in the *dextrarum junctio* scene at Lepcis Magna. The presentation has been conceived as the meeting of the representatives of the old and the new dispensations [5]. Joseph and Anna occupy the central place instead of Caracalla and Septimius Severus, while an angel replaces the tutelary gods. However Joseph and Anna do not join hands. There is no question of a *jugum* between the old dispensation and the new. Their eyes are turned towards the Mother advancing with the Child Jesus, who will reign alone.

As is wellknown, the Christian Church only gradually took an interest in the solemnization of marriages, which was regarded as above all the concern of the civil authorities [6]. Possibly the example which we have cited of the patriarch joining the hands of Maurice and his wife at the end of the sixth century was an innovation in imperial marriage ceremonial. At that time the Church had not formulated definitively the constitutive elements of her sacramental rites, while, in Byzantine imperial iconography, the emperor normally is represented, in religious ceremonies, in direct relationship with Christ. Consequently it is not

[1] ZACOS (G.) and VEGLERY (A.), *An unknown solidus of Anastasios I.* Numismatic Circular, t. 67, 1959, p. 154-155 ; *Marriage solidi of the Vth century, ibid.,* t. 68, 1960, p. 73-74 ; KANTOROWICZ, *Marriage Belts,* p. 718, fig. 21-23 *b* ; MORRISSON (C.), *De Nicéphore II Phocas à Romain IV Diogène.* Bulletin du club français de la médaille, t. 42, 1974, p. 87 and fig. 8.

[2] The best archaeological description of the mosaics is still, to my mind, that of RICHTER (J.P.) and CAMERON TAYLOR (A.), *The Golden Age of Classical Christian Art,* London, 1904.

[3] BRENK (B.), *Die frühchristlichen Mosaiken in S. Maria Maggiore zu Rom.* Wiesbaden, 1975, p. 69-70, 80-81 ; pl. 50.

[4] SCOTT RYBERG, *op. cit.* (note 8, p. 275), p. 134.

[5] GRABAR (A.), *L'empereur dans l'art byzantin,* Strasbourg, 1936, London, 1971, p. 216-220 ; BRENK, *op. cit.,* p. 21-22.

[6] ANNÉ, *op. cit.* (note 3, p. 277), p. 170-174 ; JOUNEL (P.), *La liturgie romaine du mariage.* La Maison-Dieu, 50 1957, p. 30-57.

Fig. 7. — Joseph and Anna, triumphal arch, Santa Maria Maggiore, Rome (detail).

Fig. 8. — Gold medal from marriage belt (collection de Clercq, Musée du Louvre, Paris, cliché Chuzeville).

surprising to find, on the two other Byzantine marriage issues of coins, that Christ presides the *dextrarum junctio*. The same is true on two examples of gold medals integrated into marriage belts [1] (fig. 8).

In Byzantine marriage ceremonial, the principal act was, in fact, to become the crowning of the spouses [2]. Whether it is Christ or the patriarch who crowns, this is the most common type of marriage iconography in the Byzantine tradition, although, later, in the Western tradition, the *dextrarum junctio* would be commonly represented [3]. There are only four cases of the *dextrarum junctio* in Byzantine art to be adduced for the rest of the Byzantine epoch.

The first occurs on one of the series of David plates discovered early this century in Cyprus [4] (fig. 9). They can be dated, by the stamps, to the reign of Heraclius. That is to say, they are contemporary with

Fɪɢ. 9. — Marriage of David and Michal, silver plate (Museum of Nicosia, Cyprus).

---

[1] Kantorowicz, *Marriage Belts*, p. 3, 10-11, fig. 1-2. One belt is at Dumbarton Oaks (Washington) ; the other, formerly in the De Clercq collection, is now in the Louvre.

[2] Anné, *op. cit.*, p. 172 ; Jounel, *art. cit.*, p. 37.

[3] Kantorowicz, *Marriage Belts*, p. 12.

[4] *Wealth of the Roman World* (catalogue of exhibition, British Museum, 1977), edited by J.P.C. Kent and S. Painter, n° 180, p. 103.

the description of the marriage of Maurice, which we cited earlier. However, the figure presiding the marriage between David and Michal is not a priest. The personage wears a chlamyd decorated with the badge of nobility. The figure enthroned who receives David at court on another plate is dressed similarly. Therefore this personage must be Saul. Consequently the model for the David plate must be either an Old Testament marriage, as in Santa Maria Maggiore, or an imperial marriage coin issue, such as that for Valentinian III and Eudoxia.

The *dextrarum junctio* was not retained in the Byzantine iconographical tradition regularly to illustrate marriage scenes. A number of variant formulae exist, which we cannot discuss here. Of the three other cases in which Byzantine artists used the *dextrarum junctio* two occur in the illuminated *Octateuchs* [1]. For the curious passage in *Genesis* (6, 2-4) concerning the marriage of the sons of God and daughters of man (fig. 10), it is evident that the illuminators copied models belonging to the same tradition. To the left are the sons of God, standing next to a seated, haloed personage ; to the right are the daughters of men standing beside another enthroned personage. He has no halo, and in *Vatican. graec.* 746, f. 49, he is called Cain. The Octateuch was often accompanied by a catena. It is therefore likely that the name of Cain is taken from one of these catenae. For example, Theodoret of Cyr says explicitly that the daughters of men were the daughters of Cain [2]. In the centre of the composition, a couple join their right hands. The only other example of a *dextrarum junctio* in the illustrated Octateuchs seems to be in *Vatican. graec.* 746,

FIG. 10. — Marriage of sons of God and daughters of men, Octateuch (Vatican Library).

[1] Of the five illuminated Byzantine Octateuchs known, only one, Istanbul, Topkapi Saray cod. 8, is published. The scene is represented on f. 54, USPENSKIJ (Th.), *L'Octateuque de la bibliothèque du Sérail à Constantinople*. Sofia/Munich, 1907, pl. XII 33 ; Smyrna, Evangelical School A I was destroyed in 1922 ; for Athos Vatopedi 602 (515), see LAZAREV (V.), *Storia della pittura bizantina*. Turin 1967, p. 283, p. 334 note 51 ; for *Vatican. graec.* 746 and 747, see DEVREESSE (R.), *Codices vaticani graeci* III. Vatican 1950, p. 261-263. M. Lassus lectured on the illustration of the Octateuchs at the Ecole Pratique des Hautes Etudes ; I thank him for putting photographs of unpublished miniatures at my disposal for study.

[2] Theodoret of Cyr, *Quaestiones in Genesin* 47, Quosnam Moses vocavit filios Dei ? Migne, PG 80, 150.

282

f. 96ᵛ illustrating *Genesis* 28, 9, which recounts how Esau married a daughter of Ishmaël. Why did the artist use the *dextrarum junctio* on these two occasions only, whereas there are numerous accounts of marriages, illustrated otherwise, in the *Octateuch* ?

We can only hazard an explanation. The two marriages in question may possibly have been considered to lie outside the strict tradition of the Old Testament. Theodoret speaks of contamination, when the sons of God marry the daughters of men, while the text of *Genesis* recounts that Esau already had a number of wives. In Byzantine tradition, as we have seen, crowning the couple validates the marriage. Possibly, therefore, the artist deliberately chose a noncommital formula on these two occasions ; possibly it was a deliberate archaism [1]. However, since Byzantine iconography is full of anomalies, it is difficult to be sure.

FIG. 11. — Marriage of Michael IV and Zoë, Chronicle of Skylitzes (Biblioteca nacional, Madrid).

In the illuminated manuscript of the *Chronicle* of Skylitzes at Madrid, there are numerous marriage scenes. However only once is the *dextrarum junctio* used, f. 206ᵛ, for the marriage of Michael IV (1034-1040) and Zoë (fig. 11). This was, indeed, an irregular marriage, and the patriarch Alexius had to be bribed to bless it [2]. However, since a Westernizing artist recopied this miniature from the Byzantine original, it is perhaps more likely that the insisted on what was, indeed, an Eastern practice — the joining of hands — but which was given much more importance in the West.

---

[1] For example elevation on a shield was regularly used to mark the accession of an Old Testament king in 11th and 12th-century Byzantine manuscript illumination, although it is unlikely that this practice was current then in Byzantium any more than it had been at the time of the events represented See my article, *Raising on a shield in Byzantine iconography*, Revue des études byzantines, t. 33, 1975, p. 165-167 = Studies in Byzantine Iconography. Variorum Reprints, London 1977.

[2] *Skyllitzes matritensis*, edited by S.C. Estopañan, Barcelona/Madrid 1965, p. 193 ; Ioannis Scylitzae, *Synopsis Historiarum*, edited by I. Thurn, Berlin/New York 1973, p. 391 lines 4-8 = Bonn (Cedrenus), p. 505 lines 20-25.

A Westernizing copy of a Byzantine miniature, made, probably, in the 12th century, may seem very distant from an Easternizing relief, carved at Lepcis Magna in the 3rd century according to the prevailing norms of Roman imperial imagery. The justification for so abstruse a juxtaposition may, perhaps, be found in some words penned by Monsieur Jean Lassus himself. I often had the honour of addressing his seminar at the Ecole Pratique des Hautes Etudes. In his report on a paper which I delivered on December 19th 1971, Monsieur Lassus manifested his interest in the subject of this paper : the adaptation of semiological techniques to the study of iconography in order to eliminate possible ambiguity [3].

One major hazard in the study of iconography is the temptation, in establishing the transmission of themes, to deduce the specific from the specific. However such a procedure can lead to strange results. For example, it is improbable, given the universality of the theme of motherhood, that a representation of the Virgin suckling the Christ Child should be a specific adaptation of Isis suckling Horus [4]. Both would be versions of the same generic theme of motherhood. Likewise, in the present context, it seemed necessary to show that the *dextrarum junctio*, generically, is a theme of union ; the *jugum* of marriage is only a specific case. We have attempted to do this by studying the *dextrarum junctio* of Lepcis Magna with particular reference to analogous representations of this iconographical theme on coins. This study has led us to suggest that, in the Roman iconography of marriage, whether pagan or Christian, the *dextrarum junctio* retains its generic sense ; it is not to be considered as a direct representation of the specific marriage rite of *convenire in manum*. The *dextrarum junctio* disappears from marriage iconography in the 3rd century, to be revived in the 5th century. Although the Church only gradually asserted a claim to play a determining role in the solemnization of marriage, we are inclined to attribute this revival of the *dextrarum junctio* to those who were attempting to create a specific Christian iconography from the generic themes of Antique art. We have noted that, right up to the 15th century, the *dextrarum junctio* retains the same generic sense, in Byzantine tradition, as it had at Lepcis Magna in the third century. However, since it was not the constitutive element of the Byzantine marriage rite, it was ever less frequently portrayed in Byzantine art.

---

[3] Annuaire de la 5ᵉ section de l'Ecole Pratique des Hautes Etudes, t. 79, 1971-1972, p. 308.

[4] BROWN (P.), *The World of Late Antiquity*. London 1971, p. 142-143.

Marriage crowns in Byzantine iconography

The late Professor Svetozar Radojčić's book, *Portreti srpskih vladara u srednjem veku*, published at Skoplje in 1934, was one of his earliest contributions to our knowledge of the art of the Nemanjić period in Serbia. It retains its authoritative place in the bibliography of official portraiture. I found it particularly useful when investigating the sense of the double coronation of the kralj Milutin and his Byzantine spouse at Gračanica (Fig. 1). In concluding that the basic sense of these paintings was the conferment of the *basileia*, I noted that, since coronation is an iconographical theme rich in overtones, there was no reason to exclude an allusion to the crown as a sign of immortality.[1]

One question which I did not raise in my discussion of these paintings was the possibility of an allusion to the crown as a sign of marriage. As is wellknown, the imposition of a crown is an important part of the marriage ceremony in the Byzantine rite, such that marriage is often referred to as στεφάνωμα, a word which corresponds closely enough to the modern Serbian *venčanje*[2]. Milutin took Simonida, the five-year-old daughter of the Byzantine emperor Andronicus II, as his fourth wife in 1299[3]. The marriage was intended to ratify a treaty, by which lands conquered by the Serbs in modern Macedonia were ceded to Milutin as Simonida's dowry. George Pachymeres, the Byzantine chronicler, commented sourly that Milutin had taken on Simonida not as a wife but as an estate-agent[4]. Nevertheless, Milutin was far from indifferent to the prestige which he obtained in marrying a Byzantine princess born in the purple. Obviously the painting at Gračanica, executed nearly a quarter of a century after the marriage, does not directly commemorate the event. On the other hand, given the importance of the dynastic alliance contracted, there may

Fig. 1. Milutin and Simonida (Gračanica)

be an allusion to it in the paintings. For this reason it seems worth while returnig to the subject of coronation in Byzantine iconography, but this time I propose to consider it from another angle. I propose first of all a brief conside-ration of marriage scenes in Antique, Early Christian and Byzantine art, with particular reference to the use of crowns. Next it seems advisable to turn to the use of crowns in the marriage rite and the significance attached to them. We shall then be in a position to study and interpret pictures in the Byzantine tradition, in which two spouses are crowned, and to decide whether we are entitled to see there an allusion, explicit or implicit, to marriage.

When I visited Professor Svetozar Radojčić for the last time only a few weeks before his untimely death, I had the privilege of discussing the theme of this article with him. I now dedicate the article to his memory.

I. THE WORKS OF ART

A considerable number of coins from the Roman period have survived, which were issued to commemorate a marriage[5]. Themes are represented upon them which are later taken up in Christian iconography: the *dextrarum junctio*, Juno Pronuba placing a hand on the shoulders of the two spouses, the marriage contract. However, coronation does not appear upon these coins. Moreover marriage issues become rare in the Christian epoch. One or two examples occur in the first centuries with a *dextrarum junctio*[6]. The unique example of a coinage issue upon which the spouses are crowned by Christ is that of Romanus IV Diogenes (1068—1071) and Eudocia[7] (Fig. 2). The portraits of the spouses may be represented on a Roman coin[8]. This theme recurs on other artefacts: sarcophagi, gilded glasses, rings and other objects, such as the Projecta casket, which were, presumably, destined to be wedding presents[9]. The same is true of the *dexrarum junctio*, which we also find on marriage belts.[10]

Coronation on objects commemorating a marriage seems to be introduced into iconography by Christians. We have a number of gilded glasses, upon which spouses are crowned by Christ[11] (Fig. 3). But saints may also be crowned, Peter and Paul most frequently[12]; moreover the married

Fig. 2.
Coin Romanus IV
and Eudocia (Paris,
Cabinet des médailles)

Fig. 3.
Gilded glass, Christ
crowns spouses
(London, British
Museum)

Fig. 4. Gilded
glass, putto
crowns spouses
(London, British
Museum)

Fig. 5. Ivory, putto crowns Diana and Endymion (Museo Queriniana, Brescia).

couple may also be represented with their children[13]. Sometimes the subject is more complicated as, for example, on the gilded glass in the Museo Kircheriano (Rome), where the couple join hands over an altar, while a crown »floats« between them[14]. The floating crown also figures on gilded glasses representing Saints Peter and Paul.[15]

Examples of gilded glasses upon which a putto is represented crowning are much rarer[16] (Fig. 4). Although it has been suggested that such glasses served as a model for the Christian theme of Christ crowning, I wonder whether, in fact, the opposite is not the case. Should not such an object as the gilded glass in the British Museum be associated rather with the pagan Renaissance, which produced a number of remarkable ivories?[17] One of these, which particularly concerns us here, is the diptych in Brescia, upon which two mythological couples are represented. Between Diana and Endymion stands a putto, holding crowns over their heads[18] (Fig. 5).

A unique object is the Rothschild cameo (dated about 335) (fig. 6). The emperor Constantius is represented with his spouse in the form of bust portraits[19]. What makes this cameo particularly interesting for us is the type of crown which each of them is wearing. Delbrueck has suggested that these are not imperial diadems but marriage crowns and that, consequently, this cameo is to be associated with a marriage.

Several Byzantine ivories are known to us, upon which Christ is represented crowning an imperial couple. The most remarkable is that representing Romanus and Eudocia in the Cabinet des Médailles (Paris). The identity of this couple has been the object of controversy: are they Romanus II and Eudocia (959—963) or Romanus IV Diogenes and Eudocia (1068—1071)? (Fig. 7). Recently Dr Ioli Kalavrezou-Maxeiner has produced strong arguments, in favour of the latter couple[20] for whom, as we have noted, there exists a coinage issue with the same iconographical theme as well as lead seals[21]. Moreover they also figure, crowned by Christ, upon a silver reliquary in Moscow.[22]

The argument which has told most strongly against such an attribution is the existence, in the Musée de Cluny (Paris) of a similar ivory, dated 982/3, upon which Christ crowns Otto II and Theophanes[23]. This ivory, which for stylistic reasons, must be attributed to a Western rather than a Constantinopolitan workshop, nevertheless depends iconographically on a Byzantine model. Moreover, just as with the Romanus ivory, other minor artefacts may be associated with it, notably two medallia with the same iconographical theme[24]. If then we reject the early attribution of the Romanus ivory, such that it antedates that of Otto II, we must postulate in its place the existence of a lost 10th-century Byzantine prototype.

A final Byzantine ivory associated with an imperial couple is the coffer in the Palazzo Venezia (Rome)[25]. It is decorated with a series of scenes from the Life of David, among which is that of Saul giving his daughter to David as his wife. Saul pushes Michal to wards David, who joind both hands with her. On the same ivory an identified couple is twice represented, once being blessed by Christ, who places crowns on their heads, and once in *proskynesis*.

There exists one Byzantine enamel associated with a Byzantine imperial couple, in the Museum of Tiflis[26]. On this enamel, Christ is represented crowning Michael VII Dukas (1071—1078) and Maria. The inscription reads: »I crown Michael with Maria by my hand.« Recently Ioannes Spatharakis has identified the imperial couple crowned by Christ in the frontispiece to the Homilies of John Chrysostom, Paris. Coislin. 79, f. 1 (2bis)ᵛ, as also being Michael VII and Maria rather than Nicephorus Botaniates and Maria.[27]

Historical or mythological marriage-scenes occur on Greek vases. A crown or fillet is placed upon the bride's head, sometimes by Aphrodite[28]. A description exists of a lost picture of the Marriage of Alexander, in which Alexander presents a crown to his bride[29]. In the wellknown Roman paintings of wedding scenes, such as the Nozze Aldobrandini (Vatican Museum) or those in the House of the Mysteries at Pompeii, there is no coronation. However, in a painting formerly in the House of Meleager at Pompeii, now in the Museo Nazionale (Naples), Hymen is portrayed, wearing a crown and holding another in his hands[30] (Fig. 8).

It does not seem that Christian artists used these pictures as models for representing Old Testament and New Testament marriages. The *dextrarum junctio* is preferred for marriages in the 5th-century mosaics in Santa Maria Maggiore[31]. The illuminated manuscripts of the Octateuch use a variety of formulae, which do not, however, include coronation[32]. The most frequently represented Old Testament marriage is that of David and Michal. We have already

*Fig. 6. Cameo, Constantius and spouse
(Rothschild collection, Paris)*

Fig. 7. Ivory, Romanus and Eudocia (Cabinet des Médailles, Paris).

seen that Saul pushes Michal towards David on the ivory
casket in Palazzo Venezia. On the silver plate from Cyprus,
the *dextrarum junctio* is used[33]. In the illuminated *Book
of Kings*, Vatican. graec. 333, f. 24ᵛ, Saul, seated on a throne,
places his right arm around David and his left arm around
Michal.[34]

The Psalter Vatican. graec. 752 contains two biographical series for David. In the first, f. 2ᵉ, which serves as
a kind of introduction to the Psalter and accompanies the
Paschal tables, Saul is represented crowning David and
Michal, but an inscription makes it clear that he is conferring the *basileia* upon them[35]. The second series, f. 449,
accompanies the apocryphal Psalm 151. Here two scenes
of coronation occur. In the first, which belongs to the
iconography of crowning co-emperors, David is represented,
without Michal, receiving a crown from Saul. The inscription
makes it clear that he is being crowned to the *basileia*.
However, in the second example, which resembles closely
the scene on the Romanus ivory, Saul crowns both David
and Michal. The inscription, in part effaced, seems to refer
to I Kings 18, 27: Saul blessing David with his daughter[36].

New Testament marriage scenes illustrate Lives of
Saints Joachim and Anna, or Saint Joseph and the Virgin.
An accolade is usually preferred for Joachim and Anna,
although, in one case, we may have a representation of the
High Priest placing an arm around each of the two spouses[37].
An apocryphal scene, interpolated in the Laurentian Gospels,
Florence Laur. Plut. VI 23, f. 5ᵛ, shows Zacharias pointing
out Mary, who stands to the right, to Joseph[38]. So far
as I know, coronation is not used in these apocryphal Lives.
On the other hand, on at least four occasions, the artist has
represented the two spouses at the Cana wedding feast
wearing crowns[39] (Fig. 10).

Other Byzantine illuminated manuscripts with marriage scenes are the Barlaam and Joasaph, Paris. graec.
1128, the Epithalamion Vatican. graec. 1851 and the Skylitzes
matritensis. On f. 86 of the Paris Barlaam (Fig. 11), illustrating the account of the rich young man who accepts
a poor bride, a personage wearing an unusual style of scarf
places crowns on the heads of the spouses[40]. The corresponding passage is not illustrated in Athos Iviron 463,
f. 47ᵛ, with a coronation, while, in other Byzantine manuscripts of Barlaam and Joasaph, this passage is not illustrated
at all[41]. The Epithalamion contains a unique narrative series

of miniatures illustrating the coming of the bride to Constantinople and her presentation. However no scene of coronation figures in the series.[42]

We have left till last the richest source of documentation for crowns in marriage iconography. The Skylitzes matritensis has nine illustrated accounts of a wedding; in four cases the miniature represents a coronation. We will describe first the coronation scenes (Fig. 12). On f. 53^v, a bishop places crowns on the heads of Theophobus and the sister of the emperor Theophilus (829—842)[43]. The inscription reads: »Theophobus is made a patrician and honoured with the emperor's sister«. On f. 125, a bishop crowns Constantine VII and Helen, the daughter of Romanus[44] (Fig. 13). Their marriage took place in 919. The text refers to two separate events, the giving in marriage and their coronation by the patriarch Nicolas. The miniature follows the allusion to coronation, but the epigraph accompanying it refers to marriage. Like the next two examples, it is not due to a Byzantine copyist. On f. 185, a personage, who apparently wears no omophorion, places crowns on the heads of Asotes and the daughter of Samuel of Bulgaria. The epigraphs refer to Samuel and to marriage[45]. Finally, on f. 198^v, a bishop crowns Romanus III Argyropoulos (1028—1033) and Zoë[46]. The inscription refers to marriage and coronation as emperor.

We turn now to the miniatures in which a coronation is not represented. On f. 87^v, the Byzantine copyist has represented Basil with Eudocia Ingerina[47]. Their marriage took place about 865. Basil, his head uncovered, but with an evident badge of nobility on his vestments, stands beside Eudocia, who is wearing imperial dress and crowned. A personage stands to her left with his hands on her shoulder. To the right are two priests who make a gesture of blessing. According to the text, Basil is honoured with the patriciate and allied to his wife. The epigraph refers to Basil, crowning and his wife. On f. 129, a bishop blesses Stephen, the son of Romanus Lecapenus and Anna, the daughter of Gabalas[48]. The scene is set in a church; both spouses wear crowns and imperial dress; the artist, however, was not Byzantine. The text specifies how the crown of marriage and the diadem of *basileia* were conferred at the same time upon Anna; the epigraph refers to marriage and crowning. On f. 130^v a bishop blesses Romanus II and Eudocia, daughter of Hugh of France[49]. They are imperially dressed and wear crowns;

Fig. 8. Wall-painting, Hymen,
House of Meleager, Pompeii
(Museo Nazionale, Naples)

Fig. 10. Miniature, Marriage at Cana
(Mount Athos, Iviron)

Fig. 9. Miniature, David and Michal crowned by Saul (Vatican Library)

Fig. 11. Miniature, Marriage of rich man and poor maiden
(Bibliothèque Nationale, Paris)

Fig. 12. Miniature, Marriage of Theophobus and emperor's sister (Biblioteca nacional, Madrid)

an epigraph refers to marriage. On f. 206ᵛ, Michael IV (1034—1040) is represented being blessed by the patriarch Alexius[50]. They wear imperial dress, make the gesture of *dextrarum junctio* (the only time in this manuscript) and stand before a veil. Members of the entourage hold lamps[51]. The epigraph refers simply to the beginning of the reign of Michael, son of John the Orphanotrophus of the Paphlagonians.

Finally we have two miniatures on f. 222[52]. They illustrate the accession of Constantine IX (1042) (Fig. 15). In the first miniature, Constantine is shown wearing a crown and standing at the altar; behind him is Zoë, also crowned, while another personage may be placing a hand on her shoulder. The officiating priest stands on the other side of the altar. In the next scene, a crown is placed on the head of Constantine only (Zoë was, of course, already invested with the basileia). The epigraph »marriage« has been incorrectly placed beside the second miniature, instead of properly beside the first.

Thus — to sum up briefly — coronation does not seem to figure in the Roman imperial iconography of marriage. On the other hand, crowns are found, particularly in mythological scenes, on Greek vases and in wallpaintings, although these are generally known only from descriptions. When they first appear in the Christian repertory, crowns are attributed both to saints and martyrs and to married couples. When a Byzantine imperial couple is crowned, it is not at once evident whether the scene refers to their marriage or to the conferment of the *basileia*. It is necessary to have resort to the context or to an inscription to be sure. The same is true of miniatures of David and Michal. Only in some miniatures of marriage in the Skylitzes matritensis and in one miniature illustrating the Paris Barlaam and Joasaph do we find certain examples of the use of crowns in marriage ceremonial. Finally we find an occasional echo of this use in representations of the Cana Miracle.

We must now ask what significance was attached to these crowns, firts in Antiquity and then in the Early Christian and Byzantine epochs.

II. THE USE OF CROWNS IN MARRIAGE RITES

Just as it is sometimes impossible to distinguish the

crown from the diadem, so there is a possibility of confusing the crown and the garland[53]. Garlands were used at many kinds of festivity; they were not only worn but carried in the hand or used to decorate walls and doors. Thus, on the occasion of a wedding in Ancient Greece, the house of the bride's father was covered with garlands and wreathes of myrtle[54]. At the wedding, which seems to have been more a family celebration than a civic ceremony, the bride and bridegroom wore crowns, which they exchanged[55]. The crown figured in mythological weddings; for example, Dionysius took Ariadne's crown and placed it in the sky, where it became a star[56]. This reminds us that, in Antiquity, wedding festivities had much in common with the Bacchanal. Consequently we can understand why a number of the Early Fathers of the Church, not only Tertullian who disapproved of crowns in general, discouraged Christians from celebrating their marriage with such festivities.[57]

Marriage in Roman use, from the 2nd century at least, was regarded as a civil event. The marriage of the Roman couple was assimilated to that of the emperor and his spouse. They were required to offer sacrifice before the statues of the emperor and empress, *ob insignem eorum concordiam*[58]. However, coronation did not figure in this ceremony.

Our first references to it are in the 4th and 5th centuries. According to Gregory of Nazianzus, it was the rôle of the parents to place a crown on the bride's head[59]. In the texts of John Chrysostom, it is not mentioned who imposes the crown, although it is quite clear what meaning is attributed to it[60]. The crown, for John Chrysostom, is the reward given to those who have triumphed over the flesh and maintained their virginity until marriage. This moral triumph, like that of the monk, who reaches the summit of the Heavenly Ladder of virtues, derives from Saint Paul's comparison of the Christian athlete striving for an imperishable crown with the ordinary athlete in the stadium[61]. Byzantine theology consistently attributes the same meaning to the marriage crown. The canonist Nicetas of Thessaloniki maintained, in the 11th century, that no crown should be imposed at a second marriage since it was a sign of virginity[62]. Symeon of Thessaloniki says, in the 15th century, that the crown is worn by virgins and by the pure.[63]

A confirmation of the early use of crowns by Christians is to be found in the 5th-century Syro-Roman Lawbook[64].

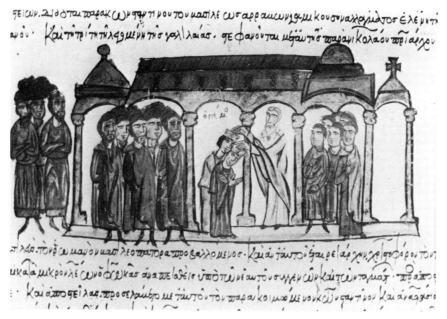

Fig. 13. *Miniature, Marriage of Constantine VII (Ibid.)*

Fig. 14. *Miniature, Marriage of Michael IV (Ibid.)*

Fig. 15. a) Marriage of Constantine IX
b) Coronation of Constantine IX

The author, when treating unwritten marriages, says that
it is sufficient that the brides give their free consent, and
»let them be crowned with the glorious crown of virginity«.
He does not, however, say who imposed the crowns. Nor
is this clear in the Reply of Pope Nicolas I to the Bulgarians
in 866. He says that the crowns were to be kept in the church,
and, after the marriage rite, the couple left the church wearing crowns on their heads[65]. Only in the 10th-century
Euchologia is the coronation of the bride and bridegroom
by the officiating priest specifically mentioned[66]. From then
on, the imposition of crowns in marriage is regularly attributed to the officiating priest in Euchologia.[67]

Our frist detailed accounts of a Christian marriage ceremony occur in chronicles. The 7th-century writer Theophylact Simocatta describes the marriage of the emperor
Maurice (583—602)[68]. The patriarch joined the hands of
the emperor and empress, pronounced the nuptial blessing
and placed the nuptial crown upon their heads. Then he
celebrated the eucharistic liturgy and gave holy communion
to the spouses. This is, of course, an imperial ceremony.
However, for the actual solemnization of the marriage, it
corresponds to the ceremony current for less exalted personages, which was, indeed, to be extended to all classes of
society[69]. The only difference for the solemnization of an
imperial marriage was that the patriarch normally presided,
and this in a palatine church — first in that of St Stephen,
built by the empress Pulcheria in 428 but later in that of the
Virgin of the Pharos, near the Chrysotriklinos, from the
time of Leo VI (886—912).[70]

However, an imperial wedding was the occasion of
other festivities besides the church ceremony, of which
Constantine Porphyrogenitus gives us an account in his
Book of Ceremonies. Unfortunately he begins only at the
moment where the church ceremony ends, saying that the
imperial couple left the church where they had been married wearing crowns[71]. He also records the acclamations
prescribed for the occasion which include an allusion to
coronation[72]. Other accounts, for example the Epithalamion
for an unknown emperor and that in the History of John
Cantacuzenus, tell us virtually nothing of the imposition
of nuptial crowns.[73]

One reason for this lacuna is the fact that coronation to
mark the conferment of the *basileia* was often closely associated with the imposition of nuptial crowns. For example

10

Heraclius (610—641) and Eudocia were crowned and married the same day[74]. The same is true for several of the marriages recounted by Skylitzes, to which we have already alluded. Generally, it seems, especially in the case of the bride, the *basileia* was conferred before marriage[75]. This was necessary, in order that she should be worthy of her imperial husband. But, equally, Theophobus and Basil are made patricians before receiving an imperial bride in marriage. This is not, however, the case, it seems, for Constantine VII and Romanus III, who were both married to their respective imperial bride before receiving the *basileia*. This was, no doubt, because it was their marriage which gave them the title to be crowned and to reign as emperor.

Thus, to conclude, coronation seems, in Antiquity, to have had a mainly festal significance. The crown is closer to a garland than a diadem. Its conferment, or the exchange of crowns, does not constitute the marriage. However, since the crown had associations with pagan rites, Christians were advised to refrain from wearing them at their wedding celebrations. It is not clear whether there was, in fact, a total cessation in the use of crowns. They were certainly used by Christians in the 4th century, but with a triumphal significance, which they keep throughout the Byzantine epoch. Moreover, as the solemnization of marriages became exclusively the responsibility of the Church, it became customary for a member of the clergy to impose the crowns. In the case of imperial couples, this was normally the patriarch himself. But imperial weddings, often contracted for political or dynastic reasons were closely associated with the *basileia*. Therefore, we have to ask whether certain representations of the coronation of an imperial couple refer primarily to their marriage or to the conferment of the *basileia*.

III. THE SIGNIFICANCE OF CROWNS IN MARRIAGE ICONOGRAPHY

The marriage crowns on gilded glasses have only a symbolical significance. We cannot affirm that they refer directly to a ceremony, any more than do the crowns offered to saints and martyrs, whether, again, on gilded glasses, or in monumental apse decorations. On the other hand, it is more difficult to be precise about the crowns offer by

a putto to Diana and Endymion. Either this is a »retake«
of the Christian motif, or it is to be associated with the
picture of Hymen wearing and holding a crown. In this case
the crown would be an attribute of the god of love.

The cameo of Honorius is too early for us to see here
a precise allusion to the triumphal crowns of Christian
marriage ritual. If, as is possible, this cameo was made to
commemorate his marriage, then we must suppose that the
crowns are part of the festal dress of the imperial couple.
In the Skylitzes miniatures where the imposition of a crown
is definitely intended to signify the solemnization of a marriage, there does not seem to be any specific distinction
between the crowns conferred and the diadems worn by
emperors in other miniatures.

In the cases of the marriage of Constantine VII with
Helen and of Samuel the Bulgar with Asotes, there is no
problem of interpretation, the more so that in the former case
the word γάμος is inscribed by the scene. However, when
the rite is represented frontally, as is the case with the marriage of Theophobus with the sister of the emperor Theophilus, we seem to be close to the model used for the ivory
of Romanus — and Eudocia, as well as to the miniature of
David and Michal in Vatican. graec. 752. Now, with regard
to the Romanus ivory, Dr Iola Kalavrezou-Maxeiner has
recently rejected the notion that it represents the blessing
of their marriage by Christ.

»Obviously«, she writes, »The notion of marriage is
there, as it is with all coronations of couples, but it can
be shown that marriage is less important as a theme in
these representations than the imperial legal status conferred
by the coronation.«[76]

There is no need to repeat Dr Kalavrezou-Maxeiner's
arguments here in detail. It suffices to recall that the theme
of coronation was used plentifully by Romanus IV and
Eudocia on works which are certainly to be attributed to
them. The aim was to present Romanus IV, who owed
his position to his marriage with Eudocia, as a legitimate
ruler, not a usurper, while Eudocia maintained the position
which she had enjoyed under Romanus's predecessor
Constantine X. These arguments help to explain our two
miniatures. In each case, a man of humble social origins
is represented as ennobled and married to a royal princess.
Theophobus is made a patrician before marrying the emperor's sister, while David, a shepherd-boy, marries Saul's

daughter and, in due course, succeeds him as king of Israël. Thus, although the artist had already represented David's coronation as co-emperor, he nevertheless used for David's marriage a model, which was associated more particularly with the conferment of *basileia*.

I am now in a position to add a precision to what I said earlier, on the occasion of the Symposium at Gračanica in 1973, about the double coronation of Milutin and Simonida. As in the imperial Byzantine pictures, the theme of *basileia* is predominant. However, while Milutin in no way owed his title to reign to his marriage with Simonida, except over the territories ceded to him as her dowry, nevertheless, in contracting this marriage, he was in the same position as David marrying Michal or Theophobus marrying the sister of the emperor Theophilus. A person of humbler social origins was being allied with an imperial bride. Thus, the painting of Milutin and Simonida at Gračanica should be more particularly associated with the group of representations of Christ crowning Romanus IV and Eudocia.

In conclusion, a few words about the relationship of marriage crowns to other coronation themes in iconography might well be appropriate. We may distinguish, in Antiquity, between the festive garland, the triumphal crown and the imperial diadem. Roman rulers receive triumphal crowns, and, in due course, this crown becomes combined with the imperial diadem, such that coronation, in Byzantine iconography, has the primary significance of conferment of the *basileia*; this is to be understood as a capacity rather than as a title to rule. In Christian religious iconography, the crown retains its triumphal sense and is used in a variety of contexts: the triumph of Christ over death, of the martyr over his persecutors, of the monk over his sinful proclivities. The garland, whose festive sense is evident in representations of weddings and Bacchanals, seems to disappear in the Christian era. In Christian tradition it becomes a triumphal crown and thus persists, both in liturgical use and in art. However, the possibility remains open of using the crown or diadem in iconography with a primary and with a subordinate significance. This seems to be what has happened in the group of pictures which I have associated more particularly with that of Milutin and Simonida. Dr Kalavrezou-Maxeiner has pointed out that the issue of coins by Romanus

IV and Eudocia on which they are represented being crowned is not strictly a marriage issue, because it was the principal issue of their reign. Their marriage alliance was the basis of government at Constantinople. If Milutin, in his old age, had himself represented, along with Simonida, being crowned by angels, might this not be in order to recall to the turbulent Serbian nobility that his alliance with an imperial princess placed him in a caste far superior to theirs?

NOTES

This article enters into a series of studies of triumphal and other themes deriving from Byzantine imperial imagery: *The coronation of a co-emperor in the Skylitzes matritensis*, Actes du 14ᵉ congrès international des études byzantines (1971), II, Bucarest 1975 (Cited: *Co-emperor*); *The iconographical sources for the coronation of Milutin and Simonida at Gračanica*, Symposium »L'art byzantin au commencement du 14ᵉ siècle«, Gračanica 1973 (cited: *Milutin & Simonida*); *The triumph of Saint Peter in the church of Saint Clement at Ohrid and the iconography of the triumph of the martyrs*, Zograf 5 (1974); *Raising on a shield in Byzantine iconography*, Revue des études byzantines 33 (1975); *The significance of unction in Byzantine iconography*, Byzantine and Modern Greek Studies 2 (1976); *The Dextrarum junctio of Lepcis Magna in relationship to the iconography of marriage* (Hommages Jean Lassus), Antiquités africaines 14 (1979) (cited: *Dextrarum junctio*). The first, fourth and fifth of these studies have been reprinted in my volume *Studies in Byzantine Iconography* (Variorum), London 1977.

  ¹ Walter, *Milutin and Simonida*, p. 183—200.
  ² The earliest recorded use of the word in this sense seems to be in the Letters of Theodore Studite (759—826), G.W.H. Lampe, *A Patristic Greek Lexicon*, Oxford 1961, p. 1258. Previously, the word signified a crown of victory. So *Methodius of Olympus, Convivium Decem Virginum (Le Banquet)*, edited H. Musurillo, Sources chrétiennes 95, Paris 1963, p. 236 line 28 (=PG 18, 161a). Methodius was martyred in 311.
  ³ M. Laskaris, *Vizantiske princeze u srednjevekovnoj Srbiji*, Belgrade 1926, p. 57—68; G. Ostrogorsky, *History of the Byzantine State* (2nd English edition), Oxford 1968, p. 489—490.
  ⁴ G. Pachymeres, *De Andronico Palaeologo*, IV 6 (Bonn II, p. 286, line 3—4).
  ⁵ L. Reekmans, *La dextrarum iunctio dans l'iconographie romaine et paléochrétienne*, Bulletin de l'Institut historique belge de Rome 31 (1958), p. 32—37.
  ⁶ Walter, *Dextrarum junctio*, p. 271—283.
  ⁷ Cécile Morrisson, *Catalogue des monnaies byzantines de la Bibliothèque Nationale*, II, Paris 1970, p. 649—650, pl. LXXXIX; Eadem, *De Nicéphore II Phocas à Romain IV Diogène*, Bulletin du club français de la médaille 42 (1974), p. 83—87. See below, p. 85, 91.

14

[8] A. Rossbach, *Römische Hochzeits- und Ehedenkmäler*, Leipzig 1971, p. 21. He cites examples from Augustus and Livia to Trajan and Plotina.

[9] O. M. Dalton, *Catalogue of Early Christian Objects . . . in the British Museum*, London 1901, № 304, p. 61—64; H. Buschhausen, *Die spätrömischen Metallscrinia und frühchristlichen Reliquiare* (Wiener byzantinische Studien 9), Vienna 1971, B 7, p. 210—214, fig. 21—26.

[10] E. H. Kantorowicz, *On the Golden Marriage Belt and the Marriage rings of the Dumbarton Oaks Collection*, Dumbarton Oaks Papers 14 (1960), p. 1—16; Walter, *Dextrarum junctio* p. 279—280 & fig. 8.

[11] R. Garrucci, *Storia dell'arte cristiana nei primi otto anni della chiesa, III, Pitture non cimiteriali*, Prato 1876, p. 104—111, fig. 195 11,12; 196 4; 197 6; 198 1—3. Dalton, *op. cit.*, № 613, p. 121. C.R. Morey & G. Ferrari, *The Gold Glass Collection of the Vatican Library* (Catalogo del Museo Sacro IV), Vatican 1959.

[12] Garrucci, *op. cit.*, fig. 181 1—6.

[13] Garrucci, *op. cit.*, fig. 199 1—6.

[14] Garrucci, *op. cit.*, fig. 195 11.

[15] Garrucci, *op. cit.*, fig. 182 5.

[16] Garrucci, *op. cit.*, 197 6; Dalton, *op. cit.* № 612, p. 121.

[17] E. Kitzinger, *Early Medieval Art in the British Museum*, 1955 (second edition), p. 4—5; Idem, *Byzantine Art in the Making*, London 1977, p. 34—38.

[18] W. F. Volbach, *Elfenbeinarbeiten der Spätantike und des frühen Mittelalters*, Mainz 1952, № 66, p. 43 (second edition 1976, p. 57), pl. 21. For a general discussion of these pagan diptychs, see H. Graeven, *Antike Diptychen*, Römische Mitteilungen 28 (1913), p. 198—304.

[19] E. Coche de la Ferté, *Le camée Rothschild, un chef-d'oeuvre du 4ème siècle après J. C.*, Paris 1957. R. Delbrueck, *Die Consulardiptychen und verwandte Denkmäler*, Berlin/Leipzig 1929, p. 258—260, pl. 66, and *Spätantike Kaiserporträts*, Berlin/Leipzig 1933, p. 206, pl. 105, had maintained that the emperor was Honorius, and that, in consequence, the cameo was executed about 398.

[20] A. Goldschmidt & K. Weitzmann, *Die byzantinischen Elfenbeinskulpturen des X.—XIII. Jahrhunderts*, II, Berlin 1934, № 34, p. 35. Their attribution to Romanus II was disputed by A.S. Keck & C.R. Morey in their review in the Art Bulletin 17 (1935), p. 398—400; it is apparently rejected by A. Volbach, *Les ivoires sculptés, de l'époque carolingienne au 13e siècle*, Cahiers de civilisation médiévale 1 (1958), p. 23. A. Grabar keeps an open mind, *L'empereur dans l'art byzantin*, Strasbourg 1936, p. 116, as does D. Talbot Rice, *Art byzantin*, Paris/Brussels 1959, № 97, p. 300. Ioli Kalavrezou-Maxeiner, *Eudokia Makrembolitissa and the Romanos Ivory*, Dumbarton Oaks Papers 31 (1977), p. 386—408.

[21] See above, note 7. G. Zacos & A. Veglery, *Byzantine Lead Seals*, I, Basle 1972, № 93 a-d.

[22] A. Grabar, *Quelques reliquaires de saint Démétrios et le martyrium du saint à Salonique*, L'art de la fin de l'Antiquité et du Moyen Age, I, Paris 1968, p. 446—63 (=Dumbarton Oaks Papers 5 1950); Ch. Walter, *St. Demetrius: The Myroblytos of Thessalonika*, Studies in Byzantine Iconography: London (Variorum) 1977, V p. 161—162 (=Eastern Churches Review 5 1973); Искусство Византии в собраниях СССР II, Moscow 1977, № 547, p. 85.

23 Goldschmidt & Weitzmann, *op. cit.*, II, № 85; P. E. Schramm & Florentine Müterich, *Denkmale der deutschen Könige und Kaiser*, Munich 1962, № 73, p. 144, pl. 73.

24 One in the National Museum, Helsinki, the other, now lost, formerly in a private collection in Leningrad. Schramm & Müterich, *op. cit.*, № 74, p. 144.

25 Goldschmidt & Weitzmann, *op. cit.*, I, № 123, p. 63, pl. LXX.

26 Ch. Amiranachvili, *Les émaux de Géorgie*, Paris 1962, p. 100; Kl. Wessel, *Die byzantinische Kleinkunst*, Recklinghausen 1967, № 38, p. 117—121.

27 I. Spatharakis, *The Portrait in Byzantine Illuminated Manuscripts*, Leiden 1971, p. 107—118, fig. 70.

28 V. Magnien, *Le mariage chez les Grecs anciens, L'initiation nuptiale*, L'Antiquité classique 5 (1936), p. 115—138, especially p. 122.

29 *Ibidem*, p. 127.

30 *ibidem*, p. 129; K. Schefold, *Die Wände Pompejis, Topographisches Verzeichnis der Bildmotive*, Berlin 1957, p. 112. Reproduction: S. Reinach, *Répertoire des peintures grecques et romaines*, Paris 1922, p. 68.

31 B. Brenk, *Die frühchristlichen Mosaiken in S. Maria Maggiore zu Rom*, Wiesbaden 1975, p. 69—70, 80—81; pl. 50; Walter, *Dextrarum junctio*, p. 280—282.

32 In Vatican. graec. 746 and 747 the usual formulae are: presentation of the spouses, dextrarum junctio and the wedding feast.

33 *Wealth of the Roman World* (catalogue of exhibition, British Museum, 1977) edited by J. Kent & S. Painter, London 1977, № 180, p. 105; Walter, *Dextrarum junctio*, p. 280.

34 J. Lassus, *L'illustration du Livre des Rois*, Paris 1973, p. 54.

35 E. De Wald, *The Illustrations in the Manuscripts of the Septuagint III, Psalms and Odes 2, Vaticanus graecus 752*, Princeton 1942, p. 4, pl. IV.

36 *Ibidem*, p. 41, pl. LIII; Walter, *Co-emperor*, p. 457 note 18.

37 I tentatively suggest this alternative interpretation of a fresco in the chapel of Saints Joachim and Anna at Kizil Çukur (Çavuşin) in Cappadocia, although Nicole and M. Thierry (*Eglise de Kizil-Tchoukour chapelle iconoclaste, chapelle de Joachim et d'Anne*, Monuments et Mémoires 50 (1958), p. 126—128) and A. Grabar (*Christian Iconography, A Study of Its Origins*, London 1969, p. 129) interpret this scene rather as Anne pregnant, supported by two attendants.

38 Jacqueline Lafontaine-Dosogne, *Iconographie de l'enfance de la Vierge dans l'Empire byzantin et en Occident I*, Brussel 1964, p. 167—168, 193, fig. 95; Tania Velmans, *Le tétraévangile de la Laurentienne*, Paris 1971, fig. 10.

39 Athos Iviron 5, f. 363ᵛ (V. Lazarev, *Storia della pittura bizantina*, Turin 1967, fig. 379; *The Treasures of Mount Athos* II, Athens 1975, pl. 38); Vienna, Library of Mechitharist Congregation, cod. 242, f. 191ᵛ (Heide and H. Buschhausen, *Die illuminierten armenischen Handschriften der Mechitharisten-Congregation in Wien*, Vienna 1976, p. 37, fig. 63); St Nicolas, Ljuboten (G. Millet and Tania Velmans, *La peinture du Moyen Age en Yougoslavie* IV, Paris 1969, fig. 7—8); St Nicolas Orphanos, Thessaloniki (A. Xyngopoulos, Οἱ τοιχογραφίες τοῦ Ἁγίου Νικολάου Ὀρφανοῦ Θεσσαλονίκης, Athens 1964, fig. 91, 92, 178).

40 Sirarpie Der Nersessian, *L'illustration du roman de Barlaam et Joasaph*, Paris 1937, p. 79—82, fig. 287.

16

41 *Ibidem*, fig. 26. Text: Migne PG *96*, 1004ᶜ—1008ᵃ.

42 Spatharakis, *The Portrait* (op. cit. note 27), p. 210—230, fig. 158—173.

43 S. C. Estopañan, *Skyllitzes Matritensis*, Barcelona/Madrid, 1965 (cited hereinafter: Estopañan) № 133, p. 80—81; *Ioannis Scylitzae, Synopsis Historiarum*, edited I. Thurn, Berlin/New York 1973 (cited hereinafter: Scylitzes), p. 67 (= Bonn, p. 120). N. Wilson, *The Madrid Scylitzes*, Scrittura e civiltà 2 (1978), p. 209—219, argues in favour of a date around 1160 for this manuscript.

44 Estopañan, № 305, p. 132—133; Scylitzes, p. 209 (= Bonn, p. 293).

45 Estopañan, № 481; Scylitzes, p. 342 (= Bonn, p. 451).

46 Estopañan, № 491: Scylitzes, p. 374 (= Bonn p. 485).

47 Estopañan, № 221; Scylitzes, p. 127 (= Bonn, p. 198).

48 Estopañan, № 321; Scylitzes, p. 228 (= Bonn, p. 315).

49 Estopañan, № 325; Scylitzes, p. 231 (= Bonn, p. 319).

50 Estopañan, № 511; Scylitzes, p. 391 (= Bonn, p. 505).

51 The use of a veil in marriage ceremonial, particularly for the bride is well attested in Western sources (R. Metz, *La consécration des vierges dans l'Eglise romaine*, Paris 1954, Appendice I, Le rituel de mariage, p. 358, 359, 383, 406, 408; P. Jounel, *La liturgie romaine du mariage*, La Maison-Dieu 50 (1957), p. 37). For Byzantine use it is less clear. L. Bréhier (*La civilisation byzantine* III, Paris 1950, p. 8) speaks of the paranymph hold a cloth over the head of the imperial couple during the marriage ceremony, but gives no adequate reference to the sources. G. Schlumberger (*L'épopée byzantine à la fin du 10ᵉ siècle* I, Paris 1896, p. 79) tells an extraordinary story of John I Tzimisces being wrapped in the Virgin's maphorion on the occasion of his marriage, but he too gives no adequate reference to the sources. Unfortunately subsequent writers have repeated what these two distinguished scholars had said, without control. For lamps, the sources are clearer. The practice of carrying lamps at a wedding must go back to Jewish usage (compare the parable of the Wise and Foolish Virgins, Matthew 25, 1—13); it is mentioned by Symeon of Thessaloniki (*De Matrimonio*, PG 155, 509).

52 Estopañan, № 548—549; Scylitzes, p. 422 (= Bonn, p. 542).

53 Walter, *Milutin and Simonida*, p. 185—198; K. Baus, *Der Kranz in Antike und Christentum* (Theophaneia 2), Bonn 1940, especially p. 93—112; R. Turcan, *Les guirlandes dans l'Antiquité classique*, Jahrbuch für Antike und Christentum 14 (1971), p. 92—139.

54 *Dictionnaire des antiquités grecques et romaines* 3 (Paris 1904), ed. C. Daremberg and E. Saglio, 1648—1649 (Matrimonium).

55 Magnien, *art. cit.* (note 28), p. 128.

56 *Ibidem*, p. 128.

57 J. Schrijnen, *La couronne nuptiale dans l'antiquité chrétienne*, Mélanges d'archéologie et d'histoire de l'Ecole française de Rome 31 (1911), p. 309—319; Baus, *op. cit.* (note 53), p. 98—99.

58 Walter, *Dextrarum junctio*, p. 276.

59 Gregory of Nazianzus, *Letter 231*, PG 37, 373; L. Anné, *Les rites des fiançailles et la donation pour cause de mariage sous le bas-empire*, Louvain 1941, p. 156, who points out that it is not clear that this »coronation« forms part of the marriage ritual.

60 John Chrysostom, *Homily 9 on I Timothy 2*, PG 62, 546.

61 *I Corinthians 9*, 24—25; Walter, *Milutin and Simonida*, p. 189—190.

[62] А. Павлов, *Сборникъ неизданныхъ памятниковъ византийс-каго церковнаго права*, Ст Петерсбург 1898, p. 30.

[63] *De Matrimonio*, PG 155, 505—508. But see also Theodore Studite (759—826), *Letters* I 50, PG 99, 1092—1093.

[64] K. G. Bruns and E. Sachau, *Syrisch-Römisches Rechtsbuch aus dem fünften Jahrhundert*, Leipzig 1880, p. 23, 26—27, 52—53, 59, 94, 128; H. J. Wolff, *Written and Unwritten Marriages in Hellenistic and Postclassical Law*, Haverford (Pennsylvania) 1939, p. 83—84; W. Selb, *Zur Bedeutung des Syrisch-Römisches Rechtsbuch*, 1964.

[65] Nicolas I, *Responsa ad Bulgarorum Consulta*, PL 119, 979—980; Metz, *op. cit.* (note 51), p. 384.

[66] A. Dmitrievsky, *Описание литургическихъ рукописей II*, Εὐχολόγια, Kiev 1901, p. 4 (Sinaït. 957, f. 22ᵛ), p. 30 (Sinaït 958, f. 78ᵛ), etc.; cf. J. Ebersolt, *Etudes sur la vie publique et privée de la cour byzantine*, Mélanges d'histoire et d'archéologie byzantines, Paris 1917— 1951, p. 31. See also (inferior editions), J. Goar, Εὐχολόγιον, Paris 1647, p. 385—390; P. Trempelas, Μικρὸν Εὐχολόγιον I, 1950, p. 23—25, p. 55—59.

[67] Basic studies: J. Zhishman, *Das Eherecht der orientalischen Kirche*, Vienna 1864, especially p. 156—160, p. 692—695; N. Politis, Γαμήλια σύμβολα, Λαογραφικὰ σύμμεικτα β′ (Δημοσιεύματα λαογραφικοῦ ἀρχείου 2). Athens 1921, especially p. 228—236 (summary in German in Jahrbuch für Liturgicwissenschaft 5 (1925), p. 208—209); M. Jugie, *Theologia Dogmatica Christianorum Orientalium III*, Paris 1930, especially p. 441—473; Ph. Koukoules, Βυζαντινῶν βίος καὶ πολιτισμὸς IV, Athens 1951, p. 70—147.

[68] Theophylact Simocatta, *Historia* I 10, edited De Boor, p. 57 (=Bonn, p. 51); Anné, *op. cit.* (note 59), p. 157.

[69] Rescript of Alexius Comnene I (1095) to the effect that the marriage of slaves must also be blessed by a priest, F. Dölger, *Regesten der Kaiserurkunden des oströmischen Reiches* II, Munich/Berlin 1925, № 1177, p. 43; text, Rhalli-Potli, Syntagma II, p. 500 (=K. Zachariä von Lingenthal, *Jus Graeco-Romanum III*, Leipzig 1857, p. 404).

[70] Constantine Porphyrogenitus, *De cerimoniis* 48 (39) & 50(41), edited A. Vogt, Paris 1939, p. 6—10, 16—23 (=Reiske, Bonn I, p. 196—202, 207—216). For the churches, R. Janin, *Les églises et les monastères (La géographie ecclésiastique de l'empire byzantin)*, Paris 1969 (second edition), p. 473 (St Stephen), p. 232 (Pharos).

[71] Vogt, *ed. cit.*, II, p. 6 (=Reiske, Bonn I, p. 196—197).

[72] *De cerimoniis* 91(82), Vogt, *ed. cit.* II, p. 181 (=Reiske, Bonn I, p. 380; P. Maas, *Metrische Akklamationen der Byzantiner*, Byzantinische Zeitschrift 21 (1912), p. 40.

[73] J. Strzygowski, *Das Epithalamion des Paläologen Andronikos II*, Byzantinische Zeitschrift 10 (1901), p. 546—567; S. Papademetrios, Ὁ ἐπιθαλάμιος Ἀνδρονίκου II τοῦ Παλαιολόγου, Byzantinische Zeitschrift 11 (1902), p. 452—460: H. Belting, *Das illuminierte Buch in der spätbyzantinischen Gesellschaft*, Heidelberg 1970, p. 26; Spatharakis, *op. cit.* (note 42). John Cantacuzenus, *Historia* I 41, Bonn I, p. 196—204.

[74] Theophanes, *Chronographia*, De Boor, p. 299 (=Bonn, p. 461).

[75] Ebersolt, *op. cit.* (note 66), p. 29.

[76] Kalavrezou-Maxeiner, *art. cit.* (note 20), p. 394—397.

PAPAL POLITICAL IMAGERY IN THE MEDIEVAL LATERAN PALACE

I. Preliminary

In one of his Homilies Gregory of Nazianzen remarks that some emperors were not content merely to have their statues set up and adored in public places. They also liked to have pictures executed of their deeds: noble cities offering them gifts, magistrates adoring them in full regalia, barbarians prostrate at their feet and various scenes of slaughter. These pictures appealed to them not only as true accounts of their deeds but also for their artistic value. Political imagery — scenes like these taken from the official biography of the emperor — played a considerable role in the decorative schemes of the imperial palaces at Constantinople. This is abundantly clear in spite of the fact that the buildings decorated with such imagery have all disappeared. One has only to turn to the Byzantine chroniclers to find numerous though generally summary accounts of these pictures. In order to recall their character I cite here one or two examples [1].

In the vestibule of the Chalké there were executed mosaic representations of Justinian's victories, scenes from the African and Italian wars and Belisarius presenting to Justinian and Theodora the kings which he had vanquished and the treasure which he had captured. The two sovereigns were also represented standing among the senators, all dressed in festal robes [2]. The emperor Maurice (582-602) had a series of frescoes executed in the Carina portico in the Blachernae region of the city. They set out the adventures of his life from his childhood till his accession to the throne [3]. In the Kainourgion the emperor Basil I (867-886) had himself portrayed seated on a throne and surrounded by the generals who had shared the fatigues of his military campaigns. The generals presented him with the

---

1. ταύταις ταῖς εἰκόσιν ἄλλοι μὲν ἄλλο τι τῶν βασιλέων προσπαραγράφεσθαι χαίρουσιν. οἱ μὲν τῶν πόλεων τὰς λαμπροτέρας δωροφορούσας, οἱ δὲ νίκας ὑπὲρ κεφαλῆς στεφανούσας. οἱ δὲ τοὺς ἐν τέλει προσκυνοῦντας, καὶ τοῖς τῶν ἀρχῶν τιμωμένους συνθήμασιν. οἱ δὲ θηροφονίας καὶ εὐστοχίας. οἱ δὲ βαρβάρων ἡττημένων, καὶ ὑπὸ τοῖς ποσὶν ἐρῥιμμένων ἢ κτεινομένων πολυειδῆ σχήματα. φιλοῦσι γὰρ οὐ τὰς ἀληθείας τῶν πραγμάτων μόνον ἐφ'οἷς μέγα φρονοῦσιν, ἀλλὰ καὶ τὰ τούτων ἰνδάλματα (Gregory of NAZIANZEN, Oratio IV, Contra Julianum I, lxxx, PG 35, 605). Charles DIEHL gives numerous examples of descriptions of such pictures in his Manuel d'art byzantin, Paris, 1925 (2nd edition), p. 225 and 404; cf. also O.M. DALTON, Byzantine Art and Archaeology, Oxford, 1911 and New York, 1961 (photographic reprint), p. 261. (This article, on account of its length, is being published in two parts, the second of which will appear in the following number of the Cahiers Archéologiques. In this number will be found: I. Preliminary; II. Description of the pictures; III. Analysis of the iconography, 1. The Triclinium of Leo III, Mission and Investiture. There will follow in the next number: III. Analysis of the iconography, 2. The Audience Hall of Callixtus II and the Lateran Portico mosaic, Triumph and Concordat; 3. The Coronation of Lotharius II, Strator; IV. Conclusion. I take the opportunity of expressing my gratitude to the staff of the photographic department of the Vatican Library for the photographs of copies of the pictures preserved in manuscripts of the Vatican.)

2. PROCOPIUS, De Aedificiis, I. 10, edited J. HAURY, Leipzig, 1913, p. 39-41; R. JANIN, Constantinople byzantine, Paris, 1964, p. 110.

3. THEOPHANES, Chronographia, edited C. DE BOOR, Leipzig, 1883, p. 261, 1. 13-16.

cities which they had conquered. In the same series of pictures were included the emperor's Herculean feats of arms, his principal deeds to bring happiness to his subjects, his battles and the victories which were granted to him by God [4]. In the palace which he had constructed in the region of the Blachernae the emperor Manuel Comnenus had represented all the exploits which he had performed against the barbarians and all that he had done for the good of the Romans [5].

It is not difficult, whether by reference to antique models or to the bas-reliefs on the base of the Column of Theodosius or to the miniatures particularly in chronicles, to reconstruct the iconography of the scenes [6]. A very slight adaptation of antique imperial imagery made it suitable for the needs of Christian emperors, when they were to be represented as triumphing over the enemies of Christendom. At the entrance to the imperial palace Constantine's victory over the enemy of the Church was, Eusebius tells us, sublimely portrayed; the enemy of the human race was represented under the form of a dragon; the emperor was surrounded by his sons; he trampled the dragon, transfixed it with a lance and threw it into the deep gulf of the sea; over the head of the emperor was represented the 'trophy of salvation' [7]. Similarly Constantine and Helena were represented as statues on top of the *Milion* holding up and presenting the Cross [8].

The distinction between political or imperial and religious or ecclesiastical imagery is never hard and fast in Byzantine art [9]. The case of Constantine is also a special one. It is consequently not surprising to find scenes from his biography, as a saint of the Church, represented in churches. In the vault of the narthex of the church of Saint Polyeuktos the princess Juliana Anicia had a series of scenes represented from the life of Constantine, among them his conversion and baptism [10]. In the room at the south west corner of Saint Sophia Constantine is included among the witnesses of Christ [11]. The *Milion* composition figures as a mosaic in the narthex of the church of Saint Luke in Phocid, and frequently in the churches of Serbia, where sovereigns of the Nemanja family may be associated with Constantine and Helena as protectors and promoters of Orthodoxy [12].

In sum we may say that there is abundant evidence that in Imperial buildings at Constantinople triumphal scenes — of victory and of the submission of captives — and official groups of the Emperor and his court continued to be portrayed. These could be merely political or they could include a symbolical allusion to a religious triumph. In the case of Constantine, however, these scenes may receive additions concerning his title to sanctity and Constantine's life cycle may then become a suitable subject for representation in churches.

It would be natural to suppose that in the papal palace in Rome there would be similar decorative schemes. That such pictures did indeed exist in the West as early as the

4. THEOPHANES CONTINUATUS (= CONSTANTINE VII PORPHYROGENITUS), *Life of Basil I*, PG 109, 348 C-D; R. JANIN, *op. cit.* (note 2), p. 115-116.

5. Nicetas CHONIATES, *Life of Manuel Comnenus*, VII. 3, PG 139, 556B.

6. The fullest study is that of A. GRABAR, *L'empereur dans l'art byzantin*, Paris, 1936.

7. EUSEBIUS, *Life of Constantine*, III. 3, edited I.A. HEIKEL, Leipzig, 1902, p. 78; PG 20, 1057; J. MAURICE, *Numismatique constantinienne*, II, Paris, 1911, p. 509; A. GRABAR, *op. cit.* (note 6), p. 43; R. JANIN, *op. cit.* (note 2), p. 110; P. COURCELLE, "Le serpent à face humaine dans la numismatique impériale", in *Mélanges A. Piganiol*, I, Paris, 1966, p. 344.

8. Ch. WALTER, "Les dessins carolingiens dans un manuscrit de Verceil", in *Cahiers Archéologiques*, XVIII, 1968, p. 106, note 29.

9. A. GRABAR, *L'art de la fin de l'Antiquité et du Moyen Age*, I, Paris, 1968, p. 189.

10. *Epigrammatum Anthologia Palatina*, I. 10, edited F. DUBNER, Paris, 1864, p. 3, l. 70-73; A. GRABAR, *op. cit.* (note 6), p. 39; R. JANIN, *Géographie ecclésiastique de l'empire byzantin*, Paris, 1969 (2nd edition), p. 405.

11. A. GRABAR, *L'iconoclasme byzantin*, Paris, 1957, p. 193; Ch. WALTER, "Two Notes on the Deësis", in *Revue des études byzantines*, XXVI, 1968, p. 330.

12. Cf. particularly the church of Saint George at Staro Nagoričino, where Milutin and Simonis are portrayed beside Constantine and Helena.

IXth century is evident from a passage in the treatise of bishop Agobardus of Lyons, *De imaginibus sanctorum,* concerning particularly the representation of synods[13]. However, if such pictures no longer exist in the papal palaces in Rome, descriptions of them are known, and, thanks to the zeal of XVIth and XVIIth century archaeologists and antiquarians, some of these pictures have been copied and the copies are available to us. Most of these drawings and sketches are wellknown. They have been reproduced by Lauer and Wilpert in their monumental studies[14]. To these must be added the important series of drawings executed for Panvinius and published by Dr. Gerhard Ladner[15].

These are the principal examples of official papal imagery at the Lateran known to us by copies: the mosaics in the Triclinium of Leo III (795-816); the paintings in the Chapel of Saint Nicolas, begun by Callixtus II (1119-1124) and finished by the antipope Anacletus II (1130-1138); the paintings in a nearby Audience Hall of Callixtus II; the coronation of Lotharius II in a nearby room, commissioned by Innocent II (1130-1144); the mosaics of scenes from ecclesiastical history in the portico of Saint John Lateran, commissioned by Alexander III (1159-1181) or Clement III (1187-1191). With these may be associated the restored mosaics of the apse of Saint Peter's, due to Innocent III (1198-1216) and the frescoes of Silvester and Constantine at the Quattro Coronati, a stone's throw the Lateran, dating from the pontificate of Innocent IV (1243-1254).

I made the acquaintance of these pictures while preparing a study of the iconography of councils in the Byzantine tradition. Professor André Grabar called my attention to the fact that, while the drawings of Panvinius in particular have been admirably published by Dr. Ladner, no full analysis of the iconographical sources of these pictures has been published. It is at his suggestion that I am attempting such an analysis in the *Cahiers Archéologiques.*

Unfortunately it is impossible to avoid a primary consideration of these pictures *en archéologue.* The reason is that since they no longer exist all depends upon how one interprets the copies and the descriptions in the written sources. It seems, particularly in the case of the mosaics of the Triclinium of Leo III, that art historians have engaged in discussion over the significance of a scene which may never have existed. I begin, therefore, with a brief description of these political scenes and of the elements composing them.

II. DESCRIPTION OF THE PICTURES

1. The Triclinium of Leo III.

The *Liber Pontificalis* records that pope Leo III built two triclinia, both of which were decorated with mosaics[16]. In one there were various scenes of the apostles preaching

13. AGOBARDUS, *Liber de imaginibus sanctorum,* PL 104, 225: "Sed causa historiae ad récordandum non ad colendum; ut verbo gratia gesta synodalia (...) iuxta morem bellorum tum externorum cum civilium ad memoriam rei gestam, sicut in multis locis videmus." Cf. A. GRABAR, *op. cit.* (note 11), p. 50.

14. Ph. LAUER, *Le palais de Latran,* Paris, 1911; J. WILPERT, *Die römischen Mosaiken und Malereien,* Freiburg im Breisgau, 1917.

15. *Vaticanus barberinus latinus* 2738; cf. G. LADNER, "I mosaici e gli affeschi ecclesiastico-politici nell'antico Palazzo Lateranense", in *Rivista di Archeologia Cristiana,* XII, 1935, p. 265-92.

16. Fecit autem et in patriarcho Lateranense triclinium maiorem super omnes triclineos nomine suo mire magnitudinis decoratum, ponens in eo fundamenta firmissima et in circuitu lamminis marmoreis ornavit, atque marmoribus in exemplis stravit et diversis columnis (...).

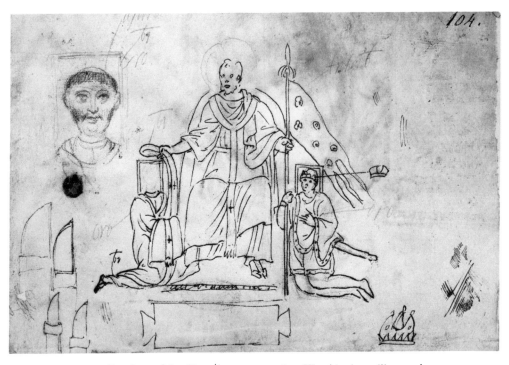

FIG. 1. — Saint Peter invests pope Leo III with the pallium and the emperor Charlemagne with the vexillum. Triclinium of Leo III. (Drawing executed for Panvinius.)

FIG. 2. — Mission of the Apostles. Triclinium of Leo III. (Grimaldi.)

FIG. 3. — Apotheosis of the victorious popes Fresco, Saint Nicholas' Chapel. (Copy made for pope Benedict XIV.)

to the Gentiles; in the other the subject of the scenes is not indicated. The first triclinium abutted directly upon the Constantinian basilica; it is the second, therefore, which is described by Panvinius [17]. He tells us that Saint Peter was represented there enthroned. On his left was Charlemagne with the vexillum and on his right Leo III with the pallium (Fig. 1).

Since Panvinius was particularly concerned with portraits of popes, he only had this scene copied. However the apse mosaic still existed in part at the beginning of the seventeenth century, and was copied and described by Grimaldi [18] (Fig. 2). The Saviour stood on a hill, from which flowed the four rivers of Paradise. He blessed with his right hand and held an open book in his left hand. He was accompanied by the apostles. The nearest on his right was represented as elderly and holding a long cross. No other held an instrument of martyrdom. Below the mosaic were remains of an inscription: *Euntes, docete omnes...* Grimaldi drew up this description in 1617 and 1621. He adds a description of the mosaic of Peter with Charlemagne and Leo III, which was to the left (spectator's right) of the apse. As to the scene on the right Grimaldi says: "*In triangulo dextro apsidae erat imago sancti Pauli apostoli, sed corruit et murus totus est rusticus.*"

In 1625 the mosaic was restored on the initiative of Cardinal Francis Barberini. He not only did this, but replaced the lost mosaic, relying on an earlier copy which '*non sine divino nutu, post diuturnam indagationem nactus est*' [19].

Cardinal Barberini's "reconstruction" after an earlier copy was retained in the final restoration of the mosaics of Leo III's triclinium by Benedict XIV (1740-1758) [20]. A group similar to that of Peter, Leo III and Charlemagne was placed in a corresponding position on the other side of the apse; one may still see it today. This time, however, it is Christ who bestows from his throne the vexillum on Constantine and the keys upon Silvester.

Such, at least, is what Alemanni says. His identification of the kneeling pope was accepted by Lauer [21], and subsequently by Schramm and by Ladner [22]. However an alternative identification of this person was proposed by Heldmann: the figure should be Peter and not Silvester [23]. Professor Deér has strongly supported this identification, although he is less

---

Et camera cum absida de musibo seu alias II absidas diversas storias pingens super marmorum constructione pariter in circuito decoravit (*Liber Pontificalis*, edited L. DUCHESNE, Paris, 1955, II, p. 3-4). Itemque fuit in patriarchio Lateranense triclinium mire magnitudinis decoratum cum absida de musibo, seu et alias absidas decem dextra levaque, diversis storiis depictas apostolos gentibus praedicantes, coherentes basilicae Constantinianae (*ibid.*, p. 11). Cf. *ibid.*, notes 14, 52 and 53.

17. Aula magna cum tribus tribunis quam a Leone III conditore Leonianam aulam veteres vocabant (...). Superest adhuc vetustum e musivo emblema circum absidam tribunae, in postico aulae, in quo sanctus Petrus sedens pictus est, qui Carolo Magno Imperatori laeva vexillum, Leoni vero Papae III dextra pallium ante se genuflexis porrigit, cum hisce inscriptionibus... Text cited by Eugène MÜNTZ in his excellent article "Notes sur les mosaïques chrétiennes de l'Italie, VIII, Le triclinium du Latran — Charlemagne et Léon III" (*Revue archéologique*, 1884, p. 1-15). The article represents an extremely valuable research. Its main conclusions are perhaps more accessible in H. LECLERCQ's article "Charlemagne", in *Dictionnaire d'archéologie et de liturgie chrétienne*, III, 663.

18. In curvatura ipsius apsidis in medio est Salvator mundi, stans supra montem, unde quattuor Paradisi flumina emanant, benedicens dextra, pollice cum annulari

conjuncto, et sinistra tenens librum apertum, indutus colore castaneo, cum apostolis (...). Salvatoris dextrae proximior, in senili aetate, longam gestat crucem et nullus alius aliquod martyris instrumentum gerit. Supra caput Salvatris extat signum Leonis papae tertiae (...). In zophoro apsidis Euntes, docete omnes (...). In triangulo ·sinistro apsidae extat imago musivea Petri in throno sedentis (...). In triangulo dextro apsidae erat imago sancti Pauli apostoli, sed corruit et murus totus est rusticus (Quoted by MÜNTZ in *art. cit.*, note 17, p. 7; cf. *art. cit.* by LECLERCQ, note 17, 664).

19. ALEMANNI, *De Lateranensibus parietinis*, Rome, 1625, p. 36-7, quoted by MÜNTZ, *art. cit.*, note 17, p. 11.

20. MÜNTZ, *art. cit.*, note 17, p. 12.

21. Ph. LAUER, *op. cit.*, note 14, p. 105-119.

22. P.E. SCHRAMM, "Das Herrscherbild in der Kunst des frühen Mittelalters", in *Vorträge der Bibliothek Warburg*, I, 1924, p. 162; *Idem, Die Zeitgenössischen Bildnisse Karls des Grossen, Beiträge zur Kulturgeschichte*, 29, Leipzig/Berlin, 1928, p. 4-16; *Idem, Die deutschen Kaiser und Könige in Bildern ihrer Zeit*, Leipzig/Berlin, 1928, p. 27-8 und fig. 4 a-m; G. LADNER, *art. cit.* (note 15), p. 267.

23. K. HELDMANN, *Das Kaisertum Karls des Grossen*, Weimar, 1928, p. 184. LADNER later round came to this view, cf. *op. cit.*, note 31, p. 118-21.

certain that the object presented to Constantine was a vexillum [24]. It now seems that opinion generally inclines in favour of this person being Peter [25].

However none of these authors attempt to refute Müntz's theory that this subject was in fact never represented in Leo III's triclinium, although Schramm does indeed refer the reader to the article by Müntz which I have already quoted [26].

To my mind Müntz's scepticism is entirely justified. He points out that the distinguished Prefect of the Vatican Library, Giuseppe Simonio Assemani, had already expressed doubts as to the authenticity of the earlier copy of the lost mosaic, upon which Cardinal Barberini's reconstruction was based. The copy was, according to Alemanni, deposited in the Vatican Library; yet it has never been found again. Besides this negative argument from the absence of any evidence for the authenticity of the subject of the mosaic, there is also a positive argument. Grimaldi, a reliable antiquarian, reported a tradition that a subject embodying Saint Paul had in fact been represented there [27]. Such a subject would enter more aptly into the iconographical structure of the decorative scheme than that chosen by Cardinal Barberini, whether the kneeling Pope be Peter or Silvester. I shall return to this point later.

2. The Chapel of Saint Nicolas.

According to the *Liber Pontificalis* pope Callixtus II (1119-1124) built and decorated a chapel dedicated to Saint Nicholas at the Lateran [28]. The first testimony to these pictures is given by Peter Sabino [29]. Panvinius describes the chapel and its decoration [30]. According to him there were represented in the apse of the chapel all the popes from Alexander II (1061-1073) up to the time of Callixtus II; that is to say, besides Alexander II, Gregory VII (1073-1085), Victor III (1086-7), Urban II (1088-99), Paschal II (1099-1118), and Gelasius II (1118-9). To these were added two former popes, Leo the Great (440-61) and Gregory the Great (590-604) and Callixtus II himself at the feet of the Saviour.

This description may be completed from many sources (Fig. 3), for the paintings were copied, and the chapel only destroyed under Clement XII (1730-40) [31]. At the centre of the

24. J. DEÉR, "Die Vorrechte des Kaisers in Rom", in *Schweizer Beiträge zur allgemeinen Geschichte*, 15, 1957, p. 37. According to Deér, "Für die Deutung der Darstellung auf der Stirnwand links von der Apsiskonche ist der Umstand entscheidend, dass die zur Rechten Christi kniende Figur nur Petrus und nicht Papst Silvester I sein kann, da sie vom Heiland mit den Schlüsseln investiert wird, war bei einem Nachfolger des Apostelfürsten undenkbar, weil jeder ikonographische Tradition widersprechend wäre".

25. Peter CLASSEN, "Karl der Grosse, das Papsttum und Byzanz", in *Karl der Grosse*, I, *Personlichkeit und Geschichte*, edited H. BEUMANN, Düsseldorf, 1965, p. 575, note 181.

26. MÜNTZ, *art. cit.* (note 17), p. 11-12.

27. MÜNTZ, *art. cit.* (note 17), p. 9.

28. *Liber Pontificalis* (cf. note 16), II, p. 323 and Duchesne's note 22, p. 325-6; *ibid.*, p. 378. It is not clear from either text whether the chapel as well as the audience hall were both painted under Callixtus II. However the decorative programmes are certainly complementary.

29. Sabino copied the inscriptions which Duchesne corrects : Sustulit hoc primo templum Calixtus ab imo/ vir celebris late Gallorum nobilitate ; Praesul Anacletus papatus culmine fretus/ hoc opus ornavit variisque modis decoravit (*op. cit.*, note 16, p. 325).

30. Callixtus II (...) aedificavit Oratorium sive aediculam in honorem S. Nicolai episcopi, pulchram et oblongam cum tecto ligneo imbricato, quam etiam totam pinxit, in cuius abside eos omnes Romanos pontifices, qui ante se fuerunt ab Alexandro II deinceps pingi iussit. Hi fuere Alexander II, Gregorius VII, Victor III, Urbanus II, Paschal II, Gelasius II. Item bis adiunxit ex antiquis sanctos Leonem et Gregorium Magnos et seipsum in absidae testudine ad pedes Salvatoris (...). Hanc porro aediculum peculiari Romani pontificis usui ipse condidit (PANVINIUS, *De praecipuis Urbis Romae sanctioribusque basilicis quas septem ecclesias vulgo vocant*, Rome, 1570, p. 173).

31. See particularly, besides LAUER, *op. cit.*, note 14, p. 162 *et seq.* and fig. 62-66, and WILPERT, *op. cit.*, note 14, p. 162 *et seq.* and fig. 43, 46, G. LADNER, *I rittrati dei Papi nell'Antichità e nel Medioevo*, Vatican, 1941, p. 202-213.

(a)

(b)

(c)

FIG. 4. — (a) Pope Alexander (Callixtus) trampling upon the emperor Otto (Henry); (b) pope Alexander (Callixtus) pointing at Burdin in prison (*Codex Toledanus*); (c) Saint Peter trampling upon Simon Magus and the patriarch Nicephorus trampling upon the patriarch Jannis (*Chludov Psalter*).

apse was the Virgin with the Child Jesus, with saints Silvester and Anastasius to their left and right. Besides Callixtus II there was at the feet of the Virgin the antipope Anacletus II (1130-38), who was responsible for completing the decoration[32].

This representation of the apotheosis, as it were, of the popes who triumphed over the emperors and their antipopes in the Investiture struggle offers an evident analogy with the representation of the Iconodule patriarchs in the room at the south west corner of Saint Sophia.

3. The Audience Hall of Callixtus II.

The same texts of the *Liber Pontificalis* attribute to Callixtus II two other rooms near to the Chapel of Saint Nicholas[33]. The paintings in one of these rooms, which was used as an audience hall, attracted far more attention than those in the chapel. There are at least four allusions to them by Medieval writers[34]. Arnulph of Lisieux saw them during the pontificate of Innocent II (1133-43), as did John of Salisbury in 1153. Suger of Saint-Denis also knew them. The significance of these paintings was not lost upon them: the Catholic Fathers of the Church were using schismatics as a footstool. Suger of Saint-Denis even says specifically that Callixtus II was trampling upon Burdin.

A further allusion to these pictures, or at least to one of them, occurs in an account of an incident at the Fourth Lateran Council in the *Codex Toledanus*[35]. Rodrigo, archbishop of Toledo, had launched a complaint against the archbishops of Braga, Compostella, Tarragona and Narbonne for refusing to acknowledge the primacy of his see. He evoked the

---

32. This transpires from Duchesne's restoration of the inscription, *vid. sup.,* note 29.

33. *Vid. sup.,* note 28.

34. "Porro schismata haec in ecclesia Romana frequentius accidisse etiam Lateranensis palatii picturae demonstrant, ubi catholicorum patrum pedibus pro scabello schismatici praesumptores adscripti sunt, ubi superborum et sublimium colla sapientia propria virtute conterit et conculcat. Quod sane ea ratione factum est, ut sanctis patribus cedat ad gloriam victoriae testis ascriptio, in qua praesumptores illi vel compressionis poenam sustinent vel praesumptionis veniam deprecantur. Unde et sancti Apostolatus vestri cathedra sine scabello esse non debuit, sed nobiliore scabello debuit illustrari. Neque enim incerta vobis est aut longinqua victoria" (Arnulf of LISIEUX, *Letter* 21, *Patres Ecclesiae Anglicanae,* ed. J.A. GILES, Oxford, 1844, I, p. 109 *et seq.*; PL 201, 34-6). Arnulf of Lisieux had been in Rome during the struggle between Innocent II and the antipope Anacletus II. This letter is addressed to pope Alexander III, who at the time was engaged in a struggle with the antipope Victor IV. He expresses his hope that Victor IV may soon serve Alexander III as a *scabellum,* as the antipopes depicted at the Lateran had served his predecessors. "Quis Teutonicos constituit judices nationum? Quis hanc brutis et impetuosis hominibus auctoritatem contulit, ut pro arbitrio principem statuant super capita filiorum hominum? (...) (Teutonicus) id enim agebat, ut in quemcumque denuntiatis inimicitiis materialem gladium imperator, in eundem Romanus pontifex spiritualem gladium exereret. Non invenit adhuc qui

tantae consentiret iniquitati, ipsoque repugnante Moyse, id est contradicente lege Domini, Balsamitam sibi ascivit pontificem per quem malediceret populo Domini (...) Sid ad gloriam patrum teste Lateranensi Palatio, ubi hoc in visibilibus picturis et laici legunt; ad gloriam patrum schismatici quos saecularis potestas intrusit, dantur pontificibus pro scabello et eorum memoriam recolunt pro triumpho" (John of SALISBURY, *Letter* 59, PL 199, 39). The context of this letter is the support given by Frederick I to the same antipope Victor IV. "Romani... intrusum ab Imperatore schismaticum Burdinum... imperante domino Papa Calixto perpetuo carcere... captivatum damnaverunt et ad tante ultionis conservationem in camera palatii sub pedibus domini papae conculcatum depinxerunt" (Suger of SAINT-DENIS, *Vie de Louis le Gros,* edited Auguste MOLINIER, *Collection de textes pour servir à l'étude de l'histoire,* IV, Paris, 1887, p. 95). In Otto of Freising's *Chronicle* there are allusions only to the inscriptions: "Unde de ipso in palatio Lateranensi scriptum repperi 'Regnat Alexander, Kadolus cadit et superatur'; unde de ipso Romae scriptum est 'Ecce Kalixtus, honor patriam decus imperiale, Burdinum nequem dampnat, pacemque reformat' *Scriptores rerum germanicarum,* XLV, *Monumenta Germaniae Historica,* edited A. HOFMEISTER, Hanover, 1912, p. 303 and p. 332.

35. The *Codex Toledanus (Matritensis vitr.* 15-3) was compiled in 1252 and 1253 (Raymonde FOREVILLE, *Latran I, II, III et Latran IV,* Paris, 1965, p. 264; *Idem,* "L'iconographie du XIIe concile œcuménique", in *Mélanges René Crozet,* II, Poitiers, 1966, p. 1125-6 and fig. 3).

personality of a former archbishop of Braga, Maurice Burdin, who under the patronage of the emperor Henry V (1098-1125) became the antipope Gregory VIII (1118-1121). After recalling his history and ultimate downfall, he implied that the case was the same for the present archbishop of Braga. The session was taking place in Callixtus II's audience hall, so that it was possible for Rodrigo then to point dramatically at the picture on the wall of Burdin's downfall and finish with the words: *"Si quis astantium hac de re dubitat, tollat oculos ad praesentis hujus loci parietes, et videbit hujusmodi historiam picturatam."* [36]

The passage in the *Codex Toledanus* gains in interest from the fact that in the margin there are two drawings, one of Alexander (an error for Callixtus) trampling upon the emperor Otto (an error for Henry V), and the other of Burdin in prison, with his mitre and crozier reversed, while Alexander (again an error for Callixtus) points at him. Could these drawings be very free copies of the original paintings? It seems unlikely, for there is no allusion in the texts to a representation of a pope actually trampling an emperor; the conquered enemy is rather the antipope. Further, although Suger refers in his account to the imprisonment of Burdin, he does not specifically say that there existed a picture of Burdin in prison [37] (Fig. 4). Examination of this manuscript in Madrid in August 1970 revealed to me the distressingly poor quality of the photograph. Burdinus is chained by the neck and the wrists. Besides the upturned mitre and crozier to the left there is also an upturned bonnet to the right; it is coloured red and similar to that which the pope above is wearing.

There is also no resemblance between these drawings and those which Panvinius had executed in the sixteenth century. According to Panvinius's account all the more important schisms which had arisen in the cause of establishing the liberty of the Church were recorded: Alexander II with Cadolus of Parma, Gregory VII, Victor II and Urban II with Guibert of Ravenna, and Paschal with three other antipopes. Finally there was the peace which Callixtus made with the emperor Henry V. To this Callixtus added the privilege conceded by the emperor, inscribed on a large plaque. Panvinius adds that the pictures in his time were hardly visible. Under the picture of Alexander II, in which he was portrayed with his cardinals trampling upon Cadolus, there was still legible an inscription [38].

These drawings having already been published in a scholarly and exhaustive manner by Dr. Gerhardt Ladner [39], it will be sufficient here to recapitulate briefly his conclusions.

The four frescoes which Panvinius (Fig. 5, 6, 7, 8) had copied have, with one exception, the same iconography. The pope in question sits on a throne wearing the pallium and a tiara; he holds a book in his left hand and blesses with his right hand. The antipope over

---

36. The account given by MANSI (22, 1073), does not, according to Mlle Foreville (cf. note 35), give an exact transcription of *Matr. vitr.* 15-3, f. 22 *et seq.* Mansi's version continues: "Erigentes autem oculos, omnia ut dixerat, viderunt, et domini Toletani subtilitatem et peritiam collaudentes, coeperunt tum admurmurare, tum etiam in domini Bracerensis faciem intendere, quae magno jam erat rubore perfusa."

37. Cf. note 34.

38. "Iuxta quam idem Pontifex duo coniuncta conclavia sive cubicula, sub quibus vestiarum, id est gardarobam, addidit, construxit. Cubiculorum vero unum iconiis picturis exornavit quod audientiae addixit et rebus publicis tractandis. In quo superiora omnia schismata, quae ecclesiasticae libertatis asserendae causa exorta fuerant, annotavit: ut Alexandri II cum Cadolo Parmense, Gregorii VII, Victoris III, Urbani II cum Ghiberto Ravennate et Paschalis cum tribus adulterinis aliis pontificibus. Postremo pacem qua ipse cum Henrico V Imperatore; eiusque imperatoris privilegium in tabula magna descriptum adiunxit: quae adhuc vetustate exolentia pene cerne possunt. Sub Alexandri itaque II tabula, in qua ipse pictus est cum cardinalibus pedibus Cadolum conculcant, sunt hujusmodi versus (...). Privilegii porro Henrici V a Calisto II concessi quod adhuc (quamquam exolescens muro pictum cernitur, exemplum sequens est: Ego Henricus... (investiture with *annulus, baculus,* etc. conceded) Callistus episcopus... (election in the emperor's presence conceded). Haec omnia in priori cubiculo annotata sunt. Alterum vero cubiculum huic proximum et variis picturis ornatum particularibus Pontificum usibus Callixtus Papa addixit, quod adhuc semifractum et sine tecto superest (PANVINIUS, *op. cit.* (note 30), p. 174-6).

39. *Art. cit.* (note 15).

FIG. 5. — Pope Alexander II with the antipope Cadolus as *scabellum*. Audience Hall of Callixtus II. (Drawing executed for Panvinius.)

FIG. 6. — Popes Gregory VII, Victor III and Urban II with an antipope as *scabellum*. Audience Hall of Callixtus II. (Drawing executed for Panvinius.)

FIG. 8. — Pope Callixtus II with Burdin as *scabellum* holding jointly with the emperor Henry V the text of the Concordat of Worms. Audience Hall of Callixtus II. (Drawing executed for Panvinius.)

FIG. 7. — Pope Paschal II with an antipope as *scabellum*. Audience Hall of Callixtus II. (Drawing executed for Panvinius.)

FIG. 9. — Pope Alexander II. Audience Hall of Callixtus II.
(Drawing executed for Panvinius by another hand.)

whom he has triumphed crouches at his feet. To left and right of the pope stand bishops in mitres and holding croziers. In the background stand other figures holding processional crosses.

This description applies exactly to the picture of Alexander II triumphing over Cadolus (f. 105 v) and to Paschal II (f. 105 v). The copy of the triumph of Gregory VII shows another figure, apparently standing, in a papal tiara to Gregory's left. If, in fact, as Panvinius says, this fresco represented together Gregory VII, Victor III and Urban II, then presumably the figure to Gregory's right would also have been enthroned and wearing a tiara. It is likely that the frescoes were already in too poor a condition in Panvinius's time for the details to be clear.

The picture of Callixtus II's triumph (f. 104) is rather different, because, while Burdin is under his feet, Callixtus sits to the left of the members of his retinue. On his right stands the emperor Henry V, wearing a short tunic, a mantle and a crown and holding in his left hand an indeterminate object. Between the pope and the emperor is an unrolled document, which the pope holds with his left hand and the emperor with his right. In the drawing half a dozen lines of text are indicated on the document by dots. This document is the Concordat of Worms; possibly it is the *tabula magna,* to which Panvinius refers, upon which the *imperatoris privilegium* was inscribed, but it seems more likely that only the beginning of the text would have been inscribed on the document in the picture, and that the *tabula magna* would have been elsewhere in the Audience Hall [40].

A drawing by another hand in Panvinius's sketch book (f. 103 v) (Fig. 9) shows that the frescoes were framed by an arcade with a rosette over each column. Ladner argues that this is authentic by pointing to the analogy of the frescoes of Saint Alexis in the church of San Clemente, executed between 1080 and 1090, and framed with similar arcades and rosettes [41].

The frescoes were accompanied by inscriptions: *"Regnat Alexander Cadolus cadit et*

40. *Vid. sup.,* note 38.
41. *Art. cit.* (note 15), p. 277.

superatur / ... nihilatur." "Gregorius Victor Urbanus cathedram tenuerunt / Gibertus cum suis tandem destructi fuerunt." "Ecclesiae decus Paschalis papa secundus / Albertum damnat Mahinulfum Theodoricum." "Ecce Calixtus honor patriae decus imperiale / Burdinum nequam damnat pacemque reformat."

We find, therefore, in these pictures two major iconographical themes: one is triumph over a vanquished enemy, the other the proclamation of a concordat.

3. The Coronation of Lotharius III.

According to the *Liber Pontificalis* Innocent II (1130-1143) built two new rooms at the Lateran [42]. In one of these rooms Innocent II had painted a series of scenes concerning the coronation of Lotharius III(Fig. 10) in 1133. They were accompanied by an inscription: *"Rex stetit* (or *venit) ante fores, iurans prius Urbis honores; / Post* (or *sic) homo fit papae sumit quo dante coronam."* [43] The pictures with their inscription were to be the occasion of misunderstanding between Frederick I and Hadrian IV (1154-59). On the first occasion in 1155 Frederick, who had come to Rome to be crowned, made a *proskynesis* before Hadrian IV and kissed his foot. However he refused to render to the pope the service of *marescalchus* — the *officium stratoris et strepae,* and consequently the pope was unwilling to give him the ceremonial kiss, for he had refused to make an act of veneration to Saints Peter and Paul [44].

An account of this incident is given by Boso in the *Liber Pontificalis,* and it is corroborated by Gerhoh von Reichersberg, who explains the reluctance of Frederick to perform this office. He was aware of the fact that, according to the text of the *Constitutum Constantini,* the emperor Constantine had performed this office for pope Silvester. But it had never been maintained, whether in words or pictures, that Constantine was Silvester's *marescalchus.* He was therefore somewhat astonished that such a picture should now exist of an emperor of the Romans. The allusion would seem to be to a picture of Lotharius as Innocent's *marescalchus* and to the inscription: *"Homo fit papae".* However, when it was explained to Frederick that the office in question was an antique custom which in no way implied that the emperor was the pope's man, he performed it joyfully [45].

42. *Liber Pontificalis* (cf. note 16), p. 384 and Duchesne's note 5. "In palatio Lateranensi duas cameras a fundamento construxit."

43. The versions of this inscription vary slightly; cf. LADNER, *art. cit.* (note 15), p. 281.

44. Eduard EICHMANN, "Das Officium Stratoris et Strepae", in *Historische Zeitschrift,* 142, 1930, p. 32. This article criticizes certain positions taken up by R. HOLTZMANN in his study *Der Kaiser als Marschall des Papstes, Eine Untersuchung zur Geschichte der Beziehungen zwischen Kaiser und Papst in Mittelalter,* Heidelberg, 1928. Holtzmann replied to these criticisms in an article "Zum Strator- und Marschalldienst", in the same review, 145, 1932, p. 301-50. The chief point of issue seems to be whether the service of *mareschalcus* differs from that of *strator.* Holtzmann maintains that it did, that it implied a feudal commendation, and that it is to be connected with the addition of the *officium strepae,* to the *officium stratoris,* the Zügel- und Bügeldienst.

45. "Beatus papa Silvester ab augusto Constantino regalis magnificentiae honoribus preditus non se honorantem inhonoravit et quamvis ei pro sui humilitate semel stratoris officium exhibuerit, non tamen eum suum esse mareschalcum vel dixit vel scripsit vel pinxit. Sed et multi post ipsum catholici leguntur imperatores monarchiam tenentes fuisse, quorum quis fuerit marescalchus dictus domni papae non invenimus. Immo certum tenemus, quod Romani pontifices et imperatores invicem se honore prevenientes pacifice vixerunt (...). Valde miramur unde nova pictura haec emerserit, qua Romanorum imperator pingitur marescalchus." GERHOH von Reichersberg, *De quarta vigilia noctis,* 12, in *Libelli de lite imperatorum et pontificum saeculis XI et XII conscripti,* III, *Monumenta Germaniae Historica,* Hanover, 1897 (photographic reprint, 1956), p. 511. "Rex Fredericus precessit aliquantulum, et appropinquante domni pape tentorio per aliam viam transiens descendit de equo, et (...) in conspectu exercitus officium stratoris cum iocunditate implevit et streuguam fortiter tenuit" (*Liber Pontificalis,* cf. note 16, II, p. 391-2).

Two years later in 1157 there was a further clash between the emperor and the pope's legates at Besançon [46]. Issue was taken over the use of the word *beneficia* in a brief of Hadrian IV, which was given by the emperor a feudal interpretation as if, by conferring benefices rather than benefits, the pope was again implying that the emperor was his man. The issue of offensive pictures was again raised but this time in a slightly different form, for, according to the description, what moved Frederick to anger was that Lotharius should be represented inclined before the seated pope in order to receive the imperial crown.

This description does not agree exactly with that of Panvinius, nor with his drawing [47]. For in each case there is a series of scenes. Lotharius is first shown at the entrance to the Lateran basilica, swearing an oath that he will maintain the privileges of the Romans; then he is shown inclined before the seated pope who embraces him; finally he is crowned at the altar by the pope who is standing. Further there is no allusion to or representation of the emperor as the pope's *marescalchus*.

I do not propose to discuss these frescoes here, but in a later study in relation to Byzantine coronation scenes. However I should like to raise again the question already put by Ladner whether a picture of Lotharius as *marescalchus* ever in fact existed. Ladner refers to an engraving of Rasponi's where Lotharius is shown on horseback approaching the gates of the city of Rome, from which the pope emerges, his arms outstretched [48]. He compares Innocent's gesture in this engraving with that which he makes in Panvinius's drawing. Rasponi's reconstructions tend to be fanciful. Ladner therefore supposes that Rasponi's picture derives from the accolade scene as Panvinius has transmitted it. However Rasponi's picture (Fig. 11) has in common with a scene of a *marescalchus* performing his office only the presence of a figure on horseback. For the rest it corresponds so exactly to the antique iconography of an *Adventus* that it must have had such a scene for its principal model [49].

These are added reasons for agreeing with Ladner that there is no direct archaeological evidence that a *marescalchus* scene ever existed. However the indirect evidence furnished by Gerhoh von Reichersberg seems too explicit to be set aside. Such a picture must, to my mind, have existed, and presumably it was destroyed, together with the offensive inscription, possibly between 1155 and 1157, since no allusion was made to either at Besançon. After the second disagreement the pope presumably considered it sufficient to explain that he had

46. "Eodem tempore inter domnum apostolicum Adrianum atque imperatorem Fridericum graves controversiae oriri ceperunt quae huiusmodi causam habuisse feruntur. Papa Innocentius, eius nominis secundus, Rome quondam in muro pingi fecerat se ipsum quasi in sede pontificali residentem, imperatorem vero Lotharium complicatis manibus ciram se inclinatum, coronam imperii suscipientem (...). Fuit et aliud incentivum et fomes discordiae (...). Affuerunt ex parte papae duo cardinales litteras apostolicae ad eum deferentes, in quibus inter alia hoc continebatur: 'beneficium coronae tibi contilimus...' Hoc verbum feodo interpres cesari interpretatus est" (*Chronica regia coloniensis, Scriptores rerum germanicarum*, XVIII, *Monumenta Germaniae Historica*, 1880, p. 93). The text of the letter is given by Otto of Freising (*Gesta Friderici Imperatoris*, III. 9, *Scriptores rerum germanicarum*, XX, *Monumenta Germaniae Historica*, Hanover, 1868, Leipzig, 1925, p. 420-421). Cf. R. FOREVILLE, *op. cit.*, note 35, p. 111-3.

47. "Innocentius II Papa in penitiori parte Lateranensis patriarchii duo alia cubicula a fundamentis fecit,

retro aediculam S. Nicolai, ea parte quae frontem basilicae Lateranensis respicit (haec adhuc semirupta supersunt) quae variis picturis ornavit, in quorum uno coronationem Lotharii Imperatoris ab se in basilica Lateranensis consecrato pinxit. In cuius tabulae prima parte pictus est Rex qui ante portas basilicae Lateranensis iurat Romanis se conservaturum consuetudines suas; post a Papa suscipitur, amplectiturque, deinde coronatur. Cui picturae hi versus suppositi fuerunt..." (PANVINIUS, *op. cit.*, note 30, p. 177).

48. RASPONI, *De Basilica et Patriarcho Lateranensi*, Rome, 1656, p. 293 ; cf. LADNER, *art. cit.*, note 15, fig. 11. Rasponi commissioned drawings of all these frescoes during the pontificate of Alexander VII (1655-67); they are to be found in *Vaticanus barberinus lat.* 4423. Long before Panvinius's drawings were rediscovered, Duchesne had rejected Rasponi's as fanciful.

49. Cf. for example the *Adventus* of Constantius Chlorus represented on a coin of his reign (305-6) in the British Museum, London, and reproduced by A. GRABAR (*Christian Iconography*, Princeton, 1968, fig. 124).

FIG. 10. — Coronation of Lotharius III. Room built for pope Innocent II at the Lateran.
(Drawing executed for Panvinius.)

FIG. 11. — Coronation of Lotharius III.
Room built for pope Innocent II.
(Drawing executed for Rasponi.)

FIG. 12. — Donation of Constantine. Portico of the
Lateran Basilica. (Painting in *Barberinus latinus* 4423,
f. 14.)

not used the word *beneficia* in a feudal sense; he certainly did not destroy the remaining pictures.

The presence of such a scene in a coronation series can be easily explained, for, according to the *Liber Censuum,* it was part of the coronation ceremony that the emperor should hold the stirrup of the pope's horse in the coronation procession from Saint Peter's to the Lateran[50]. In fact when Lotharius met Innocent at Lüttlich in 1131 he performed this service for him[51].

The significance of this ceremony could be ambiguous. The *strator* led the horse by the reins, while the *officium strepae* involved rather holding the stirrup, once this came into general use, and helping the rider to mount and dismount. But in Saxon law the *officium strepae* was, it would seem, the obligation of a vassal towards his lord[52]. It was, presumably, this aspect of the office which made Frederick I refuse to act as Hadrian IV's *marescalchus* at Sutri in 1155, and to resent the implication that he was the pope's man at Besançon in 1157. There are, moreover, indications that the coronation rite was given in Rome at certain times a sense of feudal commendation. For instance under Gregory VII a formula was proposed: "*Per manus meas miles sancti Petri et illius* (sc. *Papae*) *efficiar.*"[53]

But since no copy of this picture of Lotharius as the pope's *marescalchus* is known to us, one may only conjecture how it appeared, starting from the analogous thirteenth century picture of Constantine as Silvester's *marescalchus* in the Chapel of Saint Silvester by the church of the Quattro Coronati.

4. The Donation of Constantine in the Portico of the medieval Lateran Basilica.

In the Middle Ages the front of the Lateran basilica had attached to it an open portico, the architrave of which was divided horizontally into three narrow sections[54]. It may be conceived by analogy with the portico of the Duomo at Civita Castellana, the work of Iacopo di Lorenzo and Cosma and finished in 1210. The architrave was decorated with mosaics, already largely lost by Ciampini's time. They are known from Ciampini's engravings and from a series of water colour copies in the *Vaticanus barberinus lat.* 4423[55]. Among the scenes represented were not only ones figuring the persecutions of the saints, such as Saint John the Evangelist being tortured and boiled in oil and the martyrdom of Saint John the Baptist, but also more properly historical ones, such as the Roman fleet under Vespasian on its way to Palestine and Jerusalem besieged by Titus. To these were added scenes from the biography of Silvester: Silvester triumphing over a dragon, baptizing Constantine and

50. "Cum dominus papa venerit ad equum, Imperator teneat stapham et coronetur et intret in processionem (...). Cumpe pervenerint ad ascensorium (...). Imperator descendit, et tenet stapham domino papa descendente, deposita prius corona" (*Ordo coronationis,* in *Le Liber Censuum de l'Église romaine,* edited Paul FABRE, I, Paris, 1905, p. 6*). According to Fabre (*op. cit.,* p. 1*, n. 1) this is the most ancient *ordo coronationis* in its complete form; he supposes it to have been composed either for the coronation of Henry III (1046) or for that of Henry VI (1191); he inclines to the earlier date.
51. EICHMANN, *art. cit.,* note 44, p. 22.
52. *Idem,* p. 18; he cites the *Sachsenspiegel, Lehenrecht,* art. 66, para. 5.
53. *Idem,* p. 23.

54. A.L. FROTHINGHAM, "Notes on Christian Mosaics, II, The Portico of the Lateran Basilica," in *American Journal of Archaeology,* II, 1886, p. 414-23. He attributes the mosaics to the pontificate of Alexander III (1159-81); LAUER, *op. cit.,* note 14, p. 184, suggests rather the pontificate of Clement III (1187-91). WILPERT, *op. cit.,* note 14, I, p. 210, prefers Frothingham's attribution.
55. CIAMPINI records the inscription which accompanied the mosaic of the Donation of Constantine: Rex in scriptura Sylvestro dat jura sua. His engraving of this subject is reproduced by LAUER, *op. cit.,* note 14, fig. 71, along with the water colour in *Vat. barb. lat.* 4423, f. 14 (fig. 72). Cf. CIAMPINI, *De Sacris Aedificiis a Constantino Magno constructis,* Rome, 1693.

receiving the Donation (Fig. 12). The presence of historical scenes is worth stressing, for it brings them into line with the decoration of the Byzantine palaces. The theme of the trials and struggles of the Church before its triumph under Constantine is analogous to that of the feats performed by emperors before attaining the throne.

On the left of the copy in the Barberini manuscript may be seen a schematic representation of the Lateran basilica. Only the doorway and the campanile correspond to the Lateran basilica in Panvinius's drawing of the coronation of Lotharius III. In Panvinius's drawing, however, we probably see the open portico of the basilica, before which pope Innocent II enthroned is embracing Lotharius. In the copy of the Lateran mosaic pope Silvester, with halo, tiara and pallium, is enthroned to the right of the basilica. With his right hand he blesses; with his left he receives the document, which is presented to him by Constantine. The emperor wears a short tunic and mantle; he has no halo. Beside him stands a courtier. The concave extremities of the mosaic suggest that between each scene there was a round panel of marble. These mosaics must, then, have been unusually small, and have taken the place in normal Cosmatesque decoration, such as that on the architrave of the cloister at San Paolo fuori le Mura, of other marble panels.

III. ANALYSIS OF THE ICONOGRAPHY

1. The Triclinium of Leo III: Mission and Investiture.

As an instrument of propaganda the two triclinia which Leo III built at the Lateran are as significant as the basilica built by Constantine four centuries earlier. By making it his responsibility to provide suitable meeting places for the Christian assembly Constantine proclaimed that Christianity was the official religion of the Empire [56]. By building two triclinia on a princely scale Leo III proclaimed the independence of the Papacy with regard both to the Byzantine emperors and to the Frankish kings. It was necessary that the decorative programmes of these basilicas should underline the notion implicit in their architecture.

The independence of the Papacy could be conceived in both temporal and spiritual terms. The popes based their claims to primacy in spiritual matters upon the apostolic origin of the see of Rome. This notion is, of course, explicit in the writings of Gelasius. For example in a letter to the bishops of Dardania Gelasius claims the right of the Roman see to execute the decisions of general councils 'because of its principate, which Blessed Peter the Apostle obtained through the word of the Lord and which it has always retained and continues to retain' [57].

It was, however, quite alien to the spirit of the times for a claim to temporal authority for the pope to be based upon the fact that he was the successor of Peter. In fact it was axiomatic that temporal authority passed with the *imperium,* so that, if a pope was to exert political power, this must be delegated to him by the emperor.

In the difficult circumstances of the eighth century there could, in fact, be no question of the popes enjoying a genuine political independence. They needed a protector. In fact

---

56. R. KRAUTHEIMER, "The Constantinian Basilica", in *Dumbarton Oaks Papers,* 21, 1968, especially p. 127-30.
57. GELASIUS, *Letter* 13 to the bishops of Dardania,

PL 59, 63; cf. F. DVORNIK, *The Idea of Apostolicity in Byzantium,* Harvard, 1958, p. 117 and *Idem, Early Christian and Byzantine Political Philosophy,* Washington, 1966, p. 804 *et seq.*

from the time that the emperor was Christian there fell upon him the office of protector of the Church against its enemies. This office was the subject of the mosaic of Constantine triumphing over the enemies of Christendom at the entrance to the Imperial Palace at Constantinople.

The memory of Constantine was evoked from time to time in the West during the eighth century. Pope Hadrian I (772-95) addressed a letter to Charlemagne in May 778, inviting him to be a new Constantine and to conquer back for the Papacy the territory which the most pious emperor had bestowed upon it [58]. Charlemagne did not repudiate the comparison, for in 794 he was using a copy of Constantine's portrait on his seal and coinage [59]. But, more important than this, there existed legends and traditions which gave an explicit account of Constantine's delegations to the Papacy of privileges and authority. It seems that there is in Hadrian I's letter to Charlemagne an explicit reference to the document known as the *Constitutum Constantini*. It is to this and to the *Legend of Saint Silvester* that one must turn particularly for the ideas current in the eighth century of the spiritual and temporal status of the see of Rome. Moreover, directly or indirectly, the positions stated in the *Constitutum* are an issue in many subsequent controversies on the authority of the Papacy. For this reason also it is worth recapitulating the contents of these documents.

The *Legend of Saint Silvester* contains two parts, a prologue and a second book recounting the deeds of Silvester and Constantine [60]. The second book and the latter part of the prologue are taken up with controversies with the Jews. The prologue begins with an account of the childhood of Silvester, of his succession to pope Melchiades and his flight to a cave in Mount Soracte when the edict was published that all Christians must sacrifice to idols. Interest then passes to Constantine, his leprosy, the proposed cure by a bath in the blood of infants and the vision of Saints Peter and Paul. Constantine seeks out Silvester, recognizes their portraits on an ikon and asks for baptism. After performing penance, avowing belief in Christ the Son of God and promising to suppress the cult of idols, Constantine receives Baptism. While he is in the font there is a sensational theophany; Constantine leaves the font cured of his leprosy.

During the succeeding days Constantine confers various privileges upon the Christian Church, among which was the jurisdiction of the Roman Church. Finally, at the end of seven days, he takes off the white robe of a neophyte, and makes a solemn visit to the tomb of Saint Peter. He provides for churches to be built there and in the Lateran Palace.

58. *Codex Carolinus*, 60, *Epistolae Merowingici et Karolini Aevi*, I (= *Epistolarum Tomus* III), *Monumenta Germaniae Historica*, Berlin, 1957 (second photographic edition), p. 587: 'Et sicut temporibus beati Silvestri Romani pontificis a sanctae recordationis piissimo Constantino Magno imperatore per ejus largitatem sancta Dei catholica et apostolica Romana ecclesia elevata atque exaltata est et potestatem in his Hesperiae partibus largiri dignatus, ita et in his vestris felicissimis temporibus atque nostris id est beati Petri apostoli (...) amplius quam amplius permaneat, ut omnes gentes quae haec audierint edicere valeant: "Domine salvum fac regem et exaudi nos in die qua invocaverimus te; quia ecce novus christianissimus Dei Constantinus imperator his temporibus surrexit, per quem omnia Deus sanctae ecclesiae apostolorum principis Petri largiri dignatus est".'

59. Egen EWIG, "Das Bild Constantins des Grossen in den ersten Jahrhunderten des abendländischen Mittelalters," in *Historisches Jahrbuch*, 75, 1955, p. 36;

P. GRIERSON, "Money and coinage under Charlemagne," in *Karl der Grosse* (cf. note 25), p. 519 and plates I-IV.

60. For the *Legenda Sancti Silvestri* there is only the text edited by MOMBRITIUS, *Sanctuarium seu vitae Sanctorum*, Milan, 1480, republished by the monks of Solesmes, Paris, 1910 (second edition), II, p. 508-31. Cf., however, the critical observations of W. LEVISON, "Konstantinische Schenkung und Silvesterlegende," in *Studi e testi*, 38, 1924 (= *Miscellanea Fr. Ehrle*, II), p. 159 *et seq.* A Greek version, not earlier than the XIth century and omitting many details of the privileges conferred by Constantine upon Silvester, has been published in *Roma e l'Oriente*, VI, 1913, p. 332-67 ("Il testo greco del Βίος di S. Silvestro attribuito al Metafraste"); cf. also the article by P. SCHASKOLSKY, "La leggenda di Costantino il Grande e di Papa Silvestro," *ibid.*, p. 12-25, and the useful note by E. KITZINGER, in *Dumbarton Oaks Papers*, 21, 1968, p. 246, note 11 ("A Cross of Michael Cerularius").

The *Legend* only mentions the spiritual privileges which Constantine was reputed to have conferred upon the Church of Rome, and these are evidently related to the intervention of Saints Peter and Paul. The general theme of the *Legend* is, therefore, the recognition by Constantine of the spiritual status of the Roman see as derived from its holder's claim to be the successor of Peter, Further, although Silvester exercises an important role in the Legend, it is a secondary one.

At first sight the *Constitutum* has the appearance of merely presenting under the form of a decree a more developed version of the passages of the *Legend* concerning the privileges conferred by Constantine upon the Roman see [61]. This is, indeed, partly the case. There is the same emphasis on the role of Saints Peter and Paul, supported by quotation of the Petrine text (*Matthew* 16). The superiority of Rome to the four other patriarchal sees is explicitly stated. The clerical orders are assimilated to court orders, and the right of Silvester and his successors to legislate for the clergy is recognized. But the *Constitutum* differs from the *Legend* in the important respect that it also confers temporal power on the Pope. Thus not only does Constantine build a basilica at the Lateran but the imperial palace becomes the papal residence; the Pope's status is assimilated to that of the Emperor, with the right to wear besides the crown the *superhumerale* (pallium) and '*omnia imperialia indumenta*'. Constantine crowns Silvester himself (with the *frigium,* since the crown was too rich for the fisherman's successor), and performs the service of *strator.* Finally — and this is the most important difference between the *Legend* and the *Constitutum* — Constantine confers the sovereignty of the West upon Silvester and his successors.

The simple procession to the tomb of Saint Peter now becomes a more solemn ceremony. The text of the decree is laid by the emperor on the tomb. The document ends with a solemn warning that anyone who goes against it is going against Saints Peter and Paul.

It is clear, then, that a double theory of the status of the Papacy is expounded in these documents. Its spiritual status is derived from the apostles, and acknowledged and confirmed by the authority of the State. Its temporal status, was conferred by Constantine, out of respect for the apostles, as a free but irrevocable gift. Are these theories of the status of the Papacy manifested in the decorative programmes of Leo III's triclinia?

Of one we know only that it was decorated with various scenes of the apostles preaching to the Gentiles [62]. The other also had as its central motif a scene concerning the apostles. Below the mosaic was the text from *Matthew* 28. 19, conferring on them the mission of making disciples, baptism and instruction (Fig. 2). Leo III's conception of the

---

61. The best edition of the Donation or *Constitutum Constantini* is now that of Horst FUHRMANN, *Constitutum Constantini, Fontes iuris germanici antiqui,* X, *Monumenta Germaniae Historica,* Hanover, 1968; cf. ISIDORE MERCATOR, *Collectio Decretalium, Edictum Domini Constantini Imperatoris,* PL 130, 245-52. Among the many other editions that by Aemilius FRIEDBERG (*Corpus Iuris Canonici,* I, *Decretum Magistri Gratiani, Distinctio* 96, *cap.* 14, Leipzig, 1879, p. 342-5) is useful for its notes. The Greek text may be found in Theodore BALSAMON's *Commentary* on the *Nomocanon* of PHOTIUS (PG 104, 1075-4). He accepts it, apparently, as a genuine document, and uses it elsewhere (*In Can.* III *Concilii Constantinopolitani* II, PG 137, 321) as a model for the privileges and status of Eastern patriarchs. For general accounts of the *Constitutum,* cf. E. AMANN, "Silvestre Ier," in *Dictionnaire de Théologie Catholique,* XIV, 2072-5

and R. CESSI, "Il Costituto di Costantino," in *Enciclopedia Italiana,* XI, 606-7. For monographs, besides C.B. COLEMAN, *Constantine the Great and Christianity,* New York, 1914 and G. LAHR, *Die konstantinische Schenkung,* Berlin, 1926, the principal studies are by H. FUHRMANN, "Konstantinische Schenkung und Silvesterlegende in neuer Sicht," in *Deutsches Archiv für Erforschung des Mittelalters,* 15, 1959, p. 523-40 and by the late Werner OHNSORGE, "Das Constitutum Constantini und seine Entstehung," in *Konstantinopel und der Okzident,* Darmstadt, 1966, p. 93-162. Fuhrmann criticizes Ohnsorge's position in "Konstantinische Schenkung und abendländisches Kaisertum," in *Deutsches Archiv für Erforschung des Mittelalters,* 22, 1966, p. 103-20. R.J.H. JENKINS summarizes Ohnsorge's position in *Dumbarton Oaks Papers,* 21, 1968, p. 237, note 10 ("A Cross of Michael Cerularius").

62. Vid. sup., p. 157.

FIG. 13. — *"Traditio legis."* Sarcophagus. Ravenna.

FIG. 14. — (a) Investiture of an imperial functionary. Plate of Theodosius II, Historical Museum, Madrid; (b) Investiture of Saint Paul. Sarcophagus. Ravenna.

Church's mission is therefore directly derived from that of the apostles; as successor Peter he is responsible for the continuation of the apostolic ministry. The elements of the scene below this text, as described by Grimaldi, are extremely familiar in early Christian art: Christ on a hillock from which the waters of Paradise flow, a book in his hand, while with the other he blesses; the apostles either side of him, one of whom holds a long cross [63].

The iconography is, in fact archaic (Fig. 13). It is directly based upon models established two or three centuries earlier. Christian artists had then been in the habit of taking elements from imperial scenes of investiture or of an *allocutio* or *liberalitas,* and, by combining them with others taken from groups where a philosopher instructs his disciples, they could define the relationship between Christ and his apostles [64]. It is true that the exact significance of these scenes is not always easy to fix, owing to ambiguities in both the iconographical language and in the themes which it was to express. A scroll, for example, may represent a doctrine which is being passed on or the title to an appointment. The teacher normally sits to give his instruction, while the emperor stands to make an *allocutio.* Christ's position, therefore, and a document in his hand do not determine unambiguously the sense of a scene [65]. Similarly the 'law' which Christ confers on Peter in the socalled *Traditio legis* scene may be a doctrine, a moral law or an office. It seems, however, that the surest way of identifying these scenes, when this is possible, is to start from the central figure, Christ.

In this particular case Christ, who is standing, must be making an *allocutio,* the text of which is indeed inscribed below the scene. It is, in fact, the most general statement possible of Christ's authority and of the delegation which he makes of it to his apostles.

The following century the theme of the Mission of the Apostles, like other themes concerning their life and ministry, was increasingly used in Byzantine art [66]. This increase is no doubt to be related to the development of Byzantine missionary activity among the Slavs. The scene in *Parisinus graecus* 510, f. 426 v, has the same text inscribed, taken from *Matthew* 18. 19. Christ stands upon a hillock from which the four rivers flow, the apostles

63. *Vid. sup.,* p. 159; J. DEÉR, *art. cit.,* note 24, p. 36, writes of an investiture scene in the conch of the apse, where Christ invests Peter with the keys, the insignia of binding and loosing, and of the primacy of the Roman Church. But this description of the scene does not correspond to Grimaldi's texts and drawing.

64. Besides A. GRABAR'S general studies (*L'empereur,* cf. note 6, p. 200-2 and *Christian Iconography,* cf. note 49, p. 42-3), cf. Jo. KOLLWITZ, "Christus als Lehrer und die Gesetztübergabe an Petrus in der konstantinischen Kunst Roms," in *Römische Quartalschrift,* 24, 1936, p. 45-66; W.N. SCHUMACHER, " 'Dominus legem dat'," in *Römische Zeitschrift,* 54, 1959, p. 1-39 and "Eine römische Apsiskomposition," *ibid.,* p. 137-202; Y. M.-J. CONGAR, "Le thème du 'don de la loi' dans l'art paléochrétien," in *Nouvelle Revue Théologique,* 84, 1962, p. 915-933. This last article is remarkable not only for the richness of its iconographical documentation but also for the profound knowledge of the Patristic sources in the light of which the author interprets this subject. His conclusion is worth quoting: "Ce thème (...) traduit plastiquement l'idée de la Majesté royale du Christ lançant dans le monde, son œuvre de salut. Le Christ donne la loi; il ne transmet pas un pouvoir à Pierre spécialement; il donne au monde, par et dans l'Église, la réalité et la règle du salut ou de la vie

éternelle. Tel est le contenu du mot *lex.* (...) dans l'idéologie de l'époque constantinienne" (p. 933).

65. Two cases are known where a standing Christ hands to Saint Peter a scroll upon which are inscribed the words: 'Dominus legem dat' (Santa Costanza, Rome and the Baptistery of Soter, Naples, cf. M. van BERCHEM and E. CLOUZOT, *Mosaïques chrétiennes du IVe au Xe siècle,* Geneva, 1924, p. 6 and p. 107). But cf. also a sarcophagus at Arles, where Christ, seated with his apostles, holds a book inscribed: 'Dominus legem dat'. The first two scenes resemble an *allocutio,* the third a lesson. The variations in the scenes without an inscription are so many that it is probably fallacious to suppose that artists sought in pictorial imagery an exact equivalent to the verbal concepts of their time. It is only at the level of the general idea of the transmission to his disciples by Christ of an office that words and images exactly correspond. The sarcophagus at Arles is illustrated by J. WILPERT (*I sarcofagi cristiani antichi,* Rome, 1929, plate XXXIV. 3).

66. A. GRABAR, "L'art religieux et l'empire byzantin à l'époque des Macédoniens," in *L'art de la fin de l'Antiquité et du Moyen Age,* Paris, 1968, p. 160-3. A useful list of representations of the Mission of the apostles may be found in *The Church of Haghia Sophia at Trebizond,* edited D. TALBOT RICE, Edinburgh, 1968, p. 172-7.

are grouped each side of him, while the one nearest to Christ on his left makes an inclination towards him with arms outstretched [67]. A similar scene of Western provenance is to be found on a silver coffer dating from the pontificate of Paschal I (817-24) [68]. This time, however, the assimilation of Christ to the Emperor is even clearer, for the apostle making an inclination has his hands covered.

The particular interest of the miniature in the *Parisinus graecus* 510 is that it is accompanied by twelve scenes of the apostles baptizing; that is to say they are shown exercising the office conferred on them in the principal scene. A similar example occurs in the *Chludov Psalter*; the apostles are represented teaching all nations, while the scene of them receiving their mission is here presumed [69]. The same relationship between the reception of a mission and its exercise is present in the Triclinium of Leo III. Here, however, it is a question rather of transmitting authority. In the subsidiary scene which has survived Peter, enthroned and invested with the pallium, transmits the authority which he has received.

We have, in fact, an investiture scene. But here a slight breakaway from tradition is evident. In the investiture scene of imperial art, for example on the plaque of Theodosius at Madrid, the enthroned emperor places the *codicilli* in the covered hands of the official receiving his appointment, who makes a slight inclination towards the emperor [70]. We find the same iconography for Saint Paul on a sarcophagus at Ravenna [71]. This is perhaps the most 'imperial' example of the investiture of an apostle. And since Saint Paul in fact received his commission individually it does not cause any particular difficulty that he should be represented singly. In the scene on the wall of the triclinium, however, the pope and the emperor are kneeling. This non-classical position may be taken from contemporary forms of ceremonial (Fig. 14).

The significance of the bestowal of the pallium upon Leo by Peter is quite clear [72]. The mosaic serves as a public proclamation that the authority given by Christ to the apostles is now exercised by him. The significance of the bestowal of the vexillum upon Charlemagne is, however, less clear, and only a tentative explanation can be advanced. It must no doubt be related to the policy of the eighth century popes to look for protection to the Frankish kings rather than to the Byzantine emperors. It has been suggested that the vexillum which Charlemagne receives in this mosaic is that of the city of Rome, which Leo III sent to Charlemagne. But Professor Deér has produced a parallel example of the patriarch of Jerusalem sending Charlemagne a vexillum; it would be equivalent to the contemporary practice of conferring the freedom of a city upon a distinguished person [73]. He also makes the point that it would be unlikely, as Professor Schramm has suggested, that Leo III would have set up an official picture of Charlemagne as emperor ('ein neues fränkisches

67. H. OMONT, *Fac-similés des miniatures des plus anciens manuscrits grecs de la Bibliothèque nationale*, Paris, 1902 and 1929, plate LVI.

68. Ph. LAUER, *Le trésor du* Sancta Sanctorum, *Monuments et Mémoires, Eugène Piot*, XV, Paris, 1906, p. 67-71 and plate IX.

69. Moscow, Historical Museum *codex* 129D, f. 17; cf. the *Barberini Psalter, Vaticanus barb. gr.* 372, f. 20 and the *Theodore Psalter, Londinensis* 19352, f. 19 v.

70. R. DELBRUECK, *Die Consulardiptychen und verwandte Denkmäler*, Berlin, 1929, no. 62.

71. The Onesti sarcophagus, Santa Maria in Porto Fuori, cf. M. LAWRENCE, *The sarcophagi of Ravenna*,

College Art Association, 1945, Study Number 2, fig. 20 and p. 24. He notes two indisputable examples of Christ giving a scroll to Saint Paul and two more where Paul bends as if to receive it. A further example of an investiture of Saint Paul occurs on a bronze situla. Cf. W.L.M. BURKE, "A bronze situla in the Museo Cristiano of the Vatican Library," in *The Art Bulletin*, XII, 1930, fig. 3.

72. Cf. H. LECLERCQ, "Pallium," in *Dictionnaire d'archéologie chrétienne et de liturgie*, XIII, 931-9.

73. J. DEÉR, *art. cit.*, note 24, p. 22-3. The patriarch sent Charlemagne "claves sepulchri Dominici ac loci calvariae, claves etiam civitatis et montis cum vexillo".

Herrscherbild') in a triclinium intended to bear witness to papal sovereignty[74]. Ladner, in fact, interprets the *imperium* conferred by Leo III on Charlemagne as involving additional rights and duties, not territories and populations, and particularly 'the protection of the Universal Church, and especially the Roman Church'[75].

It seems that here again Leo III's choice is highly traditional. Charlemagne, like Constantine, receives a lance with which to transfix the enemies of the Church. For there was, of course, in this iconography of imperial origin no implication that Constantine's *imperium* derived from his option for the cause of Christianity; it was rather that he received the additional office of Protector of the Church. This was conferred upon him directly by Christ, but in the triclinium mosaic Charlemagne receives his office from Peter. But there could be only one person who made Peter's options known, his successor as bishop of Rome. The implication is that the Church of Rome henceforth chooses its protector itself.

Curiously, then, there does not seem to be any direct allusion in these mosaics to the papal claims, as set out in the *Constitutum Constantini,* to temporal authority in the West[76]. The most that can be said is that in both the *Constitutum* and the mosaic the pope's spiritual authority was made manifest. Moreover any allusion to Constantine is only implicit in the office represented by the vexillum. The case would be different if the investiture of Constantine had originally been represented the other side. But such a hypothesis seems fraught with difficulties. The theme and symmetry of the monument seem to require that the scene which is the counterpart of Peter investing Leo and Charlemagne should represent an apostle exercising the mission received in the central scene. If Christ is represented investing either Silvester and Constantine or Peter and Constantine the symmetry is destroyed. A scene, however, involving Saint Paul would not only be symmetrical but, given the status accorded to him at Rome, extremely apt. Saint Paul is not to my knowledge represented elsewhere investing another person with authority. But he is represented teaching and baptizing. Either of these subjects would fit the case, the more so as such scenes were certainly represented in Leo III's other triclinium.

---

74. *Idem,* p. 34.

75. G.B. LADNER, "Aspects of Medieval Thought on Church and State," in *Review of Politics,* IX, 1947, p. 406.

76. If Ohnsorge is right that the *Dispositio* — the part distinguishes the *Constitutum Constantini* from the *Legend of Saint Silvester* — was not composed till 804, and if the mosaics of the triclinium had already been executed by then, it is less surprising that their iconography contains no explicit reference to the ideas contained in the *Constitutum* (cf. OHNSORGE'S, *art. cit.,* note 61). However, although some do not see an evident reference to the *Constitutum* in the letter addressed by Pope Hadrian I to Charlemagne in 778 (*vid. sup.,* p. 171), as apparently Fuhrmann (cf. *art. cit.,* "Konstantinische Schenkung...", note 61, p. 121), the notions are so similar that there can be no doubt that the *Constitutum* simply puts in legal form ideas already current in the VIIIth century. It therefore remains an unsolved puzzle why Leo III in a monument intended to set forth the independent status of the papacy restricted himself to a title based uniquely upon the apostolic succession.

PAPAL POLITICAL IMAGERY IN THE MEDIEVAL LATERAN PALACE

III. ANALYSIS OF THE ICONOGRAPHY

2. The Audience Hall of Callixtus II and the Lateran portico mosaic: Triumph and Concordat.

a) Triumph.

Since the series of pictures in this audience hall proclaimed at once the triumph of the orthodox popes over the antipopes and the achievement of a concordat between the Papacy and the Holy Roman Empire, they had necessarily a solemn ceremonial setting. A similar presentation may be seen in the fresco of the Translation of the relics of Saint Clement in the narthex of the underground church of San Clemente [77] (Fig. 15 a). The pope is surrounded by clergy and in the background may be seen banners, crosses, croziers and palms. The fresco dates from about 1100 when work probably began on the upper church.

But this kind of scene derives ultimately from the official art of the Roman Empire. We may see, for example, two enthroned emperors on a bas-relief of the Arch of Galerius, surrounded with their courtiers (Fig. 15 b). They are, in fact, represented as universal sovereigns, and the allegorical persons under their feet surrounded with a cloak represent the universe. Although there is no question here of trampling a captive, the notion of domination is nevertheless implicit. The same iconography was used for the universal sovereignty of Christ on the sarcophagus of Junius Bassus in the Vatican Grottoes and on another in the former Lateran Museum [78]. It was not reserved to scenes of the sovereignty of Christ, but remained in the official repertoire of the Byzantine emperors. A good example may be

FIG. 15 a. — Translation of the body of Saint Clement (détail). Church of San Clemente, Rome.

77. The numbering of the notes and the illustrations is continuous throughout this article, of which the first part appeared in the previous number of the *Cahiers Archéologiques* (XX, 1970, p. 155-176). It contained the following: I. Preliminary; II. Description of the pictures; III. Analysis of the iconography, 1. The Triclinium of Leo III, Mission and Investiture. In this number will be found: III. Analysis of the iconography, 2. The Audience Hall of Callixtus II and the Lateran portico mosaic, Triumph and Concordat; 3. The Coronation of Lotharius II, Strator; IV. Conclusion. The analysis of the theme of Triumph and the iconography of the Strator were presented in M. Jean Lassus's seminar at the École Pratique des Hautes Études. The text has benefitted from the valuable criticisms made then. Professor J.M.C. Toynbee was kind enough to read my manuscript and to give me useful bibliographical information particularly about British funeral steles.

J. WILFERT, *Die römischen Mosaiken und Malereion* Freiburg im Breisgau, 1917, II, p. 536 and pl. 239,1968,

78. A. GRABAR, *Christian Iconography,* Princeton, p. 43 and plates 108-111.

FIG. 15 b. — Two emperors enthroned as universal sovereigns.
Arch of Galerius, Thessaloniki.

FIG. 15 c. — The emperor Theophilus surrounded by his court.
Skyllitzes matritensis.

seen in the Madrid *Skyllitzes,* portraying the emperor Theophilus (829-42) (Fig. 15 c) ; he is enthroned in the centre of the composition with guards behind the throne; to his left and right stand courtiers and in the background may be seen two banners [79].

The general setting for each representation of a triumphant pope was that which had been used in official iconography in Antiquity and which continued to be used at Byzantium whenever the sovereign dominion of the emperor

was to be particularly emphasized. We must see if the specific elements of these pictures — the humiliation of an adversary and the signature of a concordat — are also to be found in antique and in Byzantine iconography.

It would be well to examine more closely the language in which the Medieval observers of the frescoes described them [80]. Arnulf of Lisieux speaks of the *schismatici præsumptores* serving *pro scabello pedibus patrum catholicorum;* he adds that *sapientia conterit et conculcat colla superborum* and speaks also of *gloria victoriæ.* In testimony of this victory *præsumptores vel poenam compressionis sustinent vel*

79. *Skyllitzes matritensis,* I, edited S. Cirac Estopañan, Barcelona-Madrid, 1965, number 100, p. 72 and 257.
80. Cf. CA XX, 1970, p. 162, n. 34.

præsumptionis veniam deprecantur. The special interest of this passage is the variety of expressions which Arnulf uses. The notion of the *scabellum* is, of course, biblical, recalling *Psalm* 110 (109): *Sede a dextris meis, donec ponam inimicos tuos scabellum pedum tuorum, Matthew* 22.44 and *Acts* 2.34-5. The phrase *conculcat colla* may also recall a sacred text, such as *Psalm* 91 (90).13: *Super aspidem et basiliscum ambulabis, et conculcabis leonem et draconem.*

However the Old Testament contains many similar passages. For example in the Messianic *Psalm* (8.7) one reads: *Omnia subiecisti sub pedibus eius,* a passage which Saint Paul quotes at least twice[81]. It is, moreover, evident that Saint Paul understands this image as indicating conquest rather than dominion. A reference to trampling an enemy is also made by *Isaiah* (51.23): *Incurvare, ut transeamus; et posuisti ut terram corpus tuum et quasi viam transeuntibus.* A reference to the practice of trampling upon the neck of an enemy is made by the prophet *Baruch* (4.25): *Super cervices ipsius ascendes.* All these passages, which I have deliberately quoted from the Vulgate, could well have been known to Arnulf of Lisieux. They would seem to provide evidence for supposing that he read into the frescoes an allusion to the triumph of the Messianic king, prolonged in the triumph of the popes. They do not, on the other hand, completely explain his allusion to a *poena compressionis* and a *deprecatio veniæ.*

John of Salisbury's descriptive language is less rich. He speaks only of *schismatici* being a *scabellum* for the pope, and he interprets the scene as triumphal. Suger of Saint-Denis uses only one expression: *Burdinus sub pedibus domini papæ conculcatum.* Otto of Freising's Chronicle only records the inscriptions, which have a more moderate language: Alexander overcomes Cadolus, condemns him and restores peace. On the other hand the artist of the *Codex Toledanus* records a definite recollection of a trampling scene, although no actual description of the picture of Burdin's downfall appears in the text. Nevertheless on the basis of Arnulf of Lisieux's account alone a search for the origins of this iconography in Antique art is justified.

One must begin by a consideration of the victor rather than of his captive, for it was the victor who commissioned the picture, and whose tastes had to be satisfied. There were two motifs which particularly appealed to Antique taste. The first shows the victor standing in the posture of a hero. It probably dates back to the Hellenistic epoch, when it was adopted by the kings who divided among themselves the empire of Alexander. A late example may be seen in two paintings of Theseus, one from Herculaneum and one from Pompeii, in the Museo Nazionale at Naples[82] (Fig. 16).

FIG. 16. — Theseus and the Minotaur (detail). Fresco from Pompeii, Museo Nazionale, Naples.

81. Cf. *I Corinthians* 15.27 and *Ephesians* 1.22. The tradition that the Persian king Sapor used the emperor Valerian as a mounting block was also known through Lactantius and the hagiographers, to whom this humiliation undergone by a persecutor was a source of satisfaction: *Nam rex Persarum Sapor, is qui eum ceperat, si quando libuerat aut vehiculum ascendere aut equum, inclinare Romanum iubebat ac terga præbere et imposito pede super dorsum eius. Illud esse verum dicebat exprobrans ei cum risu, non quod in tabulis aut parietibus Romani pingerent* (LACTANTIUS, *De mortibus persecutorum,* V 1, ed. J. MOREAU, *Sources chrétiennes,* 39, Paris, s.d., I, p. 83; cf. II, p. 223).

82. R. BIANCHI BANDINELLI, *Storicità dell'arte classica,* Florence, 1950, fig. 169 and 170.

Theseus, naked in the heroic tradition, stands in the centre of the scene, holding a club on his shoulder. To his right is the dead Minotaur, while to his left stand those whom he has

FIG. 17 a. — Victor trampling his defeated enemy. *Signum* Neuwied.

delivered from the Minotaur; one of them is prostrate of Theseus's feet.

Theseus is not actually trampling the Minotaur in this scene, and the person prostrate at his feet has been not conquered but liberated. The standing victor actually tramples his conquered enemy upon the disc of a *signum* at Neuwied [83] (Fig. 17 a). Either side of the prostrate figure are piles of booty. The presentation of Trajan with his foot planted upon a personification of Armenia and the gods of the Tigris and the Euphrates either side is less crudely triumphal [84]. With the passage of time

83. S. REINACH, *Répertoire de reliefs grecs et romains*, II, Paris, 1912, p. 83, number 2.
84. M. BERNHART, *Handbuch zur Münzkunde der römischen Kaiserzeit*, Halle, 1936, pl. 84.2. Cf. A. GRABAR, *L'empereur dans l'art byzantin*, Paris, 1936, p. 43-4.
85. J. MAURICE, *Numismatique constantinienne*, Paris, 1911, II, p. 388-390 and pl. XII 1.
86. M. BERNHART, *op. cit.* (note 84), pl. 23.1, 6, 10, 12, 16 and 24.3 [trampling a prisoner]; pl. 23.3 [trampling a lion]; pl. 23.13, 15, 17, 18 [trampling a serpent]; P. COURCELLE, "Le serpent à face humaine dans la numismatique impériale du Vᵉ siècle," in *Mélanges André Piganiol*, Paris, 1966, I, p. 343-353. The article is concerned with a series of Vth century coins which have on their reverse side a standing emperor holding a long cross in his right hand and a globe surmounted by a victory in the left; his right foot is placed on the head of a serpent with a human face. Under the emperor Glycerus (473-4) a *scabellum* replaces the serpent, although the emperor is represented standing. Professor Courcelle suggests that there is implicit an allusion to *Psalm* 110 (109).
87. A. GRABAR, *L'empereur* (cf. note 84), p. 45-9.

symbolism or borrowings from ceremonial further modified this iconography. On a coin issued at Sirmium in 320 a personification of Victory treads upon a personification of Germany [85]. A lion, a serpent or even — the most abstract form — a *scabellum* may be substituted for the actual victim, while to the crowning Victory may be added a vexillum marked with the Chrismon [86]. Through all these representations the emperor retains his heroic stance (Fig. 18 a-d).

The second motif used to represent a victor in Antique art showed him on horseback [87]. Apart from actual battle scenes, such as those portrayed in the bas-reliefs of the Arch of Galerius and equestrian statues, of which that of Marcus Aurelius at the Capitol has

FIG. 17 b. — Victor trampling his defeated enemy. Utrecht Psalter, f. 64ᵛ.

alone survived, there is a small group of funeral steles which are perhaps less well known. A well preserved example in the City Museum of Colchester is the stele of Longinus of the

(b)

(c)   (d)

Fig. 18. — Triumphal imagery on coins: a) Valentinian II;
b) Severus III; c) Glycerus; d) Valentinian III.

first Thracian squadron (Fig. 19). Longinus, wearing a cuirasse, is seated upon his horse; at his feet is prostrated a conquered Briton. Curiously this particular version of the conqueror on horseback has mainly been found in Britain and on the German frontier; it is quite unknown in Rome or Italy [88].

The funeral stele of Dexileos, who fell in the Battle of Corinth (394 B.C.), the only fully comparable earlier instance of this composition on a tombstone that Professor Toynbee has found else where, is quite different in spirit [89]. Dexileos is on a prancing horse and about to strike a blow, from which the enemy, down on one knee, seeks to shield himself. Longinus's stele is rather of the genre of the equestrian statue, a static, formal monument. Dexileos's stele is more like the narrative scenes of actual battles. The motif can be seen on a medallion of Theodosius I, where the figure on horseback drives his spear into a fallen enemy [90].

A third motif, which does not seem to have been used earlier than the reign of Theodosius I, shows the victorious emperor enthroned [91]. In a bas-relief on the base of his obelisk in the Hippodrome at Constantinople Theodosius is seated surrounded by his courtiers. Barbarian captives, down on one knee, present him with crowns. This is an evident adaptation of an official scene, such as the *Liberalitas*. It differs from the previous ones in that, far from taking

FIG. 19. — Funeral stele of Longinus. Museum Colchester.

a heroic statue or a battle scene as its model, it clearly records a ceremony. It falls into the category of the celebration of a Triumph such as one frequently finds in the iconography of the rites of the State religion [92]. It is possible that the ceremony of the offerings was also represented in the mosaics of Justinian's victories [93]. This ceremony was obsolete by the time that Constantine Porphyrogenitus wrote the *Book of Ceremonies*. He describes, however, a more brutal one which had been developed meanwhile.

Before turning to the way these themes were treated in Byzantine art, it would be well to consider them from the point of view of the captive. The conquered person may indeed be represented simply as dead, as is the case with the Minotaur in the scene figuring Theseus mentioned above. He may be transfixed with a lance as on the medallion of Theodosius, or he may be trampled as on the Neuwied *signum*. In most portraits of the standing or equestrian victor the captive will be represented in one of these ways. For the sense is the destruction or, at the least, the subdual of an enemy rather than the extension of the victor's sovereignty. On the other hand in Antique art the seated figure of a ruler definitely signifies sovereignty, and if there is a personification of

88. J.M.C. TOYNBEE, *Art in Britain Under the Romans*, Oxford, 1964, p. 189. The stele is to be dated earlier than 61 A.D., when it was thrown to the ground during the Boudiccan revolt. Professor Toynbee calls attention to the unusual presentation: "The horse is neither galloping nor rearing... The naked barbarian is doubled up on his shield..." The enemy is also crouched on the stele of Flavinus at Hexham (*ibid.*, p. 192-3). For another crouched enemy, cf. a stele at Mainz (REINACH, *op. cit.*, p. 72, number 5; *Germania Romana, Ein Bilder-Atlas*, III, *Die Grabdenkmäler*, Bamberg, 1926², pl. IX 1). The text from Lactantius (cited note 81) suggests that the crouched barbarian may be serving as a mounting block.

89. G.M.A. RICHTER, *Sculpture and sculptors of the Greeks*, 1950, p. 44, fig. 215.

90. A. ALFÖLDI, *Die Kontorniaten*, Budapest-Leipzig, 1943, pl. XXI 1; cf. M. BERNHART, *op. cit.* (note 84), p. 121-2 and pl. 87.9 for a similar representation on a coin of Galerius Maximus.

91. A. GRABAR, *L'empereur*, p. 54 and pl. XII 2; cf. the *Liberalitas* of Constantine, pl. XXXI. These official scenes in Constantinian art may have supplied the model for the later ones figuring captives. Cf. J.M.C. TOYNBEE, *Roman Medallions, Numismatic Studies* No. 5, American Numismatic Society, New York, 1944, p. 62, 175 and 198; pl. V, VI and XXXIX.

92. I. SCOTT RYBERG, *Rites of the State Religion in Roman Art*, American Academy in Rome, Memoirs, XXII, 1955, p. 141-62 and pl. L-LVII.

93. Cf. CA XX, 1970, p. 155.

the Universe under the sovereign's feet this is to indicate the extent of his rule, not of his conquests.

The position in which captives are represented may also be considered from another point of view. They are special cases of a general way of representing an inferior. The most ordinary way of doing this is by the *proskynesis*[94]. This is not peculiar to Hellenistic tradition. For example on the Black Obelisk of Shalmaneser III, king of Assyria, now in the British Museum, Jehu, king of Samaria, or his deputy is represented making a *proskynesis* before Shalmaneser[95]. In 842 B.C. he had invaded Damascus and forced Jehu to pay tribute. The *proskynesis* is therefore used as a means of showing that Jehu is a tributary of and hence inferior to Shalmaneser. In the painting of Theseus one of those delivered by him from the Minotaur is represented making a *proskynesis*. Here the gesture implies that Theseus is of a higher order, a divine person. Similarly, as he was later to be depicted in the *Joshua Roll*, Joshua prostrates himself before the angel of the Lord (*Joshua* 5.14).

We may find all these motifs, both of the conqueror and of the conquered, in Christian art. The heroic position is used particularly for the Anastasis. It is may be combined with the trampling of Hades[96]. The normal way of representing the Resurrection in Byzantine iconography, it was also used in the West, and an example may be seen in the lower church of San Clemente in Rome. Here, however, as often in Byzantine art, Christ, although trampling Hades, is represented not in a heroic position but rescuing Adam. The same iconography was also used for king David triumphing over his enemies. In the *Theodore Psalter* (*Londin. Add.* 19352) f. 18ᵛ David is represented with a foot upon the head of each of two prostrate enemies. The text illustrated (*Psalm* 17 (18).35) runs: I smote my enemies so that they could not rise; they fell beneath my feet. Twice in the *Lichačev Psalter* David is represented in the same way[97]. But an alternative formula existed for representing the submission of a captive: the *proskynesis*; it illustrates the Byzantine tendency to tone things down. So in the frontispiece to the *San Marco Psalter*, the conquered Bulgarians are not trampled; they make a *proskynesis*. This be-

came, indeed, the regular Byzantine way of expressing inferiority in many different iconographical themes, whether of the Emperor, Christ's viceregent, before the enthroned Lord of the Universe, or again of the Emperor venerating martyrs as in *Atheniensis* 211, f. 63[98], or of a heretic submitting to the orthodox bishops in many representations of oecumenical councils[99]. Only in one case in Byzantine art is the theme of trampling regularly combined with that of the triumphal hero when a contemporary event is represented as opposed to one from sacred history. This is, of course, the Triumph of Orthodoxy, where the patriarch Nicephorus is represented trampling upon Jannis, the arch-iconoclast[100]. Even here the event is symbolic rather than historical, since Nicephorus was exiled in 815, nearly forty years before the actual Triumph of Orthodoxy. On the other hand the trampling theme appears frequently in the *Utrecht Psalter* (Fig. 17 b).

The second motif, a victor on horseback, was used in Byzantine and Romanesque art for the emperor Constantine. Examples of it may be seen in the *Chludov Psalter*, f. 58ᵛ, and on capitals in the cloister of Saint-Trophime at

94. For a general study, cf. the chapter on Submission in R. BRILLIANT's study: *Gesture and Rank in Roman Art*, Newhaven (Connecticut), 1963.

95. J. PLESSIS, "Babylone et la Bible, in *Dictionnaire de la Bible, Supplément*, I, 784.

96. Tunc rex gloriæ maiestate sua conculcans mortem... (Gospel of Nicodemus, VI, in *Evangelia Apocrypha*, ed. C. DE TISCHENDORFF, Leipzig, 1876², p. 400). This is presumably an embroidery of *I Corinthians* 15.27. For the iconography of this scene cf. C.R. MOREY, *East Christian Paintings in the Freer Collection*, New York, 1914, p. 45 et seq.; E. LUCCHESI PALLI, "Anastasis", in *Reallexikon zur byzantinischen Kunst*, I, 142-148. For the San Clemente Anastasis cf. WILPERT, *op. cit.*, note 77, pl. 229.2.

97. S. DER NERSESSIAN, *L'illustration des psautiers grecs du Moyen Age*, II, Paris, 1970, p. 22 and pl. 12, fig. 32; *Korrekturnye listy Licevaya psaltir 1397 goda prinadležaičaya Imperatorskomu Običestvu ljubitelej drevnej pismennosti*, Saint Petersburg, 1890, f. 22v and f. 61v; cf. also the miniature of Phinees trampling an enemy in the *Pantocrato Psalter* (S. DUFRENNE, *L'illustration des psautiers grecs du Moyen Age*, I, Paris, 1966, pl. 5, fig. 11).

98. A. GRABAR, *L'art de la fin de l'Antiquité et du Moyen Age*, II, p. 808 and III, fig. 190 a.

99. Ch. WALTER, *L'iconographie des conciles dans la tradition byzantine*, Paris, 1970, p. 253-256; J. WALTER, "Heretics in byzantine art," in *Eastern Churches Review*, III, 1970, p. 40-41.

100. Cf. CA XX, 1970, p. 161, fig. 4c; A. GRABAR, *Iconoclasme byzantin*, Paris, 1957, p. 218 and fig. 152, 154; J. WALTER, *art. cit.*, note 99, p. 44-45. For the *Utrecht Psalter* cf. E.T. DE WALD, *Illustrations of the Utrecht Psalter*, Princeton, 1932, f. 64ᵛ, pl. CI, etc., and, in this article, fig. 17b. Cf. also *Skyllitzes matritensis*, f. 31ᵛ (ed. cit. note 79, no. 69 and p. 64), where the soldier placing his foot upon the adopted son of Thomas preparatory to cutting off his head may recall scenes of David decapitating Goliath.

FIG. 20. — The emperor Constantine trampling Maxentius (?). Capital, cathedral Autun.

FIG. 21. — τραχελισμός or *calcatio colli*, Constantine VII and Abul Asaʾir. *Skyllitzes matritensis.*

Arles and in the cathedral of Autun (Fig. 20). The same iconography was also used for a number of warrior saints [101].

When, however, we consider the third and

101. A. GRABAR, *L'empereur*, cf. note 6, p. 47, note 6; R. CROZET, "Nouvelles remarques sur les cavaliers sculptés ou peints dans les églises romanes," in *Cahiers de civilisation médiévale*, I, 1958, p. 27-36 and fig. 1.

102. *Skyllitzes matritensis*, f. 37 (ed. cit. note 79, no. 84, p. 68 and p. 251); f. 136 (no. 343, p. 143 and 338). The first shows Michael II placing his foot upon the neck of Thomas, a Slav who proclaimed himself emperor and who fell into Michael II's hands in 823 (G. OSTROGORSKY, *History of the Byzantine State*, Oxford, 1968[2], p. 205). This is the passage of the Chronicle illustrated by the miniature: Ὁ δὲ τὸ δόξαν πάλαι τοῖς βασιλεῦσι καὶ εἰς συνήθειαν ἤδη ἐλθὸν πρῶτον τελέσας, καὶ ἐπ'ἐδάφους ἁπλώσας αὐτὸν καὶ τοῖς ποσὶ τὸν αὐχένα τούτου πατήσαι (PG 121, 973). The second shows Ἀπολασαειρ (Abul Asaʾir), the cousin of Saif-ad-Daulah, who had been taken prisoner by Leo Phocas in 956, undergoing the same treatment by Constantine VII (A.A. VASILIEV, *Byzance et les Arabes*, II 1, *La dynastie macédonienne*, edited by Marius CANARD, Brussels, 1968, p. 358). This is the passage of the Chronicle illustrated by the miniature: Ὃν ἀχθέντα πρὸς τὴν βασιλίδα ὁ · βασιλεὺς Κωνσταντῖνος θρίαμβον ποιήσας καὶ κατὰ τοῦ τραχήλου πατήσας τιμαῖς τε καὶ δωρεαῖς ἐφιλοφρονήσατο (PG 122, 65 A). Cf. the account of the ceremony for the τραχηλισμός of an Emir in the *De cerimoniis*, II 19, of Constantine Porphyrogenitus (ed. J.J. REISKE, Bonn, 1829, I, p. 610). The ceremony took place on the steps of the Column of Constantine in the Forum. The emperor placed his right foot on the head and the end of his lance on the neck of the Emir καὶ πατεῖ αὐτὸν ὁ βασιλεὺς ἐπὶ τὴν κεφαλὴν τῷ δεξιῷ ποδί.

later theme of the victorious emperor enthroned, we find that we are dealing with an iconographical subject which departs from the norms of Antique art. In the nature of things it is not easy to trample a person when one is in a seated position. It was therefore usual for submission to be manifested to an enthroned person by kneeling, as on the base of the Column of Theodosius, or by a *proskynesis,* as in the case of heretics submitting to the orthodox bishops at a general council. The only exception to this rule in Byzantine art, as far as I know, occurs in the *Skyllitzes Matritensis,* where twice a person is represented with the enthroned emperor placing his foot upon his neck [102]. This is clearly a ceremonial action: the emperor placed his foot and his lance upon the neck and shoulder of his conquered enemy, but he did not actually trample him (Fig. 21).

In Western art, rather more liberty was used, particularly for illustrating the triumphal texts in the *Psalms. Psalm* 91 (90).13 was indeed chanted at Constantinople while the emperor Justinian II, enthroned, subjected Apsimar (Tiberius II) and Leontius to the ceremony of the *calcatio colli,* but Christ trampling the asp

FIG. 22. — Enthroned Christ trampling a lion and dragon. Pignatta sarcophagus, church of San Francesco, Ravenna.

and basilisk was nevertheless represented standing in Byzantine art [103]. On the other hand the representation of Christ enthroned with one foot upon a lion and the other upon a dragon on the Pignatta sarcophagus in the church of San Francesco at Ravenna is only the first of a series in the West [104] (Fig. 22). But Christ is rarely portrayed enthroned with his feet upon these animals as a simple illustration of the text of the *Psalm*. Usually there is some added significance, Trinitarian or apocalyptic.

It is necessary always to seek the explanation of a change in iconographical practice in the first place within the tradition of art.

103. The account of Theophanes (*Chronographia*, ed. J. CLASSEN, Bonn, 1839, I, p. 574; ed. Ch. DE BOOR, Leipzig, 1883, p. 375) would have been accessible in the West in the translation of Anastasius Bibliothecarius: Porro Apsimarum atque Leontium vinctos catenis per totam urbem pompis fecit dehonestari. Cumque ludi equestres agerentur, ipseque in solio resideret, ducti sunt publice tracti et proiecti proni ad pedes eius; quorum ille colla usque ad solutionem primi bravii calcavit, universa plebe clamante: "Super aspidem et basiliscum ascendisti et conculcasti leonem et draconem". Et ita hos destinatos in vivario animantium capitis animadversione punivit (DE BOOR, *op. cit.*, p. 239). Cf. the parallels from earlier and later practice cited by Reiske (*op. cit.*, note 102, II, p. 722-3). For this incident cf. also OSTROGORSKY, *op. cit.*, note 102, p. 143. There is a coin of Valentinian III, upon which are portrayed two enthroned emperors with a bound prisoner to left and right (fig. 18d). It does not seem that they are actually trampling the prisoners, but each emperor holds a *mappa* in his hand, as if to give the signal at the Triumphal Games for the trampling to begin. In his article "The Anti-iconoclast poem in the Pantocrator Psalter" (*Cahiers Archéologiques*, XV, 1965, p. 39 *et seq.*), I. ŠEVČENKO advances the hypothesis that the poem in question was not originally intended to accompany the miniature next to which it was inscribed. In this miniature the patriarch Nicephorus is enthroned with the emperor Leo V and the patriarch Theodotus prostrate at his feet. To my mind the case for Professor Ševčenko's hypothesis is greatly strengthened by the fact that the miniature does not in fact portray a *calcatio colli*;

the emperor and patriarch are making a *proskynesis*. On the other hand the poem quite definitely alludes to a standing victor actually trampling his enemy.

104. M. LAWRENCE, *The Sarcophagi of Ravenna*, College Art Association, 1945, *Study Number*, 2, fig. 31. On the wall of the church at Stanton Saint Quintin (Wiltshire, England) Christ is sculpted in a niche enthroned with a book in his hand and his feet on an outstretched basilisk (photograph. collection Warburg Institute, London; cf. N. PEVSNER, *The Buildings of England*, Wiltshire, London, 1963, p. 431). This sculpture probably dates from the XIth century. In Cotton Julius D. vii, f. 60ᵛ, Christ is enthroned with a chalice in his left hand and blessing with his right hand; under his feet are a lion and a basilisk (cf. M.R. JAMES, *The Drawings of Matthew Paris*, *Walpole Society*, XIV, 1925-6, no. 143, p. 26 and pl. XXX). Curiously Matthew Paris also portrays Alexander the Great enthroned with his feet resting on a lion and a basilisk in his *Historia maior*, p. 24 (Corpus Christi College, Cambidge, *codex* 26; cf. *ibid.*, no. 3, p. 4 and pl. I). The apocalyptic version may be seen on a bronze door at Novgorod, where Christ is seated on a rainbow with his feet on an asp and basilisk (cf. A. GOLDSCHMIDT, *Die Bronzetüren von Nowgorod und Gnesen*, Marburg, 1932, pl. II 38); the doors date from the mid-XIIth century. Another example occurs in the painting of the Last Judgment by W. de Brailes in the Fitzwilliam Museum, Cambridge, dating from about 1240 (photograph collection, Warburg Institute). For a considerable but not exhaustive bibliography of this theme cf. F. SAXL, "The Ruthwell Cross," in *The Journal of the Courtauld and Warburg Institutes*, VI, 1943, p. 12, note 7.

(a)

(c)

(b)

FIG. 23. — The Father and the Son with the devil as *scabellum*: a) Utrecht Psalter, f. 64ᵛ; b) Cotton Titus D. xxvii, f. 75ᵛ, British Museum, London; c) Seal of Godwin, British Museum, London.

Official art is, of its nature, closely linked to ceremonial, since both seek to express a meaning by significant gestures. In antique art we find representations of mounted or standing persons trampling an enemy; however the more brutal action of trampling was replaced by a ceremonial action of placing the foot on the captive's neck. We also find representations of a figure crouched in a position resembling a mounting block, and an allusion in a text to the practice of representing a captive in this way in Roman art. However when an enthroned figure has a person under his feet, this is to indicate that he rules over the earth and the heavens. The develop-

ment of the ceremonial of the τραχελισμός at the Byzantine court explains how it came about that the antique iconography for the representation of a victor and his vanquished enemy came to be modified in illustrating the *Skyllitzes matritensis*.

On the other hand, so far as I know, the Byzantines never used the τραχελισμός as a model for illustrating *Psalm* 110 *(Sede a dextris meis, donec ponam inimicos tuos scabellum pedum tuorum)*. The explanation must be their respect for iconographical tradition (Fig. 23 a, b, c). In the West, where there was more flexibility, Christ was already represented seated with his feet upon a prostrate figure in the *Utrecht Psalter* [105]. The *scabellum* motif was therefore well established in the West before the time of Callixtus II. He could adapt an iconography hitherto reserved to Christ to express the triumph of the popes, certain that the point would be taken. This is in itself noteworthy. But Arnulf of Lisieux's description shows that he not only divined the pope's intention; he knew of analogous representations of *deprecatio veniæ* (proskynesis) and of *poena compressionis* (τραχηλισμός), and understood the iconographical tradition to which these pictures belonged.

b) Concordat.

The final picture in the triumphal series differs somewhat, as I noted, from the others, since it represents not only the defeat of an antipope but also the promulgation of the Concordat of Worms [106]. The concordat had ended — at least so Pope Callixtus hoped — the long struggle over Investitures. It was therefore fitting that a representation of it should end the series of pictures of the popes

who had been involved in the struggle. But the concordat was also something new in political and ecclesiastical history; it consisted in a mutual recognition of the respective rights of pope and emperor in the appointment of bishops. Consequently although a certain superiority is given to the pope by the fact that he is enthroned while the emperor Henry V remains standing, it is clear that both lend their authority to the document which they hold together. Upon this painted document were, apparently, inscribed the first words of the concordat, while the whole text was painted on the wall elsewhere in the audience hall [107].

Can one situate the iconography of this representation of a concordat relative to an existing tradition in political imagery, or was it a new departure?

In official representations of the empereur there is hardly any distinction between on the one hand the conferment of a privilege or of an office and on the other hand the presentation of an offering [108]. For example the emperor Theodosius I is enthroned in each case. On the base of the obelisk in the Hippodrome at Constantinople captives on their knees present an

---

105. The principal representations of Christ with a human person as *scabellum* occur in the *Utrecht Psalter* and its derivatives (cf. S. DUFRENNE, "Les copies anglaises du Psautier d'Utrecht," in *Scriptorium*, XVIII 2, 1964, p. 185-97): *Utrecht Psalter*, f. 64ᵛ (E.T. DE WALD, *Illustrations of the Utrecht Psalter*, Princeton, 1932, pl. CI); London, British Museum, Harley 603, f. 56ᵛ, dating from about 1000; *Eadwine Psalter*, Trinity College, Cambridge, *codex* R. 17.1, f. 199ᵛ, dating from about 1150 (M.R. JAMES, *The Canterbury Psalter*, London, 1935); *Parisinus latinus* 8846 (H. OMONT, *Psautier illustré (XIIIᵉ siècle)*, Paris, 1906) has illustrations only for the first 98 Psalms. The theme also appears on the matrix of the Seal of Godwin in the British Museum (O.M. DALTON, *Catalogue of the Ivory Carvings of the Christian Era in the British Museum*, London, 1909, no. 31, p. 32-3; D. TALBOT RICE, *English Art, 871-1100*, Oxford, 1952, p. 165 and pl. 36d), where a single outstretched person serves as a *scabellum* for both Christ and God the Father. In the *Ormesby Psalter* (Oxford, Bodley's Library, MS Douce 366, f. 147ᵛ), Christ's enemies make a proskynesis and do not serve as a *scabellum* (E.H. KANTOROWICZ, "The Quinity of Winchester," in *The Art Bulletin*, XXIX, 1947, fig. 9). In the Offices of Westminster, London, Maidstone Museum, MS, f. 32ᵛ, Christ has his feet placed on the shoulders of two crouching figures (*ibid.*, fig. 4). In a XIIth century Psalter (British Museum Lansdowne 383, f. 108) Christ holds an orb and is seated beside his Father on a rainbow with three prostrate figures at their feet. Two of them wear crowns. There has evidently been contamination from the apocalyptic version described earlier in this note. Finally there is the curious version in British Museum Cotton Titus D. xxvii, f. 75ᵛ with its Christological overtones. In this drawing dating from the Xth century an anthropomorphic devil with shackles and its hair standing on end serves as a *scabellum* for Christ (cf. E.H. KANTOROWICZ, *art. cit.*, and

F. WORMALD, *English Drawings of the Xth and XIth centuries*, London, no. 33, p. 69, and pl. 16 a).
106. Cf. CA XX, 1970, p. 165.
107. *Ibid.*, p. 163, n. 38.
108. For these themes in imperial and Christian art cf. A. GRABAR, *L'empereur*, especially p. 54-57, 88-89, 98-122; pl. XII and XVI. There does not seem to have been a specific formula for the bestowal of a privilege. It was conceived after the model of an investiture. Cf. representations of Moses receiving the Law (C.R. MOREY, "Notes on East Christian Manuscripts," in *The Art Bulletin*, XI, 1929, fig. 40, 43, 51 and 52). Scenes where a message is given to or received from a messenger are curiously similar. Cf. the examples in *Skyllitzes matritensis*, f. 75ᵛ (*ed. cit.* note 79, no. 191) and *Vaticanus lat.* 4939, f. 151 (G. LADNER, *I ritratti dei Papi nell'Antichità e nel Medioevo*, Vatican, 1941, pl. XXIV).
Dr Florentine Muetherich also kindly drew my attention to dedication pictures in certain manuscripts. These also resemble the iconography of an offering or the bestowal of a privilege. Normally these pictures show the author offering his work, in the form of a closed book or an unrolled roll, to his patron, whether a prince or a saint. For a little known Byzantine example cf. Dionysiou *cod.* 61, f. 1ᵛ, where Gregory of Nazianzen offers his homilies to a prince (G. GALAVARIS, *The Illustrations of the Liturgical Homilies of Gregory Nazianzenus*, Princeton, 1969, fig. 355). Two Western examples, both executed at Echternach in the first half of the XIth century, have a particular interest. In the first Abbot Gerhard, who is standing, presents an open book to Saint Peter, who is enthroned (Paris, Bibliothèque nationale f.l.n.a. 2196, f. 2, an Evangeliary dated about 1040; cf. J. PROCHNO, *Das Schreiber- und Dedikationsbild in der deutschen Buchmalerei*, Leipzig-Berlin, 1929, p. 48*). In the second a standing abbot presents to the enthroned Kind Henry II an open book upon which is inscribed a text (Bremen Stadtbibliothek *cod.* b. 21, a lectionary dated between 1039 and 1043; cf. *ibid.*, p. 50*).

offering. On the *missorium* at Madrid the official inclines his head to receive the *codicilli*. The representation of the analogous theme where the emperor makes his offering to the church differs somewhat in the two earliest examples known, those in the churches of San Vitale and Sant'Apollinare in Classe at Ravenna. However in the later examples in the church of Saint Sophia at Constantinople there is a close resemblance to the picture executed for Callixtus II of the Concordat of Worms. In the vestibule mosaic Constantine and Justinian offer respectively the city of Constantinople and the church of Saint Sophia. In the two mosaics of the south gallery, the emperor and the empress offer gifts and charters of privileges. In all these cases they stand before the enthroned figure of Christ or the Virgin [109].

109. Cf. A. GRABAR, "Quel est le sens de l'offrande de Justinien et de Théodora sur les mosaïques de Saint-Vital ?," in *L'art de la fin de l'Antiquité et du Moyen Age*, Paris, 1968, I, p. 461-468; O. DEMUS, "Zu den Apsismosaiken von Sant'Apollinare in Classe," in *Jahrbuch der österreichischen Byzantinistik*, 18, 1969, p. 229-238; Th. WHITTEMORE, *The Mosaics of Saint Sophia at Istanbul, The Mosaics of the Southern Vestibule*, Oxford, 1936, and *The Imperial Portraits of the South Gallery*, Oxford, 1942.
110. V.J. DJURIĆ, "Portraits des souverains byzantins et serbes sur les chrysobulles", in *Recueil de travaux de la Faculté de philosophie (Belgrade)*, VII 1, 1963, p. 251-272.
111. The same is, of course, true of dedication pictures. Cf. Milutin's church at Studenica (R. HAMANN - MAC LEAN and H. HALLENSLEBEN, *Die Monumentalmalerei in Serbien und Makedonien*, Giessen, 1963, fig. 246 and 249).
112. A. GRABAR, "Le portrait en iconographie paléochrétienne," in *op. cit.* note 109, p. 591-605; *Idem, Iconoclasme* (cf. note 100), p. 47-50 and 60-61. For portraits of council fathers cf. my study (*op. cit.* note 99) especially p. 61-67 and fig. 29-30 (*Vat. lat.* 1339) and my article, "The Names of the Council Fathers at Saint Sozomenos, Cyprus," in *Revue des études byzantines*, 28, 1970, p. 189-206. Cf. also the remarkable Parousia scene, in which Christ, seated on a throne, holds an unrolled scroll, upon the socalled Sarcophagus of Agilbert. Either side of Christ are standing figures in the position of Orantes. We have here an evident adaptation of a promulgation scene (B. BRENK, "Marginalien zum sog. Sarkophag des Agilbert in Jouarre," in *CA* XIV, 1964, p. 95-107). Brenk argues that it cannot be later in date than the early VIIth century.
113. *Art. cit.*, note 110.
114. After describing the position of the emperor and empress relative to the Virgin, Clavijo continues : a los pies de la imagen de Santa María estaban figurados trenta castillos e ciudades, escriptos los nombres de cada uno dellos en griego, e estas dichas ciudades e castillos dixeron que solían ser des señorio de aquella iglesia, que las hobiera dado un emperador e que la dotó, que hobiera nombre Romano, a que allí yacía enterrado a los pies de aquella imagen; e que estaban colgados unos privilegios de cuero sellados con sellos de cera e de plomo, que decían eran los dichos privilegios que aquella iglesia hobiera de los dichas ciudades e castillos (cf. S. CIRAC ESTOPAÑAN, "Tres monasterios de Constantinopla visitados por Españoles en el año 1403," in *Revue des études byzantines*, XIX, 1961, p. 374-5; V.J. DJURIĆ, *art. cit.*, note 110, p. 261 and R. JANIN, *Géographie ecclésiastique de l'empire byzantin*, Paris, 1969², p. 220-224.

This same iconography was to be used for the miniatures which were attached to Byzantine and Serbian chrysobulls [110]. Now, as Dr Djurić has pointed out, these miniatures have a common characteristic: the sovereign in question does not present the gift or privilege to a member of the clergy but to the patron of the church or monastery, whether it be Christ, the Virgin or a saint [111]. It is therefore evident that there is a basic difference between this type of scene and the one in Callixtus II's Audience Hall: no Byzantine sovereign would be represented standing and presenting a charter of privileges to a seated member of the clergy.

The presence of a portrait of the person who promulgated a document at the head of the text recalls the antique custom of representing the author at the head of the manuscript containing his treatise. The original idea in both cases would have been to offer a guarantee of the authenticity of the text. The practice was copied by Christian artists, who represented king David as frontispiece to the Psalter, an Evangelist at the head of his gospel, Saint John Chrysostom at the head of a liturgical roll and so on.

In the same way portraits of the emperor and the council fathers offered a guarantee that the doctrine promulgated under their portrait was orthodox. These portraits occur not only in monumental painting but also in manuscripts containing a brief résumé of the history of the oecumenical councils [112]. Dr Djurić has called attention to similar examples concerning gifts to churches [113]. Those at Žiča and Manasija are later than the frescoes of Callixtus II, but they must derive from earlier Byzantine models, such as the one which Clavijo describes [114]. In the church of the monastery of the Peribleptos at Constantinople, the founder Raymond III Argyrus (1028-34) was represented at the side of the Virgin in a way which recalls the mosaics of Saint Sophia. Beneath the Virgin were represented the thirty castles (estates?) and cities which the emperor had conferred upon the monastery, together with their names and a list of the monastery's privileges inscribed on metal and accompanied by seals of wax and lead. The introduction of the text changes a picture which originated as an *ex voto* into a deed of foundation; it has become a legal document placing publicly on record what are the monastery's possessions and privileges. The two themes have therefore been combined.

Professor Djurić also calls attention to the representation at Subiaco of a privilege conferred on the monastery by pope Innocent III [115]. The resemblance to Byzantine and Serbian pictures of the gift of a privilege is sufficiently evident for it to be likely that the artist had seen a Byzantine chrysobull (Fig. 24 a). However there are one or two peculiarities. Firstly

FIG. 24 a. — Privilege of Subiaco. Fresco, Subiaco.

pope Innocent III is represented above as a bust portrait with his arms apparently outstretched — a position and a gesture which in Byzantine art were used for Christ, the Virgin or a saint [116]. Secondly pope Innocent III is by some anomaly represented twice in the same picture, for he appears not only above but also to one side [117]. On the left Saint Benedict receives the charter upon which the text of the privilege is fully inscribed. Saint Benedict, enthroned, corresponds to the saint who in a Byzantine representation of this subject receives the privilege. But there is also a third peculiarity. John, who was prior at the time when the privilege was conferred, is also present in the scene; he is helping to hold the charter [118].

The combination of two disparate models in order to make a new picture is familiar in Byzantine manuscript illumination. Professor Weitzmann adduces cases where the artist, by failing to understand his model's properly, has perpetrated an anomaly [119]. However in this case the double representation of Innocent III has an evident sense: the pope at once confers the privilege and guarantees its authenticity. For the upper part of the scene the model would most probably have been a chrysobull. I would suggest that the other model would have been the representation of the Concordat of Worms in Callixtus II's Audience Hall.

I would also suggest that this picture marked a new departure in political imagery. While the scene of the Concordat of Worms resembles the conferment of a privilege and the promulgation of a document, it does not strictly enter into either category; for it is in fact the record of a contract.

It seems that this point was missed by the artist responsible for the miniature in Alexander Laicus's *Commentary on the Apocalypse* (Cambridge University Library MS Mm. 5. 31, f. 144ᵛ) (Fig. 24 b). Pope Callixtus II sits enthroned on the right with his clergy

115. V.J. DJURIĆ, *art. cit.*, note 110, p. 264; F. HERMANIN, *I monasteri di Subiaco, gli affreschi*, Rome, 1904, I, p. 462-5 and 472; R. FOREVILLE, *Latran I, II, III et Latran IV*, Paris, 1965, p. 288.

116. Cf. Djurić's examples, *art. cit.*, note 110, pl. 3 and 14; although later than the Subiaco privilege, they certainly continue a pre-existing tradition.

117. If one were to suppose that the bishop on the right of the picture is Blasius, archbishop of Torres (Turrita = Sassari, Sardinia), the *Turritanus electus* who drafted and signed the document containing the privilege (cf. P.B. GAMS, *Series episcoporum ecclesiæ catholicæ*, Ratisbon, 1873, p. 839 and L. JADIN, "Blaise, archevêque de Torres," in *Dictionnaire d'histoire et de géographie ecclésiastique*, IX, 70), then the presence of the bust of Innocent III above would present no anomaly: he would be confirming and guaranteeing the privilege accorded by the Curial official below. However there are traces of a square halo which make the pope more likely; further it seems that the letters INN can be deciphered on the dark band above the bishop's head.

118. The text of the privilege on the fresco conforms *grosso modo* with that given in the Register of Innocent III's Letters (*Innocentii II Romani pontificis Regestorum sive epistolarum Liber Sextus*, I, PL 215, 9-10). The fresco commemorates Innocent III's visit to Subiaco in 1202, when he undertook the reform of monastic discipline and promised a grant of six *libræ* annually from the Apostolic Camera. Later the Prior John, who figures in the fresco kneeling before Saint Benedict, requested that the source of revenue be fixed; this was conceded, and the charge was made upon the papal revenue from Castel Porziano (cf. R. FOREVILLE, *op. cit.*, note 115, p. 288).

119. K. WEITZMANN, *Illustrations in Roll and Codex*, Princeton, 1947, p. 178 *et seq.*

beside him. The emperor Henry stands to the left of the scene with his *spatharius* and two courtiers. Like the Lateran fresco, it is therefore an official scene. However although the emperor holds an unfolded roll upon which are inscribed the opening words of the Concordat, the pope does not hold it jointly with the emperor.

On the other hand there are examples of official pictures which one may reasonably suppose to be modelled upon the Lateran fresco. There was a need for an official imagery to portray a contract or the conferment of a privilege binding to both, the giver and the receiver (Fig. 24 c). One such picture would be the Privilege of Marbach, which, conferred by Callixtus II himself, was represented in the middle of the XIIth century [120]. It also seems likely that this fresco served as a model for the mosaic of the *Constitutum Constantini* in

FIG. 24 c. — Privilege of Marbach. *Codex* Guta-Sintram, f. 2, Grand Séminaire, Strasbourg.

FIG. 24 b. — Concordat of Worms. MS Mm. 5. 31, f. 144ᵛ, University Library, Cambridge.

120. R. FORE-VILLE, *op. cit.*, note 115, p. 80. The Privilege of Marbach was granted by Callixtus II on October 30th, 1119, but the miniature in the *codex* Guta-Sintram (Strasbourg, Grand Séminaire), f. 2, was only executed in about 1154. The Pope is represented on the left and Gerongus, provost of the Canons Regular of Marbach, on the right of the picture. Inscribed on the document which they hold are the first phrases of the privilege confirming an exemption granted by Urban II and Paschal II. For the full text cf. PL 163, 1130. The picture in the *Liber Testamentorum Regium* of bishop Don Pelayo in Oviedo cathedral and dating from about 1120 (cf. P. DE PALOL and M. HIRMER, *L'art en Espagne,* Paris, 1967, p. 164, and fig. xxxii) records a gift rather than confirms a contract. The enthroned king hands to a tonsured, haloed cleric a document inscribed TESTAMĒ. A miniature of

Lotharius III granting a privilege to the Abbey of Formbach (Munich Reichsarchiv-Formbach, *codex* Lit. 1, f. 3 a) includes the text of the conclusion of the document (cf. P.E. SCHRAMM, *Die deutschen Kaiser und Könige in Bildern ihrer Zeit*, Leipzig-Berlin, 1928, p. 150 and 221 and fig. 130). The Donation of King Aistulf in the *Chronicon*

FIG. 25. — Constantine bestowing the *frigium* on Sylvester. Chapel of Saint Sylvester, church of the Quattro Coronati, Rome.

the portico of the Lateran basilica. Again the pope is enthroned while the emperor stands; and again they hold together an unrolled document. It would then follow that the *Constitutum Constantini* was conceived in XIIth century Rome as a contract analogous to the Concordat of Worms: the pope and the emperor in both cases recognize mutually their respective rights.

It seems therefore that these frescoes commissioned by Callixtus II, while based on established traditions in official imagery, were not slavishly modelled upon a pre-existing repertoire. So far as the triumph over the antipopes was concerned, the pope was ready to be represented, along with his predecessors, after the model of the victorious Christ in Messianic imagery. For the relations between Church and Empire, he accepted a new formula, which, while giving a certain superiority to the pope and following the model of Christ as Emperor, nevertheless admitted the possibility of a contract between the Vicar of Christ and the terrestrial emperor.

3. The Coronation of Lotharius II: *Strator.*

As I stated in the first part of this study, I incline to the view that there was at one time in the room which pope Innocent II had decorated in the Lateran Palace a picture of the emperor Lotharius II performing for the pope the office of *marescalchus* or *strator* [121]. However in the absence of any description of this picture a reconstruction is necessarily hypothetical. It can only be based upon other pictures of an emperor performing the office of *strator* for the pope.

Vulturnense (Vaticanus barb. lat. 2724, f. 54ᵛ) must also derive from the fresco of the Concordat of Worms. An enthroned cleric receives an unfolded, inscribed roll from the standing king. On the other hand the forged Donation of Paschal I is represented as the conferment of a privilege. The enthroned pope hands an unfolded roll to the Abbot of San Vincenzo al Volturno (*ibid.,* f. 102). The earlier miniatures in this manuscript were, in fact, adder afterwards and date from later in the century (cf. LADNER, *I ritratti, op. cit.,* note 108, p. 232 *et seq.* and fig. 155-6).

121. Cf. CA XX, 1970, p. 167. To the bibliography of the *officium stratoris* (*ibid.,* p. 166, note 44) add O. TREITINGER, *Die oströmische Kaiser- und Reichsidee,* Jena, 1938¹ and Darmstadt, 1956², p. 225-227.

Two such pictures do exist. The earlier dates from the pontificate of Innocent IV (1243-1254), a century later, that is to say, than the paintings executed for Innocent II. It is in the Chapel of San Silvestro at the Church of the Quattro Coronati in Rome, and it forms part of the life cycle of the saint[122]. It is preceded by a representation of Constantine bestowing the *frigium* on Sylvester. This episode is taken from the *Constitutum Constantini*, although the narrative of the *Constitutum*

is not followed in every detail. For example, while in the narrative of the *Constitutum*, Constantine actually crowns Sylvester *(eius sacratissimo vertici manibus nostris imposuimus)*, in the fresco Constantine stands before the enthroned Sylvester and presents him with the tiara[123] (Fig. 25). One may, on the analogy of the representation of the τραχελισμός[124], suppose that the narrative has been modified in order to conform with ceremonial. At the coronation of a pope, the archdeacon received the tiara from the *major strator*[125]. It will be observed that in this picture a groom stands behind the principal figures holding the horse's bridle, which Constantine also holds in his left hand. The correspondence between the picture and the ceremonial is therefore close but not exact.

In the actual representation of Constantine as the pope's *strator*, Sylvester, wearing pallium and tiara, is seated upon the horse; his left hand is raised in blessing. Ahead of him rides a deacon carrying a cross and entering the gates of the city of Rome ; next comes Constantine's *spatharius*, while Constantine himself walks

122. A. Muñoz, *Il restauro della Chiesa e del Chiostro dei SS. Quattro Coronati*, Rome, 1914, p. 103 and fig. 143-4. According to an inscription the Chapel of San Silvestro was built and dedicated in 1246. Cf. also Wilpert, *op. cit.*, note 77, p. 1012 and pl. 299.

123. *Constitutum Constantini*, *Fontes iuris germanici antiqui*, X, *Monumenta Germaniæ Historica*, edited by H. Fuhrmann, Hanover, 1968, p. 91. For other editions, cf. CA XX, 1970, p. 172, note 61.

124. See above, p. 118.

125. *Celebrata missa descendit* (sc. *papa*) *ad locum ubi est equus papalis ornatus, et ibi archidiaconus recipit frigium a majori stratori de quo papam coronat;* *et sic per mediam urbem devenit ad palatium Lateranense coronatus* (From the papal coronation ceremonial, cf. *Gesta pauperis scholaris Albini*, XI, 3, in *Le Liber Censuum de l'Église romaine*, edited Paul Fabre, Paris, 1905, p. 124a). I have not seen J. Traeger's study: *Der reitende Papst. Ein Beitrag zur Ikonographie des Papsttums*, Munich-Zurich, 1970.

Fig. 26. — Constantine as Sylvester's *strator*. Chapel of Saint Sylvester, church of the Quattro Coronati, Rome.

FIG. 27. — Alexander III with the emperor Frederick I and the doge Sebastiano Ziani
as *stratores*. Palazzo della Signoria, Sienna.

beside Sylvester's horse, holding its bridle. Behind Constantine is an attendant holding an *ombrellino*; three bishops on horseback bring up the rear. This scene corresponds, therefore, more closely to the text of the *Constitutum*: *tenentes frenum equi ipsius pro reverentia B. Petri stratoris offitium illi exhibuimus* [126] (Fig. 26).

The later example is to be found in the Palazzo della Signoria at Sienna. It is in the Sala di Balia and forms part of the biographical cycle of the Sienese pope Alexander III [127]. It was executed in the XVth century by Spinello Aretino. Frederick I did not respect the Concordat of Worms. However in July 1177, having failed to sustain his opposition to pope Alexander III, he was forced to come to terms. On July 24th he prostrated himself at the

pope's feet outside the church of Saint Mark in Venice. The next day he performed the office of *strator* for the pope. On October 15th Alexander III left Venice for Rome [128].

In Spinello Aretino's picture the Venetian galleys may be seen in the background (Fig. 27). On the right are the walls of a city, presumably Rome. A figure richly dressed walks beside the pope's horse, rendering him the *officium strepæ*. Ahead of the pope's horse walk the emperor Frederick I and the doge Sebastiano Ziani, rendering him the *officium stratoris*.

This picture is perhaps the more interesting

126. *Constitutum Constantini*, ed. cit., note 123, p. 92.
127. C. RICCI, *Il Palazzo pubblico di Siena e la Mostra d'antica arte senese*, 1904, p. 17.
128. J. ROUSSET DE PINA, "La politique italienne d'Alexandre III et la fin du schisme," in *Histoire de l'Église*, IX 2, Paris, 1953, p. 143-156.

of the two, since it represents in a schematic form a number of genuine but disconnected historical events. But in both cases it is clear that the artist is working within an established tradition of political imagery. For the picture of Constantine as pope Sylvester's *strator*, Dr Kantorowicz has already suggested an origin in the classical theme of the *Adventus* [129]. The *Adventus* is the ceremonial arrival of a victorious emperor either at the city of Rome

FIG. 28. — *Adventus* at Milan of Constantine. Medal, Cabinet des médailles, Paris.

or at the city which he has conquered. He might arrive on horseback or on foot. Both kinds of *Adventus* are represented in official imagery; here however we are only concerned with the emperor's arrival on horseback. A number of variations in detail are possible. The emperor may be accompanied by a standard bearer and a personification of Victory holding a crown and a palm branch [130] (Fig. 28). A conquered barbarian may crouch before the emperor's horse; the conquered city may be represented with its *Tyche* emerging to greet the victorious emperor; alternatively a crowd may be gathered at the city gates. The theme persisted in Byzantine tradition, as for example in the curious fresco in the Church of Saint Demetrius in Thessaloniki [131] (Fig. 29). However I think that it may be said categorically that in antique representations of the *Adventus* there is *never* a person leading the victorious emperor's horse [132].

The reason is simple: in imperial ceremonial this office did not exist. It is true that the office of *strator* was known to the Greeks and Romans [133]. However he was simply a groom, who looked after his master's horses and helped his master to mount and dismount. If his master owned numerous horses, he might appoint a *tribunus stabuli*, the equivalent of the later protostrator. Obviously in a society where the

129. E.H. KANTOROWICZ, "The King's Advent and the Enigmatic Panels in the Doors of Santa Sabina," in *The Art Bulletin*, XXVI, 1944, p. 207-231; Idem, "Constantinus Strator*, Marginalien zum Constitutum Constantini," in *Jahrbuch für Antike und Christentum*, 1964 (*Mullus, Festschrift Theodor Klauser*), p. 181-189.
For a general account of this iconographical theme cf. "Epiphania", in PAULY-WISSOWA, *Supplement* IV, 310 *et seq.*; A. GRABAR, *L'empereur*, p. 47, 130-131 and 234. For an account of the iconography of the emperor's *profectio* from and *adventus* at the city of Rome cf. G. KOEPPEL, "Profectio und Adventus," in *Bonner Jahrbücher*, 169, 1969, p. 130-194.
For a description of the ceremony cf. that given by Dio Cassius of Severus's *Adventus* in 193 A.D.: Πράξας δὲ ὁ Σεουῆρος ταῦτα ἐς τὴν Ῥώμην ἐσήει [καὶ] μέχρι μὲν τῶν πυλῶν ἐπί τε τοῦ ἵππου καὶ ἐν ἐσθῆτι ἱππικῇ ἐλθὼν ἐντεῦθεν δὲ τήν τε πολιτικὴν ἀλλαξάμενος καὶ βαδίσας (After doing this Severus entered Rome. He advanced as far as the gates on horseback and in cavalry costume, but there he changed into civilian attire and proceeded on foot) *History of Rome* 75.1.3, Loeb Classical Library, London, 1927, IX, p. 162.
130. Cf. T. HOLSCHER, *Victoria Romana, Archäologische Untersuchungen zur Geschichte und Wesensart der römischen Siegesgöttin von den Anfängen bis zum Ende des 3 Jhs. n. Chr.*, Mainz, 1967, p. 48, *et seq.*
131. G.A. SOTERIOU, Ἡ Βασιλικὴ τοῦ Ἁγίου Δημητρίου Θεσσαλονίκης, Athens, 1952, I, p. 207-9 and II,

pl. 78; A. VASILIEV, "L'entrée triomphale de l'empereur Justinien à Thessalonique en 688," in *Orientalia Christiana Periodica*, XIII, 1947 (*Miscellanea Guillaume de Jerphanion*), p. 361-3; J.D. BRECKENRIDGE, "The 'Long Siege' of Thessalonika, its date and iconography," in *Byzantinische Zeitschrift*, 48, 1955, p. 116-22.
132. I think that one can afford to be categorical, because in his erudite and ingenious article "Constantinus Strator" (cf. note 129) the late Dr Kantorowicz, the assiduity of whose research is wellknown, can only cite one single example of an angel of Victory leading the emperor's horse in an *Adventus* scene, the medal minted in Tarragona on the occasion of Constantine's *Adventus* at Milan in 313 with, on its obverse, the busts side by side of Constantine and Sol Invictus. But Dr Kantorowicz was deceived by a poor photograph. According to E. BABELON, who first published the medal and knew it first hand, 'la Victoire que marche devant le cheval de l'empereur tient de la main droite levée une couronne et de la main gauche une palme' ("Un nouveau médaillon de or de Constantin le Grand," in *Mélanges Boissier*, Paris, 1903, p. 50). This is, indeed, the normal iconography for an angel of Victory. Moreover it appears evidently both in the drawing in MAURICE, *op. cit.* note 85, II, p. 239 and in the photograph in J.M.C. TOYNBEE, *Roman Medallions* (*op. cit.* note 91), pl. XVII 11 (cf. p. 108-9). It seems, therefore, that Dr Kantorowicz supposed the Victory's palm to be the bridle of the horse.
133. "Strator" in DAREMBERG-SAGLIO IV 2, 1530-1 and in PAULY-WISSOWA II vii, 329-30.

horse, whether for racing, hunting or battle, occupied a privileged place, the *strator* had opportunities for recommending himself. Bury recalls that the future Basil I passed from the stables of Theophilitzes, whose *protostrator* he had been, to the imperial stables [134].

The *protostrator* did become an increasingly important person at Constantinople from the VIIIth century. Nevertheless his functions did not include that of leading the emperor's horse on ceremonial occasions any more than in ancient Rome [135]. Only much later at Constantinople do the ceremony and the office become united. Thus we read in the *De Officiis* of the Pseudo-Kodinus that "the Count of the Imperial Horse would bring a horse and hold it when the emperor was going to mount. When the emperor had mounted the *protostrator* took the bridle and led the horse" [136]. It is hard to believe that this ceremony did not come to the Byzantine court from the West.

The *Adventus* served as a model for the representation of Christ's triumphal entry into Jerusalem [137]. The analogy is evident, and the same elements are present: Christ arriving on the ass, the city gates and a crowd acclaiming him. However here again, with one possible exception, a *strator* never leads the ass upon which Christ is mounted, at least in Byzantine art. The exception, apparently of Coptic origin, shows Christ mounted on an ass between two angels, the front one of which leads the ass [138]. It is not, however, certain that this is a representation of the Entry to Jerusalem. Christ's Entry into Egypt, an apocryphal development of the Gospel account of the Flight to Egypt, sometimes apppears as an *Adventus*. For example in the miniature in the *Menologion of Basil II* the personification of Egypt emerging from the city is conceived after the model of a *Tyche*; the figure's hands are covered, as would be the case in Imperial ceremonial when greeting a royal person. In this picture, unusually for Byzantine representations of the Flight to Egypt, Joseph is leading the mount [139].

However since the presence of a groom is not authenticated in antique representations of an *Adventus* and is unusual in Byzantine scenes derived from the *Adventus,* we must seek the origins of the *strator* in iconography elsewhere. A groom sometimes figures in triumphal processions leading the horses which draw the

chariot of the victorious emperor. In the bas-relief on the Arch of Titus the quadriga is conducted by *Roma* (or *Virtus*) carrying a tall *vexillum*. In the scene on the Arch of Septimius Severus at Lepcis, probably commemorating his victories of 203 A.D., the quadriga is led by a tunic-clad figure, for whom various identifica-

FIG. 29. — Scene modelled upon the *Adventus*. Fresco, Church of Saint Demetrius, Thessaloniki.

134. J.B. BURY, *The imperial administrative system in the IXth century*, London, 1911, p. 117.

135. R. GUILLAND, "Études de titulature et de prosopographie byzantines, Le Protostrator," in *Revue des Études Byzantines*, 7, 1949, p .156-75.

136. PSEUDO-KODINUS, *Traité des Offices*, edited by J. VERPEAUX, Paris, 1966, p. 168. It would seem that Eichmann was right (cf. E. EICHMANN, "Das Officium Stratoris et Strepæ," in *Historische Zeitschrift*, 142, 1930, p. 20) in rejecting Holtzmann's view that "der Stratordienst stammt aus Byzanz" (cf. R. HOLTZMANN, *Der Kaiser als Marschall des Papstes, Eine Untersuchung zur Geschichte der Beziehung zwischen Kaiser und Papst in Mittelalter*, Heidelberg, 1928, p. 22).

137. A. GRABAR, *L'empereur*, p. 234-236; E. LUCCHESI PALLI, "Einzug in Jerusalem," in *Reallexikon zur byzantinischen Kunst*, II, 22-30.

138. A. GRABAR, *L'empereur*, p. 235; Idem, *Christian Iconography, op. cit.*, note 78, p. 45 and pl. 123; J. BECKWITH, *Coptic Sculpture*, 300-1500, London, 1963, p. 29 and pl. 126.

139. *Il Menologio di Basilio II*, edited by C. STORNAJOLO, Vatican-Milan, 1907, I, p. 75; II, f. 274. There is no reference to the Flight to Egypt in the original text of the *Proto-Gospel of Saint-James* (cf. below p. 132 and note 154), which was apparently the best known of the apocryphal gospels in the East. In primitive Cappadocian iconography Joseph's son invariably leads the Virgin's mount.

tions have been proposed (Fig. 30). In both cases the person leading the chariot is generally given an allegorical identity [140]. Moreover the triumphal procession in a chariot does not seem

FIG. 30. — Triumph of Septimius Severus (detail). Triumphal arch Lepcis Magna.

to have continued either in ceremonial or in official imagery.

Representations of a person holding his own mount by the reins are relatively common in both classical and Byzantine art. Such a person may figure in a genre scene. For example in one of the mosaics at Piazza Armerina two young men in short tunics hold their horses by the bridle while a third offers incense before the statue of Artemis Agrotera [141]. Similarly Amazons are represented leading their horses on the diptychs of Anastasius [142]. But a representation of Constantine holding his own horse by the bridle cannot, to my mind, be cited as evidence of a traditional iconography of Constantine as *strator* [143]. The model for such a representation would have been some famous rider of Antiquity with his steed: Alexander with Bucephalus, Bellerophon with Pegasus, or — most likely of all — one of the Dioscuri (Fig. 31 b) [144].

A groom in Byzantine iconography is, it would seem, simply a groom. He has no ceremonial function. Thus in the *Sacra Parallela* at the Bibliothèque Nationale the Levite of Ephraim is represented leading his concubine on an ass [145]. In the *Skyllitzes matritensis*, a groom escorts the emperor Michael III in one miniature; in another a groom conducts Abul Asa'ir, who had been taken prisoner, to the

140. Inez SCOTT RYBERG, *Rites of the State Religion in Roman Art*, American Academy in Rome, *Memoirs*, XXII, 1955, p. 146 and 160; plate LII, fig. 79a and pl. LVII, fig. 88. Scott Ryberg is unfavorably disposed to an identification of the *strator* in the Lepcis relief as a *iuvenis* of Lepcis (*ibid.*, p. 160, note 57).

I know of no analogous scene in Byzantine art. However Theophanes tells how four *patricii* led the empress Irene's golden chariot drawn by four horses in the Easter procession of 798: προῆλθεν ἡ βασίλισσα (...) ἐπὶ ὀχήματος χρουσοῦ ἐποχουμένη τέσσαρσιν ἵπποις λευχοῖς συρομένου καὶ ὑπὸ τεσσάρων πατριχίων χρατουμένου (THEOPHANES, *Chronographia*, ed. Ch. DE BOOR, Leipzig, 1883, p. 474).

141. G.V. GENTILI, *La Villa Erculia di Piazza Armerina, I mosaici figurati*, Rome, s.d., pl. XVII.

142. R. DELBRUECK, *Die Consulardiptychen und verwandte Denkmäler*, Berlin-Leipzig, 1929, p. 75 and 125; W.F. VOLBACH, *Elfenarbeiten der Spätantiken und des frühen Mittelalters*, Mainz, 1952, numbers 17-22, p. 27-28. There seems to me to be a deliberate intention of burlesque in the representations, which in themselves derive from a more serious iconographical tradition. Cf. note 144.

143. KANTOROWICZ, *art. cit.* in *Mullus*, note 129, p. 187 and pl. X c, d.

144. K. WEITZMANN, *Greek Mythology in Byzantine Art*, Princeton, 1951, p. 102, *et seq.*, fig. 110 (bas relief of Bucephalus [?] in the Capitoline Museum, Rome) and fig. 228 (bas relief of Pegasus and Bellerophon on a sarcophagus in the National Museum at Athens); "Dioscuri", in *Dictionnaire des antiquités grecques et romaines*, edited

by C. DAREMBERG and E. SAGLIO, Paris, 1877-1910, II 1, p. 264, fig. 2448 and 2449; *idem*, in *Enciclopedia dell'arte antica*, III, p. 124 and fig. 155 (IIIrd century sarcophagus in the Palazzo Mattei, Rome).

These themes pass into early Christian and Byzantine art. Bucephalus is represented in illustrated manuscripts of the *Alexander Romance* of the Pseudo-Callisthenes; cf. WEITZMANN, *op. cit.* above, particularly in *Marcianus graecus* 479, f. 8, illustrated fig. 108. Pegasus and Bellerophon figure upon ivory caskets with genre scenes, although the person holding a horse by the bridle on the Veroli casket is not Bellerophon; cf. D. TALBÒT-RICE, *Art byzantin*, Paris-Brussels, 1959, p. 302-303 and pl. 108-109. The Dioscuri figure upon a Christian sarcophagus at Arles; cf. E. LE BLANT, *Étude sur les sarcophages chrétiens antiques de la ville d'Arles*, Paris, 1878, number XXXI, p. 38-41 and pl. XXIII, and upon another at Tortona; cf. J. WILPERT, *I sarcofagi cristiani antichi*, Rome, 1929, II, p. 349 and fig. 217. The Dioscuri would also have served as model for portraits of jockeys; cf. F. WIRTH, *Römische Wandmalerei*, Darmstadt, 1968, pl. 12. The assimilation of a triumphant emperor or a victorious jockey to the Dioscuri would be entirely in accordance with Antique tradition. Similarly a burlesque representation of Amazons with their mounts (cf. above, note 142) would be in accordance with the traditions of Hellenistic genre art.

145. *Parisinus graecus* 923, f. 371ᵛ illustrating *Judges* 19, 25-28; cf. K. WEITZMANN, "Zur Frage des Einflusses jüdischer Bilderquellen auf die Illustration des Alten Testamentes," in *Mullus* (cf. note 129), p. 408 and pl. 16 a.

FIG. 31 a. — Sarcophagus of M. Mynius Lollianus. Louvre, Galerie Mollien.

FIG. 31 b. — Rider and mount. Detail of Veroli casket.
London, Victoria and Albert Museum.

FIG. 31 c. — Journey to Bethlehem. Detail
of Throne of Maximian. Ravenna, Museo
Arcivescovile.

(a)

(b)

Fig. 32. — Aman and Mordecai: a) fresco (detail), synagogue Dura-Europos;
b) Farfa Bible, *Vaticanus latinus* 5729, f. 319ᵛ.

·T·FLAVIO·T·F·PAL·VERO·EQVITI·ROMANO·

FIG. 33. — Sarcophagus of T. Flavius.

Byzantine emperor [146]. Earlier still in the synagogue of Dura-Europos Haman is represented leading Mordecai through the streets of Babylon (Fig. 32 a, b). Dr Kraeling remarks that "in introducing at the right of the rider the man who leads the horse, the artist has made his most significant departure from the traditional composition of scenes of imperial triumph" [147]. It seems, however, clear that the Hebrew text of the *Book of Esther* countenances this departure from the traditional of Imperial iconography; perhaps it is significant that the Greek Septuagint text does not say explicitly that Haman actually leads Mordecai through

the street [148]. I know of no illuminated Byzantine text of the *Book of Esther*; I cannot therefore say how this scene would have been interpreted at Constantinople. However in two Western manuscripts Haman is represented, as at Dura-Europos, leading Mordecai's horse. The better example is in the Farfa Bible [149].

In one or two cases there may be seen in Roman funerary art a scene in which a groom is leading a mounted horse (Fig. 33). There is, for example, the sarcophagus of T. Flavius Verus, formerly at the Lateran Museum, and that of an unidentified person upon a relief in the Termi Museum [150]. The relationship be-

146. *Skyllitzes matritensis,* f. 78 (*ed. cit.* note 79, no. 198; cf. PG 122, 1062); *ibid.,* f. 136 (*ed. cit.,* no. 343; cf. here note 102). For examples of a groom leading a beast without a rider cf. Joseph's son leading a pack-mule in the Return from Egypt in the Kariye Djami (P.A. UNDERWOOD, *The Kariye Djami,* New York, 1966, p. 105 and pl. 202), and the young man holding the horses of the Magi in the Adoration scene in Saint Nicolas Orphanos, Thessaloniki (T. VELMANS, "Les fresques de Saint-Nicolas Ophanos," in CA XVI, p. 167, fig. 24).

147. C.H. KRAELING, *The Excavations at Dura-Europos, Final Report,* VIII 1, *The Synagogue,* New Haven, 1956, p. 151, *et seq.,* especially p. 154, pl. XVII and LXIV.

148. *Esther* 6, 11. The sense of the Hebrew is 'bring on horseback' (faire chevaucher). The text, however, of the Septuagint is ἀνεβίβασεν αὐτὸν ἐπὶ τὸν ἵππον καὶ διῆλθεν διὰ τῆς πλατείας τῆς πόλεως. I am grateful to Père Jean Potin for explaining to me the niceties of the Hebrew text.

149. Cf. *Vat. lat.* 5729, f. 319ᵛ (The *Ripoll* or *Farfa Bible*) which dates from the first half of the XIth century. In this example, besides Haman leading Mordecai's mount, there are three figures on the left with an arm raised in a gesture of acclamation (W. NEUSS, *Die katalonischen Bibelillustrationen,* Bonn-Leipzig, 1922, fig. 126 and p. 102).

Also the illustration to the *Gumpertsbibel* at Erlangen. Again three figures appear to the left of Mordecai's mount. Haman apparently holds the reins, but in fact his hand is slightly smudged (G. SWARZENSKI, *Die Salzburger Malerei,* Leipzig, 1913, pl. XLII, fig. 132). This example dates from the second half of the XIIth century. I am grateful to Dr Carl-Otto Nordström fo drawing my attention to these two miniatures.

150. These scenes were identified by J. WILPERT ("L'ultimo viaggio nell' arte sepolcrale romano," in *Atti della pontificia Accademia romana di archeologia, Rendiconti,* III, 1924-1925, p. 61 *et seq.,* and *I sarcofagi cristiani antichi,* III, *supplemento,* Rome, 1936, p. 18 and pl. CCLXXIII 8) and by D.E.L. HAYNES ("Mors in Victoria," in *Papers of the British School of Rome,* XV, 1939, p. 27-33) as the Journey beyond the Tomb. Haynes also cites two other sarcophagi now lost and known only from drawings. Unfortunately it does not seem possible to accept this identification, nor, by consequence, Haynes's inference that the introduction of these elements from imperial triumphal imagery into a funerary theme reflects the development of a more optimistic attitude towards death. P. VEYNE ("Iconographie de la *Transvectio equitum* et des Lupercales," in *Revue des études anciennes,* LXII, 1960,

tween these different sorts of scene which bear a resemblance to the *Adventus* needs further investigation than is possible here. For example the representation of M. Mynius Lollianus in the Galerie Mollien of the Louvre is certainly a summary version of the *Transvectio equitum* (Fig. 31 a) [151]. However it would seem that this same iconography was used in Etruscan funerary art, while upon a stele at Chester there is represented a legionary whose mount is probably

being led by a groom [152]. Again in the series of biographical scenes upon the sarcophagus of Gorgonius at Ancona there is one where the rider is preceded by a *cursor* and followed by a *pedisequus* [153].

We are up against one of the principal difficulties in the study of iconography: the ambiguity of scenes which are not accompanied by an epigraph. Only a negative conclusion can be drawn, that a *strator*, even if he figures in an official scene in Antique art, has not a clear ceremonial function. If he leads the mount of a young equestrian it is more probably for the practical reason that the mount had to be steadied. It was in fact in these terms that the office of the lay *strator* in papal ceremonial was to be explained.

The presence of a person leading the Virgin's mount in scenes of the Journey to Bethlehem and also of the Flight to Egypt is to be explained in the same way. According to the apocryphal *Proto-Gospel of Saint James* "Joseph saddled the ass and seated Mary upon it. His son led the beast and Samuel followed" [154]. This description provided the basis for the Journey to Bethlehem. Since this Gospel has no account of the Flight to Egypt, artists often adapted the scene for the Journey to Bethlehem. On the other hand the apocryphal *Gospel of Saint Matthew* [155] would have been the source for the representation of the Journey to Bethlehem on the Throne of Maximian at Ravenna (Fig. 31 c). An angel with a staff, resembling the groom on the sarcophagus of Flavius Verus, holds the reins to steady the ass while Joseph helps the Virgin to dismount [156]. Numerous examples can be cited where Joseph or his son acts as *strator* for the Virgin, particularly in Italy and Cappadocia [157].

We first hear of the ceremonial office of *strator* in Rome at the time of the pontificate of Gregory I (590-604). According to the *Ordo Romanus*, I, when the pope road on horseback *stratores laici a dextris et a sinistris equi ambulant ne alicubi titubet* [158]. In the VIIIth century king Pippin rendered the same service to pope Stephen II (752-757) at Ponthieu: *vice stratoris usque in aliquantulum locum iuxta eius sellarem properavit* [159]. In the *Constitutum Constantini*, however, as we have seen, Constantine as *strator* is said explicitly to have held the bridle of pope Sylvester's horse [160]. The change is of

---

p. 100-110 and pl. VII, VIII, IX) argues convincingly that these scenes in fact represent the ceremony by which the youth whose equestrian portrait is represented on each sarcophagus was admitted to this order. The absence of a groom leading the horse in some of these scenes suggests that he had no specific rôle in the ceremony. It also follows that we have no grounds for supposing that the presence of a groom leading the mount defines the scene in question as a journey.

151. A. HÉRON DE VILLEFOSSE, *Bulletin de la Société Nationale des Antiquaires de France*, 1904, p. 320-323.

152. R.P. WRIGHT and I.A. RICHMOND, *Catalogue of the Roman Inscribed Stones in the Grosvenor Museum, Chester*, Chester, 1955, p. 40, no. 91 and pl. 26; TOYNBEE, *op. cit.* note 88, p. 194. The attitude and proportions are highly reminiscent of Greek models, while the groom wears a pointed hat.

153. WILPERT, *op. cit.* note 150, p. 181 and pl. XIV. Monsieur Paul Veyne suggests in a private letter that this scene is the *Processus* of a magistrate.

154. Καὶ ἔστρωσεν τὸν ὄνον καὶ ἐκάθισεν αὐτὴν καὶ ἧλκεν ὁ υἱὸς αὐτοῦ καὶ ἠκολούθη Σαμουήλ (*Proto-Gospel of Saint James*, XVII 2, in *La forme la plus ancienne du Protévangile de Jacques*, edited by E. DE STRYCKER, *Subsidia hagiographica*, number 33, Brussels, 1961, p. 142-143; cf. p. 143, note 7. *Los evangelios apócrifos*, edited by A. DE SANTOS, *Biblioteca de autores cristianos*, Madrid, 1956, p. 174.

155. Iussit angelus stare iumentum, quia tempus advenerat pariendi; et præcepit descendere de animali Mariam (*Gospel of Pseudo-Matthew*, XIII 2, ed. TISCHENDORFF cf. note 96, p. 76-77; ed. DE SANTOS cf. note 15, p. 221).

156. G.W. MORATH, *Die Maximianskathedra in Ravenna*, Freiburg im Breisgau, 1940, p. 41; VOLBACH, *op. cit.* note 142, number 140, p. 68 and pl. 43; A. GRABAR, *Christian Iconography*, cf. note 78, p. 101-102 and pl. 259. Curiously the representation of this subject upon an ivory diptych at the Bibliothèque nationale, while closely resembling the Ravenna ivory in most other respects, does not include an angel *strator* (cf. VOLBACH, *op. cit.* above, number 77, p. 46 and pl. 25).

157. I am concerned here only to establish the fact that a *strator* often figures in the iconography of journeys, and particularly in the Journey to Bethlehem and the Flight to Egypt. In a subsequent article I shall attempt a closer study of place of the *strator* in these two subjects. The fact that the Virgin's mount is led sometimes by Joseph and at others by an angel or his son suggests that the artists drew their inspiration from a variety of different literary sources.

158. *Ordo Romanus* I, 8 (M. ANDRIEU, *Les Ordines Romani du Haut Moyen Age*, II, Louvain, 1948, p. 70).

159. *Liber Pontificalis*, edited by L. DUCHESNE, I, Paris, 1955, p. 447.

160. See above, p. 125. One can readily understand why the practice of the emperor acting as *strator* for the patriarch never passed into Constantinopolitan ceremonial and official art. However apparently this practice did occur in the Palm Sunday liturgy in Russia (cf. KANTOROWICZ, "The King's Advent," *art. cit.*, note 129, p. 230).

Dr Rainer Stichel kindly drew my attention to a legend

little practical importance, since in both cases the strator's office is clear: he had to steady the pope's mount. On ceremonial occasions this duty was performed by a person of rank, by a *patricius* if not by the emperor himself. It could also have a special significance: that the *strator* submitted to the person for whom he performed the service, or at least to those whom he represented.

Kantorowicz's contention, therefore, that the representation of Constantine as pope Sylvester's *strator* derives from the *Adventus* must be slightly modified. The *strator's* office at the beginning was purely functional. He had no status in imperial ceremony. His occasional presence therefore in ceremonial scenes in antique art has no special significance. The functional office of leading or steadying a mount acquired a ceremonial value first of all in the West, probably at the Papal court. But it is certainly anachronistic to represent Constantine as pope Sylvester's *strator*. The ceremonial office arrived in Constantinople from the West, but it does not seem to have been taken into Byzantine iconography. On the other hand Western political imagery has admitted once again of a development which is a departure from classical tradition.

IV. CONCLUSION

The aims of this study are modest. In the first place a reconstruction has been attempted of certain pictures embodying a theory of the political authority of the pope, pictures which no longer exist and which for the most part are known only from inadequate descriptions and from drawings executed for Panvinius when their state was already poor. Secondly an analysis of these pictures has been attempted with a view to interpreting them in the light of existing traditions in political imagery current in both East and West and deriving from the official art of the Roman Empire. This analysis has benefitted greatly from the scholarly studies of Dr Ladner; it is limited in so far as it only touches upon the possible influence of ceremonial and imagery deriving from Teutonic tradition.

There is no need today to insist upon the fact that iconography, particularly political

iconography, has its own vocabulary and structure. Nor is it necessary to demonstrate that Christian art, as all branches of Christian culture, developed in the climate of Hellenistic culture. A primary problem was to "translate" Semitic ideas into Hellenistic terms. Since Semitic culture lacked an iconographical tradition, the problem was peculiarly delicate in the realm of art.

Generally Christian artists transposed directly the themes of Imperial and pagan imagery, making Christ an Emperor or a Doctor, his Apostles courtiers or disciples and so on. However when it was necessary to state in terms of iconography the relationship between Church and Empire, difficulties arose. I have described elsewhere the solutions proposed at Byzantium for the representation of oecumenical councils, which were an institution at once of the Church and of the Empire. Here I attempt no more than to contribute some of the material necessary for the study of the imagery used at different periods to make manifest the political authority of the pope.

I have emphasized the curious anomaly that the notions expressed in the *Constitutum Constantini,* surely current at the time, find no expression in the programme of the Triclinium of Leo III. This programme is dominated by the theme of the Mission of the Apostles, an Early Christian adaptation of Antique themes: Christ as Emperor and Doctor invests and instructs his apostles. What is unusual in this programme is the insistence on Investiture. The role attributed at Byzantium to the Apostles is rather that of evangelizing and baptizing all nations.

The iconographical programme does not call in question the theory of a double authority: an *imperium* and a *sacerdotium.* Possibly this is not surprising in the VIIIth century. In his *Letter* to Leo III Charlemagne explains that his office is to defend the Church of Christ against the attacks of pagans and infidels, while the pope, like Moses, prays that the Christian people may be victorious over the enemies of

---

in the *Speculum Magnum.* In the Polish version the Virgin herself holds the reins of the horse of a young warrior whom she had cured of a criminal passion. In the Russian translation this detail is omitted as unworthy of the Mother og God (cf. O.A. DERŽAVINA, *Velikoe zercalo i ego sud'ba na russkoj počve,* Moscow, 1965, p. 31).

God, so that the name of Jesus Christ may be glorified throughout the world [161].

The inscription accompanying the Triclinium mosaic asking Saint Peter to grant victory to Charlemagne is in accordance with these sentiments [162]. However it is perhaps significant that it is Peter who in fact crowns Charlemagne in the Triclinium mosaic. In official Byzantine art this office is performed by an angel if not by Christ himself [163]. The way is therefore left open for the notion that it is the right of Peter's successors to crown those of Charlemagne, as indeed Leo III was himself to crown Charlemagne.

A timelag in the translation of ideas into imagery as well as a certain reluctance to abandon established formulae are well attested in the history of official art. It took an upheaval analogous to that of Iconoclasm in the East to modify the official imagery of the Papacy. The authority conferred by Constantine upon pope Sylvester in the *Constitutum,* particularly as manifested externally by the use of the *frigium* and the throne, was the basis of Papal propaganda during the Investiture controversy. Popes were in fact represented for the first time seated upon a throne in the second half of the XIth century [164]. This development is one of the curiosities of iconography. For the attributes of the terrestrial emperor, given in iconography to the Emperor of Heaven, are now adopted by the Bishop of Rome, who for some time had been using the title, also used by Byzantine emperors, of Vicar of Christ [165].

It seems impossible that the person who devised for Callixtus II the iconographical programme of the Chapel of Saint Nicolas and of the Audience Hall was unfamiliar with the imagery used at Byzantium to express the Triumph of Orthodoxy. I have attempted to show that Arnulf of Lisieux was aware of its overtones. Nevertheless this programme introduces certain innovations: a literal "translation" of the Jewish image of an enemy serving as a *scabellum* was contrary to the norms of Hellenistic and Byzantine art, while a Concordat between Church and Empire was unthinkable at Constantinople, where relations between emperor and patriarch were governed in theory at least by the *Epanagoge* [166].

The representation of the Donation of Constantine in the portico of the Lateran Palace seems to interpret the *Constitutum Constantini* as analogous to the Concordat of Worms. However it is only part of a programme which situates the Donation in the progressive unrolling of the Providential Plan. In fact a theory of history, the product of decadent Hellenistic Stoicism and adapted by Eusebius to the Christian Empire, has been transposed to suit the needs of Papal political propaganda [167]. Henceforth, in the West at least, it is the Pope who is the chief instrument of Providence. Basing himself upon the *Constitutum,* he exercises, parallel to the spiritual authority which he has received as successor of Peter, a temporal jurisdiction.

Evidently such an argument — that an emperor had conferred power upon a pope — became embarrassing once the popes had established themselves *de facto* as well as *de jure* as supreme authority in the West. However it does not seem to have occurred to the Latins, any more than to the Greeks, at this time to doubt the authenticity of the *Constitutum Constantini* [168]. Papal apologists sought rather to limit its significance as an argument against the *plenitudo potestatis*. So Innocent III taught that, while popes were both pontiffs and kings, they had always been pontiffs. In virtue of their pontifical authority they wore a mitre and appointed patriarchs, primates and so on. To this pontifical authority Constantine added a regal authority, in virtue of which popes appointed senators and judges. However the pontifical authority was not only anterior to

161. *Alcuini Epistolæ*, 93, *Epistolarum* IV, *Karolini Aevi* II, edited by E. DUEMMLER, Berlin, 1895, p. 136-137; cf. LADNER, *op. cit.* note 108, p. 123.
162. BEATE PETRE DONAS VITAM LEONI PAPÆ ET VICTORIAM CARULO REGI DONAS; cf. LADNER, *op. cit.* note 108, p. 118.
163. Cf. A. GRABAR, *L'empereur*, pl. XXIII.
164. LADNER, *op. cit.* note 108, p. 124.
165. Cf. M. MACCARRONE, *Vicarius Christi*, Rome, 1952.
166. Cf. A. GRABAR, "L'art religieux et l'empire byzantin à l'époque des Macédoniens," in *L'art de la fin de l'Antiquité et du Moyen Age*, Paris, 1968, p. 160-163; J. WALTER, "Staatsbevoegdheid in kerkelijke aangelegenheden volgens de Orthodoxie," in *Het Christelijk Oosten*, 22, 1970, p. 26-29.
167. F. DVORNIK, *Early Christian and Byzantine Political Philosophy*, Washington, 1966, p. 600 et seq.; cf. R.A. MARKUS, *Sæculum: History and Society in the Theology of Saint Augustine*, Cambridge, 1970, p. 1-21; cf. WALTER, *art. cit.* note 166, p. 23-25.
168. The only exception would seem to be Leo of Vercelli (died 1026), who argued the case against the authenticity of the *Constitutum Constantini* on behalf of Otto III.

the imperial authority but also wider and of greater dignity [169].

Innocent III had the mosaics of the apse of Saint Peter's restored. It is perhaps worth noticing in passing one detail of this restoration. While there is some uncertainty as to the exact programme, the resemblance between copies and the scenes on the Pola casket justify the supposition that the original programme was largely respected [170]. However there must have been one change. In the lower part there is a throne upon which is placed a cross; in front of it is a Lamb (Fig. 34). To the right of the throne stands a crowned figure with a banner; to the left stands a pope wearing a mitre, his arms outstretched in a gesture of adoration. To the right and the left are lambs. If the figure on the right existed in the original plan it might have been an emperor, while the figure on the left would have been the pope during whose pontificate the original mosaics were executed. In the restored version, however, the figure with a banner is not an emperor, as in the investiture scene in the Triclinium of Leo III, but *Ecclesia Romana*; the pope is, of course, Innocent III.

There is a further point of interest. The lambs to left and right symbolize Apostles. Innocent III and *Ecclesia Romana* are therefore integrated into a scene which belongs to the iconography of the Apostles. Further the two figures either side of Christ's throne were normally Saints Peter and Paul. Since such representations exist still — and already existed in Innocent III's time — in Santa Maria Maggiore and in the Chapel of Santo Zeno at San Prassede, the significance would not be lost upon Innocent III's contemporaries: the pope is assimilated to an Apostle and particularly to Saints Peter and Paul. In fact the popes now preferred to base their authority uniquely upon that which Christ gave to the Apostles. The notion of a secular *imperium* has been eliminated from official iconography in Rome. There was, of course, no parallel for this at Byzantium, where Constantine to the end retained his place as the paragon of the Christian emperor.

However the *Constitutum Constantini* was not forgotten. It could be used as an argument against papal claims: what an emperor had granted an emperor could withdraw. This argument was in fact used against Innocent IV. He — or one of his Curial officials — felt obliged to go even further than Innocent III in limiting the import of the *Constitutum*. From the beginning, it is argued in *Aeger cui lenia*, the Apostolic See had been endowed by Christ with both pontifical and regal authority [171]. On the other hand Constantine

FIG. 34. — Innocent III and *Ecclesia romana* assimilated to Saints Peter and Paul. Apse mosaic (detail) after Ciampini. Church of Saint Peter, Rome.

169. INNOCENT III, *Sermo VII in festo Domini Silvestris Pontificis Maximi*, PL 217, 481-484.

170. W.N. SCHUMACHER, "Eine römische Apsiskomposition," in *Römische Quartalschrift*, 54, 1959, p. 137-202; T. BUDDENSIEG, "Le coffret en ivoire de Pola, Saint-Pierre et le Latran," in CA X, 1959, p. 157-195; A. ANGIOLINI, *La capsella eburnea di Pola*, Bologna, 1970.

171. According to E. AMANN ("Innocent IV," in *Dictionnaire de théologie catholique*, VII, 1933) *Aeger cui lenia...* reflète au mieux les sentiments que l'on avait à la cour pontificale sur les rapports de l'Église et de l'État. Those who do not attribute the brief to Innocent IV himself at least suppose it to have been drawn up in the Papal Curia. Cf. J.A. CANTINI, "De autonomia sæcularis et de romani Pontificis plenitudine potestatis in temporalibus secundum Innocentium IV," in *Salesianum*, 23, 1961, p. 406-480; J.A. WATT, "The Theory of Papal Monarchy in the XIIIth Century," in *Traditio*, 20, 1964, p. 179-317, especially p. 241 *et seq.*; H. WOLTER and H. HOLSTEIN, *Lyon I*[er] *et Lyon II*, Paris, 1966, p. 116. In view of the extraordinary language used in this brief and the difficulty of access to the text, it seems worth while giving some extracts: ... Non minoris quidem, omnino longe majoris potestatis esse credendum est æternum Christi pontificium in fundatissima Petri sede sub gestis ordinatum, quam inveteratum illud, quod figuris legalibus temporaliter serviebat, et tamen dictum est a Deo illius temporis pontificату fungenti: 'Ecce constitui te super gentes et regna, ut evellas et plantas', non solum utique super gentes sed etiam super regna, ut potestas eiusdem innotesceret tradita de utrisque (...). Minus igitur acute perspiciunt qui apostolicam sedem autumant a Constantino principe primitus habuisse imperii principatum qui prius naturaliter et potentialiter fuisse dinoscitur apud eam. Dominus enim Jesus Christus (...) in apostolica sede non solum pontificalem sed et regalem

before his conversion had exercised not a legitimate authority but a tyranny. On his conversion he humbly resigned this authority to the Church together with the regalia which were its sign. Innocent IV, as Christ's Vicar and Peter's successor, continued to exercise this authority and to use the appropriate regalia.

It is possible that this interpretation of the *Constitutum Constantini* is reflected in two of

the pictures which have been described in the course of this study. In the mosaic of the Donation once in the Lateran portico, pope Sylvester is already enthroned and wearing the tiara, although the document which he is receiving from Constantine is the one which was to confer these very privileges upon him. Similarly it may be that in the fresco in the Chapel of Saint Sylvester, executed during the pontificate of Innocent IV himself, Constantine is represented not as conferring a crown upon the pope but as resigning his authority to him.

However this may be, we may see in the pictures which have been the subject of this study a wealth of interest both for the historian and for the iconographer, since by adapting traditional representations of ceremonial and symbols they reveal the changing notions of the Roman pontiffs upon what will always be a controversial question — the relationship between Church and State.

constituit monarchatum, beato Petro eiusque successoribus terreni simul ac celestis imperii commissis habenis, quod in pluralitate clavium competenter innuitur, ut per unam quam in temporalibus super terram per reliquam, quam in spiritualibus super coelos accepimus, intelligatur Christi vicarius iudicii potentiam accepisse. Verum idem Constantinus, per fidem Christi catholicæ incorporatus ecclesiæ, illam inordinatam tyrampnidem, qua foris antea illegitime utebatur, humiliter ecclesiæ assignavit, in cujus resignationis memoriale signaculum et plenum rationis mystice sacramentum relicta ab eo schematis principalis insignia pro venerabili anteriorum patrum similitudine retinemus, et recepit intus a Christo vicario, successore videlicet Petri ordinatam divinitus imperii potestatem, qua deinceps ad vindictam malorum, laudem vero bonorum, legitime uteretur et qui prius abutebatur potestate permissa deinde fungeretur auctoritate concessa... (I.B. LO GRASSO, *Ecclesia et Status : fontes selectæ historiæ iuris publici ecclesiastici*, Rome, 1952, p. 194-198).

LE SOUVENIR DU IIe CONCILE DE NICÉE DANS L'ICONOGRAPHIE BYZANTINE

Le synode, réuni à Nicée du 24 septembre au 23 octobre 787, sous l'égide de l'impératrice Irène et du patriarche Taraise, favorables au culte des icônes, a affirmé qu'il est possible de faire une représentation figurée du Christ, Homme-Dieu, ainsi que des saints. Il a affirmé aussi que la pratique d'offrir un culte aux « icônes » remontait aux origines du christianisme, et il a confirmé les six premiers conciles œcuméniques. Cependant, comme on le sait, après la mort en 802 de l'impératrice, et surtout lors de l'accession au trône de l'empereur Léon V en 813, les iconoclastes l'ont emporté à nouveau sur les iconophiles. Il fallut attendre l'accession de Michel III en 842 et la convocation d'un synode en 843 par le patriarche Méthode, qui confirma les décisions du synode de Nicée, pour que la victoire des iconophiles soit définitive.

Le synode de Nicée marque donc la fin de la période que les historiens contemporains sont convenus d'appeler celle du premier iconoclasme. Entre 787 et 813, les iconophiles ont-ils eu le temps de recommencer à peindre des icônes et de réparer les dégâts des décennies précédentes? Peu de traces nous restent de l'art de la fin du VIIIe siècle[1]. Toutefois, si mon hypothèse est correcte, le modèle pour les trois psautiers à illustration marginale, datés du IXe siècle, aurait été exécuté à cette époque en Palestine[2]. Ces psautiers nous offrent certainement le témoi-

---

1. R. CORMACK, « The Arts during the Age of Iconoclasm », *Iconoclasm*, éd. A. Bryer & Judith Herrin, Birmingham, 1977, p. 40.
2. Ch. WALTER, « ''Latter-day'' Saints and the Image of Christ in the Ninth-century Byzantine Marginal Psalters », *Revue des études byzantines* 45, 1987 (sous presse).

gnage le plus éclatant de l'existence d'un art, dont le programme reflète les préoccupations doctrinales des iconophiles[3]. L'*imago clipeata* du Christ revient dans le programme comme un leitmotiv. Les artistes s'en servent pour représenter la vision d'un prophète, ainsi que celle d'un saint. Juxtaposée à de nombreuses miniatures représentant des événements de la vie du Christ, sujets inspirés par l'interprétation typologique des Psaumes, l'*imago clipeata* n'est pas strictement une icône. Elle est plutôt un symbole de la présence virtuelle du Christ. On peut identifier dans le programme de ces psautiers plusieurs allusions aux écrits des théologiens palestiniens, notamment à ceux de saint Jean Damascène et de Jean de Jérusalem. Par ailleurs, les scènes polémiques contre l'iconoclasme — la pratique de la simonie, par exemple, et la deuxième Passion du Christ, recrucifié par les iconoclastes — reflètent surtout les préoccupations des iconophiles du VIIIe siècle[4]. Toutefois, il serait difficile d'établir une relation directe entre le programme de ces psautiers et les décisions du synode de Nicée, où l'on n'avait pas cité les écrits de saint Jean Damascène[5].

Lorsque le modèle a été recopié au IXe siècle, sans doute à Constantinople, pour nous donner le psautier Chloudov et le psautier Pantocrator, les artistes ont ajouté quelques miniatures historiques[6]. Cependant, dans ces miniatures, on ne trouve aucune allusion aux héros iconophiles du premier iconoclasme. C'est le triomphe du patriarche Nicéphore sur l'iconoclaste notoire Jean le Grammarien que célèbrent ces miniatures. Nicéphore foule aux pieds son adversaire, en portant de la main gauche l'*imago clipeata* du Christ. Ainsi est-il présenté comme le véritable triomphateur des iconoclastes. A part ces miniatures, on ne trouve que peu d'exemples d'un art triomphal au IXe siècle, comme celui situé dans la salle d'audience au palais impérial, décoré en mosaïque sous Michel III (842-867). D'après une épigramme, « le Christ a été représenté trônant. Il confond les hérésies ténébreuses. Anges, apôtres, martyrs et prêtres surveillent la salle[7]. » Les mots « hérésies ténébreuses » font, sans doute, allusion à l'iconoclasme.

Il est bien connu que l'art du IXe siècle était en général conservateur[8]. L'Église voulait affirmer la continuité et, dans ce but, les artistes recopiaient les peintures qui avaient survécu à l'iconoclasme. Toutefois, dans le même but, ils intégraient aux

3. A. GRABAR, *L'Iconoclasme, dossier archéologique*, Paris, 1957, p. 228-233.
4. J. GOUILLARD, « Art et littérature théologique à Byzance au lendemain de la querelle des images », *Cahiers de civilisation médiévale* 5, 1962, p. 5.
5. P. VAN DEN VEN, « La patristique et l'hagiographie au concile de Nicée en 787 », *Byzantion* 25-27, 1955-1957, p. 336-338.
6. GRABAR, *op. cit.* (n. 3), p. 196-202.
7. C. MANGO, *The Art of the Byzantine Empire 312-1453*, Englewood Cliffs, 1972, p. 184.
8. R. CORMACK, « Painting after Iconoclasm », *op. cit.* (n. 1), p. 147-163.

Fig. 1. IIe concile de Nicée, Ménologe de Basile II, p. 108.

2

3

Fig. 2. David prophétise le Christ. Psautier Chloudov, f° 4.
Fig. 3. Nicéphore piétine l'iconoclaste Jean le Grammairien. Psautier
Chloudov, f° 51 v°.

programmes décoratifs les saints iconophiles. Par exemple, dans une salle à côté de l'église Sainte-Sophie de Constantinople, les patriarches Germain, Taraise, Nicéphore et Méthode rejoignent, autour du Christ, la Sainte Vierge, saint Jean-Baptiste et d'autres saints[9]. Ces mosaïques auraient été exécutées vers 870 pendant le règne de Basile Ier (867-886).

L'influence des définitions de Nicée est surtout manifeste dans le nouvel essor qu'elle a donné au culte des saints. Le synaxaire des saints de l'Église de Constantinople est progressivement établi, et on y introduit les saints iconophiles qui avaient défendu, souvent de leur sang, la cause des icônes[10]. Il est à noter que l'on ne distinguait guère les saints du premier de ceux du second iconoclasme. Notre premier grand témoin dans l'iconographie de l'introduction des saints iconophiles au synaxaire est le fameux *Ménologe* de Basile II (976-1025), le *Vatic. gr.* 1613, dans lequel chaque brève *Vie* est illustrée d'une miniature[11]. Les saints iconophiles commémorés dans ce synaxaire sont les suivants : Nicétas de Paphlagonie (763-838)[12], Théodore Studite (759-826)[13], Étienne le Jeune (715-764)[14], Théodore Graptos (775-844)[15], l'impératrice Théodora (800-867)[16], et le patriarche Taraise (730-800)[17]. L'iconographie varie d'un saint à l'autre. Pour Théodore le Studite, l'artiste a représenté la translation de ses reliques. Taraise figure en prière; pour Théodore Graptos, il y a un simple portrait. Le moine Nicétas et l'impératrice Théodora, en revanche, sont représentés en véritables triomphateurs, car l'un et l'autre tiennent de la main gauche l'*imago clipeata* du Christ. Pour Étienne le Jeune et ses compagnons, il a préféré une scène de martyre. Leur commémoraison est suivie de celle d'un autre groupe de saints iconophiles, illustrée elle aussi par une scène de martyre[18].

Le plus frappant de ces types iconographiques est certainement celui du moine Nicétas et de l'impératrice Théodora. Nous voyons que, même à la fin du Xe siècle, lorsqu'on a peint les miniatures du *Ménologe* de Basile II, l'*imago clipeata* du Christ était encore le *palladium* des iconophiles triomphants. Cependant, par la suite,

9. R. Cormack, E.J.W. Hawkins, « The Mosaics of St Sophia at Istanbul : the Rooms above the Southwest Vestibule and Ramp » *Dumbarton Oaks Papers* 31, 1977, p. 231.

10. *Le Typicon de la Grande Église*, éd. J. Mateos, Rome, 1962-1963.

11. *Il Menologio di Basilio II*, éd. C. Stornajolo & P. Franchi de' Cavalieri, Vatican-Milan, 1907 (cité ci-après : *Ménologe*).

12. *Ménologe*, p. 94, le 6 octobre ; *Bibliotheca sanctorum*, Rome, 1961-1970 (cité ci-après : *BS*), 9, 892-893 ; *PG* 117, 93.

13. *Ménologe*, p. 175, le 11 novembre ; *BS* 12, 265-270 ; *PG* 117, 156.

14. *Ménologe*, p. 210, le 28 novembre ; *BS* 11, 1402-1403 ; *PG* 117, 1402-1403.

15. *Ménologe*, p. 276, le 28 décembre ; *BS* 12, 284-285 ; *PG* 117, 229.

16. *Ménologe*, p. 392, le 11 février ; *BS* 12, 222-224 ; *PG* 117, 308.

17. *Ménologe*, p. 423, le 25 février ; *BS* 12, 127-131 ; *PG* 117, 328.

18. *Ménologe*, p. 211, le 28 novembre.

Fig. 4. Évêques iconophiles. Église Sainte-Sophie, Constantinople (Dumbarton Oaks, Center for Byzantine Studies, Washington).

Fig. 5. Le patriarche Taraise, Ménologe de Basile II, p. 423. (Bibliothèque Vaticane, archives photographiques).

172

on a oublié, semble-t-il, la signification originale de cette façon de représenter le Christ. Elle est réservée à la représentation de la Sainte Face sur le *mandylion*, qui a été transféré, sous le règne de l'empereur Constantin VII, le Porphyrogénète, à Constantinople[19]. Ce thème se répand ; à partir du XIe siècle, on trouve dans presque toutes les églises une représentation du mandylion[20]. En revanche, sauf dans le cas où une miniature du IXe siècle est recopiée dans un manuscrit postérieur, l'*imago clipeata* est remplacée par la représentation d'une véritable icône. Les enlumineurs des psautiers à illustration marginale du XIe siècle ont repris beaucoup de thèmes qui figuraient déjà dans les psautiers du IXe siècle, mais, lorsqu'ils ont innové, ils ont représenté des saints qui rendent un culte à une icône de forme rectangulaire[21]. Il est significatif que, dans les psautiers enluminés du IXe siècle, personne ne soit jamais représenté en train d'offrir un culte à une icône !

Au XIe siècle, on avait presque oublié les événements traumatiques du VIIIe siècle. Il n'était plus nécessaire de défendre le culte des icônes ; tout le monde les vénérait. Par conséquent, l'iconoclaste n'est plus l'ennemi le plus redoutable de l'orthodoxie. L'on revient aux origines de l'hérésie et de la division dans l'Église. Une nouvelle hérésie était assimilée plutôt à celle qui en était l'archétype : l'arianisme[22]. Dans les psautiers du XIe siècle, et par la suite dans la décoration des églises, Arius et les ariens figurent souvent. Il est donc évident que, pour un chrétien byzantin du Moyen Age, la controverse autour des icônes était moins importante que pour les historiens de notre époque.

Le souvenir de l'iconoclasme, à partir du XIe siècle, est surtout manifeste dans le culte des saints, et notamment des moines martyrs. Parmi ceux-ci, saint Étienne le Jeune et saint Théodore Graptos étaient le plus souvent représentés. Chacun avait son iconographie particulière. Saint Étienne est représenté frontalement ; de la main gauche il porte une icône[23]. C'est l'unique saint iconophile à être représenté de cette façon, ce qui pourrait faire penser que, pour les Byzantins du Moyen Age, il est devenu le défenseur par excellence du culte de l'icône. Il est intéressant que l'icône qu'il porte soit, le plus souvent, du type *Paraclesis* (intercession)[24]. L'icône a deux volets ; l'un représente le Christ,

19. K. WEITZMANN, « The Mandylion and Constantine Porphyrogennetos », *Cahiers archéologiques* 11, 1960, p. 163-184.

20. R. CORMACK, *Writing in Gold*, Londres, 1985, p. 124-125.

21. Sirarpie DER NERSESSIAN, *L'Illustration des psautiers grecs du Moyen Age*, II, Paris 1970, fig. 27, 117, 145, 153, 176, etc.

22. Ch. WALTER, *Art and Ritual of the Byzantine Church*, Londres, 1982, p. 214.

23. GRABAR, *op. cit.* (n. 3), p. 202, fig. 141.

24. Ch. WALTER, « Further Notes on the Deësis », *Revue des études byzantines* 28, 1970, p. 167-168.

Fig. 6. L'impératrice Théodora, Ménologe de Basile II, p. 392.

Fig. 7. Fig. 8.

Fig. 7. Saint Spyridon et les Ariens, psautier Barberini, f° 138 v° (École des Hautes Études, Paris, coll. chrétienne et byzantine).

Fig. 8. Saint Étienne le Jeune. Église de Donja Kamenica, Serbie.

alors que l'autre représente la Sainte Vierge qui s'incline devant son Fils. Au début, le Christ, sur l'icône que tient saint Étienne, était représenté en portrait ; par la suite, les artistes lui ont substitué le Christ de pitié. Malgré tout la signification de cette icône à deux volets reste inchangée : la Sainte Vierge intercède pour l'humanité. Or, les iconoclastes avaient mis en cause la valeur de la prière d'intercession. Les trois cent cinquante évêques réunis à Nicée en ont réaffirmé la valeur, mais, dans les débats de l'époque, la prière occupait moins de place que l'objet auquel elle était adressée — le portrait du Christ ou celui d'un saint. Deux siècles plus tard, il semble que l'on insistait moins à Byzance sur la légitimité de l'icône même que sur la valeur de la prière.

Pour saint Théodore Graptos et son frère Théophane, la tradition iconographique est moins constante que pour Étienne le Jeune[25]. Tantôt Théodore est représenté en évêque, comme dans le *Ménologe* de Basile II, tantôt en moine, comme dans le *Métaphraste* du mont Athos, Lavra 51 D (427), folio 67ᵛ. Pour les deux frères, un cycle narratif est conservé dans le manuscrit enluminé de la *Chronique de Skylitzès* à Madrid. Curieusement, ce cycle n'inclut pas une miniature de l'incident qui a particulièrement impressionné leurs contemporains. L'empereur iconoclaste Théophile a commandé que soient tatoués sur leur front des versets, qu'il avait composés lui-même. C'est à cette torture que fait allusion leur sobriquet « *Graptoi* ». Il nous reste toutefois deux miniatures du tatouage, car la scène est représentée à la fois dans le psautier de Londres et dans le psautier Barberini[26].

Une comparaison du programme de ces deux psautiers à illustration marginale du XIᵉ siècle avec celui des psautiers du IXᵉ siècle nous offre un éloquent témoignage de l'évolution qu'avait subie la spiritualité byzantine depuis le Triomphe de l'orthodoxie. Les rares saints qui figurent dans les psautiers du IXᵉ siècle y sont présents, parce que, d'une façon ou d'une autre, ils avaient professé que, comme le Christ est visible aux yeux humains, il est possible de le représenter sur une icône. Les saints, bien plus nombreux, qui figurent dans les psautiers du XIᵉ siècle sont, pour la plupart, représentés en prière, s'adressant soit à une icône, soit directement au Christ. Le psautier, au IXᵉ siècle, était naturellement utilisé comme livre de prière, mais il est évident que, pour ceux qui l'ont enluminé, c'était surtout un recueil de prophéties[27]. En revanche, au XIᵉ siècle, l'aspect prophétique du psautier était presque ignoré ; c'était un livre de prière tout court,

25. Ch. WALTER, « Saints of Second Iconoclasm in the Madrid Scylitzes », *Revue des études byzantines* 39, 1981, p. 311-313.

26. DER NERSESSIAN, *op. cit.* (n. 21), p. 74-76, fig. 197.

27. Ch. WALTER, « Christological Themes in the Byzantine Marginal Psalters from the Ninth to the Eleventh Century », *Revue des études byzantines* 44, 1986, p. 269-284.

Fig. 9. Vierge Paraclésis. Église Saint-Néophyte, Chypre.

Fig. 10. Martyrs iconophiles, Ménologe de Basile II, p. 211 (Bibliothèque Vaticane, archives photographiques).

et les saints qui y sont représentés devaient inciter le lecteur à plus d'assiduité dans la prière.

Comme les deux psautiers ont été enluminés au grand monastère de saint Jean Stoudion, il n'est pas surprenant que les artistes aient introduit dans le répertoire des saints représentés un certain nombre de moines iconophiles. Outre Étienne le Jeune, Théodore Graptos et Théodore Stoudite, nous trouvons aussi Joannice, moine de Bithynie mort en 846[28]. Les saints iconophiles sont alors intégrés de façon permanente. Nous les rencontrons par la suite régulièrement sur les murs des églises byzantines à côté des autres saints vénérés à Byzance, mais, à l'exception de saint Étienne le Jeune qui porte toujours une icône, aucun détail iconographique ne les distingue de leurs autres confrères célestes.

Si l'influence du IIe concile de Nicée et du Triomphe de l'orthodoxie sur l'art religieux de Byzance a été modeste, et si le souvenir de la lutte contre les iconoclastes est devenu progressivement plus faible, nous n'avons pour autant aucune raison de nous en étonner. Le concile n'a pas cherché à innover ; il voulait surtout affirmer. Ceux qui ont mis fin de façon définitive à la querelle des images en 843 laissent transparaître qu'ils partageaient le point de vue de leurs illustres prédécesseurs : c'est l'orthodoxie qui a triomphé plutôt que l'icône !

Passons à présent à un examen des représentations dans l'art byzantin du IIe concile de Nicée même. Nous verrons qu'il confirmera la thèse développée dans les paragraphes précédents.

Ironiquement les plus anciennes représentations d'un concile qui nous soient parvenues sont celles du conciliabule iconoclaste de 815, conservées dans les psautiers enluminés du IXe siècle[29]. Néanmoins, de sources littéraires, nous savons que le thème iconographique existait avant le commencement de l'iconoclasme. Il y avait, par exemple, une représentation commémorative du Ier concile de Nicée dans une église de la ville où le concile s'est tenu[30]. Plus importants sont les témoignages de l'existence à Constantinople d'une série de représentations des six premiers conciles, que l'empereur iconoclaste Constantin V (741-775) a fait effacer pour les remplacer par un tableau du cirque[31].

Il convient de souligner le fait qu'il s'agissait d'une *série* de tableaux. Tous les conciles œcuméniques — il y en a eu six à l'époque — étaient représentés ensemble. Par la suite, leur nombre en sera augmenté. Déjà, semble-t-il, au IXe siècle a-t-on ajouté

28. DER NERSESSIAN, *op. cit.* (n. 21), p. 74, fig. 282.
29. Ch. WALTER, *L'Iconographie des conciles dans la tradition byzantine*, Paris, 1970 (cité ci-après : *Conciles*), p. 26-30.
30. *Conciles*, p. 21-22.
31. *Conciles*, p. 20-21.

Fig. 11. Tatouage de saint Théodore « Graptos ». Psautier Barberini, f° 155 (École des Hautes Études, Paris, coll. chrétienne et byzantine).

Fig. 12. Iᵉʳ concile de Nicée. Église d'Arbanasi, Bulgarie.

178

le IIe concile de Nicée aux six précédents[32]. Dès lors, dans la tradition orthodoxe, le nombre reste inchangé. D'autres conciles
auraient pu revendiquer l'honneur d'être appelés œcuméniques,
mais on ne les a pas pris en considération. Autour de la notion
d'un concile œcuménique, toute une mystique fut élaborée, qui
inspira le texte de la *synopsis de synodis*, où chaque concile est
présenté de la même façon : lieu où le concile s'est tenu ; nombre
des Pères ; nom de l'empereur ; noms des représentants des cinq
patriarcats ; noms des hérétiques ; définition ; condamnation[33].
Ainsi les sept conciles œcuméniques résument-ils la doctrine orthodoxe. Ils servent aussi comme paradigme pour tout autre synode.

La plus ancienne série de tableaux des sept conciles œcuméniques qui nous soit parvenue se trouve en Géorgie dans l'église
de Gelati, commencée en 1106 et terminée vers 1130[34]. Il est
très intéressant qu'un synode se soit tenu à Gelati de 1123 à
1125 pour discuter du monophysisme arménien et du chalcédo-
nisme. On devine donc facilement pourquoi on a peint cette série
de tableaux à Gelati : on voulait affirmer l'orthodoxie de l'Église
géorgienne et proclamer sa loyauté aux sept conciles œcuméniques.
D'autres exemples analogues sont connus. A Arilje en Serbie,
on a peint dans le narthex vers la fin du XIIIe siècle une série
de tableaux semblables, mais ici on leur a juxtaposé un tableau
d'un synode local, dont l'iconographie est celle des conciles
œcuméniques[35].

Nous n'avons aucune preuve que la série de tableaux des conciles,
détruite par l'empereur Constantin V, ait été restaurée après le
Triomphe de l'orthodoxie. Par ailleurs, il n'existe aucune allusion dans les sources littéraires à d'autres séries de tableaux des
conciles, érigées ultérieurement à Constantinople. La fâcheuse dis-
parition de la plupart des monuments d'antan hante à chaque
pas l'historien de l'art byzantin. Notre ignorance de l'art de la
capitale est compensée pourtant en partie par le consensus iconographique des monuments restant en province. Celui-ci rend vrai-
semblable l'hypothèse que les types iconographiques aient été
inventés dans la capitale, et ce surtout s'il s'agit de l'art « officiel ».

Le caractère étriqué de l'iconographie des conciles confirme
l'hypothèse qu'elle appartienne au genre de l'art officiel. Elle

32. J. MUNITIZ, « Synoptic Greek Accounts of the Seventh Council », *Revue des études byzantines* 32, 1974, p. 176-177 ; H. CHADWICK, « The Origin of the Title "Œcu-
menical Council" », *Journal of Theological Studies* 23, 1972, p. 132-135.
33. *Conciles*, p. 151-163, 265-273 ; Ch. WALTER, « The Names of the Council Fathers
at Saint Sozomenus, Cyprus », *Revue des études byzantines* 28, 1970, p. 189-206.
34. Tinatin WIRSSALADSE, « Fragmente der ursprünglichen Freskomalerei in der
Hauptkirche des Klosters Gelati », *Ars georgica* 5, 1969, p. 163-204.
35. *Conciles*, p. 109-111, V. DJURIĆ, *Vizantijske freske u Jugoslaviji*, Belgrade, 1974
(cité ci-après : DJURIĆ), p. 44.

aurait été inventée pour des tableaux comme ceux qu'avait détruits l'empereur Constantin V, exposés dans un lieu public, et destinés à être à la portée des provinciaux, des étrangers et des illettrés[36]. Nous nous croyons donc autorisé à nous servir de deux miniatures d'un concile œcuménique pour reconstituer l'iconographie originale. Ces deux miniatures sont bien connues. L'une, qui représente le Ier concile de Constantinople, se trouve dans le manuscrit des *Homélies* de Grégoire de Nazianze, exécuté pour l'empereur Basile Ier (867-886), le *Paris.* 510, folio 355[37]. L'autre, qui se trouve dans le *Ménologe* de Basile II, le *Vatic. gr.* 1613, p. 108, est la toute première représentation du IIe concile de Nicée[38]. La disposition des deux scènes est essentiellement semblable : les évêques et l'empereur sont assis en demi-cercle dans une exèdre ; l'hérétique condamné est placé au premier plan.

La miniature du IIe concile de Nicée accompagne le récit pour la commémoraison des saints Pères du concile, le 12 octobre. Toutefois on chercherait inutilement dans la miniature le moindre détail iconographique qui se rapporte spécifiquement au IIe concile de Nicée ! L'hérétique prosterné, qui pourrait symboliser l'ensemble des iconoclastes, fait plutôt penser à Arius. On échappe donc difficilement à la conclusion que l'artiste a calqué cette miniature sur une autre représentant le Ier concile de Nicée.

Sauf erreur, cette miniature est l'unique représentation du IIe concile de Nicée qui ne fasse pas partie d'une série. Pour l'époque byzantine, nous avons, outre celles de Gelati et d'Arilje, déjà notées, une série à Patmos dans le réfectoire du monastère (1200 environ)[39] ; à Sopoćani dans le narthex (1263-1268)[40] ; à Prizren dans l'aile sud de l'église de la Bogorodica Ljeviška (1310-1313 environ)[41] ; à Mistra dans le narthex de la métropole (1300 environ)[42] ; à Dečani dans le narthex (1348 environ)[43] ; à Dobrun dans le narthex (1343-1356)[44] ; à Ohrid à l'étage du

36. ÉTIENNE LE DIACRE, *Vie de saint Étienne le Jeune*, PG 100, 1172.

37. *Conciles*, p. 34-37 ; Leslie BRUBAKER, « Politics, Patronage and Art in Ninth-century Byzantium : The Homilies of Gregory of Nazianzus in Paris (B.N. gr. 510) », *Dumbarton Oaks Papers* 39, 1985, p. 4-7.

38. *Ménologe*, p. 108, le 12 octobre ; *Conciles*, p. 37-38.

39. A. ORLANDOS, ʽΗ ἀρχιτεκτονικὴ καὶ βυζαντιναί τοιχογραφίαι τῆς μονῆς Θεολόγου Πάτμου, Athènes, 1970, p. 243-255, 373-380 ; E. KOLLIAS, *Patmos*, Athènes, 1986, p. 25-26.

40. *Conciles*, p. 107 ; DJURIĆ, p. 39-41.

41. *Conciles*, p. 110-111 ; Draga PANIĆ, Gordana BABIĆ, *Bogorodica Ljeviška*, Belgrade 1975 ; DJURIĆ, p. 49-50.

42. *Conciles*, p. 89-90 ; Suzy DUFRENNE, *Les Programmes iconographiques des églises byzantines de Mistra*, Paris, 1970, p. 5-8, 39-40 ; M. CHATZIDAKIS, *Mistra*, Athènes, 1985, p. 42-43.

43. *Conciles*, p. 111 ; DJURIĆ, p. 63.

44. DJURIĆ, p. 63 ; Z. KAJMAKOVIĆ, *Zidno slikarstvo u Bosni i Hercegovini*, Sarajevo, 1971, p. 101-110, 313-315.

180

narthex de l'église Sainte-Sophie (1346-1350)[45] et à Mateič dans le narthex (1356-1360)[46].

La même formule iconographique est employée pour tous les conciles dans ces séries. L'empereur et les évêques président en demi-cercle dans une exèdre. C'est la même formule que celle de la miniature dans le *Ménologe* de Basile II. Souvent, au premier plan, l'artiste substitue, à l'hérétique prosterné, deux groupes d'évêques, l'un orthodoxe et l'autre hétérodoxe, qui s'affrontent[47].

Fig. 13. IIe concile de Nicée. Église d'Arbanasi, Bulgarie.

Comment, alors, peut-on distinguer le tableau du IIe concile des autres? Souvent, faut-il dire, il n'existe aucune distinction. Dans certaines séries, une légende accompagne chaque tableau, qui résume les données qui se trouvent dans la *synopsis de synodis*. La légende nous permet d'identifier le concile. Rarement — très rarement — l'artiste ajoute à la représentation du IIe concile de Nicée une icône. C'est le cas, par exemple, pour la fresque très abîmée de Mistra. L'icône ressemble à celle que porte habi-

---

45. *Conciles*, p. 114-115; DJURIĆ, p. 68; C. GROZDANOV, *Ohridsko zidno slikarstvo XIV veka*, Belgrade, 1980, p. 71-75.
46. *Conciles*, p. 113-114; DJURIĆ, p. 70.
47. *Conciles*, p. 256-258.

tuellement saint Étienne le Jeune : la Sainte Vierge s'incline devant son Fils. Citons aussi, pour l'art postbyzantin, où les séries de tableaux des conciles sont plus nombreuses, la belle fresque à Arbanasi, en Bulgarie (1632-1649)[48]. Une comparaison avec le tableau du Ier concile de Nicée dans la même église est instructive. L'empereur Constantin, entouré d'évêques, préside l'assemblée. Il tient un rouleau sur lequel sont inscrits les premiers mots du Credo. L'hérétique Arius est prosterné à ses pieds. Derrière lui est dressé un autel surmonté d'un baldaquin. L'enfant Jésus se tient debout sur l'autel. C'est la vision de saint Pierre d'Alexandrie, qu'ajoutent fréquemment les artistes à partir du Moyen Age à leur représentation du Ier concile de Nicée[49]. Dans le tableau du IIe concile de Nicée, l'assemblée est présidée par deux personnages, l'impératrice Irène et son fils l'empereur Constantin VI

Fig. 14. IIe concile de Nicée. Métropole, Mistra.

(780-797), qui n'avait en 787 que dix-sept ans. Sur le rouleau sont inscrits les mots : « Si quelqu'un ne vénère pas les saintes images, qu'il soit anathème. » Un hérétique anonyme est prosterné à leurs pieds, mais l'autel et l'enfant Jésus sont remplacés par un simple baldaquin. En revanche, l'artiste a ajouté une icône

48. *Conciles*, p. 83-87.
49. *Conciles*, p. 246-248.

182

du Christ Emmanuel, que tiennent l'empereur et l'impératrice.

Nous pouvons nous arrêter ici pour conclure. Ce rapide examen du souvenir du IIe concile de Nicée dans l'iconographie byzantine pourrait sembler décevant. L'unique reflet de la théologie iconophile se trouve dans les psautiers marginaux du IXe siècle, où l'on peut entrevoir l'influence de saint Jean Damascène, pour qui le mot *eikôn* signifiait à la fois le type du Christ dans l'Ancien Testament et le portrait du Christ[50]. Dans ces psautiers à illustration marginale, l'artiste s'est servi de l'*imago clipeata* du Christ comme symbole d'une vision prophétique et de la vision d'un saint. Il illustre aussi les psaumes de scènes typologiques de la vie du Christ. Ainsi a-t-il associé dans le même programme le Christ incarné et le Christ virtuellement présent dans une vision ou sur une icône. Les iconoclastes, qui détruisent les icônes, cherchent donc à annihiler le Christ.

Cependant, ce courant iconographique n'avait pas de suite. Après le Triomphe de l'orthodoxie, on se mettait à reconstituer un art semblable à celui des siècles qui précédaient la querelle des images. Cependant, le IIe concile de Nicée avait donné un nouvel essor au culte des saints. Surtout au Xe siècle les représentations de saints se multiplient et, aux séries de portraits des saints, on intègre les augustes défenseurs des icônes. Finalement, ils sont complètement assimilés et, à une exception près — saint Étienne le Jeune —, un saint iconophile ne se distingue pas des autres par un attribut quelconque.

Lorsque l'on se tourne vers les représentations du IIe concile de Nicée, l'on constate d'emblée que l'on ne leur a pas attribué une iconographie spécifique. Au contraire, le IIe concile de Nicée, une fois reconnu comme étant œcuménique, prend place dans les séries de tableaux, à côté des autres et au même titre que les autres. Les sept conciles œcuméniques sont vénérés comme un ensemble : ils ont défendu et promulgué la doctrine orthodoxe. Comme le Ier concile de Nicée a ouvert la série, le IIe concile de Nicée, souvent assimilé dans l'iconographie au premier, a clos la série. Ensemble, ils offrent aux défenseurs de l'orthodoxie un paradigme pour tout synode ultérieur.

---

50. JEAN DAMASCÈNE, *De imaginibus oratio* III, *PG* 94, 1341.

PHOTOGRAPHIES :
Bibliothèque vaticane, fig. 1, 5, 6, 10.
Photothèque Gabriel-Millet, Paris, fig. 2, 3, 7, 11.
Dumbarton Oaks Study Center, Washington, fig. 4, 9.
Ch. Walter, fig. 8, 12, 13.

IX

CHRISTOLOGICAL THEMES
IN THE BYZANTINE MARGINAL PSALTERS
FROM THE NINTH
TO THE ELEVENTH CENTURY*

In its pristine state, the Chludov Psalter would have contained some eighty miniatures illustrating or commenting verses of the Psalms in a Christological sense[1]. This Psalter, although now missing a number of folios, is still more complete than the Paris and Pantocrator Psalters, whose miniatures also comment Psalms with miniatures embodying a Christologi-

---

* The following abbreviations are used in this article :

WORKS OF REFERENCE
Clavis = M. GEERARD, *Clavis patrum graecorum*, I-IV, Turnhout 1974-1983.
Initia hymnorum = HENRICA FOLLIERI, *Initia hymnorum ecclesiae graecae*, I-V, Vatican 1960-1966.
Typicon = J. MATEOS, *Le typicon de la Grande Église*, I-II, Rome 1962-1963.
Typicon (Messina) = M. ARRANZ, *Le typicon du monastère du Saint-Sauveur à Messine*, Rome 1969.

PATRISTIC COMMENTATORS
Eusebius = EUSEBIUS, *Commentarii in psalmos*, PG 23 (*Clavis* 3467).
Didymus = DIDYMUS, *Fragmenta in psalmos*, PG 39 (*Clavis* 2551).
Theodoret = THEODORET, *Interpretatio in psalmos*, PG 80 (*Clavis* 6202).
« Athanasius » = ATHANASIUS, *Expositiones in psalmos*, PG 27 (*Clavis* 2140).

MONOGRAPHS
DER NERSESSIAN = SIRARPIE DER NERSESSIAN, *L'illustration des psautiers grecs du Moyen Age*, II, Paris 1970.
TIKKANEN = J.J. TIKKANEN, Die Psalterillustration im Mittelalter, *Acta societatis scientiarum fennicae* 31, 1905.

The *sigla* for the marginal psalters are those used by L. MARIÈS (Le psautier à illustration marginale : signification théologique des images, *Actes du VIe congrès*

270

cal theme. The Bristol Psalter, dating from about the year 1000, has thirty such miniatures, which resemble more particularly those in the Pantocrator Psalter[2].

The majority of the Christological miniatures in the two eleventh-century Psalters obviously derive from those in the ninth-century Psalters, particularly those in Chludov[3]. However, there are slight but significant differences. Generally Barberini is closer to Chludov than is London, in which a greater number of Christological miniatures are modified or omitted. However, in some miniatures, both Barberini and London have introduced the same modifications. For this and other reasons, art historians have argued plausibly that the two 11th-century Psalters do not depend directly on Chludov but on a lost intermediary copy into which these modifications would have already been introduced.

The distinguished Finnish scholar J.J. Tikkanen laid long ago the foundations for a study of the Christological themes in the Byzantine marginal Psalters. He recognized that the theme chosen to illustrate the verse of a Psalm was sometimes suggested by the quotation of the verse in the New Testament, sometimes by a Patristic commentator. In other cases he suggested a *rapprochement* with a liturgical text. However, he did not establish an exhaustive inventory of miniatures with Christological themes, nor did he give references to the Patristic commentators.

The aim of the present article is above all to supply for these deficiencies. The contemporary scholar is far better equipped than Tikkanen for this

---

international d'études byzantines, II, Paris 1951, p. 261-272) and by Suzy DUFRENNE (*Tableaux synoptiques de 15 psautiers marginaux*, Paris 1978) : Pc = Pantocrator Psalter (Athos Pantocrator 61) ; P = Paris Psalter (Paris *graec.* 20) ; C = Chludov Psalter (Moscow, State Historical Museum 129 D) ; 1 = Bristol Psalter (London, British Library, Additional 40371) ; L = London Psalter (London, British Library, Additional 19352) ; B = Barberini Psalter (Vatican *Barb. graec.* 372).

The numbering of the Psalm verses is that of A. Rahlfs, Septuaginta, II, 4th edition, Stuttgart 1950. The translation of the Psalms follows that of S. Bagster & J. Pott, The Septuagint Version, Greek and English, London/New York, no date.

Credit titles for the illustrations : Bibliotheca Apostolica Vaticana, figures 8, 11 ; the other figures, Collection Gabriel Millet, Paris.

1. Marfa ŠČEPKINA, *Miniatjuri Hludovskoj Psaltyri. Grečeskij illjustrirovannyj kodeks IX veka,* Moscow 1977. See R. Stichel's review, *BZ* 74, 1981, p. 357-362.

2. Suzy DUFRENNE, *L'illustration des psautiers grecs du Moyen Age,* I, Paris 1966 (Pantocrator, Paris and Bristol Psalters) ; EADEM, Le Psautier de Bristol et les autres psautiers byzantins, *CA* 14, 1965, p. 164-169.

3. DER NERSESSIAN (London Psalter) ; J.C. ANDERSON, The Date and Purpose of the Barberini Psalter, *CA* 31, 1983, p. 35-67. This manuscript, still unpublished, has a double foliation. In my references, f. 1 corresponds to the first folio, such that the frontispiece is on f. 5. Particularly in older literature, the foliation begins with the frontispiece. In referring to it, it is therefore necessary to subtract 4 from my folio numbers. I thank Cardinal A. Stickler for the free access that he has given me to this manuscript.

task. All the Psalters in question, except Barberini, have been published. Basic works of reference, not available in Tikkanen's time, facilitate such a study. Even so, it cannot be definitive for two reasons. Firstly, critical editions of the Patristic commentators are lacking, while the publication of the *Catenae* which succeeded them and which were probably, in fact, exploited by the illuminators of these manuscripts has hardly begun[4]. Secondly, although a *rapprochement* of miniatures and liturgical texts is fruitful, it cannot be taken for granted that the miniature was always inspired by the liturgical text. In general, illustrators of manuscripts and composers of liturgical texts were less rigorous than the Fathers when they interpreted a Psalm verse in a Christological sense. A simple word association was often sufficient for them. Moreover, in some cases, it might be difficult to prove that the liturgical text is more ancient than the miniature[5]. It is likely that the composition of liturgical hymns and the illumination of marginal Psalters formed part of the same movement in the Byzantine Church.

Tikkanen presented the Christological miniatures according to their theme. In this article they are presented rather according to their source of inspiration. Although the Psalter was primarily a book of worship, it was also exploited as a compendium of prophecies. I begin by listing the miniatures whose subject was suggested by the New Testament context in which the verse was quoted[6]. While the New Testament authors were mainly concerned to demonstrate that Christ's coming fulfilled the prophecies of the Old Testament, Patristic commentators went further. They sought to render explicit the prophetical content, the *sensus plenior* of the Psalms. Sometimes their exegesis overlapped with the lucubrations of those Church Fathers who interpreted and developed the « signs » of Saint John's Gospel and the τύποι dear to Saint Paul[7]. I continue by listing the miniatures whose subject was suggested by a Patristic commentator, adding, where relevant, references to the exposition of a sign or type. This accounts for nearly fifty of the Christological miniatures, which can be presented summarily.

The subjects of the remaining thirty odd miniatures were not, apparently,

4. R. Devreesse, *Les anciens commentateurs des Psaumes,* Vatican 1970 ; Marie-Josèphe Rondeau, *Les commentaires patristiques du Psautier (IIIe-Ve siècles),* I, Rome 1982 ; G. Dorival, La postérité littéraire des chaînes exégétiques grecques, *REB* 43, 1985, p. 209-226.

5. H.-G. Beck, *Kirche und theologische Literatur im byzantinischen Reich,* Munich 1959, p. 515-519, 601-609.

6. I. Saint-Arnaud, Les Psaumes dans le Nouveau Testament, *Supplément au Dictionnaire de la Bible,* IX, col. 206-210.

7. P. Bläser, Typos in der Schrift, *LTK* 10, 422-423, with extensive bibliography.

inspired by Patristic texts. In their case either the artist substituted a Christological theme, where Patristic exegesis had been moral or historical, or he extended a typological explanation, previously applied to Christ or the Church, to the Virgin. In a number of cases a *rapprochement* is possible with a later Byzantine writer. This explanation accounts for the choice of six themes. There then follow twelve for which a *rapprochement* may be made with a liturgical text.

For the choice of some themes, Tikkanen did not provide an explanation. I am obliged to do the same in eight cases. Subsequent research may fill this lacuna. However, since these themes correspond to the ninth-century *Zeitgeist,* it may have been that, as in the case of the miniatures in which a polemical anti-Iconoclast theme is linked to one which is Christological, the choice was the artist's own. Byzantine book illumination had its autonomous governing principles, such that the illuminator was free to « translate » a word into pictorial form, or to exemplify a general theme with a specific subject.

The « corpus » of Christological themes was established for the marginal Psalters in the ninth century. Although later artists adapted or omitted these themes, they added few new ones. In one case (**83**), Bristol introduces a scene of the Adoration of the Magi, which does not appear in the ninth-century Psalters. Apart from this miniature there are only four others which could be considered to be eleventh-century innovations. These five miniatures complete the inventory.

I. PSALMS QUOTED IN THE NEW TESTAMENT

1. Psalm 2,7 : « Thou art my son... » Nativity. (*Acts* 13,33 ; *Heb.* 1,5) C, 1, L, B.

2. Psalm 8,3 : « Out of the mouths of babes... » Entry to Jerusalem. (*Mat.* 21,16) 1, L, B[8].

3. Psalm 21,2 : « My God... why hast thou forsaken me ? » Crucifixion. (*Mat.* 27,46) Pc, C, B.

4. Psalm 21,19 : « They parted my garments among them. » Soldiers casting lots. (*John* 19,24) Pc, C, 1, L, B.

5. Psalm 40,10 : « The man who ate my bread. » Last Supper. (*John* 13,18) C, 1, L, B.

6. Psalm 68,10 : « The zeal of thy house... » Christ expelling merchants from temple. (*John* 2,17) Pc, C, L, B.

7. Psalm 68,22 : « They gave me gall for food. » Crucifixion[9]. (*Mat.* 27,34) C, L, B.

---

8. Folio mutilated in C. A. CUTLER (Liturgical Strata in the Marginal Psalters, *DOP* 34/35, 1980-1981, p. 25) provides a liturgical explanation of the presence of a statue of Ares above Jerusalem in London, f. 6. This also appears in the parallel miniature in Barberini, f. 14, and, in the same manuscript, f. 137ᵛ, above the edicule in which Antiochus is sitting in the scene of the martyrdom of the Maccabees.

9. See below, p. 280.

8. Psalm 80,17 : « Honey out of the rock. » Christ as the rock[10]. (*I Cor.* 10,4) (Pc), C, L, B.

9. Psalm 90,11 : « He shall give his angels charge concerning thee. » Temptation of Christ. (*Luke* 4,9) Pc, C, 1, L, B.

10. Psalm 109,1 : « The Lord said to my lord. » Christ enthroned. (*Mat.* 23,44, *etc.*) C, L, B.

11. Psalm 109,4 : « A priest for ever. » Communion of the apostles. (*Heb* 5,6) (Pc), C, P, L, B.

12. Psalm 117,26 : « Blessed is he who comes in the name of the Lord. » Entry to Jerusalem[11]. (*Mat.* 21,9) B, L.

II. THEMES COMMON TO PATRISTIC COMMENTARIES AND MARGINAL PSALTERS[12]

13. Psalm 11,6 : « Now I shall arise. » Anastasis[13]. (Didymus, 1213) Pc, 1, L, B.

14. Psalm 17,11 : « He mounted on cherubim. » Ascension. (Eusebius, 172) C, (1), L, B.

15. Psalm 21,3 : « Many bullocks have compassed me. » Christ surrounded by horned beasts[14]. (Theodoret, 1016) B, L.

16. Psalm 21, 17a : « Many dogs have compassed me. » Christ surrounded by figures with dog's heads. (Theodoret, 1017) C, L, B.

17. Psalm 21,17b : « They pierced my hands and feet. » Christ nailed to cross. (Theodoret, 1017) Pc, C, L, B.

18. Psalm 23,7 : « Lift up your gates. » Ascension. (Theodoret, 1033) C, L, B.

19. Psalm 28,3 : « The voice of the Lord on the waters. » Baptism of Christ[15]. (Theodoret, 1065) 1, L, B.

20. Psalm 34,11 : « Unjust witnesses arose. » Christ before Sanhedrin. (Athanasius, 171) Pc, C, L, B.

21. Psalm 40,8 : « Enemies whispered against me. » Judas and Jews. (Theodoret, 1164) C, 1, L, B.

22. Psalm 44,2 : « My heart has uttered a good matter. » Dove perched on clipeate icon of Virgin and Child. (Theodoret, 1187) C, L, B.

23. Psalm 46,6 : « God has gone up with a shout. » Ascension. (Theodoret, 1208-1209) C, 1, L, B.

24. Psalm 49, 1.2 : « God shall come manifestly. » Christ as midday sun. (Didymus, 1388-1389) (Pc) C, (1), L, B.

25. Psalm 55, title (David arrested by Philistines) Arrest of Christ[16]. (Didymus, 1409) Pc, C.

10. See below, p. 276.
11. Folio missing from C.
12. I have used only « samples » of Patristic commentary. My choice was principally determined by the observations of DEVREESSE and RONDEAU on the reliability of available editions. See above, note 4. Thus Eusebius is used only for Psalms 16-28 and 50-95. « Athanasius », even if spurious, provides a useful *Catena*. Reference is also made occasionally to *Homilies* by Basil and John Chrysostom on the Psalms.
13. Folio missing from C.
14. Folio mutilated in C.
15. Folio missing in C.
16. For modifications in L and B, see DER NERSESSIAN, p. 68, fig. 112, 330, 331.

274

26. Psalm 56,6 : « Be thou exalted. » Ascension. (Eusebius, 512) C, L, B.

27. Psalm 67,2 : « Let God arise. » Anastasis. (Theodoret, 1376) C, 1, L, B.

28. Psalm 67,7 : « Leading forth prisoners. » Anastasis. (Didymus, 1444) Pc, C, L, B.

29. Psalm 68,18 : « I am afflicted. » Gethsemane. (Theodoret, 1400) C, L, B.

30. Psalm 71,6 : « He shall come down as rain upon a fleece. » Gedeon before a clipeate icon of the Virgin and Child above which a dove hovers[17]. (Theodoret, 1433) Pc, L, B.

31. Psalm 73,13 : « He has wrought salvation in the midst of the earth. » Crucifixion. (Athanasius, 336) Pc, C, L, B.

32. Psalm 76,17 : « The waters saw thee. » Baptism of Christ. (Eusebius, 896) Pc, C, L, B.

33. Psalm 77,68 : « Mount Sion which he loved. » Sion with Virgin and Child. (Theodoret, 1501) C, L, B.

34. Psalm 84,3 : « Thou hast forgiven their sins. » Christ pardoning sinners. (Eusebius, 1019) (Pc), C, (L), B.

35. Psalm 84,11 : « Mercy and truth are met together. » Visitation. (Theodoret, 1549-1551) (Pc), C, L, B.

36. Psalm 85,17 : « A sign for good. » Cross with clipeate icon of Christ. (Theodoret, 1561) C, L, B.

37. Psalm 86,5 : « Such a man was born in her. » Sion with Virgin and Child. (Theodoret, 1566) Pc, C, L, B.

38. Psalm 87,7 : « They laid me in the lowest pit. » Entombment of Christ. (Didymus, 1485) Pc, C, L, B.

39. Psalm 88,10 : « Thou rulest the power of the sea. » Christ calming tempest[18]. (Didymus, 1489) (Pc) C, 1, L, B.

40. Psalm 88,13 : « Thabor and Hermon shall rejoice in thy name. » Transfiguration. (Didymus, 1489) C, 1, L, B.

41. Psalm 88,37 : « His throne is like the sun. » Christ enthroned[19]. (Theodoret, 1592-1593) C, B.

42. Psalm 101,29 : « The souls of thy servants shall dwell securely. » Christ and disciples. (Theodoret, 1684) C, (P), B.

43. Psalm 102,3 : « Who heals all thy diseases. » Christ healing. (Theodoret, 1686) (Pc), C, (P), L, B.

44. Psalm 106,16 : « He broke to pieces the brazen gates. » Anastasis[20]. (Theodoret, 1742) (P), L, B.

45. Psalm 106,20 : « He healed them. » Christ healing[21]. (Theodoret, 1741) (P), L, B.

46. Psalm 107,6 : « Be thou exalted. » Christ in mandorla[22]. (Didymus, 1533) L, B.

47. Psalm 108,1.2.4.5 : « Oh God pass not over my praise in silence. » Gethsemane[23]. (Theodoret, 1756) C.

17. Folio missing from C. For the typology of Gedeon, see below, p. 282-283.
18. For misunderstandings in L and B, see below, p. 284-285.
19. Folio mutilated in L.
20. Folio missing from C.
21. Folio missing from C.
22. Folio mutilated in C.
23. Miniature displaced in L and B. See below, p. 284.

48. Psalm 108,2 : « The mouth of the crafty man... » The devil and Judas. (Theodoret, 1756) C, B.

49. Psalm 131,11 : « The Lord swore the truth to David. » David prays before Christ enthroned[24]. (Theodoret, 1908) C, L, B.

III. THEMES COMMON TO LATER PATRISTIC WRITERS AND MARGINAL PSALTERS

50. Psalm 29,4 : « Thou has brought up my soul from Hades. » Eusebius, 260, refers this verse to David, Didymus, 1312, to Christ, Theodoret, 1071, to Hezekiah. In the marginal Psalters (Pantocrator, f. 29 ; London, f. 31^v ; Barberini, f. 48 ; the folio is missing from Chludov), the verse is illustrated by a miniature of Christ raising Lazarus from the dead (Figures 3, 4). This verse is applied by John of Euboea to the resurrection of Lazarus[25].

51. Psalm 44,11 : « Hear, daughter..., and incline thine ear. » This verse is referred by Eusebius, 401, Didymus, 1368-1369, Theodoret, 1193-1196, « Athanasius », 212, and John Chrysostom to the Church as the bride of Christ. In the marginal Psalters (Pantocrator, f. 55^v ; Chludov, f. 45 ; Bristol, f. 74^v ; London, f. 56^v ; Barberini, f. 78^v) this verse is illustrated with a miniature of the Annunciation. The verse is applied by John of Euboea to the Annunciation[26].

52. Psalm 45,7 : « The nations were troubled, the kingdoms tottered... the earth shook. » Theodoret, 1204, and John Chrysostom interpret the verse literally[27]. Eusebius, 409, and Didymus, 1376, refer it to dangers threatening the Church. « Athanasius », 216, alludes to the Crucifixion, but not to the prodigies reported in the Gospels as having occurred at the time (*Mat.* 27,45-54, etc.). Uniquely in Chludov, f. 45^v, the verse is illustrated by a miniature of the Crucifixion, while to one side stands Dionysius the Areopagite with a group of Greeks. His name and the word Ἕλληνες can be read in the much deteriorated legend. The allusion is to the *Letter* of Dionysius to Polycarp, in which he explained the phenomena which occurred at the time of the Crucifixion[28]. This verse is not illustrated in the other marginal Psalters, although, in Barberini, f. 79^v, there is a miniature of the Crucifixion, without Dionysius, illustrating verse 3 : « Therefore we will not fear when the earth is troubled. »

53. Psalm 67,17 : « This is the mountain that God has delighted to dwell in. » Eusebius, 700, and Theodoret, 1385, interpret the verse literally, while « Athanasius », 297, refers it to the Church. In the marginal Psalters (Pantocrator, f. 83^v ; Chludov, f. 64 ; Bristol, f. 105^v ; London, f. 84 ; Barberini, f. 110^v), the verse is illustrated with a particularly complex and erudite miniature. David stands while

---

24. Miniature partially mutilated in C.

25. JOHN OF EUBOEA, *Homilia in Lazarum*, edited F. DÖLGER, *An. Boll.* 68, 1950 (*Clavis* 8137 ; *BHG* 2220), p. 22.

26. IDEM, *Homilia in conceptionem deiparae*, *PG* 96 (*Clavis* 8135), 1481 ; JOHN DAMASCENE, *Sermo in annuntiationem*, *PG* 96 (*Clavis* 8118, spurious), 653-656. CHRYSIPPUS OF JERUSALEM (5th century) had already applied this verse to the Annunciation, *Oratio in sanctam Mariam Deiparam*, edited M. JUGIE, *PO* 19 (*Clavis* 6705), p. 336.

27. JOHN CHRYSOSTOM, *Expositio in Ps. 45*, *PG* 55 (*Clavis* 4413), 206-207.

28. DIONYSIUS THE AREOPAGITE, *Epistula vii ad Polycarpem antistitem*, *PG* 3 (*Clavis* 6610), 1077-1081 ; A. GRABAR, *L'iconoclasme, dossier archéologique*, Paris 1957, p. 229-230.

276

Daniel reclines on a couch beside a mountain from which a rock has fallen. Chludov, London and Barberini add, at the summit of the mountain, a clipeate icon of the Virgin and Child. The Psalm is associated with Daniel's prophecy (*Dan.* 2,34-35) by Germanus I[29]. The typology of Daniel's prophecy was frequently expounded by the Fathers, and allusions to it recur in 8th- and 9th-century texts, although only Germanus actually associates it with this Psalm[30]. Daniel's recumbent position recalls the conventional iconography of visions in dreams, although, of course, it was not his own dream which he interpreted. The rock, unmade by human hands, was interpreted as a type of Christ's birth from a virgin. The rock, assimilated to Christ, lent itself to further typological exegesis. A full account may be found Theodoret's *Commentary* on Daniel[31]. The 9th-century miniatures are accompanied by explanatory legends which are particularly developed in Bristol. Indeed it is probable that its illuminator knew Theodoret's *Commentary* on Daniel.

54. Psalm 91,11 : « My horn shall be exalted as the horn of a unicorn. » Eusebius, 1180, referred the verse to hope of the reign of Christ. Theodoret, 1620, argued that the single horn of the unicorn refers to there being only one God. « Athanasius », 405, combined both these interpretations. However, more generally in Patristic tradition the single horn of the unicorn was interpreted as a type of Christ, the only begotten son[32]. In three marginal Psalters (Chludov, f. 93ᵛ ; London, f. 124ᵛ ; Barberini, f. 160), the verse is illustrated with a miniature of a seated woman extending her right hand towards the unicorn which places its left forepaw on her knee. Above, is a clipeate icon of the Virgin and Child. The legend accompanying the miniature in Chludov reads : ὁ Χρυσόστομος ἑρμηνεύει περὶ τοῦ μονοκέρωτος εἰς τὸν υ(ἱὸ)ν τοῦ Θ(εο)ῦ. The legends in London and Barberini omit the reference to the son of God. On the other hand, they add a portrait of John Chrysostom. It does not seem that Chrysostom did, in fact, expound this type of the only son of God. If his name is introduced here, the most likely explanation for it would be that the authorship of the *Physiologus* was sometimes attributed to him. The connection is tenuous, because the attribution is made only in Western Latin manuscripts[33]. Psalm 91,11 is quoted at the beginning of the chapter in this treatise on the unicorn[34]. This exceptionally ferocious beast could only be captured by a virgin. It would leap to her bosom. She would suckle it and then take it to the king's palace. The chapter continues with an interpretation of the legend, which refers it to the Saviour, born of the Virgin Mary. A virtually identical miniature to these which illustrate the Psalm in the three marginal Psalters illustrated the chapter on the unicorn in the lost

29. GERMANUS I, *Homilia ii in praesentationem s. deiparae*, *PG* 98 (*Clavis* 8008), 306.

30. JOHN CHRYSOSTOM, *Fragmenta in Danielem*, *PG* 56 (*Clavis* 4448), 207 ; JOHN DAMASCENE, *Oratio de imaginibus tres*, edited B. KOTTER, *Die Schrifte des Iohannes von Damaskos*, III, Berlin 1975 (*Clavis* 8045), p. 140 : *PG* 94, 1354 ; IDEM, *Carmina*, *PG* 96 (*Clavis* 8070), 853 ; THEODORE STUDITE, *Oratio 5, In dormitione deiparae*, *PG* 99, 728.

31. THEODORET, *Interpretatio in Danielem*, *PG* 81 (*Clavis* 6207), 1300-1301.

32. EUSEBIUS, *Demonstratio evangelica*, X, 8, edited I. HEIKEL, *Eusebius Werke*, VI, Leipzig 1913 (*Clavis* 3487), p. 489 : *PG* 22, 785. See also COSMAS, *Hymnus 1, In natale domini*, *PG* 98, 461.

33. P. PERRY, Einhorn, *RE* XXI, 1120-1121. *Monacensis* 19419 (9th century) is the earliest manuscript in which the *Physiologus* is attributed to John Chrysostom. J.W. EIN-HORN, *Spiritalis Unicornis*, Munich 1975, p. 62-66, fig. 11, 15-17.

34. F. SBORDONE, *Physiologi graeci...*, Milan/Naples 1936, p. 78-82.

Smyrna *Physiologus*[35]. Furthermore a similar miniature occurs in Pantocrator, f. 109ᵛ, illustrating Psalm 77,69 : « He built his sanctuary as the place of unicorns. » Eusebius, 938-940, interprets this verse as referring to the firstborn in heaven. Theodoret, 1501, refers the horn of the unicorn to the one God. In the Pantocrator miniature, the seated virgin is actually suckling the unicorn, as the legend makes clear : περὶ τοῦ υἱοῦ το(ῦ) Θ(εο)ῦ καθὼς ἐθήλασεν τὴν παναγίαν θεοτόκον. This legend, which makes no reference to Chrysostom, confirms the attribution of this iconographical theme in the marginal Psalters to the *Physiologus*.

55. Psalm 98,5.9 : « Worship at this footstool... Worship at his holy mountain. » These verses are referred by Theodoret, 1665, 1668, and by « Athanasius », 421, to Jerusalem or Sion. Pantocrator, f. 140, illustrates verse 9 with a miniature of Golgotha surmounted by a sanctuary. Chludov, f. 98ᵛ, has a miniature of the empty cross, with no indicative sign referring it to a specific verse. The same subject is represented in Barberini, f. 168, illustrating verse 5. Paris, f. 6ᵛ, also has a miniature of the empty cross illustrating verse 5, together with, on f. 7, a second miniature, illustrating verse 9, of a cross upon which is placed a clipeate icon of Christ. In London, f. 131ᵛ, verse 5 is illustrated with a miniature of John Chrysostom presiding at the rite of the Exaltation of the Cross. The originality of the London miniature has not passed unobserved[36]. Most recently Cutler has pointed out that verse 9 — and later verse 5 — were used as the *prokeimenon* in the office of the Exaltation of the Cross[37]. However, he has not explained why, in three other marginal Psalters, God's footstool should have been interpreted as the empty cross. Possibly this choice was suggested by Theodore Studite's *Homily* 2, *In adorationem crucis,* preached on the occasion of the adoration of the Cross in mid-Lent, in which he quotes verse 5 of this Psalm[38].

IV. THEMES COMMON TO BYZANTINE WORSHIP AND MARGINAL PSALTERS

Besides the examples mentioned above (**13, 27, 28, 44**), where a verse is illustrated with a miniature of the Anastasis, seven others should be noted. Six times the verse contains a derivative of the verb ἀνίστημι (ἀνιστάω). All these Psalms were used in an office connected with the Resurrection.

56. Psalm 7,7 : ἀνάστηθι C, L, B. This verse was used as the *prokeimenon* before the reading of *Mark* 16,1-8 at the Ἑωθινός[39].

57. Psalm 9,33 : ἀνάστηθι Pc, C, L, B. This verse was used as *prokeimenon* in the same office before the reading of *John* 20,1-10[40].

---

35. J. STRZYGOWSKI, *Der Bilderkreis des griechischen Physiologus,* Leipzig 1899, p. 76, pl. xii ; O. DEMUS, Bemerkungen zum Physiologus von Smyrna, *JÖB* 25, 1976, p. 250-251, fig. 8-9. The second miniature was of the Annunciation. Demus argues convincingly that the Smyrna *Physiologus* was a Palaeologan copy of an earlier manuscript, *ibidem,* p. 256-257.
36. DER NERSESSIAN, p. 80 ; CH. WALTER, Biographical Scenes of the Three Hierarchs, *REB* 39, 1978, p. 255 ; IDEM, *Art and Ritual of the Byzantine Church,* London 1982, p. 154-155.
37. CUTLER, *art. cit.* (note 8), p. 22-23.
38. THEODORE STUDITE, *Oratio* 2, *In adorationem crucis,* PG 99, 693.
39. *Typicon,* II, p. 170-171.
40. *Typicon,* II, p. 172-173.

278

58. Psalm 43,24.27 : ἀνάστηθι, ἀνάστα C, (L), B. This Psalm was used at the *Orthros* of Holy Saturday[41].

59. Psalm 81,8 : ἀνάστα C, B. This Psalm was also used on Holy Saturday[42].

60. Psalm 101,14 : ἀναστάς C, L, B. This Psalm was used on Easter Sunday[43]. Once the Psalm verse contains a derivative of the verb ἐξεγείρω.

61. Psalm 77,65 : ἐξηγέρθη C, L, B. This Psalm was used on Holy Saturday[44].

It was not, of course, necessary in these cases for the artist to justify his choice of subject by referring to the liturgy. In other cases the relationship is closer.

62. Psalm 30,5.7 : « Thou shalt bring me out of the snare... I have hoped in the Lord. » Theodoret, 1080, refers this Psalm to David persecuted by Absalom. Eusebius, 265, refers it generally to protection from enemies. « Athanasius », 157, refers it to release from sin. It is illustrated in the marginal Psalters (Pantocrator, f. 30ᵛ ; Chludov, f. 26ᵛ ; London, f. 32ᵛ ; Barberini, f. 49ᵛ) by a miniature of Christ standing beside the sepulchre below which are two sleeping guards (Figures 5, 6). There is, of course, a general reference to the Resurrection, which in Chludov is rendered more explicit by the legend : περὶ τῆς ἀναστάσεως λέγει : καὶ οἱ φυλάσσοντες στρατιῶται. The vocabulary is not that of the relevant Gospel passages, *Mat.* 27, 62-66 ; 28,11-15. Actually the phrase resembles a *troparion* used on Holy Saturday. Possibly this was suggested by the word διαφυλάσσοντας which occurs in verse 7. In the London and Barberini miniatures, the iconography was modified by the introduction of a swooping angel over the sepulchre, while the legend was reduced to the words ὁ ἄγιο(ς) τάφο(ς). The full text of the *troparion,* however, needed to be known by the artist, for it explains the presence of the angel : τὸ μνῆμά σου ἐφύλαττον στρατιῶται, οἱ δὲ ἄγγελοι ἀνυμνοῦντές σε, Χριστὲ ὁ Θεός...[45]

63. Psalm 33,9 : « Taste and see that the Lord is good. » Patristic commentators referred this verse to Christ the bread of life (Eusebius, 296 ; Didymus, 1329). Theodoret, 168, and Basil add a sacramental reference. This is rendered explicit in some marginal Psalters by illustrating the verse with a miniature of the Communion of the Apostles (Pantocrator, f. 37 ; Bristol, f. 53), while in London, f. 37ᵛ, the iconography is entirely changed. In Chludov, f. 30, and Barberini, f. 55ᵛ, the verse is illustrated not with a miniature of the Communion of the Apostles but with one of the Multiplication of the Loaves and Fishes. Cutler has noted that both this Psalm and the relevant Gospel passage were used in the rite of the *artoklasia*[46].

64. Psalm 38,2.13 : « I said, I will take heed to my ways... Lord... attend to my tears. » Eusebius, 345-348, gives the Psalm a moral interpretation, while Theodoret, 1145, refers it to David. In the marginal Psalters, these verses are illustrated with two miniatures. The first (Chludov, f. 37ᵛ ; London, f. 46ᵛ ; Barberini, f. 67ᵛ) shows Saint Peter speaking to Christ. The sense of the miniature is hardly intelligible considered on its own, but only Chludov adds an explanatory legend to the effect that Saint Peter, after expressing fidelity to Christ, later denied him. Tikkanen identified the source of the legend, and hence the reason for this choice of subject[47].

---

41. *Typicon (Messina),* p. 243.
42. *Typicon,* II, p. 90-91.
43. *Typicon,* II, p. 94-95.
44. *Typicon,* II, p. 90-91.
45. *Typicon,* II, p. 82 ; *Initia hymnorum,* III, p. 69.
46. Cutler, *art. cit.* (note 8), p. 25.
47. Tikkanen, p. 55.

It is taken from the *troparion* διὰ τὸν φόβον τῶν Ἰουδαίων used at the third hour on Good Friday, in which this Psalm is actually quoted[48]. In the second miniature, Saint Peter is represented weeping, while beside him stands an enormous cock (Pantocrator, f. 48 ; Chludov, f. 38ᵛ ; Bristol, f. 65ᵛ ; London, f. 47ᵛ ; Barberini, f. 68ᵛ). Except in Barberini, the miniature is accompanied each time by a legend referring to Saint Peter's tears after his third denial of Christ. Thus the two miniatures form a sequence.

65. Psalm 50,9 : « Thou shalt sprinkle me with hyssop. » Eusebius, 440, interpreted the verse as referring to the purification of the mind and of the affections. Theodoret, 1250, adduced the parallel of sprinkling the lintels with lamb's blood at the Exodus and of the purification of Christians by the blood of Christ. « Athanasius », 241, used the first parallel but preferred the analogy of Baptism to the second. None of the illuminators of the marginal Psalters exploited these Patristic references. Instead they illustrated the verse with a miniature of Christ washing the feet of the apostles (Pantocrator, f. 63 ; Chludov, f. 50ᵛ ; London, f. 64 ; Barberini, f. 87). Their choice may have been suggested by the fact that this Psalm was recited during the rite of footwashing on Maundy Thursday[49].

66. Psalm 73,13 : « Thou didst break to pieces the heads of the dragons in the water. » Eusebius, 861, Theodoret, 1161, and « Athanasius », 337, refer the verse to Pharaoh and the Egyptians. Some marginal Psalters (Pantocrator, f. 98ᵛ ; Chludov, f. 72ᵛ ; Barberini, f. 125) include among their illustrations a scene of the Baptism of Christ. The Patristic theme of Christ purifying water by his Baptism is largely exploited in the offices of the Epiphany, in which there are frequent allusions to this Psalm, which was recited in its entirety at the sixth hour[50].

67. Psalm 113,8 : « The Lord... turned flint into fountains of water. » Patristic commentators (Theodoret, 1789 ; « Athanasius », 468 ; John Chrysostom[51]) referred the verse to the Exodus. The marginal Psalters (Pantocrator, f. 164ᵛ ; Chludov, f. 117 ; Paris, f. 26ᵛ ; London, f. 154 ; Barberini, f. 197) illustrate the verse again with a scene of the Baptism of Christ. This Psalm was, in fact, recited during Vespers on the feast of the Epiphany[52].

V. OTHER CHRISTOLOGICAL THEMES IN THE MARGINAL PSALTERS

For the following miniatures, I have not found an exact parallel either in the literary sources or in the offices of the Byzantine Church. The first two correspond to a common practice in Psalter illustration of « translating » a word literally by an image, as, for example in Chludov, f. 22ᵛ, where the words τὰ μαρτύρια αὐτοῦ in Psalm 24,10, are rendered (incorrectly) by a picture of a martyr.

68. Psalm 4,7 : « The light of thy countenance, Lord, has been manifested

48. *Typicon (Messina),* p. 239 ; *Initia hymnorum,* I, p. 309 ; Tʜ. Kʟᴜɢᴇ & A. Bᴀᴜᴍꜱ-ᴛᴀʀᴋ, Quadragesima und Karwoche Jerusalems im siebten Jahrhundert, *Oriens Christianus* 5, 1915, p. 208.

49. J. Gᴏᴀʀ, *Euchologion sive rituale graecorum,* Venice 1730, p. 591.

50. *Typicon (Messina),* p. 96 ; *Menaia,* III, Rome 1896, p. 106-107.

51. Jᴏʜɴ Cʜʀʏꜱᴏꜱᴛᴏᴍ, *Expositio in Ps. 113, PG* 55 (*Clavis* 4413), 307.

52. *Typicon,* I, p. 188.

towards us. » Didymus refers the verse to the incarnate Christ as the image of the unseen God. Theodoret, 893, refers it to divine illumination as a consolation in calamity. « Athanasius », 73, calls Christ the light of the world, while Chrysostom refers light to God's providence[53]. The marginal Psalters (Chludov, f. 4 ; London, f. 3ᵛ ; Barberini, f. 9ᵛ) illustrate the verse with a miniature of David before a cross, upon which is placed a clipeate icon of Christ[54]. In Chludov, the miniature is accompanied by a legend : Δα(υὶ)δ προφητεύει πρὸς τὸν σταυρόν. This is maintained in Barberini, while in London it is reduced to : Δα(υὶ)δ λέγ(ει). It is not immediately obvious why David should be supposed to be prophesying about the Cross. However, the almost identical miniature in Chludov, f. 86 (**36**), is accompanied by the legend : Δα(υὶ)δ σημεῖον τοῦ σταυροῦ[55]. The word σημεῖον in Patristic usage was sometimes synonymous with the Cross[56]. In Psalm 4,7, the word ἐσημειώθη occurs, and the illuminator has evidently « translated » it by this miniature (Figures 1,2).

69. Psalm 35,2 : « The transgressor says within himself... » Eusebius, 316-317, and Theodoret, 1120-1121, refer this verse to David ; Didymus, 1333, refers it to sinners in general, and « Athanasius », 175, to the Jews. The marginal Psalters (Pantocrator, f. 42 ; Chludov, f. 32ᵛ ; London, f. 40ᵛ ; Barberini, f. 60) illustrate the verse with a picture of Judas. The legends in Chludov and Pantocrator describe Judas as παράνομος. In Patristic tradition Judas was the transgressor *par excellence*[57]. Thus his portrait has been used to « translate » the word.

The other miniatures follow another common practice in Psalter illustration, particularly developed in Theodore, where portraits of saints frequently exemplify prayer and the practice of virtues. In the ninth-century Psalters, the theme of a Psalm was sometimes exemplified by a polemical picture of the Iconoclasts, which was, in its turn, referred to a Christological scene. Since this aspect of Psalter illustration has already been studied assiduously, the four miniatures in question can be presented summarily[58].

70. Psalm 25,4 : « I have not sat with the council of vanity. » Two figures are obliterating a clipeate icon of Christ. C, L, B.

71. Psalm 51,9 : « Behold the man who... has trusted in the abundance of his wealth. » Nicephorus trampling the simoniac John the Grammarian suggested a *rapprochement* with Saint Peter trampling Simon Magus. Pc, C, L, B.

72. Psalm 68,22 : « They have added to the grief of my wounds. » The obliteration of icons suggested a *rapprochement* with the Crucifixion (7). C, L, B.

73. Psalm 68,28,29 : « They add iniquity to iniquity... Let them be blotted out of the book of the living. » A simoniac ordination suggested a *rapprochement* with the bribing of the guards at the sepulchre. C, B.

In these miniatures, the theme of the Psalm has been exemplified with considerable licence. In others, the process is more conventional.

---

53. John Chrysostom, *Expositio in psalmos, PG* 55 (*Clavis* 4413), 54.

54. The subject recurs in the 12th-century Psalter, Vatican *graec.* 1927, f. 4ᵛ, E. De Wald, *The Illustrations of the Manuscripts of the Septuagint, III, Psalms and Odes,* 1, Princeton 1941, p. 4, pl. ii.

55. Tikkanen, p. 69.

56. Justin Martyr, *Dialogus cum Tryphone Iudaeo,* 94 ii, edited G. Archambault, Paris 1909 (*Clavis* 1076), p. 100 : *PG* 6, 700.

57. John Chrysostom, *In Iohannem homilia* 72, *PG* 59 (*Clavis* 4425), 391.

58. Grabar, *op. cit.* (note 28) ; Idem, Quelques notes sur les psautiers illustrés byzantins du ixᵉ siècle, *CA* 15, p. 61-82 ; Cutler, *art. cit.* (note 8), p. 19 note 9, gives further bibliography.

Pl. I

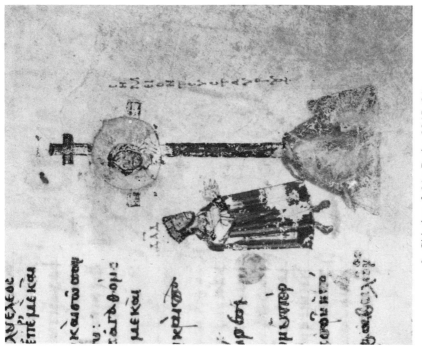

1. Chludov, f. 4 ; Psalm 4,7 (**68**)

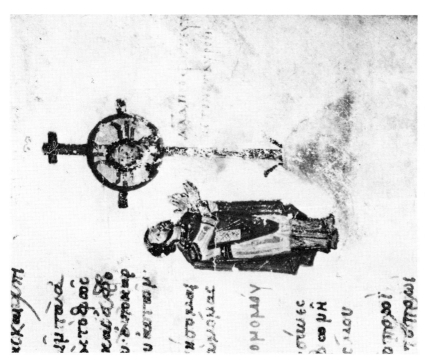

2. Chludov, f. 86 ; Psalm 85,17 (**36**)

3. Pantocrator, f. 29 ; Psalm 29,4 (50)

Pl. III

4. Barberini, f. 48 ; Psalm 29,4 (**50**)

5. Chludov, f. 26ᵛ ; Psalm 30,5.7 (**62**)

Pl. V

Κλίμον τωρρέ μβ τὸ
χυμον τοῦ δξιλέο
Γε μοῦ μοιειο θη τω
ιεαι ξο ὁι ιεορ ιεαι τα
σῶσαι μβ :·
Ὁ τι ιεραιταιϲο μαι μο
φυγη μουειου :·
Κ αι εμβ ιεβη τοῦ ὁρο
δ η γη οϲο μβ ιεαι δια
ξ αιζ ϲο μβ ικ ποψί δ
ἤ ϲε ἐκ ρυ ταψ μοι :·
Τι ου ειο τωρρααι
ιο χη ρμα ϲο υ ται
τὸ στρ μαι μου :·
Λυ τρω ϲο μβ ιεβ ὁ
Θ ειαϲ :·
μίοιοαιο τοιοδλα
ταιομμαι ταὀ τητα

6. Barberini, f. 49ᵛ ; Psalm 30,5.7 (**62**)

7. Chludov, f. 76ᵛ ; Psalm 77,24 (79)

Pl. VII

8. Barberini, f. 132ᵛ ; Psalm 77,24 (**79**)

9. Barberini, f. 39 ; Psalm 22 (**81**)

Pl. VIII

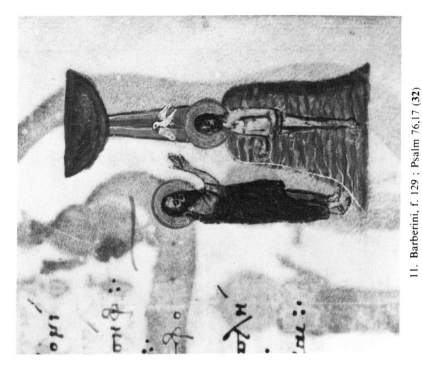

11. Barberini, f. 129 ; Psalm 76,17 (**32**)

10. Chludov, f. 75ᵛ ; Psalm 76,17 (**32**)

74. Psalm 35,10 : « For with thee is the fountain of life. » Three Patristic commentators (Eusebius, 321 ; Didymus, 1336 ; « Athanasius », 176) refer this verse to Christ. Theodoret, 1124, refers it to the Trinity. The marginal Psalters (Pantocrator, f. 42ᵛ ; Chludov, f. 33 ; London, f. 41 ; Barberini, f. 60ᵛ) illustrate the verse with a miniature of Christ and the Samaritan woman (*John* 4,5-42). The theme is typologically apt as an exemplification, but I have failed to find a formal *rapprochement* between the Psalm verse and the Samaritan woman[59].

75. Psalm 35,13 : « There have all the workers of iniquity fallen. » Eusebius, 321, and Theodoret, 1125, give this verse a moral interpretation. The marginal Psalters (Pantocrator, f. 42ᵛ ; Chludov, f. 33ᵛ ; London, f. 41ᵛ ; Barberini, f. 61) illustrate the verse with a miniature of those who came to arrest Christ falling to the ground. The legends in Pantocrator and Chludov quote from the relevant passage of the Gospel (*John* 18,6), but, again, I have failed to find the *rapprochement* made in a literary or liturgical text.

76. Psalm 38,10 : « I was dumb and opened not my mouth. » Both Eusebius, 349, and Theodoret, 1148, give this verse a moral interpretation. Three marginal Psalters (Pantocrator, f. 48 ; Chludov, f. 38 ; Barberini, f. 68) intercalate a miniature between the two episodes concerning Saint Peter (**64**), in order to illustrate this verse. The arrest of Christ is accompanied by a portrait of Isaiah. The legends in Pantocrator and Chludov quote the almost similar verse, *Isaiah* 53,7 : « He does not open his mouth. » Isaiah's prophecy was taken up in *Mat.* 26,63. It was also applied to the sacrifice of Christ in the rite of the prothesis[60]. However, I have failed to find the rather obvious *rapprochement* with the Psalm verse in any literary text.

77. Psalm 55,6 : « All day long they have abominated my words. » Eusebius, 496, and Theodoret, 1286, refer this verse to David. In two ninth-century marginal Psalters (Pantocrator, f. 69 ; Chludov, f. 54ᵛ), this verse is illustrated with a miniature of the Jews refusing to listen to Christ, as the accompanying legend explains. The miniature recurs in London, f. 70, and Barberini, f. 94, without the explanatory legend.

78. Psalm 67,13 : « Rebuke the wild beasts of the forest. » Eusebius, 713, and Theodoret, 1396, refer this verse to those who refuse the Gospel message. « Athanasius », 304, interprets the verse similarly but specifies, among those who refuse the Gospel message, evil spirits. This is exemplified in the marginal Psalters (Chludov, f. 65 ; London, f. 85 ; Barberini, f. 112) by a scene of Christ expelling the unclean spirit from the man in the country of the Gerasenes (*Mat.* 8,28-34, etc.).

79. Psalm 77,24 : « He gave them the bread of heaven ; man ate angels' bread. » Eusebius, 917, and Theodoret, 1489, comment the latter phrase. « Athanasius », 353, interprets manna as spiritual nourishment for the soul. Late the *Historia ecclesiastica* would assimilate manna to the Eucharistic bread[61]. In Pantocrator, f. 105, and Chludov, f. 76ᵛ, the verse is commented by a miniature of Christ addressing a group of figures. The legend in Pantocrator calls Christ the bread of

---

59. The typology of Christ as the fountain of life was used by Clement of Alexandria, *Protrepticus,* edited O. Stählin, Leipzig 1905 (*Clavis* 1375), p. 78²² : *PG* 8, 228.

60. Walter, *op. cit.* (note 36), p. 235.

61. Germanus I, *Historia mystica ecclesiae catholicae,* 3, edited F. Brightman, The Historia Mystagogia and Other Greek Commentaries on the Byzantine Liturgy, *The Journal of Theological Studies* 9, 1908 (*Clavis* 8023), p. 258. For manna as a type of Christ, see Origen, *Commentarii in Iohannem,* VI, edited Cécile Blanc, Paris 1970 (*Clavis* 1453), p. 308 ; *PG* 14, 280.

heaven, while that in Chludov calls him the bread of life. The illustration is typologically apt, even if the verse was not regularly explained in this sense. In Barberini, f. 132ᵛ, the same scene recurs without a legend, while London omits it altogether (Figures 7, 8).

80. Psalm 90,7.10 : « A thousand shall fall at thy side... No evils shall come upon thee. » These verses are referred by Theodoret, 1608, to the enemies of the Israelites and by « Athanasius », 400-401, to the enemies of Christ. The marginal Psalters (Chludov, f. 92 ; London, f. 123 ; Barberini, f. 158) exemplify the verses by miniatures of the Massacre of the Innocents and of the flight to Egypt respectively.

Since some forty of the Christological themes represented in the ninth-century marginal Psalters correspond to the interpretation in the New Testament or Patristic commentaries of the verse of the Psalm illustrated, it is clear that their illuminators were faithful in part to a well-established exegetical tradition. Whether there existed a parallel tradition, dating back to the epoch before Iconoclasm, for illustrating Psalters remains a matter for speculation[62]. On the other hand the Rossano Gospels provide evidence that the *rapprochement* of a Christological scene and a Psalm verse was practised, although in reverse. Six times in the Rossano Gospels, below a Christological scene, the Psalm verse is quoted which would be illustrated by the same scene in the marginal Psalters : f. 1ᵛ, Entry to Jerusalem (**2**) ; f. 3, Christ washing the feet of the apostles (**5**) ; f. 2, Christ expelling merchants from the temple (**6**) ; f. 1ᵛ, Entry to Jerusalem (**12**) ; f. 4ᵛ, Gethsemane (**47**) ; f. 3ᵛ, Communion of the Apostles (**50**)[63].

However, in the marginal Psalters, the exegetical tradition of the Fathers is carried further. It is not difficult to establish a relationship between this development and trends in Byzantine theology from the seventh century. First of all, the Iconophiles attached great importance to the revelation of Christ's humanity in the Old Testament. In his discussion of the meaning of the term εἰκών, John Damascene gave the word a far wider extension than that of the word icon as a pictorial representation[64]. He distinguished six kinds of image, of which the fourth kind was Scripture itself and the fifth kind the types which predict the future. This renewed interest in typology is also apparent in the *Historia ecclesiastica,* where it is said that the antiphons of the liturgy are the oracles of the prophets who announced in advance the coming of the Son of God[65].

As an example of a type which predicts the future, John Damascene cites that of the dew on Gedeon's fleece as predicting the Virgin and Mother of God. This type had already been expounded by the Fathers, and it figures in the illustration of marginal Psalters (**30**). However, whereas the Fathers applied it directly to Christ,

---

62. A. CUTLER, The Byzantine Psalter : Before and after Iconoclasm, *Iconoclasm,* edited Judith HERRIN & A. BRYER, Birmingham 1977 ; Suzy DUFRENNE, *Les illustrations du Psautier d'Utrecht,* Paris 1978.

63. A. MUÑOZ, *Il codice purpureo di Rossano e il frammento sinopense,* Rome 1907, p. 6-7 ; V. LAZAREV, *Storia della pittura bizantina,* Turin 1967, p. 43, 59 (dating the manuscript to the second half of the 6th century) ; WALTER, *op. cit.* (note 36), p. 185, 191.

64. JOHN DAMASCENE, *Orationes de imaginibus tres, ed. cit.* (note 30), p. 125-130 : *PG* 94, 1337-1344.

65. GERMANUS I, *Historia mystica, 32, ed. cit.* (note 61), p. 265.

John Damascene applied it to the Virgin[66]. Developments in the typology of the Virgin had begun before the Iconoclast controversy, which, nevertheless, gave new impetus to it, not only because the value of the Virgin's intercessory powers had been called in doubt, but also because it was from his mother that Christ received human form. Because he had human form, Christ could be represented in the figurative arts. Some typological shifts which bring the Virgin into greater prominence have been noted above. Psalm verses (51, 53) previously interpreted as referring to the Church were applied in the eighth century to the Virgin. Similarly the type of the unicorn, previously applied to Christ, was reinterpreted in the *Physiologus* and extended to the Virgin (54).

To the discussion by other scholars of the iconographical types created or adapted by ninth-century artists to represent these Christological themes, three complements may be added[67].

The Baptism of Christ is represented four times in the marginal Psalters (19, 32, 66, 67), but with slight variations in the iconography. Most often the posture of John the Baptist is conventional. He extends his right hand and places it on Christ's head[68]. In illustration to Psalm 113 (67), the illuminators of Pantocrator and Paris have omitted the figure of John the Baptist. In the two miniatures in Chludov (32, 67), John the Baptist is exceptionally represented not baptizing Christ but extending both hands towards him in a gesture of prayer or adoration (Figures 10, 11). In each case (67), the illuminator of Barberini has copied this gesture exactly, while the illuminator of London has returned to the traditional gesture. The unusual iconography in Chludov suggests that the ninth-century artist, as in the contemporary iconography of the Deësis, wished to call attention to John the Baptist's role as a principal witness that Christ was God incarnate[69].

The iconography of the Resurrection of Lazarus is unusual (50). The theme is presented in narrative form (Figures 3, 4). A personification of Hades grasps the souls of the dead in a sarcophagus. A diminutive figure of Lazarus, his hands outstretched, returns to earth. Christ, as in the conventional iconography of this theme, summons Lazarus, swathed in a winding-cloth, from the tomb. The miniatures in London and Barberini, while differing slightly from that in Pantocrator, resemble each other and are probably close to that which would have been painted on the lost folio of Chludov. I have already suggested that this theme was chosen, because the verse was quoted by John of Euboea. The connection between text and miniature may be yet closer, for the same narrative sequence occurs in both[70].

Grabar has noted the importance attached by the Iconophiles to the association

---

66. *Orationes, ed. cit.* (note 30), p. 129 : *PG* 94, 1341. Henceforth this type would be regularly applied to the Virgin. See THEODORE STUDITE, *Oratio 5, In dormitionem deiparae, PG* 99, 725.

67. GRABAR, *op. cit.* (note 28) ; R. CORMACK, Painting after Iconoclasm, *Iconoclasm* (note 62), p. 147-163.

68. CH. WALTER, Baptism in Byzantine Iconography, *Sobornost* 2, 1980, p. 8-25 ; IDEM, *op. cit.* (note 36), p. 125-130.

69. IDEM, Two Notes on the Deësis, *REB* 26, 1968, p. 324-336.

70. See above (note 25). (Christ) commanded the soul to come up from Hades and enter the body. (The soul) cried out : « Those murky persons are pushing me backwards. » Then (Christ) called : « Lazarus, come out. »

of the cult of the Cross with that of Christ's icon[71]. To the texts which he adduces in support of this association may be added one due to John Damascene[72]. However, he did not insist on the important place of this theme in the ninth-century Psalters. It was used to illustrate three Psalms (**36, 55, 68**). The iconographical type was not an innovation, for it had already been used in the apse of Sant'Apollinare in Classe, Ravenna, to represent the Transfiguration. However, both the context and the connotations of the icon on the Cross are quite different in the marginal Psalters (Figures 1, 2).

VI. CHRISTOLOGICAL THEMES IN THE ELEVENTH-CENTURY PSALTERS

So far as the Christological miniatures are concerned, it is not difficult to reconstruct the model on which both London and Barberini depend[73]. It would have contained the miniatures which are identical in Chludov, London and Barberini. It would also have contained the miniatures common to Chludov and Barberini but omitted or adapted in London. Besides these there would have been others which are similar in London and Barberini but different in Chludov.

One group of miniatures common to London and Barberini consists of those in which the artist has been confused by an error in his model. Most of these errors have been already noted. Twice the copyist responsible for the model misunderstood the Chludov miniatures, because they were juxtaposed on the same folio. This is evident in the two miniatures illustrating Psalms 50 and 51[74]. Psalm 108 is illustrated in Chludov, f. 113 (**47**), with a miniature of Christ at prayer in Gethsemane, which is placed beside the title of the Psalm at the top of the folio. In Barberini, f. 190ᵛ, the Psalm begins on the folio, on which Psalm 107 ends. This same scene is referred in Barberini to Psalm 107,15 (the penultimate verse) : « Give us help in tribulation ». The same displacement occurs in London, f. 149.

On three occasions, the copyist of the model failed to understand the iconography of the Chludov miniature. In Chludov, f. 48ᵛ, the illustration to Psalm 49,3 (**24**) is correctly rendered. However, the copyist failed to understand the personification of the setting sun, which in Barberini, f. 84ᵛ, has been replaced by an actual representation of the sun, while in London, f. 62, it is travestied as the head of an animal with horns[75]. In the somewhat similar miniature illustrating Habbakuk's *Ode* in Chludov, f. 154ᵛ, the sun is correctly rendered disappearing behind a hill, and the significance of the miniature is made clear by the legends. In Barberini, f. 257ᵛ, the miniature has been copied sketchily, while in London, f. 198, the hill has disappeared, making nonsense of the miniature. In both the eleventh-century manuscripts, the legend has been omitted. The third misunderstanding occurs in the copies of the miniature of Christ calming the tempest, illustrating Psalm 88,10 (**39**). In Chludov,

71. Grabar, *op. cit.* (note 28), p. 204-205.

72. *Orationes, ed. cit.* (note 30), p. 140 : *PG* 94, 1356.

73. London is dated 1066. Anderson, *art. cit.* (note 3), p. 60, dates Barberini between 1092 and 1118, perhaps around 1095. For reasons that cannot be developed here, I would propose a date around 1050 for the model. In this section, I add a few complements to Der Nersessian, p. 63-70.

74. The copyist moved David incongruously to the illustration of Psalm 51, Der Nersessian, p. 33, 68-69, fig. 105, 106, 327-329. The error is not repeated in Vatican *graec.* 1927, f. 93, De Wald, *op. cit.* (note 54), p. 18, pl. xxiii.

75. Anderson, *art. cit.* (note 3), p. 40, fig. 6-8.

f. 88, the personifications of the sea and wind are correctly rendered and identified by legends. Notably the personification of the wind holds his customary horn pointing downwards and places his hand over his mouth in a gesture of silence. In the same scene in London, f. 117ᵛ, and Barberini, f. 151ᵛ, the legends are omitted and the two figures corresponding to the personifications fall back incongruously into the sea[76].

The modern art historian, by referring back to Chludov, can decipher these miniatures and attribute a significance to them. The illuminators of London and Barberini did not have this advantage. This consideration invites one to raise a wider question : since the illuminators of London, Barberini and their common model clearly misunderstood some of the Chludov miniatures, did they really understand the other Christological miniatures, even when they rendered them correctly ? One sign of their apparent indifference to the purport of these miniatu-res is the disappearance or reduction of the accompanying legends. Often the legend which is explicative in Chludov is replaced in the eleventh-century Psalters by one which is nominative. For example, the explicative legend accompanying the miniature of the Annunciation in Chludov, f. 45 (51), is replaced in London, f. 56ᵛ, by ὁ χαιρετισμό(ς) and in Barberini, f. 78ᵛ, by ὁ χερετισμός (sic). The same occurs in the miniature of the sleeping guards at the sepulchre, illustrating Psalm 30,5.7 (62). Yet in this case, if my explanation of the swooping angel is correct, the illuminator of the model must have grasped the purport of the miniature (Figures 5, 6). In other cases, where there is no legend in the eleventh-century Psalters, the miniature is virtually meaningless ; as, for example Saint Peter's protestation of fidelity, illustrating Psalm 38,2 (64). Another example is provided by Christ explaining to his disciples that he is the bread of life, illustrating Psalm 77,24 (79). The miniature in Barberini, f. 132ᵛ, could as well represent Moses addressing the Israelites (Figures 7, 8). The illuminator of London preferred to omit this miniature, replacing it by a literal « translation » of the second phrase of the Psalm verse : « Man ate angels' bread ». It is likely that the explicative legends had already been omitted in large part in the model used by the illuminators of London and Barberini, also that in large part the copies of the Christological miniatures were executed mechanically.

There is a considerable number of miniatures common to London and Barberini which do not appear in the ninth-century marginal Psalters. However singularly few illustrate Christological themes.

81. Psalm 22,1 : « The Lord tends me as a shepherd. » All the Patristic commen-tators (Eusebius, 216-220 ; Didymus, 1289-1293 ; Theodoret, 1025-1029 ; « Athana-sius », 140) refer this Psalm to Christ as the Good Shepherd (John 10). In Bristol, f. 37, the illustration is literal. Both London, f. 24, and Barberini, f. 39, illustrate the Psalm with a miniature of Abraham seated by a river, which flows from the mouth of a personification. Lazarus, as recounted in Luke 16,23, is seated in Abraham's bosom. Abraham extends his hand towards a tree, placed by the river, in order to pluck a fruit (Figure 9). An explanation of this paradisiac interpretation of the Psalm may be found in the Byzantine rite for the funeral of a priest[77]. This Psalm

---

76. Der Nersessian, p. 66.
77. Goar, op. cit. (note 49), p. 452 ; M. Arranz, Les prières presbytérales de la 'Pannychis', La maladie et la mort du chrétien dans la liturgie, edited A. Triacca, Rome 1975, p. 73.

286

was used in the rite, while, in the prayers, there are several references to Paradise and to Lazarus seated in Abraham's bosom.

82. Psalm 44,15 : « Virgins shall be brought to the king after her. » As noted above **(51)**, this Psalm was interpreted by the Patristic commentators as referring to the Church, although it was later applied to the Virgin. In London, f. 57, and Barberini, f. 79, the verse is illustrated with a scene of the Presentation of the Virgin. This verse was used as the *koinonikon* in the liturgy of the feast[78].

83. Psalm 71,11 : « And all the kings shall worship him. » Eusebius, 309, and Theodore, 1436, interpret this verse eschatologically, while « Athanasius », in his commentary, 325, includes a reference to the Magi. In Bristol, f. 115ᵛ, London, f. 92, and Barberini, f. 120, the verse is illustrated with a scene of the Adoration of the Magi. This Psalm was used in the office of the sixth hour of the Vigil of Christmas[79].

84. Psalm 131,7 : « Let us worship at the place where his feet stood. » Didymus, 1589, and « Athanasius », 521, refer this verse to the Mount of Olives, while Theodoret, 1905, referred it to the divine temple. In London, f. 172ᵛ, and Barberini, f. 223, the verse is illustrated with a miniature of Christ, wearing a long straight colobium, attached to the Cross. To left and right stand figures inclined towards him. The verse, as well as the miniature, resemble Psalm 98,5.9 **(55)**. Yet it does not seem that this verse was used directly in any rite or celebration connected with the Cross. On the other hand, it was quoted in the *troparion* Σήμερον τὸ προφητικὸν πεπλήρωται λόγιον, which was frequently used in Byzantine worship, notably for the feast of the Exaltation of the Cross and in the rite of the veneration of the Cross on the 4th Tuesday in Lent[80].

A final Christological scene occurs only in London.

85. Psalm 2,2 : « The rulers are gathered together against the anointed. » The operative word in this verse is obviously χριστοῦ. The Psalm had already been interpreted Christologically by Hippolytus[81]. Theodoret, 869-872, and « Athanasius », 64, followed his example. In Chludov, f. 2ᵛ, it is illustrated with a miniature of a council of rulers, but with no explicit reference to Christ. In Barberini, f. 7, the miniature is similar, but the position of the figures has been reversed. In Bristol, f. 9, the verse is also illustrated by a miniature of a council, referred by the legend to Herod, Pilate and the leaders of the Jews united against Christ. In London, f. 2, a second miniature is added to that of the council. As the legend explains, it portrays Christ before Annas and Caiaphas.

In conclusion, it may be said that, so far as Christological themes were concerned, the illuminators of the eleventh-century Psalters rarely innovated. Changes made in the Christological miniatures had, for the most part, been introduced already into the model common to London and Barberini. Such changes derive either from liturgical texts or from a literal interpretation of the Psalm. This is as true for the introduction of the swooping angel

---

78. TIKKANEN, p. 49 ; CUTLER, *art. cit.* (note 8), p. 22.
79. TIKKANEN, p. 50 ; *Typicon (Messina)*, p. 81 ; *Menaion*, II, Rome 1889, p. 639.
80. *Typicon*, I, p. 28 ; II, p. 40 ; *Initia hymnorum*, III, p. 496.
81. RONDEAU, *op. cit.* (note 4), p. 33.

into the scene at the sepulchre (62) and of the statue of Ares into the scene of the Entry to Jerusalem (2). It is also true for the rare new scenes.

Lip-service continued to be paid to the prophetical nature of the Psalms. In London the legend ὁ Δαυὶδ λέγει recurs over thirty times, but what David said and why is not usually specified. Typology had been a major weapon for the Iconophiles in their polemics against the Iconoclasts. In the eleventh-century it had lost its importance. As I have observed elsewhere, Iconoclasm excited less interest among eleventh-century Constantinopolitans than among Byzantine scholars of our times[82]. In their polemics, Medieval Byzantine theologians assimilated their opponents not to Iconoclasts but to Arians. So far as the marginal Psalters are concerned, the eleventh-century *Zeitgeist* is manifest rather in iconographical themes inspired by the cult of Constantinople as the New Sion and by the cult of Constantinopolitan saints[83]. Already present in the model and Barberini, it received its fullest expression in London, in which, more than in the other manuscripts, the Messianic significance of the Psalter is rendered perfunctorily and relegated to the background.

82. WALTER, *op. cit.* (note 36), p. 214.
83. DER NERSESSIAN, p. 77-98.

"LATTER-DAY" SAINTS AND THE IMAGE OF CHRIST IN THE NINTH-CENTURY BYZANTINE MARGINAL PSALTERS

For the twelfth centenary of the Second Council of Nicaea

The introduction of miniatures of "latter-day" saints — that is to say of saints who lived in post-apostolic times — into illuminated marginal psalters marks a definite departure from the practice of literary commentators, who normally limited their typological interpretation of the Psalms to New Testament persons and events[1]. Tikkanen was already intrigued by these miniatures of "latter-day" saints[2]. He explained their presence in some cases by referring them to the use of the Psalm verse in the saint's liturgical office. Mariès first attempted to establish a comprehensive list of the saints represented in marginal psalters[3]. However he did not distinguish between New Testament saints, for whose presence a typological explanation is usually possible, those who figure as authors or commentators and genuine "latter-day" saints, for whose presence some other explanation is required.

Mariès noted that miniatures of saints are far more numerous in eleventh- than in ninth-century psalters, but he did not attempt an explanation of this increase. It is likely that it was related to modifications introduced

1. Ch. WALTER, Christological Themes in the Byzantine Marginal Psalters from the Ninth to the Eleventh Century, *REB* 44, 1986, p. 269-287.
2. J. J. TIKKANEN, *Die Psalterillustration im Mittelalter*, Helsingfors 1895-1900, reprinted Soest, Netherlands 1975, p. 74-78.
3. L. MARIÈS, L'irruption des saints dans l'illustration du psautier byzantin, *An. Boll.* 68, 1950, p. 153-162.

206

in both the eleventh-century psalters, whose overall programme is different-ly orientated from that of the earlier ones. This question cannot be treated here. André Grabar was the first scholar to investigate the reasons for introducing "latter-day" saints into the ninth-century psalters. "Je soup-çonne", he wrote, "que tous les saints précis (...) qui figurent sur les marges du psautier du 9ᵉ siècle y apparaissent en fonction de l'œuvre de restaura-tion des icônes »[4]. This explanation, which he did not develop in detail, left Jean Gouillard unconvinced. "Cette explication", wrote Gouillard, "ne nous paraît pas s'imposer, tant l'illustrateur se laisse facilement diriger dans le choix de ses figurines par des associations de mots"[5]. Yet it would seem that Grabar's and Gouillard's explanations are complementary rather than contradictory. As will be seen, it is not difficult to discern in most cases why the artist considered the saint whom he chose to be relevant to the Psalm verse illustrated. On the other hand, it is unlikely that the presence of these "latter-day" saints depends only on word associations. One would expect their choice to be relevant to the Iconophile cause, particularly if their introduction into Psalter illustration represented a new departure. There is also, in two cases, a significant iconographical link with the overall programme of the Psalters : the presence in the miniature of the clipeate image of Christ.

The article begins with a repertory of the saints, unnamed and named. The latter are, in fact, few in number : one in the Paris Psalter ; three in the Pantocrator Psalter ; six in the Chludov Psalter[6]. To these must, of course, be added the miniatures in which the Iconophile patriarch Nicephorus is represented. Their place in the overall programme is then discussed, with particular reference to the clipeate image of Christ. Finally it is argued that the presence of the "latter-day" saints — excluding Nicephorus — is best explained by the hypothesis that there was a common model for these three ninth-century Psalters, whose programme was elaborated in the late eighth century in Palestine. This was later adapted by the introduction of the miniatures concerning the patriarch Nicephorus and his adversary John Grammaticus.

4. A. GRABAR, L'iconoclasme byzantin, dossier archéologique, Paris 1957, p. 227.

5. J. GOUILLARD, Art et littérature théologique à Byzance au lendemain de la querelle des images, Cahiers de civilisation médiévale 5, 1962, p. 5, reprinted, La vie religieuse à Byzance, Variorum London 1981.

6. Paris and Pantocrator Psalters : Suzy DUFRENNE, L'illustration des psautiers grecs au Moyen Âge, I, Paris 1966. Chludov Psalter : Marfa ŠČEPKINA, Miniatjuri Hludovskoj Psaltyri. Grečeskij illjustrirovannyj kodeks IX veka, Moscow 1977. References in the text of this article to these psalters is given only by the folio number.

I. REPERTORY OF MINIATURES

i. Anonymous figures illustrating an aspect of saintliness

These miniatures are the most numerous and possibly the earliest to be introduced into psalter illustration, since they take up literally a word or phrase of the Psalm text[7]. They recall that the Byzantine vocabulary of saintliness derives for the most part from the Septuagint, notably from the Psalter itself[8].

1. The blessed man. Psalm 1,1 : Blessed is the man who has not walked in the counsel of the ungodly. C, f. 2. A haloed figure is seated, holding a codex in his hands. To the left is a clipeate image of Christ. There is a legend : μακάριος.

2. Saints. Psalm 15,3 : On behalf of the saints (τοῖς ἁγίοις) that are in his land. C, f. 11ᵛ. A group of unhaloed figures are bunched together. The front figure is represented *orans*.

3. Martyr. Psalm 24,10 : Truth to them that seek his covenant and his testimonies (τὰ μαρτύρια αὐτοῦ). C, f. 22ᵛ. A figure is lying outstretched, naked apart from a monastic scapular, with blood flowing from his wounds.

4. The just. Psalm 33,18 : The just cried and the Lord heard them. C, f. 30ᵛ. A group of monks are represented in various attitudes of prayer. Rays descend on them from a blue segment above. There is a legend : δίκαιοι.

5. Martyrs. Psalm 33,20(?) : Many are the tribulations of the just. There is a legend : οἱ ἅγιοι μάρτυρες.

6. Reliquary. Psalm 33,21 : He keeps all their bones. C, 30ᵛ. A reliquary.

7. The just. Psalm 36,39 : The salvation of the just is from the Lord. Pc, f. 46ᵛ. Two haloed figures extend their right hands in a gesture of prayer. There is a legend : δίκαιοι.

8. Martyrdom. Psalm 43,23 : For your sake we are put to death all day long. C, f. 44. Three figures are being executed with a sword.

9. Three martyrs. Psalm 67,36 : God is wonderful in his holy ones (ἐν τοῖς ἁγίοις αὐτοῦ). C, f. 65ᵛ. Three haloed figures hold a cross in their right hand. There is a legend : οἱ ἅγιοι μάρτυρες.

10. The poor man. Psalm 101, title : A prayer for the poor. C, f. 100 ; Pc, f. 141ᵛ. In C, a seated figure is represented holding his right hand to his mouth. Legend : ὁ πτωχός. In Pc, the figure kneels, his hands outstretched. There is a legend : εἰσάκουσόν μου, κ(ύρι)ε.

ii. Named "latter-day" saints

11. Symeon the Stylite the Younger (?). Psalm 4,4 : Know that the Lord has done wonderful things for his holy one (τὸν ὅσιον αὐτοῦ). C, f. 3ᵛ. A bearded figure looks from the window of his dwelling, which is placed on top of the

---

7. The hypothesis that early psalter illustration was literal is based on the lack of typological subjects in the Utrecht Psalter, which may give the most faithful reflection available of early Christian psalter illustration. See also the fragmentary Verona Psalter (7th-8th century). Suzy DUFRENNE, *Les illustrations du Psautier d'Utrecht*, Paris 1978, p. 29-30 ; A. CUTLER, The Byzantine Psalter : Before and after Iconoclasm, *Iconoclasm*, edited A. BRYER & Judith HERRIN, Birmingham 1977, p. 94-95.

8. About the only terms in the Byzantine hagiographical lexicon not already established in the Septuagint Greek are : ὁμολογητής and λείψανα.

capital of a column. Below, standing on the base of the column, a figure in a tunic extends his right hand. A receptacle hangs by a cord from the window of the stylite's dwelling. Above him is placed a clipeate image of Christ. A legend : θάμβος (miracle) has been added in a later hand. However, according to Ščepkina, the name Symeon may be deciphered on the manuscript below the later legend.

The iconography of stylites, which was well-established before Iconoclasm, has been exhaustively studied by Jacqueline Lafontaine-Dosogne. She points out that the iconography of specific stylite saints had no traits permitting one to distinguish between them. On the other hand it is only in the marginal psalters that the stylites are represented at the window of their dwelling. Normally they figure in bust form on top of their column. She suggests that the artist of the Chludov Psalter made his picture from life[9]. Another trait peculiar to psalter illustration is the clipeate image above the stylite. It still remains to decide which Symeon is represented here. Mariès suggested that this miniature would be of Symeon the Younger, of the "marvellous mountain", by reason of the word association with ἐθαυμάστωσεν in the Psalm[10].

12. Seven Sleepers of Ephesus. Psalm 32,19 : To deliver their souls from death and keep them alive in famine. C, f. 29 ; Pc, f. 36ᵛ. In both manuscripts several recumbent figures (clearly seven in Pc) are bunched together. There is a legend in both manuscripts : οἱ ἑπτὰ παῖδες (ἐν Ἐφέσῳ). The choice would have been suggested by the fact that these saints survived death, thanks to their sleeping miraculously through a period of persecution. Although this is the earliest surviving representation of the Seven Sleepers, the rudimentary iconography suggests that it is directly copied from an existing model, possibly even in a simplified form.

13. George. Psalm 43,23 : For your sake, we are put to death all day long. C, f. 44. Saint George, naked apart from a loincloth, lies upon a wheel, fixed to a trestle upon the upper beam of which are seven knives pointing downwards. Blood flows from his back. To either side of the trestle stand figures in tunics who pull on cords attached to George's hands and feet respectively. There is a legend : ὁ ἅγιος Γεώργιος. This is the "typical" torture scene for Saint George[11]. The scene was probably considered apt to illustrate this Psalm verse, because, in his *Passion*, George is said to have succombed to and recovered from a whole series of tortures[12]. Again, this is the earliest surviving example of the iconography of George on the wheel.

14. John Chrysostom. Psalm 48,2 : Hear this, all the nations. C, f. 47ᵛ. A frontal portrait of a bishop holding a book is accompanied by the inscription : ὁ Χρυσόστομος. John Chrysostom inherited the title of apostle of the

9. Jacqueline LAFONTAINE-DOSOGNE, *Itinéraires archéologiques dans la région d'Antioche. Recherches sur le monastère et sur l'iconographie de S. Syméon Stylite le jeune*, Brussels 1967, p. 199.

10. MARIÈS, *art. cit.* (note 3), p. 161.

11. Temily MARK WEINER, *Narrative Cycles of the Life of St. George in Byzantine Art*, doctoral dissertation, New York 1977 ; Ch. WALTER, The Cycle of Saint George in the Monastery of Dečani, *Symposium Dečani and XIVth-century. Art in the Byzantine World*, Belgrade & Dečani 1985 (printing).

12. MARIÈS, *art. cit.* (note 3), p. 159.

Gentiles from Saint Paul. He also commented this Psalm. The portrayal of John Chrysostom is rudimentary, and would have been copied from an earlier model. For the general presentation, the icon of Saints Paul, Peter, Nicolas and John Chrysostom at Saint Catherine's, Mount Sinaï, offers an obvious parallel, although John Chrysostom's facial features are represented differently[13].

15. Constantine. Psalm 59,6 : You have given a sign to them that fear you, that they may flee from the bow. C, f. 58ᵛ. Constantine, seated on a prancing horse, holds a shield and a lance on top of which is a cross. A fallen figure is trampled by the horse, while two others are aiming arrows from their bows. There is a legend : ὁ ἅγιος Κωνσταντῖνος. The word σημείωσιν probably suggested an association with the prophecy to Constantine : In this sign you will conquer[14] (Figure 1).

16. Eustace. Psalm 96,11 : Light has sprung up for the righteous and gladness for the upright in heart. C, f. 97ᵛ ; Pc, f. 138 ; P, f. 5ᵛ. This is the only theme concerning a named saint of which an illustration has survived in all three ninth-century psalters. The iconography varies slightly from manuscript to manuscript. The simplest version is that in the Pantocrator Psalter, in which Eustace, in armour and mantle, kneels facing towards the stag, his arms outstretched. The fleeing stag turns its head back towards Eustace. Between its antlers is placed a clipeate image of Christ. Eustace's prancing horse is placed to the left ; his spear and shield have fallen to the ground. There is a legend : ὁ ἅγιος Εὐστάθιος.

In the Paris Psalter, the scene is reversed, such that the stag appears on the left. There was also a further detail, now cut out, although the accompanying legend has survived : Πέτρος ἐν τῇ φυλακῇ. Thus the lost detail would have been a representation of Saint Peter in prison (*Acts* 17,7).

The scene in the Chludov Psalter closely resembles the preceding one, except that Eustace is placed behind rather than beside his horse. Next to the stag's antlers, a bust figure is represented in a rectangular frame whose triangular top ends in a pinnacle. There are two legends : φῶς ὁ Χ(ριστὸ)ς εἰς τὸν ἅγιον Πέτρον — φῶς ὁ Χ(ριστὸ)ς εἰς τὸν ἅγιον Εὐστάθην (*sic*).

The iconography of the conversion of Eustace is well attested for this early period. Two examples in Georgia dating from the seventh or eighth centuries,

13. K. Weitzmann, *The Monastery of Saint Catherine at Mount Sinaï. The Icons*, volume one, Princeton 1976, n° B. 33 (7th-8th century ?).

14. A later hand has added a scholion to this folio, which is made up of two passages from the *Expositio in Psalmos* of Nicephorus Blemmydes, PG 142, 1481-1482. Since there are only slight variants from the published text, I have not transcribed the scholion, but give, with his kind permission, the translation established by Joseph Munitiz :

1. οἰονεὶ ἐνσεσημασμένοι... ποικίλου τόξ(ου), commenting Psalm 59,6 : As if marked with a sign were *those who fear you* and (they) have not been destroyed. By *the bow* he refers to the warlike weapon. The *marking* on the faithful, however, (is) the seal of holy baptism, and the imprint of the life-giving cross, by means of which we escape from the devils' varied *bow*.

2. ἀγαλλιάσομαι τῇ εὐαρεστήσει... τ(ὴν) ἰουδαίαν ἐδήλωσ(εν), commenting Psalm 59,8 : *I shall rejoice* in the well-being of my people, and I shall allot to them the city of the tribe of *Ephraim* ; the city called *Sikima*, and the place that formerly was of the Sikimians, which is called the *valley of dogs* ; by these (terms), however, he refers to the whole of Judaea. — The words in italics are quotations from the Psalm commented.

the relief from Cebeldi and the stele of Davit Gareža (Figure 5), show a bust of Christ between the antlers of the stag which he has been pursuing[15]. In early Cappadocian frescoes a cross between the antlers was preferred[16]. The miniatures of the three ninth-century psalters are, therefore, in this respect, closer to the Georgian iconography, although only in the psalters does the bust image of Christ take on clipeate form. Another detail peculiar to the ninth-century psalters is the association with Saint Peter. In the *Life* of Eustace, his conversion is contrasted with that of Cornelius (*Acts* 10). Whereas Eustace was directly illuminated by Christ, Cornelius was converted by the intermediary action of Saint Peter[17]. If the Chludov miniature is considered in isolation, it could be supposed that this contrast is implicit in its iconography, for the sense of the triangular frame surrounding the bust of Saint Peter is not immediately evident. Ščepkina considered it to be a cabinet for icons (*kiota*). Its form also resembles that of a Byzantine lantern. The nearest analogy in the Chludov Psalter is the stylite's dwelling (f. 3ᵛ). This, taken in conjunction with the legend for the missing detail in the Paris Psalter, makes the interpretation of the frame as a schematic prison the most plausible. The operative word in the Psalm verse illustrated is φῶς, which is taken up in both legends. Consequently the spiritual illumination of Eustace is being compared with the illumination of Peter's prison when he was rescued by an angel[18].

17. Panteleimon. Psalm 123,6 : Blessed be the Lord who has not given us for a prey to their teeth. Pc, f. 182. The folio for this Psalm is missing from the Chludov Psalter, but, since the miniature recurs in both the Barberini and London Psalters, it is reasonable to suppose that it once figured there. Panteleimon, haloed, kneels beside a rudimentary hillside, his hands covered and outstretched in prayer. To his left is a panther. Above, Daniel is represented standing, while two lions lick his feet. There are two legends : Δανιήλ — ὁ ἅγιος Παν(τελεήμων). It is told in the *Life* of Panteleimon, whose original name was Pantoleon, that in the arena the wild beasts refused to devour him[19]. Thus the association with the Psalm verse is as appropriate for him as for Daniel.

15. N. A. ALADAŠVILI, *Monumentalnaja skulptura Gruzii*, Moscow 1977, p. 60 ; Nicole THIERRY, Essai de définition d'un atelier de sculpture du Haut Moyen Âge en Gogarène, *Revue des études géorgiennes et caucasiennes* 1, 1985, p. 178-179.

16. At Saint John the Baptist, Çavuşin, Nicole THIERRY, *Haut Moyen Âge en Cappadoce*, Paris 1983, p. 97 ; at Mavrucan, church n° 3, EADEM, Art byzantin du Haut Moyen Âge en Cappadoce : l'église n° 3 de Mavrucan, *Journal des savants*, octobre-décembre 1972, p. 255 ; at Davullu kilisesi, EADEM, Mentalité et formulation iconoclastes en Anatolie, *Journal des savants*, août-juin 1976, p. 85-87. See also Anita COUMOUSSI, Une représentation rare de la vision de saint Eustache dans une église grecque du XIIIᵉ siècle, *CA* 33, 1985, p. 51-60.

17. *S. Eusthatii acta antiqua* (*BHG* 641), *PG* 105, 377-381 = JOHN DAMASCENE, *Orationes de imaginibus tres* (*Clavis* 8045), B. KOTTER, *Die Schriften des Iohannes von Damaskos*, III, Berlin 1975, p. 177-178 ; *PG* 94, 1381.

18. GRABAR, *op. cit.* (note 4), p. 227, wrote in error that this comparison also occurs in the text of the *Acts* of Eustace.

19. *Passio* (*BHG* 1414m), *Menologii anonymi byzantini saeculi X quae supersunt*, edited B. LATYŠEV, II, Petrograd 1912, § 12, p. 220. *Passio* (*BHG* 1412z), Hagiographica graeca inedita, ed. B. LATYŠEV, *Mémoires de l'Académie impériale de St-Pétersbourg*, VIIIᵉ série, 12, 2, 1914, § 20, p. 49-50.

There is little consistency in the way that these saints are represented. Only three are haloed (John Chrysostom, Eustace, Panteleimon) ; only four are called saints in the accompanying legends (George, Constantine, Eustace, Panteleimon). There are also clear differences in the quality of their rendering. John Chrysostom and the Seven Sleepers seem to be mechanical copies from a current model. The scene of George in the wheel is more developed, but remains independent of the text. On the other hand, the scene of Constantine, while recalling the traditional triumphal imagery of emperors on horseback, has been made relevant to the Psalm verse by the introduction of figures aiming arrows from their bows (Figure 1). Two "latter-day" saints — Eustace and Panteleimon — have been coupled with a biblical saint, as if to render them more respectable. This might be considered an answer to the Iconoclast challenge to the cult of "latter-day" saints, which, if ancient, had yet to be systematized. It might well be — although there is no possibility of certitude — that the introduction of named saints into Psalter illustration was a recent initiative. They do not, of course, figure in the aristocratic psalters ; in the Utrecht Psalter only one "latter-day" saint is represented, Saint Laurence along with Saints Peter and Paul[20] ; in the Bristol Psalter, the unique hagiographical miniature occurs on f. 24, where Psalm 15,3 is illustrated by a group of anonymous martyrs[21].

Two points made by Gouillard are not in doubt[22]. All these named saints were aptly chosen, and, as is evident from the small number compared with those whose *Lives* are cited in the Iconophile *florilegia*, the representation of saints has not been undertaken systematically. Nevertheless, a fairly strong case can be argued in favour of Grabar's proposition that these saints *do* appear in the Psalters, as in the *florilegia*, as witnesses to Iconophile doctrines challenged by the Iconoclasts. There is, indeed, little overlap with the *florilegium* compiled for the second Council of Nicaea, which cites passages concerned only with two of the saints represented here : John Chrysostom and the two Symeons[23]. On the other hand four saints represented are cited in the *florilegium* compiled by John Damascene. Twice the passage cited corresponds directly to the scene represented : the triumph of Constantine[24] and the conversion of Eustace[25]. In the other two cases — John Chrysostom and the two Symeons — the artist has not established a direct relationship.

The passage quoted by John Damascene from the *Life* of Symeon the Younger is the account of the merchant of Antioch who set up Symeon's icon in a public place[26]. When three men tried to take it down, they were miracu-

---

20. DUFRENNE, *op. cit.* (note 7), p. 149-150.

21. DUFRENNE, *op. cit.* (note 6), p. 50.

22. GOUILLARD, *art. cit.* (note 5), p. 5-6.

23. P. VAN DEN VEN, La patristique et l'hagiographie au concile de Nicée de 787, *Byz.* 25-27, 1955-1957, p. 357-358 n⁰ˢ 63, 73, 74.

24. JOHN DAMASCENE, *op. cit.* (note 17), edited KOTTER, p. 173, *PG* 94, 1373-1376 = EUSEBIUS, *Historia ecclesiastica* (*Clavis* 3495), 9, 9, edited G. BARDY, *Histoire ecclésiastique*, II, Paris 1958, p. 63-64, *PG* 20, 824.

25. See above, note 17.

26. JOHN DAMASCENE, *op. cit.* (note 17), *PG* 94, 1393-1394 = La vie ancienne de S. Syméon Stylite le Jeune (BHG 1689), edited P. VAN DEN VEN, I, Brussels 1962, p. 139-141 ; II, Brussels 1970, p. 164-165.

lously hurled to the ground. He also quoted two passages about John Chrysostom[27] : a resurrection miracle performed by the saint's icon, and the apparition of Saint Paul, whom Proclus could recognize from the resemblance with an icon suspended on the wall. In the *Lives* of the other saints represented in the ninth-century psalters, similar incidents occur. Saint George had visions of Christ and performed resurrection miracles[28]. The miraculous sleep and awakening of the Seven Sleepers of Ephesus was considered to be a witness to the resurrection[29]. Panteleimon restored life to a child bitten by a snake, and had a vision of Christ[30]. Such is the evidence for supposing that these particular saints were chosen, not only because they could be aptly associated with the Psalm verse, but also because their *Lives* could be quoted in favour of doctrines challenged by the Iconoclasts : resurrection and immortality ; the utility and efficacity of the cult of icons ; the physical visibility — and hence representability — of Christ. However, it does not seem that the psalter illustrations are intended to affirm the intercessory powers of saints, although this was, in fact, one of the first doctrines to be challenged by the Iconoclasts[31]. The programme of the ninth-century psalters is Christocentric : the prophetical visions of Old Testament "saints" ; the New Testament theophanies and finally the witness of "latter-day" saints. In two cases, their witness is particularly important. The clipeate image of Christ — a *leit-motiv* of these psalters — is included in the miniatures of Symeon and Eustace. It provides the link between the miniatures of saints and those which are more strictly Christological. The importance and significance of this link will be considered in due course.

iii. Miniatures of the patriarch Nicephorus

The miniatures of Nicephorus differ from the preceding ones in two respects. Firstly, all the other "latter-day" saints had a well-established cult before Iconoclasm, while Nicephorus was a contemporary. Secondly, the miniatures of Nicephorus set him in the historical context of the Iconoclast controversy. He figures there less as a witness to the truth of a disputed doctrine than as the ultimate vindicator of the cult of icons, triumphing over his adversaries.

18. Nicephorus is contrasted with the council of the impious. Psalm 25,4.9-10 : I have not sat with the council of vanity... Do not destroy my

---

27. *Ibidem, PG* 94, 1410, 1277 (= 1364-1365) = GEORGES D'ALEXANDRIE, *Vie de Jean Chrysostome* (*BHG* 873), ed. F. HALKIN, *Douze récits byzantins sur saint Jean Chrysostome*, Brussels 1977, p. 142[5-6], p. 147[5-6].

28. Especially in the earliest version of the *Passion* (*BHG* 670 ; *BHL* 3363-3383). Cf. H. DELEHAYE, *Les légendes grecques des saints militaires*, Paris 1909, p. 50-51 ; F. CUMONT, *La plus ancienne légende de saint Georges*, *Revue de l'histoire des religions* 114, 1936, p. 6-41.

29. In the earliest surviving witness to their *Passion*, their miraculous survival and awakening is already described as evidence in favour of the doctrine of the Resurrection of the dead. PHOTIUS, *Bibliothèque*, VII, edited R. HENRY, Paris 1974, p. 209-211 ; *PG* 99, 102. Compare *Syn. CP* 155-156 (October 22nd).

30. *Passio* (*BHG* 1414m), *ed. cit.* (note 19), § 3, p. 217 ; § 11, p. 220. *Passio* (*BHG* 1412z), *ed. cit.* (note 19), § 4, p. 42 ; § 17, p. 48.

31. *Regestes*, n°s 327-332. N° 332 is published in this number of *REB*, p. 8-11. Cf. V. GRUMEL, L'iconologie de saint Germain de Constantinople, *EO* 21, 1922, p. 165-175 ; J. DARROUZÈS, Germain Ier de Constantinople, *Dictionnaire de spiritualité* 6, 309-311.

soul together with the ungodly... C, f. 23ᵛ ; Pc, f. 16. There is no need to give here a full account of these two miniatures, which have been so often described and analysed³². It will suffice to recall that these two representations of a historical event, the assembly of the synod of St Sophia in 815, if similarly structured in that in both Nicephorus is contrasted with his adversaries, nevertheless differ significantly in a number of details. The miniature in the Chludov Psalter is more straightforward. Nicephorus is represented frontally, haloed and holding a clipeate image. He is contrasted with the figures below ; indeed his triumph is only implicit. The two figures to the right of the members of the synod who are blotting out an icon closely resemble the same figures in the miniature on f. 67, illustrating Psalm 68,22. In both miniatures, one figure is episcopally dressed while the other has his hair standing on end, so that it is likely that they are portraits of Theodotus Melissenus (816-821) and John Grammaticus. The miniature in the Pantocrator Psalter is more erudite. Again Nicephorus holds a clipeate image, but now he is enthroned, with his two enemies, Theodotus Melissenus and the emperor Leo V, at his feet ; his triumph is explicit. The representation of the synod, where the members are inspired by John Grammaticus, would seem to lend itself to an elaborate exegesis. The vituperative poem inscribed on the folio does not correspond exactly to the miniature : Nicephorus is seated, not standing ; he is not stopping the mouth of John Grammaticus ; it also implies that the triumph of Nicephorus over John Grammaticus was not yet complete. The legend in both the Chludov and Pantocrator Psalters describes Nicephorus as the patriarch, without the title of saint ; yet in both psalters he is haloed. Unfortunately, as has been noted above, there is not yet a standard iconography for the representation of saints in these psalters. Consequently it cannot be argued from the absence of the word saint that Nicephorus was still living when the miniatures were executed, nor from the presence of a halo that he had already been canonized.

19. Nicephorus tramples John Grammaticus. Psalm 51,9 : Behold the man who put trust in the abundance of his wealth. C, f. 51ᵛ. The primary illustration to this Psalm verse in both the Chludov and Pantocrator Psalters shows Saint Peter trampling Simon Magus, who is surrounded by scattered coins. The scene of the triumph of Nicephorus, holding a clipeate image and trampling John Grammaticus, is accompanied by a legend : Νικηφόρος πατριάρχης ὑποδεικνοίω(ν) Ἰάννην τὸν δεύτερον Σίμονα κ(αὶ) εἰκονομάχ(ον).

This miniature does not occur in the Pantocrator Psalter. As Grabar noted, the iconography is borrowed from the repertory of imperial triumphal imagery³³. Yet, as with the synod of St Sophia there may be a historical allusion. It is told that Nicephorus engaged John Grammaticus on one occasion in

---

32. GRABAR, *op. cit.* (note 4), p. 198-201 ; Suzy DUFRENNE, *op. cit.* (note 6), p. 21‑22 ; I. ŠEVČENKO, The Anti-Iconoclastic Poem in the Pantocrator Psalter, *CA* 15, 1965, p. 39-60 ; Ch. WALTER, *Iconographie des conciles dans la tradition byzantine*, Paris 1970, p. 26-29.
33. GRABAR, *op. cit.* (note 4), p. 217-218.

214

controversy, utterly routing him[34]. John Grammaticus was assimilated to Simon Magus for his dabbling in magic rather than for his practice of simony[35]. This calumny, which was repeated in the Canon of Methodius, seems to be gratuitous[36]. It is told that on one occasion John Grammaticus distributed bribes in order to gain supporters, but it does not seem that he performed simoniac ordinations[37].

In both manuscripts, John Grammaticus emerges as a more picturesque figure than Nicephorus. One might almost suppose that the artists were more intent to vilify the Iconoclast than to celebrate the Iconophile. Again there is a contrast between the Chludov and the Pantocrator Psalters. Psalm 36,35 is illustrated in C, f. 35ᵛ, by a caricature of John Grammaticus, in which allusion is made again to his love of money. On the other hand the miniature in the Pantocrator Psalter, f. 165, illustrating Psalm 113,12-16, in which John Grammaticus is contrasted with Bezalel is among the most erudite in the ninth-century psalters[38].

II. THE PLACE OF SAINTS IN THE PROGRAMME OF NINTH-CENTURY PSALTERS

So far as "latter-day" saints are concerned, their only iconographical link with the programme of the psalters is the clipeate image of Christ. This recurs thirteen times in the Chludov Psalter. In six cases it is the object of a prophetic vision : f. 4, David ; f. 12, David ; f. 48ᵛ, David and Habbakuk ; f. 86, David ; f. 90ᵛ, Moses ; f. 154ᵛ, Habbakuk. In most of these miniatures a legend confirms that the prophet is foreseeing Christ. Never does he address prayer to a clipeate image. The only doubtful case is that of Moses, f. 90ᵛ, since there is no legend

34. The sources refer to three disputations between John Grammaticus and the Iconophiles, in all of which, naturally, he came off worst : 1. with Nicephorus, C. MANGO, *The Homilies of Photius*, Cambridge (Mass.) 1958, p. 243 ; cf. *Epistola ad Theophilum imperatorem* (*BHG* 1387 ; *Clavis* 8115), *PG* 95, 372. 2. with the monk Methodius, F. DVORNIK, The Patriarch Photius and Iconoclasm, *DOP* 7, 1953, p. 67-97 ; *Acta graeca SS. Davidis, Symeonis et Georgii Mytilenae* (*BHG* 494), edited J. VAN DEN GHEYN, *An. Boll.* 18, 1899, p. 248-250. 3. with Constantine/Cyril, S. GERO, John the Grammarian, the Last Iconoclast Patriarch of Constantinople, *Byzantina* (Uppsala) 3-4, 1974-1975, p. 27-28.

35. GERO, *art. cit.* (note 34), p. 28 ; P. LEMERLE, *Le premier humanisme byzantin*, Paris 1971, p. 135-146.

36. *Canon in erectione SS. imaginum*, Ode 4, *PG* 99, 1772 ; GERO, *ibidem*, p. 27. However, Gero is wrong in supposing that John Grammaticus is represented in the Chludov Psalter performing simoniac ordinations. The miniature in question, f. 67ᵛ, is anonymous.

37. The only concrete case mentioned in the literary sources of John Grammaticus exercising venality occurs in the *Acta graeca SS. Davidis...*, ed. cit. (note 34), p. 245, where he is accused of distributing bribes to gain clerics to the Iconoclast cause. According to I. ŠEVČENKO, Hagiography of the Iconoclast Period, *Iconoclasm, op. cit.* (note 7), p. 117-118, this is a late text, perhaps as late the 11th century.

38. Suzy DUFRENNE, Une illustration « historique » inconnue du Psautier du Mont Athos, Pantocrator n° 61, *CA* 15, 1965, p. 83-95 ; Élisabeth REVEL-NEHER, *L'arche d'alliance dans l'art juif et chrétien du second au dixième siècles*, Paris 1984, p. 175-178.

and the miniature is placed beside the title of the Psalm : *Prayer of Moses.* However, in the parallel miniature in the Pantocrator Psalter, f. 128, there is a legend, which explains that Moses is prophesying (Figure 2). There are, indeed, prayer scenes in the ninth-century psalters, but, if the miniaturist shows the destination of the prayer, he does so by a segment, from which rays of light or a hand may emerge.

This *imago clipeata* with a bust of Christ is not an icon, in the sense of a portrait to which cult is offered, although it may, particularly in the miniatures explicitly concerned with Iconoclasm, have the connotation of an icon. It signifies rather, as Grabar expressed it, "présence virtuelle du Christ"[39]. Since Christ is represented physically on the clipeate image, he is visible to human eyes. Since he is virtually present in the image, any act concerned with it is concerned with Christ. Those who see the clipeate image see Christ ; those who destroy it destroy Christ.

In pre-Iconoclast art there are three main iconographical variants of the clipeate image of Christ. In one, the *clipea* serves as a frame for the bust portrait ; in the second, the *clipea* is commensurate with Christ's nimbus. In the third, there is a cross behind Christ's head but no nimbus. An example of the first variant is provided by the Cross of Justin II (565-578) at the Vatican[40] ; an example of the second by the icon of Saint Peter at Mount Sinaï (*ca* 600)[41] ; an example of the third by the coins of Justinian II (685-695)[42]. So far as the two first variants are concerned, it is unlikely that there is a difference in their meaning, since both are found on ampoules[43] (Figure 4). After Iconoclasm, the first variant, in which Christ is haloed while the *clipea* serves as a frame, figures regularly in cupolas ; the earliest surviving example is that in the chapel of Santo Zeno (San Prassede), Rome, executed between 817 and 824[44]. The second variant is maintained in the eleventh-century psalters, particularly where the miniature is recopied from the earlier ones, and in the two portraits of Iconophile saints in the Menologium of Basil II[45]. It is used once in the Homilies of Gregory Nazianzus, *Paris. graec.* 510, f. 264[v], for the scene of the

---

39. GRABAR, *op. cit.* (note 4), p. 219. For a penetrating analysis of the theological issues concerning the image of Christ, see C. SCHÖNBORN, *L'icône du Christ, fondements théologiques,* third edition, Paris 1986. Schönborn calls the image the *sainte face,* which is convenient if not strictly accurate.

40. M. ROSENBERG, Ein goldenes Pektoralkreuz, *Pantheon* 1, 1928, p. 151ff. (this article has been inaccessible to me) ; E. KITZINGER, Byzantine Art in the Period between Justinian and Iconoclasm, *Berichte zum XI. Internationalen Byzantinisten-Kongress,* 4/1, Munich 1958, p. 18, fig. 18, reprinted *The Art of Byzantium and the Medieval West, Selected Studies,* edited W. E. Kleinbauer, Bloomington/London 1976, p. 174.

41. WEITZMANN, *op. cit.* (note 13), n° B. 5.

42. GRABAR, *op. cit.* (note 4), p. 37-45, fig. 13, 14, 17-19 ; R. CORMACK, *Writing in Gold,* London 1985, p. 96-97.

43. A. GRABAR, *Ampoules de Terre Sainte,* Paris 1958. Nimbus and clipea commensurate : Monza, n[os] 6-9, 14, 15. Nimbus for head only : Monza, n[os] 10, 11 ; Bobbio, n[os] 1, 6, 18 ; cf. Dumbarton Oaks, n° 48.18, Gary VIKAN, *Byzantine Pilgrimage Art,* Washington 1982, p. 22.

44. V. LAZAREV, *Storia della pittura bizantina,* Turin 1967, p. 122 note 57.

45. *Il Menologio di Basilio II,* edited C. STORNAJOLO & P. FRANCHI DE' CAVALIERI, Vatican/Milan 1907, p. 94, 392, depicting the monk Nicetas and the empress Theodora ; GRABAR, *op. cit.* (note 4), p. 219.

conversion of Saint Paul[46] (Figure 3). Here it is evidently used to signify that Christ is physically present and visible. It is also used, from the eleventh century, for representations of the Holy Face, in Moscow Historical Museum cod. 386, f. 192[v], dated 1063, and regularly on the Mandylion in monumental painting[47] (Figure 6). However, it is unlikely that the Holy Face of Edessa was really represented on the relic in this way, because, in other early versions — there are none, it seems, prior to the relic's translation to Constantinople in the mid-10th century —, the image of Christ conforms to the third variant, that which is found on Justinian II's coins[48]. Thus, although the Mandylion of Edessa, with its miraculously imprinted image of Christ not made by human hands, was naturally exploited by the Iconophiles in their polemics, the clipeate image of the ninth-century psalters does not reproduce it.

Nevertheless the clipeate image of Christ, in which the nimbus is commensurate with the *clipea* is a central element of the programme of the ninth-century psalters. This has a clearly defined binary structure. The protagonists are divided into two camps : those who accept the physical visibility — and hence representability — of Christ, before, during and after the Incarnation ; those who refuse to acknowledge the message of the prophets, who crucify the incarnate Christ, and who, by destroying his image, attempt to crucify him again. In the development of this programme, the clipeate image is used for the visions of the prophets and of "latter-day" saints. Thus Symeon the Stylite and Eustace carry the witness of the prophets into post-apostolic times.

On the other hand, the Iconoclasts are represented as emulating the Jews who crucified Christ. Psalm 68,22 : They gave me gall for food and they made me drink vinegar for my thirst, is illustrated in the Chludov Psalter, f. 67, by two scenes. (The folio is missing from the Paris and Pantocrator Psalters). The representation of Christ on the cross being offered a sponge on a rod corresponds to the typological interpretation of the Psalm (*Matthew* 27,34). In the parallel scene, two Iconoclasts are represented obliterating an icon. This miniature has often been discussed by scholars, who have recognized that it refers to the theme of the Second Passion of Christ[49]. This theme was first developed in a letter attributed to John of Jerusalem and written about 780[50].

46. H. Omont, *Miniatures des plus anciens manuscrits grecs de la Bibliothèque Nationale*, second edition, Paris 1929, p. 24-25, pl. xlii ; Leslie Brubaker, Politics, Patronage and Art in Ninth-century Byzantium : Homilies of Gregory of Nazianzus in Paris (B.N. gr. 510), *DOP* 39, 1985, p. 7.

47. K. Weitzmann, The Mandylion and Constantine Porphyrogennetos, *CA* 11, 1960, p. 163-184, reprinted, *Studies in Classical and Byzantine Manuscript Illumination*, Chicago/London 1971, especially p. 234, fig. 220 ; Cormack, *op. cit.* (note 42), p. 124-125.

48. For example on the 10th-century Sinaï icon, Weitzmann, *op. cit.* (note 13), n° B. 58.

49. Gouillard, *art. cit.* (note 5), p. 3. The Second Passion also figures in the polemics of Second Iconoclasm, Grabar, *op. cit.* (note 4), p. 229.

50. *De sacris imaginibus contra Constantinum Cabalinum* (*Clavis* 8114), *PG* 95, 333-336. The passage in question : καὶ καθὼς οἱ ἄνομοι ὄξος καὶ χολὴν μίξαντες, προσήνεγκαν τῷ στόματι τοῦ Χριστοῦ, οὕτως καὶ οὗτοι μίξαντες ὕδωρ καὶ ἄσβεστον..., προσήνεγκαν τῇ σαρκομοιομόρφῳ ὄψει τῆς τιμίας εἰκόνος, καὶ ἐνέχρισαν αὐτήν. Gouillard, *art. cit.* (note 5), p. 3 note 26. S. Gero, *Byzantine Iconoclasm during the Reign of Constantine V*, Louvain 1977, p. 27, points out that, although the text, in its original form, dates from First Iconoclasm, the attribution to John of Jerusalem is not absolutely certain.

1. Constantine, Chludov Psalter, f. 58ᵛ.

3. Saint Paul, *Paris. graec.* 510, f. 264ᵛ.

2. Moses, Pantocrator Psalter, f. 128.

Pl. III

5. Eustace, stele of Davit Gareža.

4. Ampoule, Dumbarton Oaks.

6. Mandylion, Kato Lefkara (Cyprus).

However, so far as I am aware, no one has recognized to date that the legend accompanying the miniature is taken from this letter. The legend reads : οὗτοι ὄξος κ(αὶ) χ[ολὴν μίξαντες] — κ(αὶ) οὗτοι μήξαντες (sic) ὕδωρ κ(αὶ) ἄσβεστον ἐπὶ τὸ πρόσωπον. The presence of this legend beside the miniature makes it clear that the illustrators of the Chludov Psalter were familiar with the letter. It could well also be that the iconographical theme was first elaborated at about the time of John of Jerusalem, that is to say at the end of First Iconoclasm, in the last decades of the eighth century.

III. THE DATING OF THE NINTH-CENTURY PSALTERS

There have been many attempts to attribute a precise date to these psalters. The task is most difficult for the Paris Psalter, which, in its present fragmentary state, contains no miniatures referring directly to events of Second Iconoclasm. For the Chludov and Pantocrator Psalters, on the other hand, a *terminus post quem* is available ; they must have been painted later than the synod of St Sophia in 815. A. Frolow, whose case is the most closely argued, placed them between 815 and the election of John Grammaticus as patriarch in 837[51]. A number of scholars have found this dating acceptable[52]. André Grabar, however, rejected it, opting rather for the first patriarchate of Photius (858-867)[53]. Ševčenko preferred the patriarchate of Methodius (843-847)[54]. All these datings depend on *argumenta ex convenientia* ; each case, taken on its own, is argued convincingly. Yet, when they are taken together, the arguments tend to cancel each other out. In other words, there is no insuperable obstacle to any of these datings.

It is unlikely that the illuminated psalter, as an artistic genre, was a ninth-century creation. Many scholars have suggested that psalter illustration began, in fact, very early. Notably, in her analysis of the Utrecht Psalter, Suzy Dufrenne has distinguished between the iconographical elements which can be traced back to at least the fifth century and those which were added in the Carolingian epoch[55]. The late Viktor Lazarev maintained that the essential traits of the illustrated marginal psalter were fixed at the end of the Early Christian epoch on Syrian territory, although, unfortunately, he did not develop this hypothesis[56].

The process of accretion in Psalm interpretation may be discerned in literary Psalm commentaries. Thus, for Christological themes, it is possible to distinguish between New Testament, Patrological and later interpretations of the

51. A. FROLOW, La fin de la querelle iconoclaste et la date des plus anciens psautiers à illustrations marginales, *Revue de l'histoire des religions* 163, 1963, p. 201-223.

52. Ch. DELVOYE, Chronique archéologique, *Byz.* 46, 1976, p. 198-199, lists the scholars favorable to Frolow's dating.

53. GRABAR, *op. cit.* (note 4), p. 196 ; IDEM, Quelques notes sur les psautiers illustrés byzantins du 9ᵉ siècle, *CA* 15, 1965, p. 75-82.

54. ŠEVČENKO, *art. cit.* (note 32), p. 57.

55. DUFRENNE, *op. cit.* (note 7), p. 219.

56. LAZAREV, *op. cit.* (note 44), p. 116.

218

Psalms. In general, the themes chosen for the illustration of Psalm verses with Christological scenes were taken from the literary commentaries. In one or two cases the commentary exploited dates from the eighth century : Germanus I (died 733) and John of Euboea[57]. It would therefore be reasonable to suppose that the illustrators of Psalm verses enriched and extended their repertory of scenes by a similar process of accretion. However it also seems clear that the overall orientation of the illustrative programme of these ninth-century psalters was modified, in order to bring it into line with Iconophile polemics. Points of contacts with Iconophile writings are easily established. Yet the use of typology as an argument against the Iconoclasts in the illustrations of these psalters has its closest literary equivalent in the writings of John Damascene (died *ca* 750)[58].

Some scholars — Ševčenko for example — take it for granted that the surviving ninth-century psalters derive from a lost "archetype"[59]. This would have already had an anti-Iconoclast slant. Gouillard observed that the Iconoclast miniatures — with the exception of those concerned with Nicephorus and John Grammaticus — reflect the disputed issues of First rather than Second Iconoclasm[60]. The date which would seem to have been the most propitious for the production of this "archetype" is the last decades of the eighth century, while the most propitious place would be Palestine.

This hypothesis is also necessarily based on *argumenta ex convenientia*. There is first of all the strong anti-Jewish bias, which has its literary counterpart in the writings of George of Cyprus and John of Jerusalem, notably in the *Nouthesia*[61]. For example, *Isaiah* 1 is a text which combines a diatribe against the Israelites who have forsaken the Lord and a prophecy of the birth of the Messiah. It is quoted in the *Nouthesia* and applied to the Iconoclasts[62]. Psalm 2, the Messianic interpretation of which is very ancient, is illustrated in the Chludov Psalter, f. 2ᵛ, by two miniatures. The lower one, referring to verse 7 : You are my son ; today I have begotten you, is a representation of the Nativity. The upper miniature refers to rulers united against the Lord and his anointed (verse 2). It is accompanied by a legend : λέγει ὅτι οὐαὶ ἔθνος ἁμαρτωλόν. This is a quotation of *Isaiah* 1,4 : Ah sinful nation !

The binary contrast between the Jews who reject the Messiah and those who recognize that the incarnate Christ is God, so frequent in the typological miniatures of these psalters, could have been elaborated before Iconoclasm. However it becomes peculiarly apt to the Iconophile cause, when these miniatures are doubled with ones in which the Iconoclasts figure. The key theme, that of the Second Passion, is safely linked, if not with John of Jerusalem, at least with Palestine in the late eighth century — by the accompanying legend. Another example is provided by the miniatures illustrating

---

57. WALTER, *art. cit.* (note 1), p. 275-277.

58. *Ibidem*, p. 282.

59. ŠEVČENKO, *art. cit.* (note 32), p. 39.

60. GOUILLARD, *art. cit.* (note 5), p. 5.

61. B. M. MELIORANSKIJ, *Georgij Kiprjanini i Ioanni Ierusalimljanini*, Saint Petersburg 1901, p. XI-XIII, XVII ; GERO, *op. cit.* (note 50), p. 32 ; Kathleen CORRIGAN, Anti-Jewish Polemics in the 9th-century Marginal Psalters, *Annual Byzantine Studies Conference*, Chicago 1982, p. 48-49. I have not had access to Corrigan's doctoral dissertation, *Byzantine Marginal Psalters of the Ninth Century*, U.C.L.A. 1984.

62. MELIORANSKIJ, *op. cit.* (note 61), p. XXXVIII.

Psalm 68,28-29 : Add iniquity to their iniquity... Let them be blotted out of the book of the living. In the Pantocrator Psalter, f. 89, the Psalm verse is illustrated by a miniature of the Jews bribing the guards at the sepulchre (Matthew 27,62-66 ; 28,11-15). This theme could also have been exploited much earlier. In the Chludov Psalter, f. 67ᵛ, the scene is doubled with one of a simoniac ordination, accompanied by the following legends : διὰ ἀργύρια ἐψεύσαντο καὶ προσέθηκαν ἀνομίαν ἐπὶ ἀνομίας — καὶ τὴν τοῦ Χ(ριστο)ῦ εἰκόνα ἀτιμάζοντο προσθήκην τῆς ἀνομίας αὐτῶν ἐργάζοντο.

I have failed to identify the source of the legends and to find a literary analogy for the assimilation of simoniac bishops to the guards at the sepulchre who accepted bribes. Yet the issue of simoniac Iconoclasts is far more relevant to the patriarchate of Tarasius (784-806) than to Second Iconoclasm[63].

A final argument in favour of a Palestinian provenance for the "archetype" is provided by the "latter-day" saints themselves. As has been noted above, extracts from texts referring to four of these seven saints are included in the *florilegium* of John Damascene, and, in two cases, the miniature corresponds exactly to the quoted text. This could be dismissed as a coincidence. Alternatively, the artist could have been familiar with John Damascene's *florilegium.* However, if the second explanation is preferred, he could hardly have been working in Constantinople, where, it seems, John Damascene's *Orationes de imaginibus* were not known. At least, they were not cited at the Second Council of Nicaea, nor were they exploited by later Iconophile polemical writers living in the capital[64].

If the postulate that the three surviving ninth-century marginal psalters copy and adapt a late eighth-century model reflecting the preoccupations of First Iconoclasm is accepted, then the problem of dating them is largely reduced to deciding what date and milieu were most propitious for adding the miniatures of Nicephorus and John Grammaticus. Since nothing precise can be said about the Paris Psalter, it is best left aside ; there is no reason to refuse Weitzmann's suggestion, however, that it is the earliest of the three[65]. As for the Chludov and Pantocrator Psalters, there is no necessary reason to suppose that both were illuminated at the same date and in the same milieu.

The greatest difficulty to overcome is that, of all the Iconophile heroes, only Nicephorus is celebrated. That the artists should have restricted their vituperation almost exclusively to John Grammaticus is less embarrassing, because, in all the anti-Iconoclast writings of the ninth century, he was the principal target for calumny and detraction[66]. On the other hand texts like the Canon of Methodius and the Synodikon of Orthodoxy, even if there are evident similarities between their language and the imagery of the miniatures of Nicephorus, do not reserve their aureoles exclusively to him[67].

---

63. *Regestes,* nᵒˢ 361-364.

64. Van den Ven, *art. cit.* (note 23), p. 336-338.

65. K. Weitzmann, *Die byzantinische Buchmalerei des 9. und 10. Jahrhunderts,* Berlin 1935, p. 53.

66. See above, note 34.

67. Gouillard, *art. cit.* (note 5), p. 4-6. In fact, Nicephorus is not specifically named in the Canon of Methodius, *PG* 99, 1767-1780. Idem, Le synodikon de l'orthodoxie, édition et commentaire, *TM* 2, 1967, p. 50-51, where his eternal memory is evoked, together with that of Germanus, Tarasius and Methodius.

220

This exclusivity is the strongest — if not totally convincing — argument in favour of Frolow's date and provenance for the Chludov Psalter. The updating would have consisted in the introduction of the miniature of the synod of St Sophia(18),doubling, according to the established procedure, the miniature of Saint Peter trampling Simon Magus with one of Nicephorus trampling John Grammaticus (**19**), adding a caricature of John Grammaticus (f. 35ᵛ), and attributing the features of Nicephorus and Theodotus Melissenus to the figures who are blotting out icons in the miniature of the Second Passion (f. 67). However, if the updated Psalter was produced to celebrate the rehabilitation of Nicephorus, it becomes easier to understand how he was introduced into the category of "latter-day" saints. He had already been "canonized" by his biographer, although, admittedly, the assimilation of Nicephorus to saints of the Old and New Testament, was rather a matter of literary convention than a witness to his already established cult[68]. This date has a further advantage that it is subsequent to the composition of the Synodikon and of the Canon of Methodius. Literary *rapprochements* are now possible, which were not available at the earlier date.

However, for the Pantocrator Psalter, it could well be that the updating of the illustrations was undertaken rather later, in the entourage of the patriarch Photius. Evidence is available of the esteem in which Photius held Nicephorus. There is, for example, the passage in *Homily* 15, delivered during his first patriarchate (858-867), possibly in 867, in which Photius said : "So the wondrous Nicephorus with a prophetic eye barred the entrance of the Church to John and his fellow leaders in heresy"[69]. The erudite character of the two miniatures,of the synod of St Sophia(**18**)and of the contrast between Jannis and Bezalel (f. 165), has already been noted[70]. It distinguishes them from all the other miniatures and invites a *rapprochement* with those in the Homilies of Gregory of Nazianzus, *Paris. graec.* 510.

68. IGNATIUS, *Vita* (*BHG* 1335), edited C. DE BOOR, *Nicephori archiepiscopi Constantinopolitani opuscula historica*, Leipzig 1880 ; *PG* 100, 147-160.

69. MANGO, *op. cit.* (note 34), p. 239-243 ; DVORNIK, *art. cit.* (note 34), p. 87.

70. See above, p. 214. DUFRENNE, *art. cit.* (note 38), plausibly adduces the commentary on Psalm 113,12-16, in the *Amphilocia*, Q. 111, *PG* 101, 653-664, as a point of contact between the miniature and the erudition of Photius. However, the status of the furniture of the Tabernacle (*not*, as Dufrenne writes, the Temple !) as images in Jewish cult was a constant subject of controversy in both First and Second Iconoclasm. Nicephorus himself dilated interminably on the subject. Yet I have only found one text of the period in which Bezalel is actually named : *Epistula synodica ad Theophilum imperatorem* (*BHG* 1386), edited L. DUCHESNE, L'iconographie byzantine dans un document du IXᵉ siècle, *Roma e l'Oriente* 5, 1912/3, p. 278. For a new assessment of this curious document as a source for Iconophile iconography, see CORMACK, *op. cit.* (note 42), p. 121-131. See also M. AUBINEAU, Le cod. *Dublin, Trinity Coll. 185*, Textes de Christophe d'Alexandrie, d'Éphrem et de Chrysostome, *Le Muséon* 88, 1975, p. 114-116.

IV. CONCLUSION

The presence of "latter-day" saints in the illustrative programme of the ninth-century psalters can be explained more easily if it is assumed that these psalters are not entirely original creations but belong to a tradition of psalter illustration, in which the programme was progressively updated, both by accretion and by adaptation to their milieu and times. These miniatures of saints fall into three categories : the anonymous saints (**1-10**), who illustrate literally, if anachronistically, a word of the Psalm verse ; the named saints whose cult was long established (**11-17**), for whom a connection with the Iconophile polemics of First Iconoclasm can be, in some cases, argued ; the patriarch Nicephorus (**18-19**).

Apart from the blessed man (**1**), beside whom there is a clipeate image of Christ, the anonymous saints are not closely integrated into the illustrative programme of the psalters. There is consequently no obvious indication as to the stage in the development of the programme when this kind of accretion began. This clipeate image, in which the *clipea* is commensurate with the nimbus, was one of several variants in pre-Iconoclast art of the bust portrait of Christ. It is used exclusively in the ninth-century psalters to signify the virtual presence of Christ, but, although the Holy Face of Edessa was exploited in controversy by the Iconophiles, it is unlikely that Christ was, in fact, represented in this way on the Mandylion. Earlier representations of the vision of Eustace do not exploit the clipeate image ; the adaptation of this iconographical theme to the programme of these psalters by introducing the clipeate image was therefore intentional. The artists were intent on giving its full force to the argument that, since Christ was physically apprehended in a vision, he was, in consequence, representable.

This group of miniatures of "latter-day" saints, some of whom are likely to have been chosen because texts about them are quoted in the *florilegium* of John Damascene, is only one element of the updated programme which may be associated with this writer. Another is the εἰκών as an Old Testament type of the New Testament event. This argument in favour of the use of images was further developed by other Palestinian Iconophiles, notably John of Jerusalem, to whom may be due the notion of the Second Passion of Christ. Thus many aspects of the programme of these psalters suggest that it was elaborated in the late eighth century in Palestine.

The next updating would have taken place in the ninth century, when the binary contrast between Jews and Christians, extended already to the first Iconoclasts and Iconophiles, received a new accretion with the addition of miniatures of John Grammaticus and Nicephorus. It is not possible to fix with precision when the surviving adaptations of the eighth-century "archetype" were made. For the Paris Psalter, in its mutilated condition, the necessary elements are lacking. The Chludov Psalter could well have been painted during the lifetime of Nicephorus or, perhaps more plausibly, during the patriarchate of Methodius. The more erudite character of the added miniatures in the Pantocrator Psalter suggests that this copy was made later, perhaps during the first patriarchate of Photius.

« LATTER-DAY » SAINTS
IN THE MODEL FOR THE LONDON
AND BARBERINI PSALTERS*

A LOST ELEVENTH-CENTURY MARGINAL PSALTER

Unless I am mistaken, Sirarpie Der Nersessian first postulated the existence of an illuminated marginal psalter, now lost, which served as a model for both the London and the Barberini Psalters[1]. Her hypothesis, formulated in the chapter of her study of the London Psalter in which she discusses its relations with other illuminated marginal Psalters, has been

---

* The following abbreviations are used in this article :

DER NERSESSIAN = Sirarpie DER NERSESSIAN, *L'illustration des psautiers grecs du Moyen Age*, II, Paris 1970.

Menaia = *Menaia* (Grottaferrata edition), 6 volumes, Rome 1888-1901.

Typicon = J. MATEOS, *Le typicon de la Grande Église*, I-II, Rome 1962-1963.

The usual *sigla* are used for the marginal psalters :

C = The Chludov Psalter (Marfa ŠČEPKINA, *Miniatjuri Hludovskoj Psaltyri...*, Moscow 1977).

Pc = The Pantocrator Psalter (Suzy DUFRENNE, *L'illustration des psautiers grecs du Moyen Age*, I, Paris 1966).

L = The London Psalter (DER NERSESSIAN).

B = The Barberini Psalter (unpublished).

For *Lives* of saints only a reference is given to *BHG*, unless an allusion is made to a specific passage.

Dr Jeffrey C. Anderson read a first draft of this article. I thank him for valuable suggestions.

Credit titles for the illustrations : Biblioteca Apostolica Vaticana, figures 1-4, 9-11, 14, 15 ; Collection Gabriel Millet, Paris, 5-8, 12, 13, 16.

1. DER NERSESSIAN, p. 70.

confirmed by subsequent research[2]. However, to date, scholars who have affirmed the existence of this lost psalter have not taken the next step ; they have not attempted to characterize it in detail. They concentrate their attention on the London Psalter, largely ignoring the Barberini Psalter, which is, in fact, a closer copy of the lost psalter. Yet such a characterisation is not a mere academic exercise. It is really a necessary prelude to the characterisation of the London Psalter. Many traits of this psalter, often assumed to be original, can be shown to have been already introduced into the lost psalter. It was in this lost manuscript that a radical reorientation of the illustrative programme of marginal psalters took place earlier than 1066 when the London Psalter was painted.

The arguments in favour of the existence of this lost psalter may be summarized as follows : both L and B depend ultimately on C ; however, although B was painted later than L, it is not a copy of L, even abridged, because in many of its miniatures B is closer than is L to C. However, L and B have common characteristics which distinguish them from C. The iconography of a subject whose significance is clear in C is sometimes misunderstood in both L and B in the same or a similar way. Also in both L and B a subject, present in C, may be modified in the same or a similar way. Moreover both L and B contain a number of new subjects, similarly represented in the two manuscripts, which do not occur at all in C. The simplest explanation of the changes common to L and B with respect to C is that they were introduced into an earlier manuscript, itself closely dependent on C, which served, in fact, as the model for L and B.

A reconstruction of the model's illustrative programme would include, therefore, miniatures common to C and B (and often to L), modifications common to L and B of subjects already in C, and, above all, the new subjects common to L and B. There was, indeed, a considerable increase in the number of miniatures in eleventh-century illuminated psalters. Whereas there were originally less than two hundred miniatures in C, there are more than three hundred in L and B. This increase is not proportionately distributed between themes. Old Testament subjects were taken over almost *en bloc* ; only four new Christological themes were introduced, which, unlike the earlier typological ones, have their literary point of reference rather in liturgical texts[3].

By far the largest number of new miniatures are concerned with named « latter-day » saints. Mariès long ago contrasted the « invasion » of saints

2. J. ANDERSON, The Date and Purpose of the Barberini Psalter, *CA* 31, 1986, p. 39-40 ; Ch. WALTER, Christological Themes in the Byzantine Marginal Psalters from the Ninth to the Eleventh Century, *REB* 44, 1986, p. 284-285.

3. *Ibidem*, p. 285-286.

in the ninth-century psalters (nine miniature subjects) with the « irruption » of saints in the London Psalter (nearly seventy miniature subjects)[4]. Since he erroneously supposed the Barberini Psalter to be a copy of the London Psalter, he had no explanation for the fact that it contains only about forty miniature subjects in which « latter-day » saints are named. However, once it is realized that B copies faithfully a psalter illuminated earlier than L, the discrepancy is easily explained. B witnesses to an intermediate stage in the development of psalter illustration between C and L, even though it was painted much later than L, between 1092 and 1118, perhaps around 1095[5].

However, the introduction of a greater number of miniatures of saints was tributary of a far more important innovation in this lost psalter. The new programme is characterized above all by its moralizing tone. Miniatures exemplifying this theme concern the blessed man, the just man, the sinless man, the poor man. Frequently in the eleventh-century psalters — but exceptionally in the earlier ones — he is represented at prayer. Most prayer scenes in the ninth-century psalters have David or Christ for their subject. They persist into the eleventh-century psalters, in which, in fact, the number of scenes of David at prayer increases.

To accommodate these prayer scenes a new iconographical formula was developed. In C, when David is represented at prayer, he is usually making a proskynesis (seven times), accompanied by a legend : $\Delta\alpha(\upsilon\grave{\iota})\delta$ $\varepsilon\mathring{\upsilon}\chi\acute{o}\mu\varepsilon\nu o\varsigma$, but the artist does not always make it clear that David's prayer is addressed to God. Since David is represented once in C standing before a segment from which light descends (f. 13^v ; Psalm 17,1), the formula of the segment representing heaven was available in the ninth century, but its use was exceptional[6]. In the eleventh century it became just one of several related formulae. Prayer might also be addressed to a bust figure of Christ, possibly within a blue segment, or to an icon of Christ.

The representation of figures — David, the anonymous just and named « latter-day » saints — addressing their prayer to an icon does not occur in Byzantine art earlier than the eleventh-century psalters. In the ninth-century psalters, the clipeate image of Christ recurs as a *leitmotiv*, occasionally with the connotation of an icon but always with the primary significance of the virtual presence of Christ. *Never* is prayer actually addressed to a clipeate image of Christ[7]. Many of these ninth-century miniatures

---

4. L. Mariès, L'irruption des saints dans l'illustration du psautier byzantin, *An. Boll.* 68, 1950, p. 153-162.

5. Anderson, *art. cit.* (note 2), p. 60.

6. Compare with the monks at prayer, C f. 30^v.

7. Ch. Walter, « Latter-day » Saints and the Image of Christ in the Ninth-century Byzantine Marginal Psalters, *REB* 45, 1987, p. 214-215.

214

embodying a clipeate image of Christ were recopied mechanically into the eleventh-century psalters. Artists may have been ignorant of or indifferent to their significance, for they placed alongside them other miniatures in which prayer is definitely being addressed to a clipeate image.

Consequently it is clear that the new saints introduced into the eleventh-century psalters also have a new function. Those who figure in the ninth-century psalters witness, in my opinion, to iconophile doctrines, concerning notably the visibility and consequent representability of Christ[8]. The new saints exemplify the just man and his activities, particularly his assiduity in prayer. The important rôle attributed to the just man in the eleventh-century psalters reveals the change which had occurred in the conception of the Psalter : it is no longer a compendium of prophecies to be interpreted typologically ; rather it is a book of prayer and of edification. This change in orientation had occurred before the London Psalter was painted, precisely in the lost illuminated psalter on which it and the Barberini Psalter depend.

It is important to stress the fact that this was an overall change, not peculiar to representations of « latter-day » saints. This point may be exemplified by an examination of modifications introduced in the iconography of David. Most of the miniatures of David at prayer in C are taken over in L and B, but they are slightly modified : it is made clear that David's prayer is addressed to God. Thus for Psalm 27,1 (C f. 25 ; B f. 46), B adds a portrait of Christ in a segment extending his hand towards David. For Psalm 50 (C f. 50 ; L f. 63^v ; B f. 86^v), David's penitence is conveyed by a proskynesis, to which L and B add a hand emerging from a segment. The same modification is made to the miniature illustrating Psalm 53,1 (C f. 52^v ; L f. 67 ; B f. 90^v).

This point may be further exemplified by the new miniatures introduced portraying David at prayer. In illustration to Psalm 7,13 (L f. 7^v ; B f. 13^v), David prays to a clipeate icon while below a figure shoots an arrow at another who is falling into an abyss. In illustration to Psalm 9,14 (L f. 15^v ; B f. 26), David makes a proskynesis before the enthroned Christ. In illustration to Psalm 16,23 (L f. 15^v ; B f. 26), David prays before an icon of Christ while below an angel spears his enemies. This list is not exhaustive. However, it is sufficient to make clear that David himself is not conceived so much as a prophet but as the just man of the Old Testament *par excellence* and more particularly a man of prayer. He addresses his prayer to God or to Christ, who responds, since rays of light frequently descend from heaven towards him.

8. *Ibidem*, p. 211-212.

The anonymous just are treated in the same way. For example Psalm 101, whose title is « The prayer of the poor man », is appropriately illustrated with the poor man at prayer (C f. 100 ; Pc f. 141^v ; L f. 133^v ; B f. 170). In C he is grieving ; in Pc he kneels with his hands outstretched ; in L and B a hand is added, emerging from a segment. Psalm 10,1-2 is illustrated with a miniature of the just man persecuted by the impious (C f. 10 ; L f. 10^v ; B f. 19). The miniature in C interprets the Psalm verse literally, while L and B introduce a clipeate image of Christ.

New scenes of the anonymous just were introduced. Psalm 5,10 (L f. 4^v ; B f. 10^v) is now illustrated with a miniature of the just man stopping the mouths of his calumniators and addressing his prayer to a bust image of Christ[9]. For Psalm 118,1 the blameless are introduced (B f. 202^v), facing an icon of Christ (Figure 6).

NAMED « LATTER-DAY » SAINTS IN THE LOST MARGINAL PSALTER

If the overall motive is clear for introducing nearly forty new miniatures of saints into the illustrative programme, it is not always easy to know why one saint, or group of saints, was preferred to another.

i. Copies or adaptations of ninth-century miniatures

A move away from anonymous just to named saints may be observed in a few adaptations of ninth-century miniatures.

1. Psalm 15,3. The anonymous saints in C (f. 11^v) become the three warrior saints, Theodore, George and Demetrius, in L (f. 13^v) and B (f. 23).

2. Psalm 67,36. The anonymous martyrs in C (f. 65^v) are replaced by the vision of Saint Procopius in B (f. 112^v) and L (f. 85^v). Saint Procopius, seated on a prancing horse and haloed, raises his left hand towards a bejewelled cross which hangs from a segment (Figure 12). The iconography is identical in B and L. The account of his vision, which led to his conversion, was introduced into the second state of his *Life*[10]. It was cited at the second council of Nicaea[11]. The Psalm verse was used in the office of Procopius[12].

In one other case the anonymous just who illustrate Psalm 36,39 in Pc (f. 46^v) are replaced by named just of the Old Testament : Abraham, Isaac, Jacob and Job (B f. 65 ; L f. 44^v).

---

9. My interpretation of the miniature is based on the fact that Saint Paul quotes this Psalm verse, *Romans* 3,9-19, adding : « The Law speaks for those under the Law, so that every mouth is closed ».

10. A. PAPADOPOULOS-KERAMEUS, Ἀνάλεκτα ἱεροσολυμιτικῆς σταχυολογίας, V, Petrograd 1898, p. 5-6 (*BHG* 1577).

11. MANSI 13, 89.

12. *Typicon*, I, p. 332-333 (8 July), synaxis in his martyrium. The only other representations of the vision of Procopius seem to be those in Cappadocia : Göreme n° 5, n° 10, n° 11 & n° 32, Nicole THIERRY, Vision d'Eustache, vision de Procope, Nouvelles données sur l'iconographie funéraire byzantine (printing).

216

The saints who already figured in the ninth-century Psalters were all maintained. With one exception, there were only minor modifications in their rendering in the eleventh-century versions.

3. Psalm 4,4. Symeon the stylite (?). B f. 9 ; L f. 3. There is no legend, which suggests that the one apparently in C (f. 3ᵛ) was already hardly legible when this miniature was copied in the model. That the stylite was assumed to be one of the Symeons may be inferred from the fact that two others were introduced with their names into L (**58, 59**).

4. Psalm 32,19. The Seven Sleepers. B f. 54ᵛ ; L f. 36ᵛ. Both B and L introduce the sleepers' staffs and haversacks, placed outside the cave, a detail which is already present in the *Menologium of Basil II*, p. 133[13]. More significantly, they also introduce a bust figure of Christ extending his hand, from which fall rays of light (Figures 15, 16).

5. Psalm 43,23. George. B f. 77 ; L f. 55.

6. Psalm 48,2. John Chrysostom. B f. 82ᵛ ; L f. 60. Here the portrait in C (f. 47ᵛ) is replaced in both B and L by a scene of John Chrysostom preaching to the nations. This change may be explained by the fact that the Psalm verse in question, 'Hear this, all the nations', was used as the *stichos* for the two principal feasts of John Chrysostom, November 13th and January 27th[14].

7. Psalm 59,6. Constantine. B f. 100 ; L f. 75. In both B and L the presentation is slightly modified in the same way : the figure which Constantine's horse is trampling in C f. 58ᵛ has been eliminated, while Constantine wears conventional imperial dress. In B, Constantine's standard has been made more like the Cross, with two bars on the lower of which is placed the crown of thorns (Figure 11)[15].

8. Psalm 96,11. Eustace. B f. 160ᵛ ; L f. 130ᵛ. In the versions of both B and L, the prancing horse more closely resembles that of Procopius (**2**), while the representation of Saint Peter in prison has been eliminated (Figure 13).

9. Psalm 123,6. Panteleimon. B f. 218ᵛ ; L f. 169. This folio is missing from C. In Pc, f. 182, the Psalm verse is illustrated with two parallel scenes, one of Daniel and the other of Panteleimon. In both B and L the two scenes have been combined into one.

Even these minor changes witness to the general trend in renewal in the eleventh-century : the importance attributed to prayer themes (**4**), and reference to liturgical texts (**2, 6**).

10. Psalm 25,3.4.9. Nicephorus. B (f. 43ᵛ) is close to C. In L (f. 27ᵛ), the iconography is modified considerably, in order to give prominence to Theodore Studite[16]. B undoubtedly faithfully follows the model, even to including

---

13. *Il Menologio di Basilio II*, edited C. Stornajolo & P. Franchi de' Cavalieri, Vatican/Milan 1907.

14. *Typicon*, I, p. 100, 212-214.

15. In the eleventh century, representations of the Cross of the Hetoimasia with the crown of thorns are found. This may have been the model for Constantine's standard in B. Th. von Bogyay, Hetoimasia, *Reallexikon zur byzantinischen Kunst*, II, 1197.

16. Der Nersessian, p. 24, 73.

the falling blood, a detail probably omitted from L because it had become unintelligible.

11. Psalm 51,9. Nicephorus trampling Jannis. B (f. 89ᵛ) is again close to C. The scene is omitted in L.

ii. Saints at prayer

Although their iconography is banally similar, the twenty miniatures of saints at prayer, common to B and L but not in C, are iconographically important, because they define so clearly the new orientation of the Psalter. In thirteen cases, there is no detail which might define the occasion of their prayer. There is consequently no reason to suppose that the presence of each saint requires a specific explanation. They must have been chosen, more or less at random, to exemplify the just man.

12. Psalm 16,7 : 'Show the marvels of your mercy'. Athanasius. B f. 25 ; L f. 15. He extends his hand towards an icon of Christ[17].

13. Psalm 54,2 : 'Listen, Lord, to my prayer'. Macarius. B f. 91 ; L f. 67ᵛ. In B he extends his hand towards a segment, from which rays of light emerge ; in L Christ extends a hand towards him from a clipeate icon[18].

14. Psalm 54,17 : 'I cried to God and the Lord listened to me'. Sabas. B f. 92ᵛ ; L f. 68ᵛ. In B he extends his hands towards a segment from which emerge a hand and rays of light. In L Christ extends his hand from a segment[19].

15. Psalm 60,2 : 'Oh God, listen to my petition'. Arsenius. B f. 100ᵛ ; L f. 75ᵛ. In B and L he extends his hands towards a segment from which a hand emerges ; L omits the descending rays of light[20].

16. Psalm 63,2 : 'Hear my prayer, Oh Lord'. Theodosius. He extends his hands towards a hand emerging from a segment. L adds a demon attacking him with a spear[21].

17. Psalm 69,2 : 'Draw close, Oh God, to my help'. Theodore Studite. B f. 116 ; L f. 88ᵛ. In B he extends his hands towards Christ represented in bust form. In L Christ is placed inside a clipeate icon (Figure 2)[22].

18. Psalm 70,14 : 'I will hope continually and praise you more and more'. Gregory of Nyssa. B f. 118 ; L f. 90. In B he extends his hands towards a rectangular icon of Christ. In L the icon is clipeate in form (Figure 5)[23].

17. *Typicon*, I, p. 200 (18 January), synaxis in the Great Church. Metaphrastic *Life* (*BHG* 183).

18. *Typicon*, I, p. 202 (19 January). No shrine at Constantinople and no Metaphrastic *Life*. Mariès, *art. cit.* (note 4), p. 161, followed by Der Nersessian, p. 89, explains the presence of Macarius by a pun on his name. The work *makarios* occurs in 19 Psalms, but not in the two illustrated with a portrait of this saint !

19. *Typicon*, I, p. 122 (5 December), synaxis in his martyrium. Metaphrastic *Life* (*BHG* 1609).

20. No reference to a synaxis in the *Typicon* (8 May). Metaphrastic *Life* (*BHG* 168), also a *Laudatio* by Theodore Studite (*BHG* 169), with a reference to his assiduity in prayer, *PG* 99, 880.

21. *Typicon*, I, p. 194 (11 January), synaxis in church of Saint Peter. Metaphrastic *Life* (*BHG* 1778).

22. *Typicon*, I, p. 98 (11 November). No Metaphrastic *Life*.

23. *Typicon*, I, p. 192 (10 January), synaxis in the Great Church. No Metaphrastic *Life*.

19. Psalm 74,3 : 'We will give thanks to you, Oh God'. Ephraim. B f. 125^v ; L f. 97. In B he extends his hands towards a segment. In L Christ is placed in a clipeate icon[24].

20. Psalm 76,2 : 'I cried to the Lord'. Macarius. B f. 128 ; L f. 98. In B he extends his hands towards a segment. In L Christ is placed in a clipeate icon[25].

21. Psalm 79,20 (?) : 'Turn towards me, Lord of hosts'. Amphilocius. B f. 140^v ; L f. 109. In B he raises his hands towards a segment. In L Christ is placed in a clipeate icon, and the saint is accompanied by two smaller figures[26].

22. Psalm 88,2 : 'I will declare your truth for all generations'. Stephen Neos. B f. 151 ; L f. 117. In B he extends a hand towards a segment. L substitutes a frontal portrait of the saint, holding an icon[27].

23. Psalm 118,93 : 'I will never forget your decrees'. Clement and Agathangelus. B f. 209 ; L f. 163. The two saints are facing a segment in both manuscripts[28].

24. Psalm 118,132 : 'Look upon me and have mercy on me'. Alexius. B f. 212 ; L f. 165. In B he extends his hands in prayer ; L adds a segment[29].

As the painter of L tends to amend and modify, where there are slight differences it is likely that B is closer to the model. Miniatures in which the saint turns towards a segment from which a hand and rays of light descend are much commoner in B.

There are two further prayer scenes of the same kind in B which, since they are not in L, may not have already been present in the model. On the other hand they conform to the iconography of the miniatures listed above.

25. Psalm 71,18 : 'Blessed is the Lord God of Israel'. Nicolas. B f. 121. He extends his hands towards a segment[30].

26. Psalm 119,2 : 'Deliver my soul, Oh Lord, from unjust lips'. Gregory of Agrigentum. B f. 215^v. He raises his hands towards a segment (Figure 4). There is a possible reference to the calumny of which Gregory was the victim[31]. This receives more developed illustration in L, f. 29^v, in illustration to Psalm 26,12 (**68**)[32].

In seven cases the prayer miniature common to B and L is differently conceived or more developed.

24. *Typicon*, I, p. 214 (28 January), synaxis in the church of Saint Aquilina. Metaphrastic *Life* (*BHG* 584).

25. See note 18.

26. No reference to a synaxis in the *Typicon* (23 November). Metaphrastic *Life* (*BHG* 72).

27. *Typicon*, I, p. 115 (28 November), synaxis in his martyrium. Metaphrastic *Life* (*BHG* 1667).

28. *Typicon*, I, p. 208 (23 January), synaxis in their martyrium. Metaphrastic *Life* (*BHG* 353).

29. *Typicon*, I, p. 248 (17 March). Tomb in Saint Peter's, Rome. No Metaphrastic *Life* but many others (*BHG* 51-56h).

30. *Typicon*, I, p. 124 (6 December), synaxis in the Great Church. Metaphrastic *Life* (*BHG* 1349).

31. *Typicon*, I, p. 112 (24 November), synaxis with other bishops of Agrigentum. No shrine at Constantinople. Metaphrastic *Life* (*BHG* 708).

32. See below.

Pl. I

1. Theodore Studite, Menologium of Basil II, p. 175.

2. Theodore Studite, Barberini Psalter, f. 116.

Pl. II

4. Gregory of Agrigentum,
Barberini Psalter, f. 215ʳ.

3. Gregory of Agrigentum,
Menologium of Basil II, p. 203.

6. The Blameless,
Barberini Psalter, f. 202.

5. Gregory of Nyssa,
Barberini Psalter, f. 118.

8. Theodora,
   Barberini Psalter, f. 201.

7. Antony,
   Barberini Psalter, f. 193.

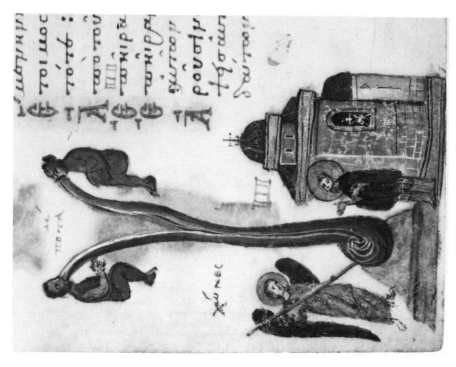

10. The Miracle of Chones,
Barberini Psalter, f. 160ᵛ.

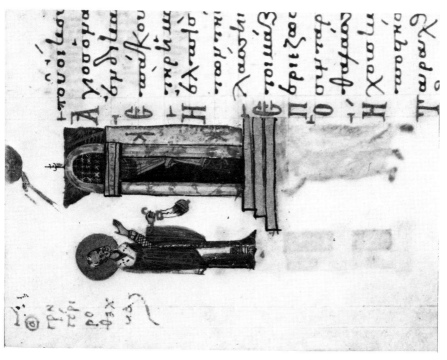

9. Gregory the Wonderworker,
Barberini Psalter, f. 105ᵛ.

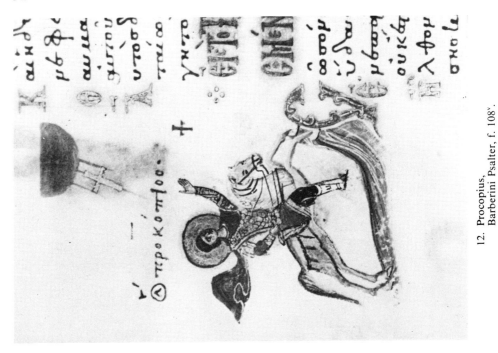

12. Procopius,
Barberini Psalter, f. 108v.

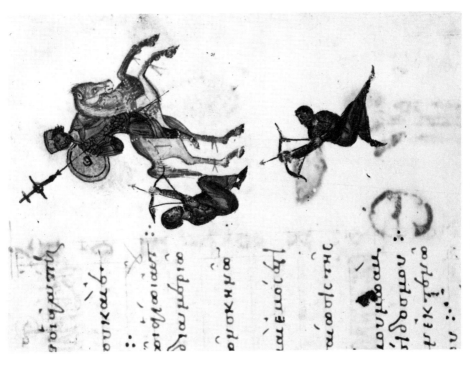

11. Constantine,
Barberini Psalter, f. 100.

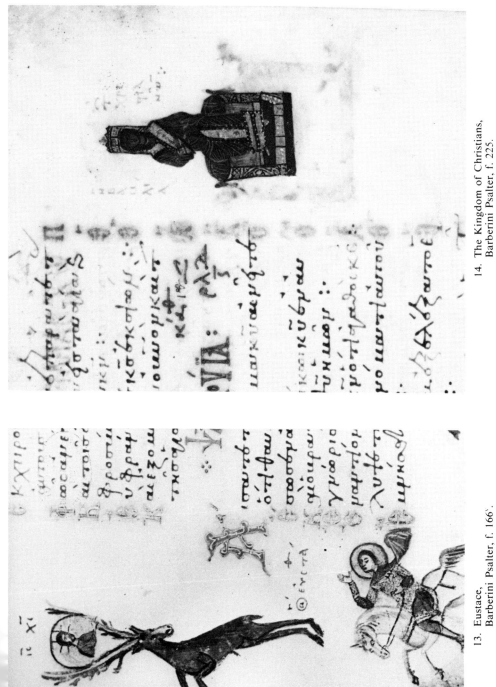

14. The Kingdom of Christians,
Barberini Psalter, f. 225.

13. Eustace,
Barberini Psalter, f. 166ᵛ.

15. The Seven Sleepers,
Menologium of Basil II, p. 133.

16. The Seven Sleepers,
Barberini Psalter, f. 54ᵛ.

27. Psalm 5,4 : 'In the morning you will hear my voice'. Basil. B f. 9ᵛ ; L f. 3ᵛ. Basil stands before a building, facing a lectern on which a book is placed. There is no evident personal reference to Basil, but, since he holds a taper in his left hand, he is probably reciting the Orthros[33].

28. Psalm 64,5 : 'Blessed is he whom you have chosen... Your temple is holy'. Gregory the Wonderworker. B f. 105ᵛ ; L f. 79ᵛ. He stands before a building, a censer in his left hand while his right hand is raised towards a segment (Figure 9). Mariès suggested a play on the word θαυμαστός which occurs in the Psalm verse[34]. There may also be an allusion to an incident which Gregory of Nyssa recounts in his *Life* : Gregory the Wonderworker once entered a temple and purged it of demons[35].

29. Psalm 70,1 : 'Oh God, I have hoped in you'. James the Persian. B f. 117 ; L f. 89ᵛ. The saint is represented frontally in exotic costume as an *orans*. There is no evident connection between him and the Psalm verse. On the other hand the account of his Passion is full of quotations from the Psalter. He was put to death by being cut to pieces. As each limb was amputated, he recited a Psalm verse, but never the one which is illustrated here[36]. Consequently it is clear that, in choosing saints to illustrate Psalm verses, the artist responsible for the model did not systematically seek out a connection between the Psalm and the saint.

30. Psalm 78,12 : 'Repay our neighbours seven times... their reproach'. Spyridon. B f. 138ᵛ ; L f. 107ᵛ. The saint extends his left hand towards an icon of Christ. He points with his right hand to a group of Arian bishops below. The incident of Spyridon's dispute with the Arians is recounted in the Metaphrastic *Life*, but there is no evident connection between it and the Psalm verse[37].

31. Psalm 108,28 : 'Let those that rise up against me be ashamed'. Antony. B f. 193 ; L f. 151. The saint stands before his cell, extending his hands towards a segment. Behind the cell stands a large demon holding a staff ; before Antony, two smaller demons are fleeing. References to Antony's combat with demons occur in his *Life* and office, but there is no evident connection with the Psalm verse (Figure 7)[38].

32. Psalm 117,11 : 'They completely surrounded me'. Theodora. B f. 201 ; L f. 157. The iconography is similar to that in the miniature of Antony. The saint stands before her cell, raising her hands towards a segment. Large demons stand before her and behind the cell : two smaller ones stand below. This time

---

33. *Typicon*, I, p. 170 (1 January), synaxis in the Great Church. No Metaphrastic *Life*.
34. MARIÈS, *art. cit.* (note 4), p. 161.
35. *Typicon*, I, p. 106 (17 November), synaxis in the Great Church. The incident is recounted in his Metaphrastic *Life* (*BHG* 715), *PG* 46, 916.
36. *Typicon*, I, p. 114 (27 November), synaxis in his martyrium. Metaphrastic *Life* (*BHG* 772b). A. DEVOS, Le dossier hagiographique de S. Jacques l'Intercis, *An. Boll.* 71, 1953, p. 172-173, 189-191, 204-205 ; 72, 1954, p. 244-245.
37. *Typicon*, I, p. 128 (12 December), synaxis in the church of Saint Peter. Metaphrastic *Life* (*BHG* 1648). P. VAN DEN VEN, *La légende de S. Spyridon évêque de Trimithonte*, Louvain 1953, p. 125*-141* ; *PG* 116, 429-436.
38. *Typicon*, I, p. 200 (17 January), synaxis in the Great Church. Metaphrastic *Life* (*BHG* 140), *PG* 26, 845-852.

a connection can be established, for, according to her Metaphrastic *Life*, Theodora recited this Psalm verse in order to ward off demons (Figure 8)[39].

33. Psalm 139,2 : 'Rescue me, Oh Lord, from the evil man'. Hermolaus. B f. 232 ; L f. 178ᵛ. The saint raises his left hand towards a segment. He points with his right hand towards the evil man below. L represents the evil man armed with a shield and club. There is no evident connection between the Psalm verse and the saint, but it is recounted in his *Life* that he was denounced to the emperor Maximian[40].

iii. *Other representations of saints*

These miniatures described above make up the bulk of illustrations of Psalm verses with a named « latter-day » saint common to B and L and hence already present in the model. Other iconographical forms than prayer scenes, common to B and L, are rare for saints. They are only five in number : a group portrait ; two scenes of martyrdom ; one miracle ; one cycle.

34. Psalm 32,1 : 'Rejoice in the Lord, you just'. A group of named saints. B f. 53 ; L f. 35ᵛ. In B four saints have been chosen to exemplify the just : John Chrysostom, Gregory of Nazianzus, Cosmas and, probably, Damian (The legend in the margin to the right of him is very rubbed). For Cosmas and Damian, L substitutes Basil, so making up a group of the Three Hierarchs.

35. Psalm 88,51 : 'Remember, Oh Lord, the reproach... which I have borne in my bosom'. Theodore Graptus. B f. 155 ; L f. 120ᵛ. Theodore is prostrate on a couch ; a figure leans towards him, tattoing verses on his head. There is no explicit connection between the incident and the Psalm verse, but no doubt Mariès was right in suggesting that the tattoed verses were the reproach which Theodore 'bore in his bosom'[41].

36. Psalm 92,3 : 'The rivers have lifted up their voices'. The Miracle of Chones. B f. 160ᵛ ; L f. 125. Archippus stands before his cell. An angel stops with a staff the flood of water descending from two personifications of rivers. Here a connection can be established, because the Psalm verse is quoted both in the account by Archippus of the miracle and in the office of the archangel Michael (Figure 10)[42].

37. Psalm 93,20 : 'Shall the throne of iniquity have fellowship with you ?' The Martyrdom of Ignatius. B f. 162ᵛ ; L f. 127. Ignatius, his hands raised in prayer, is in the arena being devoured by lions. The judge sits above at the *kathisma*. In B he is named : Trajan, while in L he is simply called the eparch.

39. *Typicon*, I, p. 24 (11 September), commemoration. Metaphrastic *Life* (*BHG* 1730), *PG* 115, 681. MARIÈS, *art. cit.* (note 4), p. 161.

40. *Typicon*, I, p. 350 (26 July), commemoration. No Metaphrastic *Life*. His denunciation to Maximian is recounted in *Syn CP*, 843.

41. *Typicon*, I, p. 163 (27 December), commemoration in the Great Church. Metaphrastic *Life* (*BHG* 1746). MARIÈS, *art. cit.* (note 4), p. 160. Ch. WALTER, Saints of Second Iconoclasm in the Madrid Scylitzes, *REB* 39, 1981, p. 311-313.

42. *Typicon*, I, p. 17 (6 September), synaxis of Michael in Anaplous. Metaphrastic account (*BHG* 1284), edited M. BONNET, *An. Boll.* 8, 1889, p. 314. MARIÈS, *art. cit.* (note 4), p. 162. Ch. WALTER, The London September Metaphrast Additional 11870, *Zograf* 12, 1981, p. 19.

The judgment seat is no doubt the throne of iniquity, but there is no explicit connection with the martyrdom of Ignatius[43].

38. Psalm 65,12 : 'We went through fire and water'. The Forty Martyrs of Sebaste. B f. 107[r-v] ; L f. 81[r-v]. The cycle is represented virtually identically in both manuscripts. All the scenes have been identified by Sirarpie Der Nersessian[44]. The application of this Psalm verse to the Forty Martyrs dates back to Basil's eulogy, which was quoted by John Damascene in his *Florilegium*[45]. The account of the recovery of their relics by Peter of Sebaste is already in the earliest *Passion*. One incident in the cycle — the exposure of the martyrs on the icy lake — is framed. This suggests that it was copied from an icon. The iconography of the exposure of the martyrs on the icy lake is ancient and attested in pre-iconoclast art[46]. Unfortunately the corresponding folio is missing from C. It is possible that this scene had already been represented on it in illustration to this Psalm verse. However, the full cycle is not attested earlier than the eleventh century[47]. Why a full cycle of the Forty Martyrs — and no other cycle for saints — should have been chosen to illustrate the model is an intriguing question[48].

This « collation » of the two eleventh-century illuminated psalters shows clearly that the new « redaction » represented by their lost common model is to be situated in the movement well attested for the period towards a more assiduous cult of saints in the Church's worship. The Metaphrastic *Lives* were already available, arranged according to the Church's calendar, as was the selection of *Homilies* of Gregory Nazianzenus. The standard text of the *Menaia* was being prepared[49]. Moreover, in monumental painting, portraits of saints were being grouped in echelons, the bishops in the apse and other saints, according to their station in life, along the walls of the nave. Their iconography was also being standardized[50]. In the Chludov Psalter, their iconography is less formal : they may or may not have a halo and, in the accompanying legend,

---

43. *Typicon*, I, p. 140 (20 December), synaxis in the Great Church. Metaphrastic *Life* (*BHG* 815).

44. DER NERSESSIAN, p. 36, 92-93.

45. BASIL, *In sanctos quadraginta martyres* (*BHG* 1205), *PG* 31, 421. JOHN DAMASCENE, *Orationes de imaginibus tres* (*BHG* 1391e-g), *PG* 94, 1361.

46. O. DEMUS, Two Palaeologan Mosaic Icons in the Dumbarton Oaks Collection, *DOP* 14, 1960, p. 101-102 ; H. MAGUIRE, *Art and Eloquence in Byzantium*, Princeton 1981, p. 36-41.

47. Compare the slightly different version in Saint Sophia, Ohrid, Gordana BABIĆ, *Les chapelles annexes des églises byzantines*, Paris 1969, p. 117-119.

48. *Typicon*, I, p. 244 (9 March), synaxis in their martyrium. The Psalm verse is used in their office. Metaphrastic *Life* (*BHG* 1284). See also Ch. WALTER, The Iconography of the Forty Martyrs in the Marginal Psalters, *Belfast Byzantine Colloquia on the Forty Martyrs*, 1986 (printing).

49. M. ARRANZ, Les grandes étapes de la liturgie byzantine : Palestine-Byzance-Russie. Essai d'aperçu historique, *Liturgie de l'Église particulière et de l'Église universelle*, edited A. TRIACCA, Rome 1976, p. 62-63.

50. Anna CHATZINIKOLAOU, Heilige, *Reallexikon zur byzantinischen Kunst*, II, 1034-1093.

there is not necessarily an epithet for saint[51]. By contrast in the Barberini and London Psalters — and hence in the model — they are invariably haloed, and an epithet for saint is invariably used in the accompanying legends.

In choosing a saint to illustrate a Psalm verse, the artist was rarely motivated by an explicit association — the use of the Psalm verse in the saint's *Life* or office — between the two. Such an explicit association can only be demonstrated in five cases (**2, 6, 32, 36, 38**). In four further cases an association may be implicit (**26, 28, 33, 35**). This is a further reason for maintaining that the painter of the model drew upon a general repertory, the same one as was used by artists who decorated churches. Various criteria may be suggested for the establishment of this repertory. Of those saints selected by the painter of the model, all, of course, figure in the Byzantine calendar. The selection corresponds broadly to that which had already been made for the Metaphrastic *Lives*. Six saints represented in the model do not have a Metaphrastic *Life* : Macarius (**13, 20**) ; Theodore Studite (**17**) ; Gregory of Nyssa (**18**) ; Alexius (**24**) ; Basil (**27**) ; Hermolaus (**33**). However, with the exception of Macarius and Hermolaus, all these saints had wellknown *Lives* outside the Metaphrastic collection.

Another possible criterion for inclusion in the general repertory was their cult at Constantinople. Most of the saints represented in the model were entitled to a synaxis either in a shrine in the city or in the Great Church itself. There are eight exceptions : Macarius (**13, 20**) ; Arsenius (**15**) ; Amphilocius (**21**) ; Alexius (**24**) ; Gregory of Agrigentum (**26**) ; Theodore (**32**) ; Hermolaus (**33**) ; Theodore Graptus (**35**). Of these saints, two were bishops, who were regularly included in the apse echelon ; three were monks. There remain the popular Alexius, « man of God », the nun Theodora, for whom the Psalm verse illustrated is quoted in her *Life*, and the more obscure Hermolaus.

THE CHARACTER OF THE LOST MARGINAL PSALTER

It is certain that the lost psalter was in the monastery of Saint John Studius in 1066, when the London Psalter was painted. It was also there in the last decade of the eleventh century, when it was faithfully copied to make the Barberini Psalter. Consequently the lost psalter was in all likelihood destined to remain in the Studite monastery, but only tenuous arguments can be advanced in favour of its actually having been painted there.

In general, the pictures of saints belong to the mainstream of Constantinopolitan eleventh-century art, without its being possible to link them closely with any other work. Possibly there is some connection with the *Menologium of Basil II*, but certainly not a direct relationship of dependence. The formula of saints addressing their prayer to a hand emerging from a segment which recurs a number of times in the *Menologium*, might

---

51. WALTER, *art. cit.* (note 7), p. 211.

be used for the same saints (Figures 1, 3). One or two scenes are closely similar in the *Menologium* and in B and L, notably the Seven Sleepers (Figures 15, 16) and the Miracle of Chones[52]. The scene of the tattooing of Theodore Graptus may be an adaptation of the blinding of an iconophile martyr in the *Menologium*[53].

A more fruitful line of enquiry might be to examine the cycle of the Forty Martyrs (**38**). It has been suggested that manuscripts with a developed cycle of a saint was, like a biographical icon, destined for a shrine in which the saint in question was particularly venerated. There were at least eight shrines dedicated to the Forty Martyrs at Constantinople[54], but, if the lost psalter remained in the Studite monastery, it was hardly destined for one of them. On the other hand, it seems that Theodore Studite had a special devotion to the Forty Martyrs. He recommended forty as the ideal number for a religious community, like the Forty Martyrs[55]. Further, in the *Parva catechesis*, when exhorting his monks to imitate the sufferings of the Lord, he holds up as example the perseverance of the Forty Martyrs[56]. This tradition of a special devotion to them may have still been alive when the lost psalter was illuminated.

A further connection with the Studite monastery might be implicit in two miniatures concerning Constantinople itself, although the sentiments which they express were not the monopoly of the Studite monks. David, it has been noted, does not figure in the miniatures common to L and B as the paragon of the Byzantine emperor. With one exception, when he is teaching[57], he figures as the just man *par excellence* of the Old Testament, and he is represented at prayer.

However, in the miniature illustrating Psalm 50,20 : 'Do good, Oh Lord, to Sion' (L f. 65 ; B f. 88), which results from a misunderstanding of the Chludov miniature (f. 51), there does seem to be a direct assimilation of Sion to Constantinople. A personification of Sion, imperially dressed, stands before the city. In B, but not in L, there is a legend accompanying the miniature : ἡ ἁγία πόλις. Another miniature is more remarkable. It illustrates Psalm 133,3 : 'May the Lord... bless you out of Sion' (L f. 173ᵛ ;

52. *Menologio, op. cit.* (note 13), p. 17, 133.
53. *Ibidem*, p. 211. Ch. WALTER, Le souvenir du IIᵉ concile de Nicée dans l'iconographie byzantine, *Nicée II 787-1987*, edited F. BOESPFLUG & N. LOSSKY, Paris 1987, p. 170, 174 ; fig. 10, 11.
54. R. JANIN, *Les églises et les monastères [de Constantinople]*, Paris 1969, p. 482-486.
55. THEODORE STUDITE, *Epistula* II 59 *Monialibus*, PG 99, 1273.
56. IDEM, *Parva catechesis*, edited E. AUVRAY, Paris 1981 (*BHG* 1208b), p. 217-220.
57. Illustrating Psalm 17,26, L f. 17ᵛ, B f. 29.

B f. 225). In B, a female personification, imperially dressed, is seated on a throne, accompanied by the legend : ἡ βασιλ(ε)ία τ(ῶν) Χριστιανῶ(ν) (Figure 14). In L, curiously, the personification is male, although the legend is the same.

Both the miniature and the legend are unusual. *Basileia* was rarely personified. Once, however, the name is attributed in a legend to a female figure, draped *all'antica*, who crowns David in the Bristol Psalter, London Additional 40731, f. 33, illustrating Psalm 20,4[58]. Yet she does not have much in common with the personification of the kingdom of the Christians. The formula was not in common use, the normal one in patristic writings being the kingdom of heaven[59]. However, the significance is clear. Epiphanius had explained how Christ, who inherited the throne of David, transferred regal and high-priestly status to the archpriests of the Church[60]. An eleventh-century analogy may be noted in an anonymous treatise on the prerogatives of metropolitan bishops ; it dates from about 1050. According to this treatise, the see of Rome had lost its privilege of primary and its universal jurisdiction. These now belonged to Constantinople, because the *basileia* had been transferred there[61].

This text would be about contemporary with the illumination of this lost psalter, if it is to be associated with the rare dated manuscripts, earlier than 1066, in which saints are represented : the Metaphrastic volumes *Paris. graec. 580 + 1499 (1055-1056)* and *Mosqu. graec. 9 (1063)*[62] ; the *Homilies* of Gregory of Nazianzus, *Vatican. graec. 463 (1062)*[63].

NAMED « LATTER-DAY » SAINTS IN THE LONDON PSALTER

When Theodore set out to illuminate his psalter, he had before him a model with a fully articulated programme. He followed this programme in its general lines, maintaining, with some exceptions, the Old and New Testament scenes, presenting the just man and his deeds, who was frequently exemplified by David or the « latter-day » saints. However, he gave the

---

58. Ch. WALTER, Raising on a Shield in Byzantine Iconography, *REB* 33, 1975, p. 153, reprinted in *Studies in Byzantine Iconography*, London 1977.
59. *A Patristic Greek Lexicon*, edited G. LAMPE, Oxford 1961, *sub verbo : basileia.*
60. EPIPHANIUS, *Adversus haereses*, I ii, *PG* 41, 391-397.
61. ANONYME, Sur les prérogatives des métropolites; edited J. DARROUZÈS, *Documents inédits d'ecclésiologie byzantine*, Paris 1966, p. 146.
62. Nancy P. ŠEVČENKO, Illustrated Editions of the Metaphrastian Menologium, *JÖB* 32/4, 1982, p. 187-188. Nancy Ševčenko has identified other volumes of these two collections, which would presumably be of about the same date.
63. G. GALAVARIS, *The Illustrations of the Liturgical Homilies of Gregory Nazianzenus*, Princeton 1969, p. 250-252.

programme, as Sirarpie Der Nersessian has shown, an original politico-mystical slant[64]. Three new miniatures of David were introduced, two of his imperial unction (f. 19, f. 97ᵛ), and one of him trampling his enemies (f. 18ᵛ). Moses and Aaron lead the Israelites (f. 99ᵛ, f. 155). The investiture of the hegumen is represented (f. 192) ; an angel brings him his *rhabdos* directly from Christ, while Saints John the Baptist and Theodore Studite stand either side of him in prayer. According to Der Nersessian, these new miniatures establish a parallel between ecclesiastical and imperial investiture, exalt David as prefiguring the Christian *basileus* and exemplify the « symphony » of powers. Theodore also introduced a new miniature assimilating Constantinople to Sion (f. 57ᵛ), and gave greater prominence to the monastery's founder, Theodore Studite. In the lost psalter, he had figured only once at prayer (**17**). In the London Psalter, he was represented alongside Nicephorus in the modified iconoclast miniature (f. 27ᵛ), as well as in the investiture scene mentioned above.

So far as « latter-day » saints are concerned, Theodore also modified his model's programme quantitatively. He introduced nine new simple representations of saints at prayer[65]. He developed sometimes the setting of the prayer miniature in his new additions[66]. He represented more frequently the evil, from which the saint prayed for protection[67]. Sometimes — and this was an innovation — he represented the actual event which was the occasion of the saint's prayer[68]. Besides these miniatures, he introduced new portraits[69], new scenes[70], five of martyrdom, and two new cycles[71].

All the new « latter-day » saints belong to the Byzantine liturgical calendar. Theodore, therefore, drew upon the same repertory as the illuminator of the lost psalter. However, although it does not seem that his choice of a specific saint to illustrate a specific Psalm verse was invariably

---

64. DER NERSESSIAN, p. 107.

65. **39.** Psalm 21,2, Chariton (f. 22) ; **40.** Psalm 30,2, Abercius (f. 32ᵛ) ; **41.** Psalm 30,19, Artemius (f. 33ᵛ) ; **42.** Psalm 31,1, Barlaam (f. 34ᵛ) ; **43.** Psalm 45,2, Cyrus & John (f. 57ᵛ) ; **44.** Psalm 61,2, Patricius (f. 76ᵛ) ; **45.** Psalm 108,1, Epiphanius (f. 149ᵛ) ; **46.** Psalm 118,58, Euthymius (f. 161) ; **47.** Psalm 140,58, Joannicius (f. 179ᵛ).

66. **48.** Psalm 83,3-5, Blasius (f. 112) ; **49.** Psalm 110,5, Onuphrius (f. 152ᵛ) ; **50.** Psalm 118,1, Holy Five (f. 159) ; **51.** Psalm 118,35, Xena (f. 160).

67. **52.** Psalm 34,5-6, Auxentius (f. 38ᵛ) ; **53.** Psalm 72,18, Mocius (f. 94) ; **54.** Psalm 73,19, Auxentius (f. 96ᵛ).

68. **55.** Psalm 73,7, Anthimus (f. 95ᵛ) ; **56.** Psalm 82,3-4, Monks in Sinaï & Raïthou (f. 111) ; **57.** Psalm 93,1, Demetrius & Nestor (f. 125ᵛ).

69. **58.** Psalm 17,2, Alypius the stylite (f. 16) ; **59.** Psalm 24,13, Daniel the stylite (f. 26ᵛ) ; **60.** Psalm 118,144, Thecla (f. 165ᵛ).

70. **61.** Psalm 21,25, John the Almoner (f. 23ᵛ) ; **62.** Psalm 33,30, Stephen (f. 38) ; **63.** Psalm 34,15, Theodore Stratilates (f. 39ᵛ) ; **64.** Psalm 34,22-23, Eleutherius (f. 40) ; **65.** Psalm 54,8, Mary the Egyptian & Zosimus (f. 68) ; **66.** Psalm 118,100, Euphemia (f. 163ᵛ) ; **67.** Psalm 119,1-2, Catherine of Alexandria (f. 167).

71. **68.** Psalm 26,12, Gregory of Agrigentum (f. 29ᵛ) ; **69.** Psalm 39,3, Gregory the Illuminator (f. 49).

motivated, there are indications that he was more frequently inspired than his predecessor by the kind of literature which would be available to a Studite monk : *Lives* of saints and their office in the *Menaia*, which, at that time, was being systematized. For two of the newly introduced « latter-day » saints, the Psalm verse which they illustrate was used in their office or their *Life*. For others, it seems possible to pick up the association which inspired Theodore's choice. The following list of examples does not pretend to be exhaustive.

50. Psalm 118,1 : 'Blessed are the blameless in the way, who walk in the law of the Lord'. In B f. 202ᵛ, the blameless are anonymous (Figure 6). Theodore substituted the Holy Five, variously dressed and moving towards the right, their arms outstretched in prayer (f. 158). Orestes, in his account of the death of Auxentius, one of the Holy Five, tells how he chanted this Psalm verse on the way to martyrdom[72].

65. Psalm 54,8 : 'I have fled far off and lodged in the desert'. Mary the Egyptian and Zosimus (f. 68). The Psalm verse is quoted in the *Life* of Mary the Egyptian[73].

The following examples of a choice motivated by association must be judged on their merits.

48. Psalm 83,3-5 : 'My soul longs for the courts of the Lord... The turtle dove (has found) a nest for herself... even your altars, Oh Lord'. Blasius extends his right hand towards a clipeate icon of Christ. With his left hand, he points to a bird nesting in a tree and a church (f. 112). In B f. 144ᵛ, the Psalm verse is illustrated literally by a miniature of a nesting bird. Theodore may have been inspired to develop the miniature by references in the office of Blasius to a phoenix in the courts of the Lord and a tree in the house of the Lord[74].

49. Psalm 110,5 : 'He has given food to those who fear him'. Onuphrius, naked, stands beside a river ; before him is a palm tree (f. 152ᵛ). There are references in his office to his nourishment in the desert with bread from heaven and to the tree of life[75].

51. Psalm 118,35 : 'Guide me in the paths of your commandments'. Xena (Eusebia) with two other figures, all dressed as nuns, move towards the right, their hands outstretched in prayer (f. 160). The miniature is the counterpart for women saints to that of the Holy Five. In the office of Xena, there is a reference to her respect for the Lord's commandments[76].

52. Psalm 34,5-6 : 'Let them be as dust before the wind and an angel of the Lord afflicting them'. Auxentius raises his right hand towards a clipeate icon

---

72. Metaphrastic *Life* (*BHG* 646), *PG* 116, 488. Compare *Menaia*, 2, p. 485, Ode 7. Psalm 118 in L is illustrated with seven miniatures of « latter day » saints as well as Saint Paul. According to the *argumentum* of « Athanasius » with regard to this Psalm, it describes the saints, their struggles, torments, trials and assaults from demons, as well as the help which comes from above and their rewards, *La chaîne palestinienne sur le Psaume 118*, edited Marguerite HARL, I, Paris 1972, p. 184-185 = *PG* 27, 480.

73. Metaphrastic *Life* (*BHG* 1042), *PG* 87³, 3716. Compare *Menaia*, 4, p. 224.

74. *Menaia*, 3, p. 563, *Echos* 2 ; p. 565, *Echos* 4.

75. *Menaia*, 5, p. 274, *Echos* 4 ; p. 275, Ode 1, *Echos* 2 ; p. 278, Ode 5.

76. *Menaia*, 3, p. 352, Ode 6.

of Christ, and, with his left hand, points towards an angel spearing fallen enemies (f. 38ᵛ). This miniature replaces the one in B f. 57ᵛ of Christ directing an angel to spear a group of men.

54. Psalm 73,19 : 'Do not deliver to the wild beasts a soul who gives praise to you'. Auxentius, again, raises his right hand towards a clipeate icon of Christ, while pointing with his left hand towards two demons (f. 96ᵛ).

Michael Psellus (1018-ca 1078) wrote a *Life* of Auxentius, in which he made much of the saint's struggles with demons and of the help which he received from angels. He said that angels accompany the saints in their struggles, and that if one sang a Psalm of David demons were like corpses[77].

61. Psalm 21,25 : 'He has not despised... the supplications of the poor'. John the Almoner gives alms (f. 23ᵛ). He was the obvious saint to exemplify the just man's duty of charity towards the poor.

63. Psalm 34,15 : 'Scourges were brought against me'. Theodore Stratilates is beaten with sticks (f. 39ᵛ). The scourging of Theodore Stratilates is described in his *Passion*[78].

66. Psalm 118,100 : 'I understood more than the ancients'. Euphemia stands in prayer between two lions (f. 163ᵛ). Theodore may have been inspired by the prodigy attributed to her. According to the earlier version of the prodigy, the orthodox and heterodox bishops at the council of Chalcedon went to the tomb of Saint Euphemia. Each party presented its *tomos*, whereupon Euphemia seized the orthodox *tomos*, placed it to her lips and returned it to the bishops[79].

67. Psalm 119,1-2 : 'Deliver my soul, Oh Lord, from unjust lips'. Catherine of Alexandria disputes with rhetors before the emperor. This miniature replaces Gregory of Agrigentum at prayer in B f. 215ᵛ (**26**). Rhetors, it seems, were ill-reputed. In the *Souda* they are said to have forked tongues like dragons[80].

68. Psalm 26,12 : 'Unjust witnesses have risen up against me'. The calumny of Gregory of Agrigentum (f. 29ᵛ). If Theodore placed Gregory of Agrigentum here, it may have been because the calumny was based on false testimonies[81].

69. Psalm 39,3 : 'He brought me up out of a pit of misery'. The rescue of Gregory the Illuminator from the pit in which he had been imprisoned (f. 48). Theodore's legend accompanying the miniature establishes the connection between this event in Gregory's *Life* and the Psalm verse[82].

CONCLUSION

The principal aim of his article has been to reconstruct in outline the programme of the lost model for the London and Barberini Psalters and to define the place of the « latter-day » saints in this programme. Although,

77. P.-P. JOANNOU, *Démonologie populaire-démonologie critique au XIᵉ siècle. La vie inédite de S. Auxence par M. Psellos*, Wiesbaden 1971 (*BHG* 203), p. 118, 120.

78. L'éloge de saint Théodore le Stratélate par Euthyme Protasecretis (*BHG* 1753b), edited F. HALKIN, *An. Boll.* 99, 1981, p. 231.

79. Ch. WALTER, *L'iconographie des conciles dans la tradition byzantine*, Paris 1970, p. 248-249.

80. *Suidae Lexicon*, edited A. ADLER, II, Leipzig 1931, p. 139.

81. DER NERSESSIAN, p. 96-97.

82. *Ibidem*, p. 96.

in accordance with normal Byzantine practice, the painter of the model recopied many miniatures, notably the Biblical ones, already established in the Chludov Psalter, he also innovated by introducing a considerable number of new scenes of a moralizing nature. By so doing he reinterpreted the Psalter as a book of edification and of prayer. He introduced a new iconographical formula, according to which prayer was addressed to Christ or an icon. In some cases he modified prayer scenes in the Chludov Psalter by adding an icon or a hand emerging from a segment.

To judge by the number of prayer scenes introduced into the model, assiduity in prayer was the primary duty of the just man. The « latter-day » saints, like David, exemplify the just man, sometimes replacing the anonymous just of the Chludov Psalter. For his choice of saints, the illustrator of the lost psalter drew on the established calendar of the Byzantine Church, but he did not systematically select saints for whom a connection with a specific Psalm verse was already made in their *Life* or office. Thus, for Macarius (**13, 20**) and James the Persian (**29**), he ignored obvious connections.

The Barberini Psalter seems to be a close copy of this lost Psalter. The London Psalter also depends on it in its main lines. Theodore, its illustrator, even reinforces its moralizing programme by introducing more saints at prayer and underlining the importance of prayer as a source of protection against evil.

The Barberini and London Psalters were illuminated in the Studite monastery. It is likely that the lost model was also illustrated there, although allusions in it to a possible Studite « ideology » are discreet. In the lost psalter, Constantinople had already been assimilated to Sion, and, by implication, is presented as the kingdom of Christians, although David is regularly presented as the paragon of the just man. Theodore, however, introduced new miniatures, implying that David was also the paragon of the Byzantine emperor, anointed and victorious. In other new, or adapted, miniatures, he laid more stress on the cult of the monastery's founder Theodore Studite. Also, in his investiture scene, he implied that the authority of the hegumen came directly from Christ, so that he enjoyed a measure of autonomy relative to the emperor, in spite of the fact that his authority also derived directly from Christ.

XII

The Aristocratic Psalters and Ode Illustration in Byzantium

A century ago, the Finnish scholar J. J. Tikkanen identified a family of illuminated Byzantine Psalters, which he called "aristocratic".[1] More recently, Sirarpie Der Nersessian described the characteristics of this family as follows: they comprise scenes from the Life of David and his portrait, which precede Psalm 1; a miniature of David's penance illustrates Psalm 50; a series of scenes illustrates the apocryphal Psalm 151, which briefly recounts David's Life; there is a frontispiece for the Psalms of Asaph before Psalm 77, as well as for each of the Odes.[2]

Tikkanen knew only seven illuminated Psalters of this family. In the course of this century, many others have been discovered. In fact A. Cutler has assembled fifty-one examples (counting separately folios removed at some time from a Psalter and now held in other libraries).[3] He has also taken note of seven other Psalters, which in some way are related to the "aristocratic" family. He has described all these manuscripts, and reproduced their figurative miniatures as well as a number of non-figurative headpieces or headbands. He has also established their bibliography up to 1982.

Cutler, like other art historians, accepts that the term "aristocratic" is not exact, and like them also he has failed to find a better one. He maintains Der Nersessian's description as corresponding to "an ideal Psalter to which, as it were, all extant examples aspire." However, he is not, it seems, implying that the description could be applied to a lost "archetype." The scholar who sets out to establish pre-Iconoclast exemplars would be attempting "to resolve insoluble questions with unverifiable answers." He plans to publish a general study of the aristocratic Psalters in a subsequent volume. His first volume assembles the relevant data for such a study; it also "makes available to scholars material which has long been witheld from them."[4]

I am certainly not the only scholar to be grateful to Cutler for his generosity and to wish to take advantage of this material which he has now made available. In this present article I am more particularly concerned with the illustration of the Odes. Whatever the differences between the aristocratic Psalters, the marginal ones and those which are less easily classified, they all have one feature in common: they tend to include illustrations to many, if not all, of the Odes. It is true that for the aristo-

---

[1] J. J. TIKKANEN, *Die Psalterillustration im Mittelalter*, Helsingfors 1895—1900, reprinted Soest 1975, 112—134.

[2] Sirarpie DER NERSESSIAN, *A Psalter and New Testament Manuscript at Dumbarton Oaks*, Dumbarton Oaks Papers 19 (1965) 166—167.

[3] A. CUTLER, *The Aristocratic Psalters in Byzantium*, Paris 1984. I presented this volume briefly in the Revue des études byzantines 43 (1985) 304—305. Cutler's studies of illuminated Psalters are listed in the bibliography. See particularly his paper *The Aristocratic Psalter: The State of Research*, in: XVᵉ congrès international d'études byzantines, Rapports et Co-rapports, III, Art et archéologie, 231—257.

[4] CUTLER, *Aristocratic Psalters*, 7—9.

44

tic family this is an ideal towards which it aspires. Fifteen of the Psalters which Cutler has published carry no illustration to the Odes, although of these ten carry headbands. A further eleven Psalters have an illustration only for the first Ode of Moses. Of the three earliest — and closely related — aristocratic Psalters (Paris. graec. 139, ca 975; Paris. suppl. graec. 610 ca 1050; Washington Dumbarton Oaks cod. 3, ca 1084), only the third has a full complement of Ode illustrations. Another closely related group — the "Family 2400" dating from the twelfth century and containing eleven members — has numerous Ode illustrations. They also occur in five others from the twelfth century, four from the thirteenth century and one from the fourteenth century, whose affinities are less evident. Incidentally one may wonder why Cutler did not include the eleventh-century Psalter Leningrad graec. 214 among those which are in some way related to the aristocratic family.

The study of Ode illustration, curiously neglected by Byzantinists, is greatly facilitated by Cutler's publication.[5] It may now be undertaken, in all its breadth, as a common element of all kinds of illuminated Psalters Several questions come at once to mind: Was the choice of Ode illustrations determined by the overall conventions of Byzantine bookmaking? Were there common principles specific to Ode illustration as such? To what extent was Ode illustration influenced by the programme of the kind of Psalter in which it appears? Were there cross-influences in Ode illustration between the aristocratic and marginal families? However, i is not my intention, in this brief article, to attempt to answer all or any of these questions. I prefer rather to offer the reader three notes: on the significance of the Odes for the Byzantine illuminator; on prayer themes in the early marginal and aristocratic Psalters; on the possible sources for miniatures in which the subject rather than the author of the Ode is portrayed.

1. The Significance of the Odes for the Byzantine Illuminator

The word Ode (ῷδή), which in classical Greek means song, recurs fre quently in the Septuagint, some thirty times in the title of a Psalm. It was also applied to the first and second Odes of Moses (Exodus 15,1—19 Deuteronomy 32,1—43) quite independently of their later use in the worship of the Christian Church. One cannot know whether Saint Paul was referring to one of these texts when he wrote of "spiritual odes" (Ephesians 5,19; Colossians 14,3). However, there is an explicit reference to the first Ode of Moses in Apocalypse 15,3, while, in the late second century, Clement of Alexandria referred to the second Ode of Moses.[6] By the fifth century, the socalled "Nine Odes", together with those of Manasseh, Hezekiah and Symeon, had been grouped together after the Psalms in the Codex Alexandrinus.[7]

Sacred songs are numerous in the books of the Old Testament. Some were selected for Christian worship, others rejected, but the date and exact criteria for the choice are not known. This choice was certainly

[5] The principal studies to date of Ode illustration as such are by K. WEITZMANN The Ode Pictures of the Aristocratic Psalter Recension, Dumbarton Oaks Papers 30 (1976 65—84, and Sirarpie DER NERSESSIAN, L'illustration des psautiers grecs du Moyen Age, II, Londres, Add. 19.352, Paris 1970, 102—106.
[6] Clement of Alexandria, Paedogogus, I, PG 8, 317.
[7] J. MEARNS, The Cantic(l)es of the Christian Church, Cambridge 1914, 9.

eclectic, although certain themes recur: divine intervention to rescue victims of persecution; typological reference to the Messiah; answer to personal prayer. Thus, the first Ode of Moses, celebrating the delivery of the Israelites from the Egyptians, was early used in the Paschal vigil, which Schneider thought to have been the place of origin of the use of Odes in Church offices.[8] The Ode of Jonah (Jonah 2,3—10) was at once a personal prayer for delivery and a sign of the death and resurrection of Christ (Matthew 12,40). The Ode of the Three Youths in the Furnace (Daniel 3,26—88) expresses confidence in delivery.

Three other Odes are personal acts of thanksgiving for answer to prayer: Hannah, who was barren but conceived Samuel, also prefigured the Virgin Mary (I Samuel 2,1—10); Hezekiah, who was dying but whose life was prolonged (Isaiah 38,10—20; cf II Kings 20,1—11); Manasseh, who having abandoned the cult of the God of Israel for that of idols, repented and was forgiven (cf II Paralipomena 33).[9]

The remaning Odes are more heterogeneous. The second Ode of Moses extols the fidelity of the God of Israel in spite of the rebelliousness of the Chosen People, recalling certain Psalms with the same theme, notably 77, 104 and 105. The Ode of Isaiah (Isaiah 26,9—20) may have recommended itself during times of persecution, with its reference (verse 10) to the putting down of the ungodly man. The Ode of Habakkuk (Habakkuk 3,2—19) was interpreted as a prophecy of the coming of the Messiah. Finally the three New Testament Odes, of the Theotokos (Luke 1,46—55), of Zachariah (Luke 1,68—79), of Symeon (Luke 2,29—32) were presumably also chosen for their Messianic content.

It will be possible to form a more precise notion of the Byzantine interpretation of the Odes when their Catenae have been published in a scholarly edition.[10] Meanwhile something may be learned from the titles given to the Odes in illuminated manuscripts, although, unfortunately, in Cutler's edition of the aristocratic Psalters, as in those of other illuminated Psalters, these titles are by no means consistently reproduced or transcribed. In the ninth-century Chludov Psalter, of ten titles reproduced, only three designate the poem specifically as an ode: Moses I, Isaiah, the Theotokos. For Hannah, Jonah, Hezekiah, Manasseh and Symeon, προσευχή (prayer) was preferred, while Zachariah's Ode is called a prophecy. These titles, so far as can be judged, were maintained fairly consistently, although Hannah, Habakkuk and Isaiah's poems may be designated as an ode or a prayer, while Zachariah's poem is also called thanksgiving.

In some manuscripts, notably in the Dumbarton Oaks Psalter, the title to each Ode is a dodecasyllable: "Moses speaks, Pharaoh totally drowning" (Moses I); "Writing of the Law, again an Ode of Moses" (Moses II); "The barren woman strangely giving birth honours God" (Hannah); "Habakkuk demonstrating the abasement of the Logos" (Habakkuk); "The prediction of Isaiah, fulfilment of prayer" (Isaiah); "From the monster Jonah cried out, saying..." (Jonah). For the Three Youths, there is no title but three subtitles: "The praise of the Three Youths quenches the

---

[8] H. SCHNEIDER, *Die biblischen Oden in christlichen Altertum,* Biblica 30 (1949) 28—65, especially 37, 41.

[9] For this apocryphal Ode, see particularly, *Les constitutions apostoliques,* I, edited M. METZGER, Paris 1985, 211—223; H.-P. RÜGER, *Apokryphen des Alten Testaments,* Theologische Realenzyklopädie 3, 304, 313.

[10] For the status quaestionis of editions of Catenae for the Odes, see M. GEERARD. *Clavis patrum graecorum* IV, Turnhout 1980, 212—213.

flames"; "The praising of the virtuous was the delight of the youths"; "Created nature exalting the Lord". The rest of the titles are as follows: "The Virgin Mother hymns the Son and God" (Theotokos); "Prayer of Zachariah, the father of the Prodromos" (Zachariah); "She (?) beholds Hezekiah praising me" (Hezekiah); "The redeemed Manasseh magnifies God" (Manasseh).

I do not know whether these dodecasyllables are attested in nonillustrated Psalters earlier than Paris suppl. graec. 610.[11] They do, however, resemble other poems about the Odes, for example two attributed in the manuscripts to Elias of Jerusalem or Andrew of Crete published by Sophronius Eustratiades.[12] They suggest that, while the two Odes of Moses were considered significant for their historical context and the Ode of Habakkuk for its Messianic content, the others were valued rather as acts of prayer, praise and thanksgiving.

2. Prayer Themes in the Early Marginal and Aristocratic Psalters

As has been noted, five of the Odes in the Chludov Psalter are called a prayer in their title.[13] Jonah, Hezekiah and Manasseh are indeed represented at prayer. On the other hand, for Hannah the artist had chosen a frontal portrait, holding the infant Samuel, and for Symeon the "festival scene" of the Presentation of the child Jesus in the temple. He has also represented Isaiah frontally in illustration to his "prophecy". This relative lack of interest in prayer themes is evident in the illustration of the Psalms in this Psalter. However, the Chludov Psalter is remarkable for the number of miniatures which interpret Psalm verses typologically.[14] Yet only one Ode, that of Habakkuk, is illustrated typologically. Moreover, apart from the Ode of Isaiah, in which the ungodly man is represented being dragged away by an angel, each Ode has only one illustration, an "author portrait" or a scene referring to its theme. These may be combined, since Jonah prays inside the whale and Hezekiah prays on his sickbed. It seems that the Odes, unlike the Psalms, were treated as individual compositions by different authors.

The two eleventh-century marginal Psalters, London and Barberini, maintain, sometimes with slight modifications, the subjects used in Chludov to illustratte many of the Odes.[15] Thus Hannah holds the infant Samuel, although in London she is now turned towards an edifice surmounted by a cross. Zachariah holds the infant John, with again the introduction into London of an edifice representing the temple. For the Ode of Symeon, the scene of the Presentation is also maintained in both Psalters (figure 1). Hezekiah and Manasseh are represented at prayer in Barberint, although they are missing from London.

There are, however, certain changes and more significant modifications. For the first Ode of Moses, the Egyptians falling into the Red Sea have been added to the Israelites crossing on dry land (figure 2). Both eleventh-century Psalters also add miniatures of Moses at prayer (figure 3).

---

[11] Ch. ASTRUC, *Un psautier byzantin à frontispices: le suppl. gr. 610*, Cahiers archéologiques 3 (1958) 106—113, refers to "le traditionnel vers de 12 syllables," without further development.

[12] S. EUSTRATIADES, Εἱρμολόγιον, Chennevières-sur-Marne 1932, 238—239.

[13] Marfa ŠČEPKINA, Миниатюры Хлудовской псалтыри, Moscow 1977.

[14] Ch. WALTER, *Christological Themes in the Byzantine Marginal Psalters from the Ninth to the Eleventh Century*, Rev. des ét. byz. 44 (1986) 269—287.

[15] DER NERSESSIAN, op. cit. (note 5); J. ANDERSON — P. CANART — Ch. WALTER, *The Barberini Psalter*, Stuttgart (printing).

Figure 1. The Presentation, Barberini Psalter, fol. 271^v.

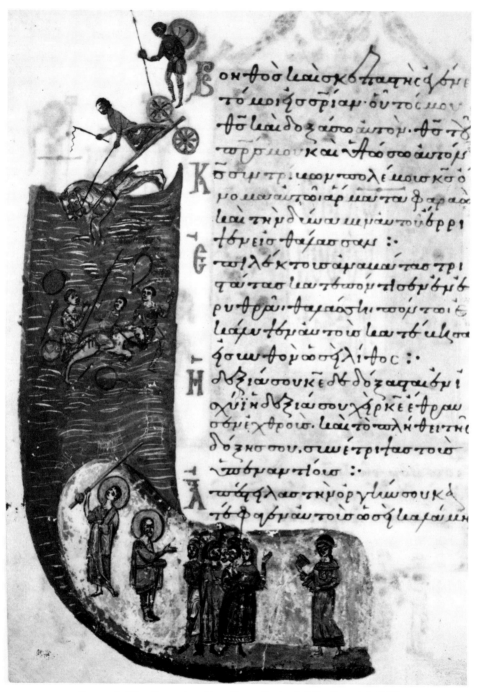

Figure 2. The Drowning Egyptians, Barberini Psalter, fol. 249ᵛ.

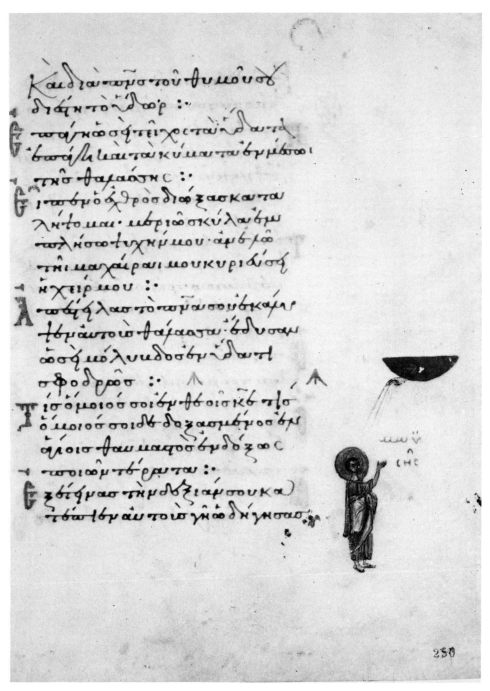

Figure 3. Moses at Prayer, Barberini Psalter, fol. 250.

XII

Figure 4. Jonah cycle, Vatican graec. 1613, p. 59.

The second Ode of Moses receives extensive illustration along the lines of that of the Psalms which it resembles. In London, a second miniature has been added to the Ode of Habakkuk, in which the prophet addresses prayer to an icon of Christ while extending a hand towards an angel spearing fallen figures designated as lawless in the accompanying legend. This miniature comments verse 13: "You brought death on the heads of the lawless."

For the Ode of Isaiah the frontal "author portrait" has been modified in both eleventh-century Psalters; Isaiah is now represented at prayer. In Barberini, the ungodly man still resembles that in Chludov, but in London he is named Julian the Apostate. Further, he has been integrated into the miniature of Isaiah as the object of his prayer, a characteristic procedure of the painter of London. In this same Psalter a second miniature has been added to the Ode. Isaiah prays to a clipeate icon of Christ, while before him stands a youth holding a torch, a personification of Dawn. In both eleventh-century Psalters, a miniature of Jonah at prayer has been introduced, while in Barberini Jonah is also represented being spewed by the whale and in London a full Jonah cycle has been added.

The increased importance attached to the Psalter as a book of prayer and edification distinguishes the eleventh-century illuminated examples from the ninth-century ones.[16] Their overall programme has been re-structured in accordance with this idea. However it should also be asked whether, in modifying the illustrations to the Odes, the eleventh-century artists were not influenced by a model of the aristocratic family. The Bristol Psalter provides evidence that an artist might seek inspiration in Psalters belonging to both families.[17] While many of its miniatures resemble those in the Pantocrator Psalter, others, not found in the marginal Psalters, occur in the aristocratic Psalters. Thus the painter of the Bristol Psalter introduces personifications into his miniatures: Basileia into the coronation of David (Psalm 20,4); Metanoia into the penitence of David (Psalm 50); Dynamis and Alazoneia (arrogance) into the duel between David and Goliath (Psalm 143); Night and Day into the scene of the blessed man meditating the Law (Psalm 1,1—2) and again into the illustration of the Ode of Isaiah.

One modification in the programme of the eleventh-century marginal Psalters which may be noted in passing is the introduction of a frontispiece to Psalm 77, the first of the Psalms of Asaph. In the Chludov and Pantocrator Psalters, only the title is indicated, with, in the Pantocrator Psalter, a miniature in the margin of Asaph blowing a horn. In the Bristol Psalter, Psalm 77 is preceded by a framed frontispiece of Christ teaching. In Barberini and London, the Psalms of Asaph are preceded by an elaborate headpiece and illustrated by a miniature. In Barberini, Christ giving the Law is acclaimed by two groups of figures with outstretched hands. In London, Asaph is seated, like Christ in Bristol; he holds an open book upon which the word νόμος (law) is inscribed, while Christ Emmanuel is represented above in a clipeate image. Athough the iconography does not resemble that of frontispieces to the Psalms of Asaph in Psalters of the aristocratic family, in which the theme of Moses receiving or giving the

---

[16] Ch. WALTER, 'Latter-day' Saints in the Model for the London and Barberini Psalters, Rev. des ét. byz. 46 (1988) 213—215.

[17] Suzy DUFRENNE, L'illustration des psautiers grecs du Moyen Age, I, Paris 1966, 49—51.

Law is preferred, it could nevertheless have been an aristocratic Psalter which inspired the painters of the eleventh-century manuscripts to give greater prominence to this section of the Psalter.

In the London Psalter, Moses receiving the Law illustrates the second Ode of Moses as sometimes in the aristocratic Psalters. For the first Ode of Moses, the addition in London and Barberini of the Egyptian chariots falling into the Red Sea to the Israelites crossing on dry land might have been inspired by the prominence given to the drowning of Pharaoh in the aristocratic Psalters. Thus there is some reason to suppose that the illustrators of the two eleventh-century marginal Psalters had some familiarity with the aristocratic family.

In the miniatures illustrating Odes in the three earliest aristocratic Psalters, considerable prominence is given to the theme of prayer. In the Dumbarton Oaks Psalter, sometimes the authors of the Ode are represented at prayer in the scene which illustrates it. This is the case for Isaiah, the Three Youths, Hezekiah and Manasseh. However in others the praying figure is doubled with the scene within the same frame. This is the case for Hannah, Habakkuk and Jonah. The same device was used in the miniatures of Hannah and Habakkuk in Paris. suppl. graec. 610, where they are iconographically very close to the Dumbarton Oaks Psalter. It had already been used in Paris graec. 139 for Jonah and Hezekiah, while, in this Psalter, Hannah is represented only at prayer without a scene.

To raise the question whether the practice of doubling a scene with a praying figure had occurred in earlier lost aristocratic Psalters is no doubt to risk providing an insoluble problem with an unverifiable answer, However, it is more than plausible to suppose with Weitzmann that the four scenes grouped together in the ninth-century Homilies of Gregory of Nazianzus, Paris graec. 510, fol 435^v, figuring Habakkuk bringing food to Daniel in the lions' den, the Three Youths in the furnace, Hezekiah on his sickbed and Manasseh beside a brazen bull, were copied from illustrations to Odes in an aristocratic Psalter, even if they have not survived together in any extant example.[18]

These four scenes are not accompanied by a portrait of the author of the Ode at prayer. However, in another ninth-century manuscript, the Sacra Parallela, Paris. graec. 923, fol. 252^v, Hezekiah is represented on his sickbed, doubled with a portrait of him placed lower in the margin, in which he is represented at prayer. There has been some confusion, since the title of the passage illustrated refers it to the Book of Kings, although, in fact, the parallel passage, the one used for the Ode, taken from Isaiah, has been written out.[19] It is therefore possible that both text and miniatures were copied from an illuminated Psalter rather than from a Book of Isaiah.

The next step would be to combine the scene and praying figure in the same framed miniature. This practice occurs in the Menologium of Basil II. This manuscript, Vatican graec. 1613, was no doubt painted later than the Paris Psalter.[20] However, it bears witness to the custom in tenth-

---

[18] K. WEITZMANN, *Illustrations in Roll and Codex*, Princeton 1947, 149.

[19] K. WEITZMANN, *The Miniatures of the Sacra Parallela, Parisinus graecus 923*, Princeton 1979, 148—150, fig. 357.

[20] *Il Menologio di Basilio II*, edited by C. STORNAJOLO and P. FRANCHI de' Cavalieri, Vatican/Milan 1907; Sirarpie DER NERSESSIAN, Московский менологий, in: Византия. Южные славяне и Древняя Русь. Западная Европа. Сборник статей в честь В. Н. Лазарева, Moscow 1973, 94—111.

Figure 5. Matrona at Prayer, Vatican graec. 1613, p. 169.

Figure 6. Theodore Studite, Vatican graec. 1613, p. 175.

century Constantinople of placing a single framed miniature at the head of a text; within this frame, one or more subjects could be represented. Some subjects, Jonah and Habakkuk for example, are common to the Vatican Menologium and to the aristocratic Psalters. However, their iconography does not correspond closely. Jonah (p. 59) is represented twice in the miniature, once asleep in his arbour and once being spewed by the whale (figure 4). Habakkuk (p. 219) is represented frontally against an architectural background. The common point of contact would be rather the formulae used than the person represented. Thus Matrona at prayer (p. 169) before a domed church is represented according to the same formula as Hannah at prayer before the temple in Paris graec. 139 (figure 5). Among the examples of a saint at prayer represented beside a scene in the Vatican Menologium may be mentioned Philip the Deacon (p. 107), Cornelius (p. 125) and Theodore Studite (p. 175) (figure 6).

This examination of prayer scenes in illustration to Odes in the earliest aristocratic Psalters and their antecedents may help to understand the evolution of Ode illustration in the marginal Psalters from the ninth to the eleventh century. The painters of London and Barberini took over the practice of doubling a scene with a figure at prayer from the aristocratic Psalters, but did not follow the practice of combining both in a single miniature.

It is also possible that, in the Dumbarton Oaks Psalter, the opposite occurred. That is to say that its artist was influenced by a Psalter of the marginal type. Besides the framed frontispieces to the Odes, the Dumbarton Oaks Psalter carries eleven historiated initial letters. Such letters are somewhat rare in Psalter illustration. Within the aristocratic family, almost the only other Psalter with historiated initial letters is the thirteenh-century Spencer cod. graec. 1 in the New York Public Library. Here three authors of Odes — Hannah, Habakkuk and Isaiah — are represented holding the infant Christ in their hands. This suggests that the artist wished to underline the prophetic character of these Odes. Closer to the historiated initials in the Dumbarton Oaks Psalter are those in Sinaï graec. 61, dated about 1274, which Cutler related to the aristocratic without actually including this Psalter among its members. Here Moses, Habakkuk and Isaiah are represented in the initial letter of their Ode, their arms extended in prayer while light falls toward them from a segment. Closer still, and, since Lazarev dates it about 1080, almost contemporary with the Dumbarton Oaks Psalter, is Leningrad graec. 214.[21] In this Psalter, apart from the frontispiece to the Ode of Jonah, fol. 313, all the figurative illuminations are initial letters. In two cases — Hannah and Isaiah, fol. 306^v and fol. 311^v — Christ is represented within the letter, blessing the author of the Ode.

The formula used in the Dumbarton Oaks Psalter is to place the author in the initial letter with his arms outstretched in prayer, facing a bust portrait of Christ in the right hand margin. It may be noted that, in the case of Hannah, the formula is slightly different, since Christ is enthroned. Christ is not represented as the person to whom prayer is addressed in Byzantine miniatures earlier than those represented in the eleventh-century marginal Psalters. The iconographical formula may have been

[21] V. N. LAZAREV, Царьградская лицевая псалтирь XI в., Виз. врем. 3 (1950) 211—217. Excellent reproductions in V. N. LAZAREV, История византийской живописи, new edition, Moscow 1986, fig. 221—229.

invented specifically to emphasize the fact that these Psalters were conceived to be primarily books of prayer and edification. It was taken up by the illuminator of the Dumbarton Oaks Psalter, but, here again, it is necessary to distinguish between the content and disposition of the miniatures. Historiated initials were not used in this way in the eleventh-century marginal Psalters.

3. The Sources for the Subjects of Ode Illustration

Cutler's publication of the aristocratic Psalters makes it clear that, so far as the illustration of the Odes is concerned, the family connections are less close than in the marginal Psalters. For the latter, it is possible to trace their iconographical development fairly straightforwardly from the ninth-century examples down to the fourteenth-century Kiev Psalter. However, the connection between the three earliest aristocratic Psalters, which have particularly concerned us in this article, and the later ones are much less easy to trace. Indeed it may be asked whether it is correct to treat the aristocratic Psalters as a single recension, in spite of the fact that they aspire to a common ideal.

The three earliest aristocratic Psalters, together with the later copies of the Paris graec. 139, might be better considered as a "subrecension". Another "subrecension" would be constituted by the Psalters of the so-called Family 2400. This group is marked by its distinct preference for author portraits and by the banality of its rare scenes.

Yet the illuminators of Odes in general did not exercise much initiative in their choice of a subject. Only the painter of Vatican graec. 1927, who grouped in one miniature subjects suggested by different verses of the Ode, displayed outstanding originality.[22] The general lack of originality of choice is not, however, surprising. The themes of many of the Odes belong to the mainstream of Christian spirituality. They have their counterpart in early Christian art, the subjects appearing in various media: the Israelites crossing the Red Sea, the drowning of the Egyptians, Moses receiving the Law, the Three Youths in the Furnace and the Jonah cycle. Only variations in the detail of the iconography can be used for establishing connections. The New Testament scenes — the Annunciation, Visitation, Presentation in the Temple and Zacharias — present similar difficulties, although for these it should be possible in some cases to suggest connections with Gospel Books or Lectionaries painted by the same group of artists. This fascinating but arduous task cannot be tackled here. I prefer to limit myself to a consideration of some of the more original subjects used to Ode illustration.

Possibly the finest illustrates Isaiah's Ode. This begins: Ἐκ νυκτὸς ὀρθρί-ζει τὸ πνεῦμά μου πρὸς σέ, ὁ Θεός, words which may be translated as: Out of night my spirit rises at dawn towards you, Oh God. The connotation of rising for morning prayer was well-established in Christian tradition, as is apparent in a poem by Andrew of Crete (ca 660—740), paraphrasing this first verse of the Ode.[23] It therefore seems likely that the iconographical type of Isaiah at prayer between personifications of Night and Dawn was elaborated specifically to illustrate the Ode. It had a certain success, being used in the Bristol Psalter as well as the three earliest

---

[22] E. T. De WALD, *The Illustrations in the Manuscripts of the Septuagint III, Psalms and Odes 1, vaticanus graecus 1927*, Princeton 1941; Suzy DUFRENNE, *Les illustrations du Psautier d'Utrecht*, Paris 1978, 38, etc.

[23] Andrew of Crete, *Magnus canon*, PG 97, 1353.

Figure 7. Hannah Presents Samuel to Eli; Sacrifice of a Calf, Hamilton Psalter, fol. 250ᵛ.

Figure 8. Isaiah between Night and Dawn, Vatican graec. 755, fol. 107.

Credit lines:
Figures 1—6, 8: Biblioteca apostolica vaticana
Figure 7: Centre d'étude Gabriel Millet

aristocratic Psalters. Outside Ode illustration, the only example known to me is that in a Book of Isaiah with Catenae, Vatican graec. 755, fol. 107, a manuscript dated by R. Devreesse to the eleventh century (figure 8).[24]

The early marginal Psalters do nót have a scene for the Ode of Isaiah. In the London Psalter, fol. 199ᵛ, the theme is adapted by omitting the personification of Night. This is followed in the Kiev Psalter, fol. 218ᵛ, where the personification of Morning leads Isaiah towards a temple.[25] The only comparable miniature in the later aristocratic Psalters is in Athens National Library 15, fol. 122ᵛ, dated about 1180. Here a youth holding a taper leads Isaiah through a mountainous landscape. Is this adapted from the edited version of the London Psalter, or does it follow a primitive "narrative" version, from which the type of Isaiah between Night and Dawn was constructed? The question remains open.

Other later aristocratic Psalters, when they include a scene for the Ode of Isaiah, have Isaiah and the seraph, as in Athens National Library 7, fol. 243ᵛ, or Vatopedi 760, fol. 280ᵛ, where the Vision of Isaiah is included. The artist's intention must have been to underline the prophetic nature of the Ode, but the scene would have been borrowed from Isaiah 6,7, which is, in fact, inscribed on the Vatopedi miniature.

The scene of Habakkuk being carried by an angel, which has survived in the Dumbarton Oaks Psalter, fol. 76, and Paris suppl. graec. 610, fol. 252ᵛ, has been excerpted from the early Christian model, in which Daniel in the lions' den is also normally the dominant element. That the full scene may have originally been used to illustrate the Ode is made likely because it appears in the miniature in Paris graec. 510, fol. 435ᵛ, to which allusion has already been made. It then disappears from Psalter illustration, except for the Serbian Psalter, fol. 201, where the full scene is used to illustrate the Ode of the Three Youths.[26] The marginal Psalters introduce a scene of Habakkuk prophesying the coming of Christ. The later aristocratic Psalters invariably use an author portrait. However, the curious twisted position often attributed to Habakkuk requires some explanation. I would suggest that it has been borrowed from the representations of Habakkuk's vision which illustrate the Homily of Gregory of Nazianzus for Easter Sunday. Here Habakkuk is turned towards Gregory but looks back at the vision.[27]

When Hannah is not represented at prayer, she is accompanied by the infant Samuel, both in the aristocratic and in the marginal Psalters. However, two variants merit a special mention. One is in the aristocratic Psalter, Athens National Library 7, fol. 237ᵛ. Here the artist has represented Hannah facing the infant Samuel. Both hold up their hands towards the hand of God blessing them from a segment. The scene is not strictly relevant to the Ode. However, in the Book of Kings, Vatican graec. 333, fol. 5, there is a curiously similar scene, in which Hannah and another figure face each other with their hands raised.[28] The Ode of Hannah is

[24] R. DEVREESSE, *Codices vaticani graeci* III, Vatican 1950, 271—272.

[25] G. VZDORNOV, *Исследование о Киевской псалтири*, Moscow 1978, 143.

[26] J. STRZYGOWSKI, *Die Miniaturen des serbischen Psalters*, Vienna 1906, 72—73, fig. 117; Suzy DUFRENNE and R. STICHEL, *Der serbische Psalter, Inhalt und Ikonographie der Bilder*, Wiesbaden 1978, 255—256.

[27] Ch. WALTER, *The Iconography of Habakkuk*, Rev. des ét. byz. 46 [1989] 251—260; see also my communication Η εικονογραφία του προφήτη Αββακούμ στο αριστοκρατικό Ψαλτήρι της Εθνικής Βιβλιοθήκης των Αθηνών, κωδ. 15, Ὄγδοο Συμπόσιο Βυζαντινής και Μεταβυζαντινής Αρχαιολογίας και Τέχνης, Athens 1988, 97—98.

[28] J. LASSUS, *L'illustration byzantine du Livre des Rois*, Paris 1973, 31—32.

not illustrated in this manuscript. Lassus has related the miniature to I Samuel 1,14 (in the Septuagint not the Hebrew version), in which it is told how Eli's servant, believing Hannah to be drunk, wished to turn her away. It seems that the painter of the Athens manuscript, misunderstanding this or a similar miniature, used it as a model for Hannah and Samuel at prayer.

In the Hamilton Psalter, fol. 250^v, two scenes illustrate Hannah's Ode. In the first Hannah is presenting the child Samuel to Eli; in the second a calf is being sacrificed (figure 7). Neither is strictly relevant to the Ode. However, again both incidents are recounted, I Samuel 1,24—26 (Septuagint version). Again they are also illustrated in the Vatican Book of Kings.

Conclusion

The Odes were added to the Psalter as an appendix and used in Byzantine worship many centuries before the earliest surviving illuminated Psalter was produced. However, the Odes were not strictly assimilated to the Psalms. The latter had been taken over en bloc from Israelite worship. By contrast, each Ode was an individual composition. Consequently the author, the author's status and the occasion of the composition of the Ode were in each case a matter of concern both for the commentator and for the artist.

Some, like the two Odes of Moses and the New Testament Odes, were valued particularly as narratives of signal events in the history of salvation. These are the ones which most frequently receive a subject picture. Their subjects, with similar iconography, recur not only in illuminated manuscripts of the Pentateuch or the Gospels but also in other genres of early Christian and Byzantine art. Consequently the immediate model used by artists is difficult to establish.

As for the other Odes, it seems that the commentators and artists treated most of them as individual prayers. Thus, in their titles, they are usually called prayers, while the author, from the tenth century, was regularly represented at prayer. The practice of representing the author at prayer was general in the earliest aristocratic Psalters, from which it may have been taken over in the eleventh-century marginal psalters. On the other hand, the addition in the Dumbarton Oaks Psalter of historiated initials of authors of Odes addressing their prayer to Christ is likely to have been inspired by the example of the London and Barberini Psalters.

Two "subrecensions" of aristocratic Psalters can be easily identified: those related to Paris graec. 139 and those which are members of the Family 2400. Ten aristocratic Psalters dating from the twelfth to fourteenth centuries do not enter into either of these "subrecensions". They also have individual features which distinguish them from each other as well as from the rest. The task of establishing their relationship with manuscripts of other genres painted by the same group of artists will be greatly facilitated by Cutler's publication.

INDEX OF MANUSCRIPTS

INDEX